A Documentary Companion to *Storming the Court*

ASPEN PUBLISHERS

A Documentary Companion to *Storming the Court*

Brandt Goldstein

Visiting Associate Professor of Law
New York Law School

Rodger Citron

Associate Professor of Law
Touro Law Center

Molly Beutz Land

Associate Professor of Law
New York Law School

Foreword by Harold Hongju Koh

Wolters Kluwer

Law & Business

AUSTIN   BOSTON   CHICAGO   NEW YORK   THE NETHERLANDS

To contact Customer Care, e-mail customer.care@aspenpublishers.com, call 1-800-234-1660, fax 1-800-901-9075, or mail correspondence to:

Aspen Publishers
Attn: Order Department
PO Box 990
Frederick, MD 21705

Printed in the United States of America.

1 2 3 4 5 6 7 8 9 0

ISBN 978-0-7355-6317-9

Library of Congress Cataloging-in-Publication Data

Goldstein, Brandt.
  A documentary companion to Storming the court / Brandt Goldstein, Rodger Citron, Molly Beutz Land; foreword by Harold Koh.
    p. cm.
  Includes index.
  ISBN 978-0-7355-6317-9
  1. United States—Trials, litigation, etc.   2. Haitian Centers Council, Inc.—Trials, litigation, etc. 3. Refugees—Legal status, laws, etc.—United States.   4. Detention of persons—United States. 5. Haitians—Cuba—Guantánamo Bay Naval Base.   I. Citron, Rodger, 1966-   II. Land, Molly Beutz, 1974-   III. Goldstein, Brandt. Storming the court.   IV. Title.
  KF228.U5G648 2006
  342.7308′3—dc22

                                                                                    2009018259

Cover Images:

Photo of the camp: Members of the Joint Task Force and Haitian nationals at Camp McCalla, Guantánamo Bay, Cuba, Spring 1992. Photograph courtesy of Stephen Kinder.

Photo of the team: Plaintiffs' counsel and Yale law students on the steps of the United States Supreme Court on the day of oral arguments in Sale v. Haitian Centers Council, March 2, 1993, Photograph courtesy of Harold Koh.

About Wolters Kluwer Law & Business

Wolters Kluwer Law & Business is a leading provider of research information and workflow solutions in key specialty areas. The strengths of the individual brands of Aspen Publishers, CCH, Kluwer Law International and Loislaw are aligned within Wolters Kluwer Law & Business to provide comprehensive, in-depth solutions and expert-authored content for the legal, professional and education markets.

CCH was founded in 1913 and has served more than four generations of business professionals and their clients. The CCH products in the Wolters Kluwer Law & Business group are highly regarded electronic and print resources for legal, securities, antitrust and trade regulation, government contracting, banking, pension, payroll, employment and labor, and healthcare reimbursement and compliance professionals.

Aspen Publishers is a leading information provider for attorneys, business professionals and law students. Written by preeminent authorities, Aspen products offer analytical and practical information in a range of specialty practice areas from securities law and intellectual property to mergers and acquisitions and pension/benefits. Aspen's trusted legal education resources provide professors and students with high-quality, up-to-date and effective resources for successful instruction and study in all areas of the law.

Kluwer Law International supplies the global business community with comprehensive English-language international legal information. Legal practitioners, corporate counsel and business executives around the world rely on the Kluwer Law International journals, loose-leafs, books and electronic products for authoritative information in many areas of international legal practice.

Loislaw is a premier provider of digitized legal content to small law firm practitioners of various specializations. Loislaw provides attorneys with the ability to quickly and efficiently find the necessary legal information they need, when and where they need it, by facilitating access to primary law as well as state-specific law, records, forms and treatises.

Wolters Kluwer Law & Business, a unit of Wolters Kluwer, is headquartered in New York and Riverwoods, Illinois. Wolters Kluwer is a leading multinational publisher and information services company.

For all those who have taught me, and especially for Judge Harry T. Edwards,
Dr. Amitai Etzioni, and Professor Harold Hongju Koh.
B.J.G.

For my parents, Carl and Jane Citron.
R.D.C.

For the students and teachers of international human rights clinics.
M.B.L

Summary of Contents

Contents

CHAPTER NINE

Appeal and Settlement   201

CHAPTER TEN

Preclusion   235

Preface

Brandt Goldstein's book *Storming the Court* tells a story that is significant both because it involves one of the most dramatic human rights cases of its time—*Haitian Centers Council v. McNary*—and because law students played an indispensable role in the litigation. Law students not only did much of the legal work in the case; they also dreamed up the idea of filing it, despite considerable skepticism from their professor and experienced litigators. The students' remarkable dedication was one of the inspirations behind *Storming the Court*, and Brandt hoped his book would be a case study about the extraordinary things law students can achieve even before they graduate.

What Brandt did not originally anticipate was that *Storming the Court*, together with litigation materials from the *McNary* case, might also serve as key components in an introductory civil procedure course. But in conversations with his Yale Law School classmate Rodger Citron, it became apparent that the book was remarkably well-suited to this purpose, for several reasons. First, the case covers almost every phase of civil litigation in the federal courts, from the filing of a complaint to appeal, in the astonishingly brief period of one year. Second, *Storming the Court* relies heavily on primary sources from the case—filings, transcripts, discovery documents—and Brandt and Rodger recognized that they could readily situate court filings and other documents in the context of the narrative, providing a rich background for each civil procedure concept presented to the reader. Third, and perhaps most important, while other narrative nonfiction books about civil litigation have served as the basis for teaching aspects of civil procedure (perhaps most notably, *A Civil Action* by Jonathan Harr), books in this genre rarely feature law students in such a major role. It seemed obvious to both Rodger and Brandt that students learning civil procedure would have a natural affinity for the protagonists in the book.

With these ideas in mind, Brandt and Rodger decided in early 2006 to write a civil procedure teaching text as a companion to *Storming the Court*. Along the way, they had the pleasure of welcoming aboard a third co-author, Molly Beutz Land. All three co-authors not only teach civil procedure, but also have a special connection to the *McNary* case and the individuals involved in it. In addition to researching and writing about *McNary* for over six years, Brandt Goldstein was Professor Harold Koh's civil procedure student. Rodger Citron was one of the law students who worked on *McNary*, and he appears "off-screen" in Chapter 4 of *Storming the Court*, as one of the people involved in the discovery process before the preliminary injunction hearing. Molly Land was a student director of the Lowenstein Clinic (some years after Brandt and Rodger) and later co-taught the Clinic with Jim Silk and International Human Rights with Harold Koh at Yale. This documentary companion is the result of the co-authors' collective efforts over the past several years.

We had several aims in writing this book. First, we hoped to bring to life the topic of civil procedure by presenting it in the context of a fast-paced, high-stakes case in which law students played meaningful roles. It is one thing to read a casebook's edited version of an opinion about the sufficiency of allegations in a complaint for negligence. It is quite another to read the actual complaint from a case in which law students helped draft the document—with the lives of several hundred people hanging in the balance.

Second, we wanted to explore civil procedure in a single case from start to finish to show how strategic choices made based upon the rules of civil procedure play out over the course of a case. Too often in teaching, individual concepts of civil procedure are explored as part of a particular phase of litigation and then left behind as a course moves on to other issues. Yet every decision that litigants make at a particular point has potential consequences at later stages of the case, from the way the plaintiffs initially draft their allegations to the scope of the matters the judge allows into evidence. Casebooks also typically make litigation look quite tidy by presenting little more than an appellate opinion focused on a single issue, when the truth is that during a case, the outcome is usually very much in doubt and the litigants generally face great uncertainty about how best to proceed. The uncertainty about the best way forward often comes to the fore in this book.

Third, we wanted to use several distinctive features of the *McNary* case to investigate aspects of civil procedure that are often neglected in first-year courses, such as trial, appeal, and preliminary relief. We devote individual chapters to all three of these topics, in addition to exploring matters typically considered in more depth in a first-year course, such as pleading, Rule 11, and the principles of preclusion. We also wanted to emphasize not just doctrine but practice-based learning. To that end, we have incorporated a number of exercises that call for students to do practice-oriented work, such as taking a deposition or preparing an oral appellate argument. And at many junctures, we have described for the student how a practitioner actually goes about the day-to-day work of litigating.

Fourth, and finally, we simply wanted to make civil procedure more fun. We think *Storming the Court* tells a fascinating story—and that the pleadings from the case and the civil procedure issues that played out over the course of the litigation provide a rich, fascinating story of their own, posing manifold questions to the student about civil procedure, and, more generally, the work of litigation and representing clients. To further develop the story we tell here, we have conducted new interviews with key participants from the *McNary* case—people such as Michael Ratner, Lisa Daugaard, Robert Begleiter, and Judge Sterling Johnson, Jr. These interviews offer additional insight into the proceedings and the challenges and rewards of complex civil practice.

We hope the stories told in this companion will help in teaching law students the meaning and significance of our system of civil procedure. More broadly, we hope that *Storming the Court* and parts of the companion will find their way into other courses, from trial practice and advanced civil procedure to clinical practice and legal ethics. However *Storming the Court* and the companion are used, though, we do recommend one thing: The class should read *Storming the Court* itself *before the course begins*. It is a quick, easy—and inspiring—read, and it will give students in the course a common set of facts and a narrative to share and discuss from the first day of class forward.

We are eager to hear your thoughts about this book and welcome your comments, suggestions, and corrections for the second edition. Please send them to us at stormingthecourt@gmail.com.

Brandt Goldstein
Rodger Citron
Molly Beutz Land

New York, New York, May 2009

Acknowledgments

In preparing this book, we have benefitted from the comments, suggestions, research assistance, and support of many people. We owe special thanks to Judge Sterling Johnson, Jr., Ronald Aubourg, Robert Begleiter, Sarah Cleveland, Lisa Daugaard, Harold Koh, Michael Ratner, Joe Tringali, and Mike Wishnie for taking the time to be interviewed. We would also like to thank Andrew Baron, Lenni Benson, Natalie Behm, Stella Burch, Kasi Carson, Henry Dunow, Bram Elias, Jay Galik, Matt Goodro, Yevgenia Gorbacheva, Jillian Howell, Jessica Kasman, Nicole Kennedy, Jamie Kleidman, James Lucarello, Danielle Morris, Jeremy Neil, John Pollack, Ed Purcell, Gary Rowe, Matthew Russo, Michael Seitzman, Justin Sherman, Edit Shkreli, Nicole Spence, Melissa Stevenson, Vivian Tseng, Rose White, and Don Zeigler for their invaluable contributions. Ms. Behm, Ms. Morris, and Mr. Russo deserve special thanks for their devotion to the project. Our thanks also to the students in Prof. Land's fall 2008 Civil Procedure sections who took this book for a "test run" prior to publication.

Brandt Goldstein and Molly Land would like to thank Dean Richard Matasar, Joyce Saltalamachia, Camille Broussard, Grace Lee, and the staff at the New York Law School library. Rodger Citron would like to thank Dean Lawrence Raful, Beth Mobley, April Schwartz, the staff at Touro Law School library, and The Touro Law Center's Summer Research Fund.

We are also grateful to everyone at Aspen and in particular to Steve Errick and Carol McGeehan for seeing the potential of this project, and to Eric Holt and Peter Skagestad for guidance, patience, and good humor in helping us reach the finish line.

Finally, loving thanks to our family and friends, and especially Alexa and Amelia Citron and Andrea Cohen; Irwin Goldstein, Jone Rymer, and Garth Goldstein; and Emily and Thomas Land.

Brandt Goldstein
Rodger D. Citron
Molly Beutz Land

FOREWORD

Storming the Court, with Procedure

Harold Hongju Koh[+]

When I first began studying law more than three decades ago, I never really thought of the cases we studied as stories about real people. Sometimes the facts were memorable or amusing. Occasionally, I would recognize the name of a living attorney or judge. But I knew no courtroom lawyers personally, and to be honest, I had never been in a real courtroom, even though I had certainly watched more than my share of courtroom dramas on television.

Nor did I have the slightest inkling about what the course in Civil Procedure was about, much less why (as I now firmly believe) it is easily the most important course in law school. My first day in Civil Procedure smacked uncomfortably of John Jay Osborn's *The Paper Chase*, with the legendary Harvard Professor Arthur Miller grilling students like Professor Kingsfield.[1] Most of us were too afraid to remember our own names, much less the facts or the confusing holding of *Capron v. Van Noorden*.[2] Although I found the theatrics of the Procedure class exciting and dutifully memorized many fact patterns and rules, it all remained abstract to me—even after I had graduated and become a judicial law clerk. In particular, I found cloudy the connection between doing Procedure and achieving justice. On my first reading of the Federal Rules of Civil Procedure, Rule 1 haunted me: Was it really possible for procedural rules to be "construed and administered to secure the just, speedy, and inexpensive determination of

---

+ Dean and Gerard C. & Bernice Latrobe Smith Professor of International Law, Yale Law School; Legal Adviser designate, United States Department of State; Counsel of Record for Plaintiffs in *Haitian Centers Council v. McNary* (later *Sale v. Haitian Centers Council*); Assistant Secretary of State for Democracy, Human Rights and Labor, 1998-2001.

1. *Cf.* JOHN JAY OSBORN, JR., THE PAPER CHASE (1973).

2. 6 U.S. (2 Cranch) 126 (1804) (holding that, on direct attack before the U.S. Supreme Court, a plaintiff may challenge a federal court's lack of subject matter (diversity) jurisdiction, even if the plaintiff chose to file in that federal court in the first instance).

every action . . . ?"[3] How, I wondered, could a man-made system of Procedure really secure justice?

It was not until I became a law professor at Yale in 1985, teaching Procedure myself, that the subject finally came to life. At Yale, we call the course "Procedure," not "Civil Procedure," to introduce students to the relationships among civil, criminal, and administrative procedure, all subsumed under the umbrella concept of due process. We also use the course to explore the important but fuzzy distinction between procedural and substantive law. After a few years, it dawned on me that any Procedure course really revolves around four core ideas: *jurisdiction* (or the exercise of judicial authority), *due process* (fairness), *roles* (professional and institutional), and the *relationship among procedural systems*, whether state to federal, state to state, or national to international. Procedure, I began to realize, was not just black-letter doctrine, but a living process. For Americans, the overarching concept of *adjudication* had emerged as our chosen social tool for facilitating dispute resolution, norm enunciation, and political bargaining. Through procedure, litigation became not just a tool for private dispute resolution, but also an important constitutional vehicle for transforming public policy, in both the domestic and the transnational realms.

By the late 1980s, again without fully realizing it, I had become a human rights litigator, bringing transnational cases in domestic courts on behalf of the newly founded Allard K. Lowenstein International Human Rights Clinic at Yale Law School.[4] In "transnational public law litigation,"[5] I came to see that domestic courts function not simply as passive umpires, but as important transnational actors, wielding significant "power to persuade, with the formal powers of legal office serving as leverage points and bargaining chips in a discursive, norm-creating process."[6]

And so it was that in 1991, my co-teacher Michael Ratner, an extraordinary group of Yale law students, and I began the work that led to *Haitian Centers Council v. McNary*, the case grippingly detailed in Brandt Goldstein's nonfiction novel, *Storming the Court: How a Band of Yale Law Students Sued the President— and Won.*[7] *Storming the Court* recounts how, in the early 1990s, we sued two U.S. Presidents on behalf of thousands of Haitian refugees fleeing from political violence on small boats, many of which came to be held at the U.S. naval base at Guantánamo Bay, Cuba.

This Documentary Companion, ably prepared by Professors Brandt Goldstein, Rodger Citron, and Molly Beutz Land, reminds us that at bottom, the Haitian refugee story was not just a human rights story, a human interest story, or a clinical legal education story, but a Procedure story. College students "storm the court" after a winning basketball game in a chaotic expression of unfocused, uproarious exuberance, whereas law students "storm the court" through a flurry of disciplined actions guided

---

3. Fed. R. Civ. P. 1.

4. For a summary of lessons learned in this capacity, see generally HAROLD HONGJU KOH, TRANSNATIONAL LITIGATION IN UNITED STATES COURTS (2008). For a history of human rights clinics, see generally Deena R. Hurwitz, *Lawyering for Justice and the Inevitability of International Human Rights Clinics*, 28 YALE J. INT'L L. 505 (2003).

5. Harold Hongju Koh, *Transnational Public Law Litigation*, 100 YALE L.J. 2247 (1991).

6. Harold Hongju Koh, *Why Do Nations Obey International Law?*, 106 YALE L.J. 2599, 2638 (1997).

7. BRANDT GOLDSTEIN, STORMING THE COURT: HOW A BAND OF YALE LAW STUDENTS SUED THE PRESIDENT—AND WON (2005). [For the Scribner paperback edition published in 2006, Goldstein changed the subtitle to "How a Band of Law Students Fought the President—and Won."—Eds.]

by Procedure: filing motions, taking depositions, and writing briefs. In the Haitian refugee case, we stormed the courts first and foremost by using the tools and lessons taught in the traditional first-year law school course in Procedure.

If you have read *Storming the Court*, you should know that it is remarkably true to life. The story of the Haitian litigation has now been recounted in many places, and I have done my share of the recounting.[8] Where Brandt Goldstein's book succeeds best is in bringing home viscerally the raw emotions that pervaded the Haitian litigation. While the suit was unfolding, there were many dark days when we had absolutely no idea whether things would end up well, or we or our clients would make it safely through the experience. Even so, we all quickly realized that we were living through something very special.

Few lawyers get the chance to take a single case from preliminary injunction to class action complaint to Supreme Court judgment to full bench trial to settlement, but that is precisely what we did in the Haitian litigation. During the 15 months during which that case unfolded, the suit went to the Second Circuit five times and the Supreme Court eight times, including once as a full oral argument before the Court. On at least one occasion, we filed litigation papers at the district, circuit, and Supreme Court on the same day! In 1992, we were among the first civilian lawyers to travel to Guantánamo—which back then, almost no one had heard of—as well as to Haiti.[9] And, as Goldstein's book recounts, we found ourselves caught up in an extraordinary public event that brought us into daily contact not just with lawyers, but with public figures and celebrities like Hillary Clinton, Jesse Jackson, Harry Belafonte, and Susan Sarandon.

Before the Haitian case, my total courtroom experience had been my law school moot court appearance. Over the next year and a half, I argued more times than I can remember, on one occasion arguing a motion before Judge Sterling Johnson on a conference call, standing at a speakerphone at a *maitre d*'s station at a New York hotel, with Michael Ratner participating by cellphone from the bleachers at a Mets game. When I later recounted the scene to one of our students, Ray Brescia, he retorted jovially (and perhaps presciently), "No surprise, man! It's all just part of the movie!"[10]

The Haitian refugee case taught me many things about Procedure that I had never fully grasped in law school. First, learning Procedure is what it means to speak, write, and think like a lawyer. Becoming a lawyer is like becoming bilingual. When you

---

8. For an account from the students' perspective, see Victoria Clawson, Elizabeth Detweiler & Laura Ho, *Litigating as Law Students: An Inside Look at* Haitian Centers Council, 103 YALE L.J. 2337 (1994). For a review of the litigation strategy and the human rights lessons, see Harold Hongju Koh & Michael J. Wishnie, *The Story of* Sale v. Haitian Centers Council: *Guantanamo and* Refoulement, *in* DEENA HURWITZ, DOUGLAS FORD & MEG SATTERTHWAITE, HUMAN RIGHTS ADVOCACY STORIES 385 (2008). For analysis of the policy implications, see Harold Hongju Koh, *The "Haiti Paradigm" in United States Human Rights Policy*, 103 YALE L.J. 2391 (1994); and Harold Hongju Koh, *America's Offshore Refugee Camps*, 29 U. RICH. L. REV. 139 (1994). For contemporaneous accounts, including some of the appellate briefs, see The Lowenstein International Human Rights Clinic (including Koh & Wishnie), *Aliens and the Duty of* Nonrefoulement: Haitian Centers Council v. McNary, 6 HARV. HUM. RTS. J. 1 (1993); and Harold Hongju Koh, *Reflections on* Refoulement *and* Haitian Centers Council, 35 HARV. INT'L L.J. 1 (1994).

9. Like most Americans, I had first heard about Guantánamo through the popular folk song *Guantanamera* ("The Girl from Guantánamo") and Jack Nicholson's unforgettable performance as a Guantánamo naval commandant ("You can't handle the truth!") in the Rob Reiner/Aaron Sorkin film *A Few Good Men*.

10. At this writing, Brandt Goldstein's book STORMING THE COURT is apparently being adapted for the screen by writer-director Michael Seitzman.

shift from the discourse of life to the discourse of law, you must practice shifting ways of thinking and talking as seamlessly as you do when you switch from speaking English to French, once you cross the English Channel.

Second, you can never know too much procedure. Knowing more procedure gives you broader options in litigating, in the same way as knowing more vocabulary gives you broader options in verbal expression. Time and time again during the Haitian case, we thought we had hit a wall—with venue, claim preclusion, standing, and injunctive relief—only to discover, through a flurry of frantic research, an unseen procedural avenue forward. Often you have only one chance to get it right. You never know when you may suddenly be called upon to recall a point of procedure from memory. In one of my oral arguments before the Second Circuit, for example, I suddenly found myself reciting canons of *res judicata* that I had first memorized as a first-term law student.

Most of the procedural documents you will read here were drafted under extreme time pressure, under strict court deadlines, during caffeine-driven all-night sessions. What bears remembering is that they were written before today's age of e-mail, the World Wide Web, cell phones, text messaging, or laser printers, and in the relatively early days of laptops and word processing. Students downloaded their research onto 3.5" floppy drives, and we merged them and edited them into the documents you see during intense all-nighters. Some of the research and writing was done by students only a few months into law school, written at the same time as they were attending classes, writing law school memo and brief assignments, and participating in moot court. Some students did legal research between trips to Miami or Guantánamo, taking depositions, or while fasting in protest against the government's Haitian policies. At times, we attached to pleadings handwritten declarations transcribed in airplane hangars and faxed from Guantánamo. Upon rereading, our litigation documents hardly seem as elegant or as tightly edited as they should have been. Nevertheless, they did the job—and, more important, they capture the passion that we all felt about our clients' plight: an urgency that drove the entire Haitian litigation.

Third, I learned that success in Procedure is *situational*: what John McPhee once called "having a sense of where you are."[11] In explaining why some people succeed where others fail, Malcolm Gladwell highlights what psychologist Robert Sternberg called "'practical intelligence,' knowing what to say to whom, knowing when to say it, and knowing how to say it for maximum effect."[12] Through the course of intense litigation, lawyers similarly develop a "procedural intelligence": the awareness that the same set of arguments that may fail in one litigation setting (*HRC v. Baker*) may, with thoughtful tweaking, just as easily succeed in another (*HCC v. McNary*). If you are a new law student more comfortable with expressing yourself through dance, basketball, or chamber music rather than law, you may be surprised to think of litigation as a form of human expression. Like inspired music or art, inspired litigation means fusing passion with practical judgment in an effort to achieve meaningful human results.

Fourth, and most important, the Haitian refugee litigation taught me that our procedural system is not an impersonal machine. It is a human system populated by courageous clients like Yvonne Pascal; idealistic students like Mike Wishnie, Sarah

---

11. John McPhee, A Sense of Where You Are: Bill Bradley at Princeton (1965).
12. Malcolm Gladwell, Outliers: The Story of Success 101 (2008).

Cleveland, Lisa Daugaard, Tory Clawson, and Ray Brescia;[13] heroic judges like Sterling Johnson, Jr.; principled government lawyers like Bob Begleiter; savvy trial lawyers like Joe Tringali; and tireless human rights advocates like Michael Ratner and Lucas Guttentag.

Litigating the Haitian case fundamentally changed the way I teach Procedure. When I teach the subject now, sometimes using illustrations from the Haitian case, I try to teach it less as a collection of doctrinal rules and more as a process of human decision. I try to show that abstract procedural choices have stark human consequences. For example:

- I used to teach pleading as a kind of historic ritual, which evolved from writ pleading to Code pleading to the Federal Rules; I now teach it as an occasion for genuine complaint and answer, telling the kind of human and legal story that the pleadings told in this case.
- I used to teach temporary restraining orders and injunctions as a historical invention of equity; I now teach injunctive relief as a means by which even a dramatically overmatched David can stop a Goliath (or a government policy) in its tracks.
- When I teach "forum-shopping," I no longer routinely treat it as an abuse of process, but as it so often is, an understandable quest for a friendly forum at trial and on appeal, often chosen less for litigation purposes than to create a political focal point to bring local communities (e.g., Haitian-Americans) and local press into the courtroom.
- When I teach discovery, I now give less emphasis to the "no surprises, open disclosure" philosophy of American procedure and more attention to the adversarial use of discovery as part of a resource-sapping war of attrition.
- When I teach claim preclusion, I speak less of "doctrine" and more of "representation," noting that in the Haitian case, we successfully argued that our clients could not be denied their day in court by prior litigation. Their interests as "screened-in" plaintiffs with credible claims to political asylum, we argued, had never been adequately represented by a prior class judgment against "screened-out" plaintiffs who had been found to be lacking those claims.[14]
- When I teach Rule 11, which has now been modified partly in response to the publicity over this case,[15] I place less stress on its formal character as a tool for judges to control overreaching litigants. Instead, I stress the ways in which

---

13. Many of the Yale law students who worked most intensively on the Haitian case have gone on to pursue careers in human rights, international law, or public interest law, including Michelle Anderson, Ethan Balogh, Michael Barr, Graham Boyd, Ray Brescia, Sarah Cleveland, Tory Clawson, Chris Coons, Lisa Daugaard, Liz Detweiler, Margareth Etienne, Carl Goldfarb, Adam Gutride, Laura Ho, Anthony K. (Van) Jones, Christy Lopez, Catherine Powell, Steve Roos, Veronique Sanchez, Paul Sonn, Cecillia Wang, and Jessica Weisel.

14. [*See* Chapter 10.—Eds.]

15. Cf. Neil Lewis, *House Approves Measure To Limit Federal Lawsuits*, N.Y. TIMES, March 8, 1995 ("[M]any civil rights lawyers have challenged the penalties, known in the legal profession as [Rule] 11 sanctions, because they are open to abuse. As an example, the Justice Department in the Bush Administration sought to have $10 million in [Rule] 11 sanctions imposed in 1992 against a Yale Law School professor, Harold H. Koh, and his students for lawsuits they brought on behalf of Haitian detainees. The effort was dropped after Federal courts upheld Professor Koh's suits and the Justice Department faced mounting criticism that it was abusing the sanctions to intimidate its opponents.").

defendants can use Rule 11 to drive a wedge between a public interest lawyer and his client, by encouraging the lawyer to divert resources to his own Rule 11 defense, and away from his ethical commitment to the undivided and zealous representation of his client.

- Finally, the Haitian case illustrated the four core ideas that pervade any Procedure class:
  - *Jurisdiction*, or how we invoked the power of the court to bring the exercise of judicial authority to bear on U.S. interdiction policy;
  - *Due process* of law owed to alien detainees on Guantánamo, an issue that seized global attention in the years after September 11, 2001;
  - Our professional *roles*, as advocates and teachers, and the institutional roles we were urging upon the district, circuit and Supreme Courts; and
  - The *relationship among procedural systems*, particularly the stark contrast between the established system of justice in Brooklyn federal court and the total absence of procedural rules on Guantánamo (another issue that graphically resurfaced during the post-9/11 "War on Terror").

Most fundamentally, the Haitian case revealed how the concept of *adjudication* has transformed over time. What started as traditional private dispute resolution evolved during the civil rights era into a form of public law norm enunciation, and has now mutated again in the age of human rights into a transnational device that can give voice to the powerless by empowering them to demand answers and bargain with even the most powerful governments.

To me, the most thrilling moment in the Haitian case came not in any courtroom, but in June 1993, at Kennedy Airport, when Michael Ratner and I watched a planeload of our clients, freed by Judge Johnson's court order, arrive from Guantánamo. While we watched the military transport plane taxi in, as Brandt Goldstein describes, I turned to Michael, pounded him on the back and shouted, "Law made this happen!"[16] When we started the case, it seemed that the Haitians would be trapped indefinitely on Guantánamo. By the end, through Procedure, a significant number had found hope and new lives in America. A friend who excelled in the sport of fencing once told me, "We learn to practice our technique over and over every day, because in a real match, fear robs you of 99% of your skills. And so the person with the larger one percent wins." During much of the Haitian case, I must admit, I was afraid: for my clients' well-being, for the students and colleagues who were relying on me, and for the future and family I was putting in jeopardy. More poetically, Archimedes once said, "Give me a place to stand on, and I can move the world." Looking back, as we stormed the court, my "one percent of Procedure" became my place to stand on. From that place, Procedure helped us to move the world, just a little bit, and maybe even to secure some justice.

---

16. GOLDSTEIN, *supra* note 7, at 291.

CHAPTER ONE

Introduction

How did a group of human rights lawyers and law students manage to shut down the first Guantánamo detention camp and free the 300 refugees who had been detained there for over a year? A layperson who has read *Storming the Court* might well say something about hard work and dedication. True, the victory against the White House could not have been achieved without great effort. But an experienced litigator might well point to another factor: litigation strategy, including a thorough understanding and sophisticated use of the rules and doctrines of our system of civil procedure.

This response might be less dramatic than talk of passion and commitment, but the fact is that the strategic use of federal civil procedure had an incalculable impact on the structure, development, and outcome of *Haitian Centers Council v. McNary*, the civil action at the center of *Storming the Court*. Consider just three of the most significant ways that the Yale team's use of civil procedure rules and doctrines affected the case:

- Harold Koh and the students relied on a provision of the federal venue statute—which helps determine where a case should be filed—to bring their case in the U.S. District Court for the Eastern District of New York. Had the Yale team not been able to choose this forum, Judge Sterling Johnson, Jr. would not have been assigned to the case and appeals would not have gone to the U.S. Court of Appeals for the Second Circuit, which proved as sympathetic to the Haitians as Judge Johnson did.
- The Yale team cited a critical exception to the doctrine of claim preclusion (what Koh calls "res judicata" in *Storming the Court*) to argue that Judge Johnson should allow *McNary* to go forward—despite the fact that the remarkably similar case of *Haitian Refugee Center v. Baker* had just been decided in favor of the government. Without this exception to claim preclusion, the plaintiffs might have been barred from bringing the *McNary* suit.
- After the government filed a Rule 11 sanctions motion against Harold Koh for bringing an allegedly frivolous lawsuit, Koh feared that his family's financial security was on the line. But he persuaded the government to drop its motion by threatening to file a Rule 11 motion of his own against the government—for filing a frivolous Rule 11 motion.

Similarly, the Justice Department lawyers in the *McNary* case relied on various civil procedure rules and doctrines to achieve many important victories of their own:

- Led by Paul Cappuccio, the Justice Department filed an application for a stay of Judge Johnson's preliminary injunction and managed, through an interlocutory appeal, to obtain the stay from the Supreme Court. This enabled federal immigration authorities to send back to Haiti many Haitians on Guantánamo who, under the preliminary injunction, might have remained there and later entered the United States.

- Government lawyers used numerous tactics to prolong the discovery process, making fact-finding difficult for the Yale team; yet, by never disobeying the rules, they largely managed to avoid answering in court for their strategic slowdown.

- After the government lawyers had lost at trial, they used the threat of an appeal as leverage to convince the Yale team to settle the case. As part of the settlement, Yale agreed to file a joint motion requesting that Judge Johnson vacate his final decision. The judge approved the settlement and granted the motion, and, as a result, his ruling that the due process clause applies on Guantánamo was stripped of any precedential value.

There are numerous other examples of how the use of civil procedure by counsel on both sides affected the case, and we'll explore them over the course of this book. Taken together, they show that the rules and procedures for litigating a civil action can affect its outcome as much as the substantive law that applies to the underlying dispute.

Demonstrating the importance of effectively using the tools of civil procedure in litigation is the first of this book's three overarching goals. The second goal is to present the structure and "life cycle" of a lawsuit in more depth than is possible in a traditional casebook. We aim to do that by working through a single case from beginning to end, an approach very different from that generally taken in casebooks. Most such books, as you are no doubt finding, ask you to focus on tightly edited versions of important Supreme Court and other appellate court opinions. They demand, primarily, that you learn to extract the holding and rationale of a decision, analyze the development of a particular area of the law from one major case to the next, and then apply your knowledge of legal doctrine to new factual situations. These skills are, of course, fundamental to any new lawyer's development. But if one spends too much time thinking about lawsuits only as they are presented in a casebook, it is difficult to acquire a broader understanding of the litigation process.

The reason, as Harold Koh himself was reminded when the team was struggling to draft the complaint in *McNary*, is that cases have a way of looking nice and neat (relatively speaking) when presented in the form of judicial opinions. The relevant facts are conveniently laid out in a page or two, followed by a discussion of the applicable law and the court's holding. In the most persuasive judicial decisions, the ruling—and often the arc of the whole case—can seem almost inevitable.

The outcome in most cases, however, is anything but foreordained. Indeed, before Koh and the students filed *McNary*, most immigration experts were sure they were going to lose. If we rewind the litigation process back to the start of a suit, we find that things look drastically different than they do after final judgment. The facts, the law, and the real dispute at issue can seem hazy at best—and the way forward very uncertain. When the Yale team was initially researching *McNary*, the circumstances surrounding the screening and detention of the Haitian refugees were only dimly apparent to the students, and some of the key events that would later be at the center of the case had not yet even occurred. The team was unsure about what legal claims to make, where to file the case, and—given that Yale had no access to the Haitians—even whether the putative plaintiffs wanted a case filed on their behalf.

What was the best way to proceed? At every stage of the litigation—from pre-complaint investigation and the filing of the complaint all the way through the post-trial appeal and settlement—there were many possible answers, and the lawyers and students had to make decisions and act on them while confronted with a huge array of unknowns. On top of the manifold uncertainties of the case, they had to operate (as lawyers often do) under great time pressure, not to mention work stress and numerous other competing obligations and concerns. All told, when litigation is seen from the perspective of an attorney in the middle of the fight, it looks and feels completely different from the way it does in casebooks.

This brings us to the third purpose of this book. In short order, law students grow familiar with terms like "complaint," "motion to dismiss," and "discovery request." After hearing them in class over and over, most students know—vaguely—what they are about. But unless you've worked as, say, a paralegal in a litigation firm, chances are you don't know what most of these documents actually look like or how you would go about drafting or reviewing one of them. In metaphorical terms, the doctrinal training most first-semester students receive can make one a bit like a chef who learns her profession by studying recipe books, but is never allowed into the kitchen.

As a third goal, then, we hope to offer a sense of what litigation is like from the nuts-and-bolts perspective of the lawyers involved in *McNary*—a taste of the real day-to-day legal work that is required when you are on a case. With this book, you'll be able to delve into the actual documents from the litigation: the complaint, the answer, the motion to dismiss, the Rule 11 motion, discovery requests, deposition transcripts, and many of the other key filings and materials from both the plaintiffs and the defendants. We'll discuss how you go about filing a complaint with the court, drafting a Rule 11 motion, taking and defending a deposition, preparing for trial, handling appeals, settling cases, and dealing with opposing counsel and your clients.

We begin with the assumption that you've read *Storming the Court*, which will give you a working understanding of the *McNary* case. From there, we will get into the nitty-gritty of the litigation, starting with a chapter about the complaint and then working our way through the entire case. Each chapter covers a stage in the litigation process and contains the following three elements: (1) the introduction to the procedural stage of the case, (2) a reproduction of part or all of one or more key documents from that stage, and (3) a series of questions, comments, and, in some instances, exercises, all relating to the document(s) and the relevant rules and doctrines of civil procedure. The chapters are designed to help you understand what was at stake at each stage in the case, the rules and doctrines that govern that stage, the choices the plaintiffs' attorneys and government lawyers faced, the decisions they made, the papers they filed with the court, the challenges those decisions and filings presented for the other side, and some of the many nuances of the applicable principles of civil procedure.

Before we start, though, we will quickly review the circumstances that gave rise to the *McNary* case, the course of the suit, the individuals involved in the litigation, and the courts in which the case was litigated. This should help you recall the basic outline of the lawsuit, stimulate your thinking, and, thanks to some photographs, give you a fuller sense of the people and places that helped make *McNary* such a fascinating lawsuit.

EVENTS LEADING UP TO *McNARY*: THE *BAKER* LITIGATION

Let's start by reviewing the situation prior to the filing of *McNary*. You'll recall that Yvonne Pascal and thousands of other Haitians worked to help make Jean-Bertrand Aristide—a radical, charismatic priest from the slums—the first democratically elected president in Haiti's history. Despite enjoying huge support among ordinary Haitians, Aristide was ousted in a military coup on September 30, 1991, and he ultimately fled to the United States. Following the president's forced departure, Haitian soldiers and paramilitary forces persecuted pro-Aristide elements among the citizenry, particularly in Aristide strongholds such as Cité Soleil,[1] the sprawling, fetid slum where Yvonne Pascal and her family lived.

Cité Soleil, Port-au-Prince, Haiti—one of the most impoverished neighborhoods in the Western Hemisphere's poorest country. Photograph by Daniel Morel.

---

1. Cité Soleil (pronounced "Si-tay So-lay") means "Sun City" in French.

Several months after the coup, Yvonne was arrested and tortured for her pro-democracy activities. Believing she would be killed if she remained in Haiti, she fled the country on a sailboat with hundreds of her fellow citizens, seeking safe haven from the military regime. From late October 1991 through May 1992, about 35,000 other Haitians did the same thing, cramming themselves into any vessel that would float and heading into the Windward Passage between Haiti and Cuba. Concerned that most of the Haitians wanted to reach the United States, the Bush administration ordered Coast Guard cutters into the Caribbean Sea to intercept all the Haitian boats. This policy was possible only because former Haitian dictator "Baby Doc" Duvalier had signed a treaty with the Reagan administration allowing the United States to stop Haitian vessels in international waters. *See Storming the Court (STC)*, p. 18. Acting on the Bush administration's orders, the American cutters took all of the Haitians on board and then blew up their boats as so-called "hazards to navigation."

In the first weeks after the coup, with only a thousand or so Haitians having fled, the Coast Guard simply kept everyone on the cutter decks and waited for further orders. But with more and more people fleeing Haiti, the Bush administration decided to forcibly send back to Port-au-Prince all those who did not qualify as potential refugees (meaning people who feared persecution in Haiti). Assisted by Creole inter-preters, Immigration and Naturalization Service (INS)[2] officials on board the cutters began interviewing the Haitians and dividing them into two groups: the potential refugees, who had what is called a "credible fear" of persecution, and the "economic migrants," who were supposedly trying to reach the United States solely in search of greater economic opportunity. Those deemed "economic migrants" were sent back to Port-au-Prince and handed over to the Haitian military. Those who established a credible fear of persecution were flown to the United States to file a formal asylum application.

This is where lawyers first entered the picture. American immigration attorneys and Haitian refugee advocates believed that the federal government's interviews of the Haitians were inadequate—too quick, too cursory. The result, they feared, was that the United States may have been returning bona fide political refugees to Haiti. Hoping to improve the interview process, immigration specialist Ira Kurzban and other attorneys filed the first case for the Haitians, *Haitian Refugee Center v. Baker*, in Miami in November 1991. Days after the lawsuit was filed, the government decided to move the Haitians off the Coast Guard cutters and onto the American naval base at Guantánamo Bay, where they were housed in military tents and surrounded by razor wire on the tarmac of an unused airfield.

The *Baker* lawsuit played out very fast—and, if you were a Haitian at Guantánamo, not very favorably. A lower court in Miami briefly halted the interview process and granted the plaintiffs' lawyers access to Guantánamo to investigate the situation there, but the case was ultimately dismissed by a federal appeals court in Atlanta. The Supreme Court denied certiorari (meaning it refused to hear the case) on February 24, 1992, putting an end to the litigation just three months after it began. *See STC*, Chapter 2. As disappointed as Kurzban and his colleagues were, the Justice

---

2. The INS ceased to exist on March 1, 2003, and most of its functions are now handled by three agencies within the Department of Homeland Security: U.S. Citizenship and Immigration Services (USCIS), U.S. Immigration and Customs Enforcement (ICE), and U.S. Customs and Border Protection (CBP).

Camp McCalla, Guantánamo Bay, most likely spring 1992. Photograph courtesy of Stephen Kinder.

Department was equally relieved, and the government lawyers in Washington believed that they could now direct their energy to other matters.

A QUICK REVIEW OF *McNARY*

Almost immediately, the students at Yale were talking about picking up where the *Baker* lawyers had left off. The first serious meeting about filing a new case took place just days after the Supreme Court's February 1992 decision, and *McNary* was filed on March 17, 1992. Judge Johnson issued a temporary restraining order in favor of the plaintiffs on March 27. *See STC*, Chapter 3.[3] Yale Law students Mike Wishnie and Sarah Cleveland then flew down to Guantánamo Bay to meet with the Haitians, including Frantz Guerrier, for the first time. The preliminary injunction hearing was held on April 1, and Judge Johnson issued the preliminary injunction on April 6; the Supreme Court then stayed the preliminary injunction order on April 22. *See id.*, Chapter 4.

Following the stay, the INS began holding asylum hearings on Guantánamo—without lawyers—for screened-in, HIV-positive Haitians. This was a result of a new policy instituted by the government on February 29, 1992, providing that individuals who had demonstrated that they had a "credible fear" of persecution in the initial screening process but who tested positive for HIV would not be allowed to enter the United States. Prior to the institution of this policy, individuals with a credible fear of

---

3. The endnotes to STORMING THE COURT provide comprehensive citations to the published decisions.

persecution would have been transported to the United States where they would have undergone a second interview, with access to legal representation, to determine whether they had a "well-founded fear" of persecution (which is a more stringent standard than the "credible fear" standard). Those Haitians who did not establish a "well-founded fear" of persecution or refused to participate in the hearing process, as did Frantz Guerrier, were sent back to Port-au-Prince.

Subsequently, the White House decided to take a much harder line in the crisis. On May 24, President George H.W. Bush issued an executive order authorizing the Coast Guard to return to Port-au-Prince, without a screening interview, *all* Haitians fleeing Haiti. The Yale team immediately moved for a temporary restraining order against the direct return policy, and on May 29, Judge Johnson heard arguments by Harold Koh and Kenneth Starr on the motion. Judge Johnson ruled for the government on June 6, and after Yale appealed,[4] the Second Circuit reversed his decision and instructed Judge Johnson to enter a preliminary injunction to halt the direct return policy. On August 1, the Supreme Court issued a stay preventing enforcement of the injunction, thus allowing the direct return policy to continue. *See id.*, Chapter 5.

By mid-July, Haitians had largely quit trying to flee Haiti, and the only Haitians left at Guantánamo were HIV-positive screened-in individuals who had either (1) proved a well-founded fear of persecution in an asylum hearing or (2) not yet undergone an asylum hearing for various reasons. (Yvonne Pascal fell into the latter category.) Camp McCalla was closed down, and all remaining Haitians at Guantánamo were detained at Camp Bulkeley, located on a remote part of the naval base. *See id.*

A few words about Bulkeley's layout: The barracks (called *kay-o* by the Haitians) are the long, narrow buildings in the lower right-hand quadrant of the picture on the next page. The camp entrance is just below and to the left of the large white building with dark windows near the top middle of the picture. Although it is hard to see them because of the scale, most of the Haitians are gathered near the camp entrance. They appear as a blurry spot immediately to the bottom left of the large white building. They had assembled to protest the restrictive camp policies of Colonel Joe Trimble, who preceded Colonel Stephen Kinder as the military official in charge of Bulkeley. *See id.*, pp. 144-46, 151-54.

In mid-September 1992, Paul Cappuccio met with the Yale team to offer a settlement proposal in the Guantánamo case, and on October 16 and 17, Harold Koh, Lisa Daugaard, and others presented the settlement offer in person to the Haitians on Guantánamo. The offer would have allowed the detainees access to lawyers on Guantánamo in connection with their asylum hearings. Based on the Yale team's view that Bill Clinton, the Democratic presidential nominee, would likely end the ban on HIV-positive foreigners if he won the election, the Haitians rejected the offer. *See id.*, Chapter 6.

By agreement of the parties, all proceedings in the Guantánamo case were postponed ("continued," in legal parlance) until after the election. Clinton was elected president on November 3, 1992. On January 14, 1993, six days before his inauguration, President Clinton went back on an earlier promise to reverse the Bush administration's direct return policy. *See id.*, Chapter 7. He subsequently refused to rescind the HIV ban,

---

4. Judge Johnson treated the plaintiffs' motion as one for a preliminary injunction, which allowed them to appeal his denial of the motion under 28 U.S.C § 1292(a)(1). *See* Chapter 9.

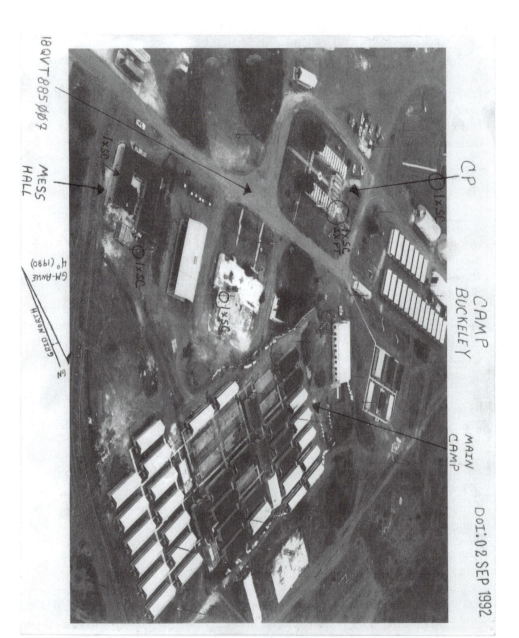

Camp Bulkeley, September 2, 1992 (misspelled as "Buckeley" at the top of the picture; the handwritten notes were made by someone in the military or the government). Photograph courtesy of Stephen Kinder.

and Congress then voted to make the ban—which at the time was only a federal regulation—federal law. The Haitians launched their hunger strike on January 28, 1993. *See id.*, Chapter 8.

Harold Koh argued the direct return case before the Supreme Court on March 2. *See id.*, Chapter 9. The trial for the release of the Guantánamo Haitians began in Brooklyn on March 8, and on March 11, eleven Haitians broke out of Camp Bulkeley, leading to the March 13 pre-dawn military effort to account for the whereabouts of the entire Bulkeley population. The trial in Brooklyn essentially ended on March 18,[5] and on March 26, Judge Johnson issued an interim order requiring the government to either free all Bulkeley Haitians not receiving adequate medical care on Guantánamo or provide them adequate care while still in confinement. The Justice Department opted to evacuate the Haitians, and the first group of them arrived in the United States on April 5, 1993. Judge Johnson issued his final order and decision in the Guantánamo case on June 8, 1993, and the last of the Haitians were released on June 21, 1993. *See id.*, Chapter 10. Also on June 21, the Supreme Court reversed the Second Circuit in the direct return case, ruling that the direct return policy was permissible under both federal and international law.

---

5. On March 25, the Court heard the testimony of one government rebuttal witness; this testimony is not described in *Storming the Court.*

In early August, the government appealed Judge Johnson's final order in the Guantánamo case. Settlement negotiations then ensued, and in late October, the Yale team and the Department of Justice signed a final settlement agreement. The agreement called for the government to drop its appeal and to reimburse plaintiffs' counsel $634,100 for litigation costs and attorneys' fees. In exchange, plaintiffs' counsel joined a motion by the government to vacate Judge Johnson's final order, stripping it of any precedential value. On February 22, 1994, Judge Johnson approved the settlement and vacated his final order. *See id.*, Chapter 11.

THE FOCUS OF THIS BOOK

As the previous summary should remind you, the *McNary* litigation ultimately split into two cases: the suit challenging the detention of HIV-positive Haitians held at Guantánamo and the suit challenging the Bush administration's direct return policy. For several reasons, this book focuses largely on the Guantánamo case. The Guantánamo case went through almost all of the key stages of a civil action: the filing of a complaint and a request for preliminary relief, a motion to dismiss and an answer, multiple forms of discovery and pretrial preparation, trial, appeal (both interlocutory appeal and appeal from a final order), and, finally, settlement. In contrast, the direct return case involved little more than a motion for preliminary relief, an interlocutory appeal, and a Supreme Court argument. The Guantánamo case therefore provides a much better opportunity to explore the life cycle of a lawsuit.

Further, most of the documents in the litigation relate to the Guantánamo case; the story of the documents is therefore largely the story of the Guantánamo suit. Finally, there were almost no facts in dispute in the direct return case. It was almost entirely focused on the law—and combined with its truncated procedural path, the direct return case boils down to a legal argument about the interpretation of federal and international laws protecting refugees. Thus, although we will draw on the direct return case in several places, it will play far less of a role in this book than it does in *Storming the Court*.

THE MAIN PLAYERS

After reading *Storming the Court*, you should be familiar with the team of lawyers and law students representing the Haitians. Here are many of them, assembled on the steps of the Supreme Court the day of oral argument in the direct return case, March 2, 1993. *See STC*, p. 229.

As for the Haitians themselves, although almost 35,000 Haitian citizens were processed at Guantánamo Bay in 1991 and 1992, the *McNary* case ultimately focused on the fate of the last 300 Haitians who remained at Camp Bulkeley after July 1992. Of those 300 Haitians in Bulkeley, perhaps 230 were HIV-positive; the remaining 70 were dependents of the HIV-positive detainees. As you know, *Storming the Court* concentrates on one of the HIV-positive Haitians—Yvonne Pascal.

The following is a partial list of those pictured. Front row (from left to right): ACLU attorney Lucas Guttentag, Yale Professor Harold Koh, Center for Constitutional Rights lawyer Michael Ratner, Yale graduate Catherine Powell, and Simpson Thacher & Bartlett partner Joe Tringali. Second row: Yale graduate Graham Boyd, Yale graduate Michael Barr, Yale graduate Paul Sonn, Yale student Mike Wishnie (dark curly hair, leaning a bit to his right and partly obscured by Joe Tringali), Yale student Lisa Daugaard (partly obscured). Third row: Yale graduate Ray Brescia, Yale student Tory Clawson (with bangs, slightly behind Brescia), Yale graduate Chris Coons (with beard). Near the back in the middle is Yale graduate Sarah Cleveland (with hat); at the very back in the middle is Yale student Veronique Sanchez; and in the back right (with an opening to his left) is Yale student Steve Roos. (Note: Those identified as "graduates" were students at the time the case was filed—March 1992—but had finished law school by the time this picture was taken.) Photographer unknown.

Camp Bulkeley, most likely autumn 1992. Photograph courtesy of Stephen Kinder.

McNARY AND THE FEDERAL COURT SYSTEM

McNary was a federal court case. The federal court system has three levels: district (trial) courts, circuit (appellate) courts, and the Supreme Court. The *McNary* litigation played out on all three levels, moving from the district court in Brooklyn all the way to the Supreme Court and back again with extraordinary speed. You would be hard pressed to find another case that covered so much ground so quickly, and this is one of the features of *McNary* that makes the suit so remarkable. To provide some additional context as you work your way through this book, here is a brief introduction to the three courts involved in deciding *McNary*.

The District Courts

The *McNary* case was filed in the U.S. District Court for the Eastern District of New York. District courts are the trial courts of the federal system; the term "district" is a geographic one. Each state has between one and four federal judicial districts, depending on the state's size and population, for a total of 94 districts, including the districts in Puerto Rico, Guam, and other U.S. territories. The largest states, such as California and New York, have four judicial districts, while states with particularly small populations, such as Rhode Island and Alaska, have one. The number of judges per district varies, from two judges in Idaho, North Dakota, and Vermont, to 60 in California. 28 U.S.C. § 133.

District court judges, like judges on the courts of appeals and Justices on the Supreme Court, are Article III judges. This means that they are nominated by the President and confirmed by the Senate, and, once confirmed, they have life tenure subject to good behavior,[6] which essentially means they can keep their position so long as they are not convicted of a serious criminal offense. Only seven federal judges in American history have been removed from the bench.

The Eastern District of New York is one of the state's four federal judicial districts and encompasses all of Long Island, including Brooklyn and Queens Counties, as well as the New York City borough of Staten Island. There are 52 federal judges in New York's four judicial districts, but almost all the action is in the Eastern District and the Southern District (which encompasses Manhattan and the Bronx). In fact, more than 75 percent of New York's federal judges sit in those two districts. In addition to regular (or active) judges, most districts also have a number of senior judges serving on the courts. Senior judges have reached retirement age but choose to keep working on a reduced schedule. Judge Sterling Johnson, Jr., for example, took senior status in the Eastern District several years ago.

The Eastern District's courthouse is located in Brooklyn, just across the East River from Manhattan. A new, ultra-modern courthouse was completed some years after the *McNary* case ended. Judge Sterling Johnson, Jr.'s chambers and courtroom are now in the new addition, but at the time of *McNary*, Judge Johnson heard cases in the fluorescent-lit basement of a temporary annex. There was not enough space for all of the trials that were scheduled, and Judge Johnson once went so far as to hold a civil trial in the park across the street when the weather was nice.

The Circuit Courts

Appeals of decisions by judges in the Eastern District are heard by the U.S. Court of Appeals for the Second Circuit, one of the 13 appellate courts in the federal system. All of the circuit courts encompass specific groups of states, except for two appellate courts in Washington: the D.C. Circuit, which hears appeals from the U.S. District Court for the District of Columbia, as well as many federal agency matters, and the Federal Circuit, which has exclusive jurisdiction over patent cases and certain other cases involving claims against the federal government. The Second Circuit, located in Manhattan, hears appeals from the federal district courts in New York, Connecticut, and Vermont. The circuit courts have between six and 28 judges; as of May 2009, the Second Circuit had 12 active judges and nine senior judges. The Second Circuit is one of the best known and historically most influential of the federal appeals courts, and some of America's greatest jurists—Thurgood Marshall, Learned Hand, and Henry Friendly, to name just three—have served on the court. Guido Calabresi, Yale Law School's dean during the *McNary* case, is now a judge on the Second Circuit.

---

6. "The Judges, both of the supreme and inferior Courts, shall hold their Offices during good Behaviour, and shall, at stated Times, receive for their Services, a Compensation, which shall not be diminished during their Continuance in Office." U.S. Const. art. III, § 1.

The U.S. Supreme Court

The Supreme Court, established on February 2, 1790 and located in Washington, D.C., is the oldest federal court in the United States and the only court required by the Constitution.[7] The only required position on the Supreme Court is that of Chief Justice; Congress designates the number of Associate Justices by statute. That number is currently eight, giving us a total of nine Supreme Court Justices. The Court has the power to review the judgments of all the federal circuit courts as well as the power to hear appeals from the highest court of each state if a question of federal law is at issue. Unlike the federal courts of appeals, the Supreme Court's appellate jurisdiction is discretionary. In other words, it is not required to review cases; it chooses the ones it will review. Each year, the Court receives approximately 7,500 petitions for writs of certiorari (a request to review a case). But the Court grants these petitions and invites attorneys to make arguments (typically in both written and oral form) in only about 80 cases annually.[8] As you will recall from *Storming the Court*, the Court also hears emergency applications for stays (temporary suspensions) of lower court orders.

The Honorable Sterling Johnson, Jr.

The Honorable Sterling Johnson, Jr. was the judge in the Eastern District who issued most of the rulings in the *McNary* case. Born in 1934 and raised in the hardscrabble Bedford-Stuyvesant neighborhood of Brooklyn, New York, Johnson served in the Marine Corps and later attended Brooklyn Law School at night while working as a New York City police officer. After law school, he became a prosecutor in the U.S. Attorney's Office in the Southern District of New York, and after two other government posts, he assumed the position of Special Narcotics Prosecutor for New York. He held that post from 1975 to 1991, supervising attorneys and investigators collectively responsible for preparing and prosecuting over 7,000 criminal cases each year. A lifelong Democrat, he was nominated to the bench in May 1991 by President George H.W. Bush in large part because of support from U.S. Senator Alfonse D'Amato (R-N.Y.), a longtime friend of Johnson's.

---

7. "The judicial Power of the United States, shall be vested in one supreme Court, and in such inferior Courts as Congress may from time to time ordain and establish." U.S. Const. art. III, § 2.

8. The Supreme Court also has original jurisdiction, meaning that it can serve as a court of first instance in certain cases, but this jurisdiction (set forth in Article III of the Constitution) is exceedingly narrow.

Judge Sterling Johnson, Jr., 2003. Photograph by Michael Spano.

MOVING FORWARD

With the next chapter, we'll begin to work our way through the stages of the *McNary* case document by document. (Although the documents in this volume have often been edited in the interest of space, unedited versions are available on the companion website, along with other case documents and materials. *See* www.aspenlawschool. com/books/stc.) Over the course of the book, our focus will largely be on the Federal Rules of Civil Procedure. Those rules determine much of the structure and shape of federal litigation, and every chapter will discuss and analyze one or more of the Federal Rules. In addition, the book will cover a number of congressional statutes, judicially fashioned principles and doctrines, and traditional practices of lawyers and judges, all of which bear on the process of federal litigation. Along the way, we'll also present interviews with key figures from the case, such as Lisa Daugaard, Joe Tringali, and Judge Sterling Johnson on issues related to the litigation. Some of the material you will encounter in the forthcoming chapters, such as the government's motion for sanctions under Rule 11, will sound familiar because *Storming the Court* discusses it in some detail. Other material will no doubt prove new to you. We hope you find all of it interesting—and helpful in your development as a lawyer.

CHAPTER TWO

The Complaint

INTRODUCTION

Most every form of combat has a ritual that marks its start. Medieval battles had their horns and drums; boxing has the clang of a bell; chess has the opening move of a pawn or knight. In the American system of litigation, the fight formally begins with the filing of a complaint with the court. This chapter will focus on the drafting and filing of that critical document, as well as on a series of closely related topics.

Because the *McNary* case was filed in federal court, most of our attention in this chapter—indeed, in the entire book—will be on litigation in the federal courts. Cases filed in federal court are governed by the Federal Rules of Civil Procedure, and, accordingly, those rules will be our focus. They are, in essence, the rules of the road for litigation in federal court. Our aim is to help you to understand their basic operation, as well as the operation of other key principles and doctrines of civil procedure.

We begin by introducing you to one of the simplest of the Federal Rules: Rule 3, which provides that a plaintiff initiates a civil action in federal court by filing a complaint with the court. *See* Fed. R. Civ. P. 3. (The complaint also must be served on the other parties to the case. *See* Fed. R. Civ. P. 4.) The first document you will read from *McNary* is the original complaint, filed in March 1992. Reproduced below is a short excerpt from the complaint; selected additional excerpts appear later in this chapter. (If you would like to review the complaint in its entirety, it is available on the companion website for this book.)

What must the complaint contain? Rule 8 provides that information, and we will examine that rule's requirements in the Notes that follow. Briefly, the complaint must state the jurisdictional basis of the suit, the nature of the claims at issue, and the type of relief sought. Over the course of this chapter, we will explore how the Yale team sought to satisfy Rule 8. As you start to familiarize yourself with the complaint, ask yourself what other objectives Koh and the students might have been trying to achieve. Begin to think, as well, about how you would respond to the complaint if you were one of the Justice Department lawyers representing the government. Would you take issue with the factual allegations of the complaint, or perhaps just the legal arguments? What else would you contest? Under the Federal Rules, the Justice Department lawyers had a number of options for responding to the complaint; we will discuss those options in Chapter Three. (Note: The asterisks that appear throughout the excerpted documents in this book indicate where we have omitted material from the original.)

UNITED STATES DISTRICT COURT
EASTERN DISTRICT OF NEW YORK

- x

Haitian Centers Council, Inc. National Coalition for :
Haitian Refugees, Inc., Immigration Law Clinic of
the Jerome N. Frank Legal Services Organization, of :
New Haven, Connecticut; Dr. Frantz Guerrier, Pascal
Henry, Lauriton Guneau, Medilieu Sorel St. Fleur, :
Dieu Renel, Milot Baptiste, Jean Doe, and Roges Noel
on behalf of themselves and all others similarly :
situated; A. Iris Vilnor on behalf of herself and
all others similarly situated; Mireille Berger,   :
Yvrose Pierre and Mathieu Noel on behalf of
themselves and all others similarly situated,   :

                    Plaintiffs,   :

vs.   :

Gene McNary, Commissioner, Immigration and   :
Naturalization Service; William P. Barr, Attorney
General; Immigration and Naturalization Service; :
James Baker, III, Secretary of State; Rear Admiral
Robert Kramek and Admiral Kime, Commandants,   :
United States Coast Guard; and Commander, U.S.
Naval Base, Guantanamo Bay,   :

                                 :

                    Defendants.
- -x

COMPLAINT
92 Civ. **CV-92 1258**

JOHNSON

Plaintiffs Haitian Centers Council, Inc., National Coalition for Haitian Refugees, Inc.,

Immigration Law Clinic of the Jerome N. Frank Legal Services Organization, of New Haven,

Connecticut (hereinafter "Haitian Service Organizations"); Dr. Frantz Guerrier, Pascal Henry,

Lauriton Guneau, Medilieu Sorel St. Fleur, Dieu Renel, Milot Baptiste, Jean Doe, and Roges Noel on

behalf of themselves and all others similarly situated (hereinafter "screened in plaintiffs"); A. Iris

Vilnor on behalf of herself and all others similarly situated (hereinafter "screened out plaintiffs"); and

Mireille Berger, Yvrose Pierre and Mathieu Noel on behalf of themselves and all others similarly

situated (hereinafter "immediate relative plaintiffs"), by their undersigned attorneys, as and for their

complaint, allege as follows:

A reproduction of the first page of the actual McNary *complaint. For legibility purposes, the case documents in the book have been retyped.*

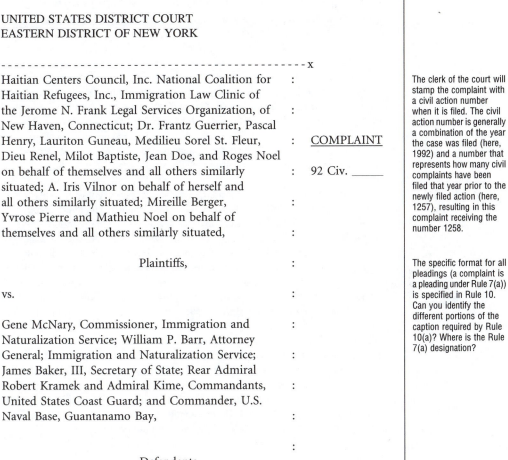

UNITED STATES DISTRICT COURT
EASTERN DISTRICT OF NEW YORK

- -x

Haitian Centers Council, Inc. National Coalition for   :
Haitian Refugees, Inc., Immigration Law Clinic of
the Jerome N. Frank Legal Services Organization, of   :
New Haven, Connecticut; Dr. Frantz Guerrier, Pascal
Henry, Lauriton Guneau, Medilieu Sorel St. Fleur,   :   COMPLAINT
Dieu Renel, Milot Baptiste, Jean Doe, and Roges Noel
on behalf of themselves and all others similarly   :   92 Civ. _____
situated; A. Iris Vilnor on behalf of herself and
all others similarly situated; Mireille Berger,   :
Yvrose Pierre and Mathieu Noel on behalf of
themselves and all others similarly situated,   :

                    Plaintiffs,   :

vs.   :

Gene McNary, Commissioner, Immigration and   :
Naturalization Service; William P. Barr, Attorney
General; Immigration and Naturalization Service;   :
James Baker, III, Secretary of State; Rear Admiral
Robert Kramek and Admiral Kime, Commandants,   :
United States Coast Guard; and Commander, U.S.
Naval Base, Guantanamo Bay,   :

                                                         :

                    Defendants.
- -x

The clerk of the court will stamp the complaint with a civil action number when it is filed. The civil action number is generally a combination of the year the case was filed (here, 1992) and a number that represents how many civil complaints have been filed that year prior to the newly filed action (here, 1257), resulting in this complaint receiving the number 1258.

The specific format for all pleadings (a complaint is a pleading under Rule 7(a)) is specified in Rule 10. Can you identify the different portions of the caption required by Rule 10(a)? Where is the Rule 7(a) designation?

      Plaintiffs Haitian Centers Council, Inc., National Coalition for Haitian
Refugees, Inc., Immigration Law Clinic of the Jerome N. Frank Legal Services
Organization, of New Haven, Connecticut (hereinafter "Haitian Service Organizations"); Dr. Frantz Guerrier, Pascal Henry, Lauriton Guneau, Medilieu Sorel
St. Fleur, Dieu Renel, Milot Baptiste, Jean Doe, and Roges Noel on behalf of
themselves and all others similarly situated (hereinafter "screened in plaintiffs");
A. Iris Vilnor on behalf of herself and all others similarly situated (hereinafter
"screened out plaintiffs"); and Mireille Berger, Yvrose Pierre and Mathieu Noel
on behalf of themselves and all others similarly situated (hereinafter "immediate
relative plaintiffs"), by their undersigned attorneys, as and for their complaint,
allege as follows:

PRELIMINARY STATEMENT

      1. This is a complaint for declaratory and injunctive relief arising from
defendants' illegal and arbitrary actions against Haitians and Haitian Service
Organizations following the military coup that overthrew the government of

The Federal Rules do not require that a complaint include a preliminary statement. What might be the purpose of drafting one?

Jean-Bertrand Aristide on September 30, 1991. Following the coup, many Haitians fled their country because of a well-founded fear of political persecution. Defendants have all but ignored those fears. Although binding domestic and international law mandates that refugees, such as the Haitian plaintiffs in this action, shall not be returned to countries where they face death and political persecution, defendants have interdicted numerous vessels on the high seas carrying the Haitian refugees to freedom. Defendants have detained those refugees at Guantanamo Bay Naval Base and subjected them to screening procedures nowhere mentioned in the Immigration and Nationality Act (INA). Refugees who have been "screened out" are then forcibly repatriated to Haiti to face death, injury or political persecution. Those who have been "screened in" remain detained and uncounseled for the most part, even as they await further proceedings that may lead to their forced repatriation.

2. Although the First Amendment protects the right of lawyers to talk with their clients, defendant officials have barred plaintiff legal and advocacy groups from speaking to Haitian refugees held incommunicado within U.S. jurisdiction, based solely upon the content of the message those representatives would communicate. Defendants simultaneously have barred plaintiff Haitian refugees from communicating with their retained counsel, even while subjecting those refugees to screening and exclusion proceedings that may lead to their death or serious injury. Since the September coup, lower executive officials have acted arbitrarily and capriciously and in violation of unambiguous constitutional, statutory, presidential, and administrative mandates to coerce and detain plaintiff refugees and to diminish their right to resist forced repatriation to a brutal regime the United States Government has called illegitimate. In so doing, defendants have ignored binding international obligations that have been executed as United States law and which deny them discretion to return political refugees to a country where those refugees have a well-founded fear of political persecution. Finally, defendants impermissibly have applied these unauthorized, ad hoc procedures solely against Haitian refugees, based on their race and national origin.

JURISDICTION AND VENUE

* * * *

PARTIES

A.   Plaintiffs

5. Plaintiff Haitian Centers Council ("HCC") is a not-for-profit corporation organized and existing under the laws of the State of New York, having its principal place of business at 50 Court Street, Brooklyn, New York. It provides a variety of services to the Haitian community, particularly the refugee community. Its clients have included thousands of Haitian refugees, including many that have fled Haiti by boat. Among its services HCC provides pro bono legal counsel on immigration questions for refugees seeking political asylum. HCC also provides services concerning employment, family counseling, job placement, AIDS education and prevention, education and health. It represents all Haitians that need its services, and part of its mission is advocacy on behalf of Haitian refugees. It has sought and continues to seek to provide services, legal and otherwise, to Haitians who have fled Haiti and been interdicted by defendants since the September 1991 coup. Defendants have denied HCC access to its clients on Guantanamo Bay

The Federal Rules do not require that the plaintiffs provide so much information about themselves in the complaint. It is common practice, however, for the complaint to list the plaintiffs, their domiciles (identifying them as citizens of a particular state or foreign country), and, when relevant to the case, their job titles and descriptions. Note that identifying citizenship *is* required when plaintiffs are trying to establish federal diversity jurisdiction. See Note 5 below.

Naval Base, thereby hindering its ability to provide effective representation to its interdicted clients.

6. Plaintiff National Coalition for Haitian Refugees, Inc. ("NCHR") is a not-for-profit corporation organized and existing under the laws of the State of New York, having its principal place of business in New York City.

* * * *

7. The Immigration Law Clinic of the Jerome N. Frank Legal Services Organization, of New Haven, Connecticut was organized in 1989 at the Yale Law School as a faculty-supervised clinical course designed to render pro bono legal assistance to refugees filing asylum claims.

* * * *

[The Complaint lists several other plaintiffs, as identified in the caption above.]

* * * *

B.   Defendants

14. Defendant Gene McNary is the Commissioner of the Immigration and Naturalization Service ("INS"). He is in charge of implementing the practices and procedures under which plaintiffs are denied their statutory and constitutional rights. The INS officers on board the United States Coast Guard cutters and at the U.S. Naval Base at Guantanamo Bay are acting under his direction and supervision. Defendant McNary is being sued in his official capacity.

15. Defendant William P. Barr, III, is the United States Attorney General and in that capacity has ultimate responsibility for the enforcement of the immigration laws of the United States. Defendant Barr is being sued in his official capacity.

16. Defendant James Baker, III, is the United States Secretary of State and in that capacity has the final decision-making authority within his department. Upon information and belief, the State Department has directed other United States agencies forcibly to repatriate Haitian refugees. Defendant Baker is being sued in his official capacity.

17. Defendants Kramek and Kime are Commandants of the United States Coast Guard. Other Coast Guard officers implementing the interdiction program are acting under their direction and command. These defendants are being sued in their official capacity.

Working under immense time pressure, the Yale team forgot to obtain Admiral Kime's first name before filing the complaint (not a fatal flaw). They had Rear Admiral Kramek's first name, as indicated in the caption.

18. Defendant Commander of the United States Naval Base has general jurisdiction over the United States' military operations at Guantanamo.

19. Defendant Immigration and Naturalization Service (INS) is the agency charged with direct responsibility for enforcing the immigration laws of the United States.

STATEMENT OF FACTS

Notice how the statement of facts seeks to present the case in simple, clear terms. Legal writing has a reputation for being dense and difficult to follow, but a well-written complaint (like a well-written brief) should be easy to read and understand.

20. On September 30, 1991, a military coup ousted Haitian President Jean-Bertrand Aristide. President Aristide had been elected in December 1990 in the first fully democratic elections to take place in Haiti in over 200 years.

21. The United States government refused to recognize the military junta which succeeded President Aristide. President Bush issued Executive Orders freezing all assets of Haiti in the United States and prohibiting U.S. citizens from transacting any business with the military junta. In Executive Order 12779, the President recognized that "the grave events in the Republic of Haiti . . . are continuing to disrupt the legitimate exercise of power by the democratically elected government of that country."

22. The September 1991 coup triggered a continuing, widely publicized reign of terror in Haiti. On information and belief, in the past five months, over fifteen hundred Haitians, many of them supporters of the Aristide government, have been killed or subjected to violence and destruction of their property because of their political beliefs and affiliations, producing fear and desperation throughout the country.

23. As a result of these grave conditions, thousands of Haitians have fled the brutality of the illegal Haitian regime. Thousands of refugees have fled to the Dominican Republic. Thousands more have set out in small boats that are often overloaded, unseaworthy, lacking basic safety equipment, and operated by inexperienced persons, braving the hazards of a prolonged journey over high seas in search of safety and freedom.

24. United States Coast Guard cutters on patrol in the international waters of the Windward Passage near Haiti have intercepted and are intercepting vessels carrying Haitians fleeing political persecution, many of whom have no desire to enter the United States and either have no specific destination in mind or are fleeing to a particular third country.

25. To date, countless vessels carrying Haitian refugees have been intercepted and more than 16,000 Haitians from these vessels have been detained since the coup. Initially, interdicted Haitians were taken to Guantanamo, where, after being denied procedural safeguards, including the right to counsel, the Haitian detainees were interviewed summarily and classified as "screened in" or "screened out." The "screened out" detainees thereby lost any opportunity to demonstrate that they were political refugees who should not be forcibly returned to Haiti because of a well-founded fear of persecution. The "screened in" detainees were supposed to be brought to the United States and afforded the full panoply of procedural safeguards in asserting their political asylum claims, including the right to counsel, although only a small number have apparently been so treated.

26. Well over 14,000 Haitians have been taken to the United States Naval Base at Guantanamo Bay, where they have been detained incommunicado week after week. Guantanamo Naval Base and the Coast Guard cutters on which the Haitians were originally detained are wholly within the jurisdiction of the United States.

This paragraph is to set up the claim that the government has denied the institutional plaintiffs (the legal and advocacy groups) their claimed First Amendment rights of access to their clients on Guantánamo.

27. Despite repeated attempts by legal and advocacy groups to gain access to Haitian refugees on the Coast Guard cutters or at Guantanamo Bay, defendants have barred such access completely. At the same time, however, defendants have granted access to numerous other individuals, including clergy and church groups, the press, and even piano-tuners.

28. Although the forcible repatriation of the "screened out" Haitian detainees was for a period preliminarily enjoined by the United States District Court for the Southern District of Florida, the United States Court of

Appeals for the Eleventh Circuit ultimately vacated all injunctions on February 4, 1992. On February 26, 1992, the Supreme Court denied certiorari, permitting the forcible repatriation of the "screened out" Haitian detainees to continue unchecked.

29. After the Supreme Court's denial of certiorari, defendants changed their screening policy by resuming screening on Coast Guard cutters and forcing some "screened in" Haitian refugees to undergo multiple layers of review before being brought to the United States. At present, defendants are purporting to adjudicate fully some Haitians' political asylum claims on Guantanamo while denying them access to counsel, the opportunity to rebut and submit evidence and other procedural safeguards. As a direct result of these procedural changes, the percentage of Haitians "screened in" has dropped precipitously. Defendants have provided no public notice in the Federal Register or otherwise to plaintiff Haitian Service Organizations, to plaintiff Haitian refugees, or to any one else in the United States or elsewhere of these drastic changes in procedure that directly affect the life and liberty of plaintiff Haitian refugees and that continue to thwart the organizational purposes of plaintiff Haitian Service Organizations.

* * * *

FIRST CLAIM FOR RELIEF

(Content-Based Denial of First Amendment Rights)

42. Plaintiffs repeat, reallege and incorporate paragraphs 1 through 41 above as though fully set forth herein.

> Rule 10(c) permits incorporation by reference, which enables the litigants to avoid repetitive allegations.

43. Plaintiff Haitian Service Organizations are legal and advocacy groups formed for the organizational purpose of providing counseling, advocacy, and legal representation, without remuneration, to refugees, including Haitian refugees.

44. In furtherance of their organizational purposes, plaintiff Haitian Service Organizations seek to communicate with Haitian citizens, including the individual named plaintiffs, who are held at the United States Naval Base on Guantanamo Bay, and on Coast Guard cutters off Guantanamo, and elsewhere, for the purpose of providing them legal counsel, advocacy, and representation.

45. Defendants' refusal to allow plaintiff Haitian Service Organizations to have access to communicate with Haitian refugees being detained by the U.S. government at the U.S. Naval Base at Guantanamo Bay on Coast Guard cutters and elsewhere, denies plaintiffs' First Amendment rights. Defendants' allowing other individuals and organizations who are not competent to counsel plaintiff Haitian refugees on their asylum claims to gain access to those refugees, is a content-based restriction on the free speech and association rights of plaintiff Haitian Service Organizations and therefore violates plaintiffs' rights under the First Amendment of the U.S. Constitution.

> The complaint should identify the legal basis for the plaintiff's claim, but it is not necessary to make legal arguments in a complaint. As you can see, the plaintiffs simply described the government conduct that allegedly violated their First Amendment rights and stated the nature of this violation. They did not discuss First Amendment doctrine in detail.

SECOND CLAIM FOR RELIEF

(Denial of Statutory Rights to Obtain and Communicate with Counsel)
* * * *

THIRD CLAIM FOR RELIEF

(Denial of Constitutional Rights to Obtain and Communicate with Counsel)

* * * *

FOURTH CLAIM FOR RELIEF

(Failure to Follow Rulemaking Procedures)

* * * *

FIFTH CLAIM FOR RELIEF

(Arbitrary and Capricious Agency Action Not in Accordance With Law)

* * * *

SIXTH CLAIM FOR RELIEF

(Judicial Enforceability of Duty of Non-Refoulement)

* * * *

SEVENTH CLAIM FOR RELIEF

(Equal Protection)

* * * *

Respectfully submitted,

This reproduction of the complaint is unsigned. The real complaint would need to have been signed for it to have been accepted by the court. *See* Rule 11(a). Documents filed electronically— something that is possible today but was not available at the time of *McNary*—are often "signed" by placing a "/s/" followed by the signing attorney's name on the signature line.

_____

MICHAEL RATNER #3357
SUZANNE SHENDE
Center for Constitutional Rights
666 Broadway
New York, NY 10012
(212) 614-6464

_____

HAROLD HONGJU KOH*
CARROLL D. LUCHT
Lowenstein International
Human Rights Clinic
Allard K. Lowenstein
International Human Rights Law
    Project
127 Wall Street
New Haven, CT 06520
(203) 432-4932

NOTES AND COMMENTS

1. Notice Pleading.   The complaint can be a very simple document. According to Rule 8(a), there are only three things that it must contain: (1) a short and plain statement establishing the grounds for the court's jurisdiction, (2) a short and plain statement of the claim, explaining why the plaintiff is entitled to relief, and (3) a demand for relief, explaining what the plaintiff wants the court to do—for example, award damages or enter an injunction. *See* Fed. R. Civ. P. 8(a). In short, Rule 8 asks the plaintiff for only the most basic information—enough to tell the court that it has the authority to hear the dispute and to put the defendant on notice of what the case is essentially about. To see just how brief a complaint can be under the Federal Rules, go to the Appendix of Forms mentioned in Rule 84 and examine Form 11, which is a model complaint for a negligence action arising from a car accident. The whole document is only four paragraphs long!

This minimalist approach to the complaint in Rule 8 is a reflection of the modern "notice pleading" approach that forms the basis of the Federal Rules. This approach is based on the assumption that it should be relatively simple and easy to get into the courthouse—in sharp contrast to the earlier common-law pleading system inherited from England. Under that earlier system, litigants had to classify their dispute with extreme precision and often found their claims dismissed because of the most minute of technicalities. Our modern system of notice pleading, in contrast, is less focused on form than on substance.

One purpose of notice pleading is to allow more cases to be considered on the merits. Notice pleading ensures that fewer cases are dismissed for failure to comply with technical requirements and more cases are decided based on the substantive claims at issue. As a result, the modern system of notice pleading tends to wait until later stages in the litigation process to weed out cases as unmeritorious. From a system-wide perspective, what might be some of the costs and benefits of such an approach? The notice pleading system worked to the Yale team's advantage in the *McNary* case because the lawyers and students were trying to extend some legal theories beyond their existing contours, and also because they were not altogether sure of some of the facts of the case when they filed the complaint.

2. Drafting Strategy.   Although we have a notice pleading system, that does not mean that Koh and the students could simply throw a few things down on paper and stroll into court. They expended great effort preparing the complaint in this case—researching potential legal claims, marshalling facts, and structuring the presentation to give it the greatest possible credibility and impact. Indeed, while Rule 8 speaks of "short and plain" statements, the plaintiffs' complaint was neither short nor plain.

Why do you think Koh and the students included more in the complaint than was absolutely necessary? What were they trying to accomplish, beyond simply putting the court and the defendants on notice about the case? To help answer that question, consider this one: Who were the various "audiences" the Yale team might have been trying to reach? Think of the complaint as a narrative. What kind of story does it tell? Is it an effective story? How should "effective" be defined here?

Drafting a complaint sometimes also requires an attorney to make choices about what *not* to say. Consider, in this regard, the following two paragraphs from the complaint.

8. The individual named plaintiffs Dr. Frantz Guerrier, Pascal Henry, Lauriton Guneau, Medilieu Sorel St. Fleur, Dieu Renel, Milot Baptiste and Roges Noel, on information and belief, are Haitian refugees who have been "screened in" and are being held in detention at Guantanamo Bay Naval Base. They have retained plaintiff Haitian Service Organizations as their counsel. These named plaintiffs also represent other similarly situated persons detained within U.S. jurisdiction on Coast Guard cutters or at Guantanamo Bay Naval Base (the "screened in plaintiffs"). On information and belief, defendants have screened in some 6,000 Haitian detainees as having credible claims for political asylum. Although the "screened in" Haitians were supposed to be brought to the United States and afforded full procedural safeguards, including the right to counsel, many of them have languished at Guantanamo Bay and have not been informed of their screened-in status or of their procedural rights. They seek, and are entitled to seek, political asylum in the United States. They have a substantive right not to be forcibly returned to Haiti, where they face persecution because of their political opinions and risk unlawful arrest, detention, persecution and possible death. They also seek the enforcement of the U.S. government's obligations under domestic and international law. Plaintiff Haitian Service Organizations consider the above named plaintiffs and similarly situated persons to be clients of their organizations by virtue of their seeking asylum status. These "screened in" Haitians are being detained incommunicado at Guantanamo and denied their right to communicate with retained counsel and/or to communicate with counsel they wish to retain. Contrary to defendants' previous assertions that asylum processing would take place in the United States with lawfully guaranteed procedures, including right to counsel, some of these "screened in" Haitians are being processed for political asylum on Guantanamo.

9. Jean Doe, a Haitian presently detained on Guantanamo, is one of the "screened in" plaintiffs who, along with at least 200 others, is being processed by INS asylum officers for political asylum at Guantanamo. This processing is taking place contrary to defendants' previous assertion that such processing would take place in the United States where plaintiffs would clearly have substantial statutory procedural rights, including the right to counsel. This change in policy and practice occurred on or about March 10, 1992. Despite the fact that he is being processed for political asylum, plaintiff is not being provided with any counsel, any right of rebuttal or any of the other procedural safeguards required by the Immigration and Nationality Act, regulations and due process. On information and belief, plaintiff wishes to challenge the arbitrary and ad hoc procedure which he confronts, and has made a written objection to defendants or their agents regarding the additional tier(s) of screening to which he is being subjected. On information and belief, he has refused to be "rescreened," on the grounds that defendants or their agents promised that he and others similarly situated would be processed for asylum on Guantanamo, and that to be rescreened on Guantanamo deprives him of the right to consult with counsel regarding his rights in such a proceeding. Plaintiff Haitian Service Organizations consider the above-named plaintiff and similarly situated persons to be clients and constituents of Haitian Service Organizations by virtue of their seeking refugee or asylum status. The above-named plaintiff sues under a pseudonym because, on information and belief, he fears retaliation against himself and/or his family for participation in this legal challenge. He sues on behalf of himself and other detainees similarly situated.

Can you identify the difference between the plaintiffs described in paragraph 8 and those described in paragraph 9 of the complaint? Yvonne Pascal actually arrived on Guantánamo after the complaint had been filed; had she arrived beforehand, which of these two categories would she have fallen into and why? The plaintiffs described in paragraph 9 were those Haitians who were HIV positive, a subset of the "screened-in" plaintiffs described in paragraph 8.[1] Can you think of reasons why the Yale team might have left such a significant fact out of the complaint? Do you agree or disagree with the decision?

   3. Alternatives to Litigation.   Although the Yale team ultimately filed the complaint and litigated the *McNary* case, there are many ways in which a dispute can be resolved without ever going to court. Indeed, litigation is only one tool in the arsenal of a good lawyer. Recall, for example, that the plaintiffs in *McNary* considered possible political solutions for freeing the Guantánamo detainees, believing that a change in administration would likely result in a change in policy. *See STC*, pp. 178-80. Lawyers, particularly those involved in public interest work, may seek relief for their clients either directly through the political process or through pressure on that process from public opinion, together with or even in lieu of a lawsuit. What non-litigation strategies might have been available to the *McNary* plaintiffs? Do you think, viewing the situation from the perspective of the Yale team in March 1992, that a lawsuit was necessarily the most likely means of obtaining the relief the plaintiffs sought? Why or why not? In this connection, recall the argument between Koh and a lobbyist for the NAACP regarding whether to file a second case to challenge President Bush's direct return order. *See STC*, pp. 135-36.

   Another far more common way in which disputes are resolved is settlement, particularly in cases involving private parties.[2] Before filing a complaint, a plaintiff might first send the defendant a "demand letter" that spells out the relief desired by the plaintiff. In private suits (that is, one private party suing another), the parties sometimes engage in prefiling negotiations, and the plaintiff may decide to go to court only if the parties fail to resolve the dispute on their own. In addition, there are many private disputes in which there is no pre-filing settlement, but the potential plaintiff simply decides, after drafting (or even serving) the complaint, that it is not worth the time, effort, and expense to litigate the case.

   Settlement is also a possibility when a private plaintiff intends to sue the government; however, the government's decision about whether to settle a case of the magnitude of *McNary* can be highly complex, involving a variety of political, strategic, and policy considerations that extend far beyond the concerns of private defendants. What might some of those factors be?

   In *McNary*, the Yale team made a token effort to settle the case prior to filing suit. Several days before heading to federal court in Brooklyn, Harold Koh sent a demand letter to Gene McNary, secretary of the INS, seeking access to the Haitians at Guantánamo.[3] *See STC*,

---

   1. A further complication to be aware of: The Haitians in paragraph 9 can be separated into those who were willing to undergo the second asylum interview (that is, the more formal asylum hearing) and those who refused to do so. A third sub-category can also be added: Haitians who were screened in, found to be HIV positive, and then simply detained at Camp Bulkeley without ever being subjected to the more formal asylum hearing. Yvonne Pascal fell into this third group. *See STC*, pp. 121-22.

   2. Very few of the cases that do make it to court ever reach trial, in large part because many of them are settled. Recent statistics indicate that only between two and four percent of all filed civil cases are tried. *See* Chapter 8, Note 7.

   3. Koh sent a demand letter less because he actually believed the INS would capitulate than because he believed he had to satisfy the "administrative exhaustion" doctrine. This doctrine requires the putative plaintiff to seek redress before the relevant administrative agency prior to suing that agency in court. Administrative exhaustion gives the agency in question a chance to correct its mistakes before it is sued, promotes efficiency by fostering settlements, and creates a record for any court that later considers the case.

pp. 50-51. As it turned out, no one with any real authority at the INS even saw the demand letter—perhaps unsurprising in a massive organization processing millions of pieces of paper—and Yale filed suit just days after Koh sent the letter. Moreover, when Brandt Goldstein later interviewed federal officials and Justice Department lawyers about the case, they said the government never would have agreed to Yale's demands. Why do you think the government would have been so uninterested in settling the case? How might the resolution of the *Baker* lawsuit, which the Supreme Court refused to hear, bear on this question?

4. Early Decisions.   Among the many decisions that must be made early in the case is the question of whom to sue. Review the excerpted portions of the complaint at the beginning of this chapter. Whom did plaintiffs' counsel name as defendants in *McNary*? Why do you think that Koh and the students decided to sue those particular defendants? Note that the government officials that the *McNary* plaintiffs sued are named in their official capacity. This means that the officials are not being sued as private individuals. Instead, the "real" defendants are the federal government and the specific agencies the officials represent.

Another critical question that must be addressed at the outset of the litigation is who the plaintiff or plaintiffs should be. In some cases, the choice is obvious: the person who was injured. In other cases, however, there may be more than one possible plaintiff, each of whom would be able to request the desired relief. This is often the case in class actions such as *McNary*—lawsuits in which a few representative plaintiffs bring suit on behalf of a larger group of plaintiffs. Reproduced below are a few of the class action allegations from the *McNary* complaint.

CLASS ACTION ALLEGATIONS

36. The named Haitian plaintiffs bring this action pursuant to Rule 23(a) and (b)(1)(2) on behalf of themselves and all other persons similarly situated in the following presently ascertainable classes:

37. All Haitian refugees who previously have been "screened in" and are now detained on Guantanamo, including those who may face or who have faced additional screening procedures, including but not limited to, those whose political asylum status defendants are purporting to adjudicate fully on Guantanamo, without right to counsel or other protections as required by law (hereinafter "screened in plaintiffs"). On information and belief, this group currently numbers over 6,000.

* * * *

39. All Haitian refugees who are awaiting screening or have been "screened out" and currently are awaiting forcible repatriation, while being detained within territory subject to U.S. jurisdiction, whether on Coast Guard cutters, on Guantanamo Bay Naval Base, or outside the continental U.S. (hereinafter "screened out plaintiffs"). On information and belief, this group currently numbers approximately 200.

* * * *

See *Woodford v. Ngo*, 548 U.S. 81, 88-92 (2006). You can learn more about the doctrine in a course on administrative law.

> 41. Plaintiff classes warrant class action treatment because: they are sufficiently numerous; defendants have acted or threatened to act on grounds generally applicable to each member of each class, thus making final declaratory and injunctive relief with respect to each class as a whole appropriate; the plaintiffs are adequate representatives of their classes and the claims of the named plaintiffs are both common to and typical of the claims of members of each class.

As set out in Rule 23, there are a number of requirements imposed on the "named" or representative plaintiffs in a class action, and the plaintiffs must be chosen with those requirements in mind. We will discuss class actions in Chapter Ten.

5. Subject-Matter Jurisdiction.   As noted earlier, Rule 8(a)(1) also requires the plaintiff to include a short and plain statement of the court's jurisdiction. The reason for this requirement stems from one of the most important principles of federal civil procedure: Federal courts are courts of *limited* subject-matter jurisdiction. This means federal courts are limited in the kinds of cases that they can hear. Article III, Section 2 of the Constitution sets forth the outer boundaries of the federal courts' subject-matter jurisdiction. There are nine categories of jurisdiction described in Article III, Section 2, including, for example, cases arising under the Constitution, laws, or treaties of the United States, and cases between citizens of different states.

But just because a case falls within the limits of Article III, Section 2 does not necessarily mean that the federal courts can hear the case. Operating within the confines of Article III, Section 2, Congress has the authority to select which categories (or subsets of categories) of cases the federal courts can hear. In other words, the federal courts can hear those types of cases that Congress chooses, but Congress is limited in its choices—it can only choose from what is included in Article III, Section 2 and cannot confer on the federal courts any category of jurisdiction that does not appear there.

For purposes of this case and civil procedure generally, a particularly important category of federal jurisdiction is "federal question" jurisdiction. Federal question jurisdiction involves cases "arising under the Constitution, laws, or treaties of the United States." 28 U.S.C. § 1331. This basis of jurisdiction is called "federal question" because a federal law is at issue. By far the most common example of a claim "arising under" federal law is when federal law creates the cause of action—that is, when it is a federal law that grants the plaintiff her right to sue.

In federal question cases, federal law must not only be at issue in the case; it must be the *basis for the claim asserted by the plaintiff.* That is, the grounds for federal question jurisdiction must appear on the "face" of the plaintiff's complaint. *Louisville & Nashville Railroad v. Mottley,* 211 U.S. 149 (1908). A case does not "arise under" federal law if the only way in which a federal issue would appear in the case is as a defense. For instance, if a case involves an action by a city against a bookstore for violating a local civil ordinance against pornography, and the bookstore's defense is based on the First Amendment, the case does not raise a federal question under *Mottley.* One might think, based on this rule, that the plaintiff could obtain a federal forum simply by mentioning federal law in the complaint. Courts, however, are not bound by the allegations in the plaintiff's complaint and will focus on what the plaintiff would have included if the complaint were "well-pleaded"—that is, if it included only what was necessary to establish the plaintiff's claim and nothing else. This rule, set out in *Mottley*, is known as the "well-pleaded complaint" rule.

A second important category of federal subject-matter jurisdiction is diversity jurisdiction. Diversity jurisdiction covers disputes regarding substantive state law (such as tort law and contract law) in which the plaintiff and defendant are "citizens" of different states *and* more than $75,000 is in controversy. *See* 28 U.S.C. § 1332. For purposes of diversity jurisdiction, "citizenship" for natural persons is equivalent to domicile—that is, the place where the person maintains a physical presence and has an intent to remain indefinitely. A corporation is a citizen of the state in which it is incorporated and in which it has its principal place of business. *See* 28 U.S.C. § 1332(c).[4]

Review the following excerpt from the *McNary* complaint. Can you identify the grounds for federal jurisdiction?

JURISDICTION AND VENUE

3. Plaintiffs' claims arise under the Immigration and Nationality Act, 8 U.S.C. Sections 1101(a)(43), 1157(c), 1158, 1182, 1225, 1226, 1253(h), 1362, the Refugee Act of 1980, 8 U.S.C. Section 1521, regulations promulgated thereunder, the Administrative Procedure Act, 5 U.S.C. §§ 551 et seq., Executive Order No. 12324 of September 1981, 46 Fed. Reg. 48107, the INS's Interdiction Guidelines and Operations Instructions of October 6, 1981, the First and Fifth Amendments to the United States Constitution, the Agreement Effected by Exchange of Notes Between the United States and the Republic of Haiti of September 23, 1981, the United Nations Protocol Relating to the Status of Refugees, and principles of customary international law. Jurisdiction is based on 28 U.S.C. § 1331, as a civil action arising under the Constitution, laws, or treaties of the United States; 8 U.S.C. § 1329, as a civil action arising under the Immigration and Nationality Act, as amended; 5 U.S.C. § 702 as a civil action arising under the Administrative Procedure Act; and 28 U.S.C. § 2201, 2202 as a civil action seeking, in addition to other remedies, a declaratory judgment.

As you may have noted, diversity jurisdiction was not at issue in *McNary*. The complaint makes no reference to the diversity statute, 28 U.S.C. § 1332. This is because the United States is not a "citizen of any state" for the purpose of diversity jurisdiction, and, as a result, neither it nor its agencies can be sued in diversity. *See General Ry. Signal Co. v. Corcoran*, 921 F.2d 700, 703 (7th Cir. 1991). Instead, the main basis for federal jurisdiction in *McNary* was federal question jurisdiction under Section 1331. Paragraph 3 of the complaint also alleges several bases of federal jurisdiction other than those discussed in this Note. Can you identify the statutory sections in paragraph 3 that provide those bases?

6. Personal Jurisdiction. In addition to subject-matter jurisdiction, a federal court must also have personal jurisdiction over the defendant—that is, the power to

---

4. In addition, 28 U.S.C. § 1367 allows federal courts under certain circumstances to hear supplemental claims that do not themselves provide a basis for federal subject-matter jurisdiction as long as those claims form part of the same constitutional case—that is, arise out of the same transaction—as the claim that does have such a basis. Supplemental jurisdiction was not at issue in *McNary* because the case did not involve any claims under state law.

require the defendant to submit to the court's judgment. A common defense in cases involving private defendants is that the court lacks personal jurisdiction, and the Supreme Court has developed a sophisticated and highly nuanced doctrine regarding when a court may assert personal jurisdiction over private defendants. Generally, a court only has the power to require a defendant to submit to the court's judgment if the defendant has enough of a connection with the forum state in which the court sits to render the exercise of this power fair and reasonable. Consider one simple example: If you get into a car accident in Arizona, it makes intuitive sense that you could be sued in Arizona for injuries resulting from that accident. Similarly, it makes intuitive sense that you could not be sued in, say, Maine for that car accident if you have no other contacts with Maine. The basis of the modern jurisprudence in this area is *International Shoe v. Washington*, 326 U.S. 310 (1945).

The traditional rules of personal jurisdiction do not apply in cases in which the federal government, its agencies, or its officials, are sued in an official capacity. A suit against a federal government official in her official capacity is generally considered a suit against a federal agency or the United States. These types of cases can be brought in any judicial district in which a defendant resides, a substantial part of the events giving rise to the lawsuit occurred, or a plaintiff resides (as long as no real property is involved in the suit). *See* 28 U.S.C. § 1391(e).[5] Because some of the plaintiffs resided in Brooklyn, New York, including Haitian Centers Council, the Yale team was able to file suit against the government there.

7. Forum Shopping and Judge Shopping.   In choosing where to file the complaint, parties and their attorneys will often seek a jurisdiction that they believe will be favorable, whether because of convenience, the case law of that circuit, the political leanings of members of the bench, the composition of the jury pool, or any number of other reasons. This is often called "forum shopping."

As you saw in *Storming the Court*, however, plaintiffs' counsel in *McNary* went one step beyond forum shopping, trying to choose not only the forum state but also the specific judge assigned to the case—a process known, not surprisingly, as "judge shopping." As you will recall, Koh was focused on Judge Jack Weinstein because of his reputation as a plaintiff-friendly, left-leaning jurist with the habit of pressuring powerful defendants to accept settlements that the judge considered fair. Although most judges at least nominally seek to encourage settlement between the parties, Weinstein is particularly notable for his aggressive involvement in the negotiation process. *See* Peter Schuck, *Agent Orange on Trial: Mass Toxic Disasters in the Courts* (1986). Should Koh and the students have been able to shop around this way? Do you see a distinction between forum shopping and judge shopping? Is one more objectionable than the other? Why or why not?

In order to have the case assigned to Judge Weinstein, the Yale team had to avoid the local rules of the Eastern District of New York that govern how judges are assigned to incoming cases. Every federal judicial district enjoys the power to establish local

---

5. When government officials are sued in their private capacity—that is, for actions they engage in as private individuals, not actions they undertake on behalf of the government—they can be sued only where they have sufficient contacts under the traditional test for personal jurisdiction described above. *See, e.g., Islamic American Relief Agency v. Unidentified FBI Agents*, 394 F. Supp. 2d 34, 55-60 (D.D.C. 2005), *aff'd in part, remanded in part*, 477 F.3d 728 (D.C. Cir. 2007) (dismissing claim against Internal Revenue Service agent in his individual capacity for lack of personal jurisdiction).

rules governing that district's case assignment system. *See* Fed. R. Civ. P. 83(a). While specific case assignment systems vary from district to district, the two basic considerations in making assignments remain the same everywhere: assuring equitable distribution of caseloads among judges and avoiding judge shopping. *See* http:// www.uscourts.gov/faq.html. Maneuvering of the sort found in the *McNary* case is not common at the federal level, both because it is impermissible and because it is almost guaranteed to fail. Should judge shopping be subject to a sanction—that is, a penalty? If so, what should the appropriate sanction be?

   8. Venue.   The section of Yales's complaint that sets forth the basis for the court's subject-matter jurisdiction also discusses what is known as "venue." Venue refers to the specific judicial district within the federal system in which the suit should be brought.[6] To understand the concept of venue, consider a federal age discrimination case that arises from events in the state of New York. The plaintiff may decide to file in federal court because her claim arises under a federal law and she believes that a federal forum will be more favorable to her claims. And she may decide to file suit in New York because that is where the defendant would be subject to personal jurisdiction and it is a convenient forum for the plaintiff. Those decisions, however, do not help her decide *which* of the United States district courts in New York she should choose. Remember that there are four such districts: the Southern District of New York, the Eastern District of New York, the Northern District of New York, and the Western District of New York. Venue refers to the rules that help the plaintiff identify the appropriate *district* in which to sue.

   When a case in federal court involves only private parties, there are often a number of potential judicial districts in which the plaintiff may properly file suit. *See* 28 U.S.C. § 1391(a), (b). Section 1391(a) and section 1391(b) authorize venue based on several alternative factors, including the judicial district in which a defendant resides (if all defendants reside in the same state) or in which a substantial part of the events giving rise to the lawsuit occurred. Sections 1391(a) and (b) did not apply in *McNary*, however, because the defendants were federal agencies and employees. When the defendant is an officer or employee of the United States government, venue is determined by section 1391(e).[7] As described in Note 6 previously, section 1391(e) permits suit not only in any judicial district in which a defendant resides, but also in any district in which *plaintiff* resides. Below is the paragraph of the complaint regarding venue.

> 4. Venue is proper in this district under 28 U.S.C. Section 1391(e)(3) because the defendants include officers and employees of the United States and agencies thereof acting in their official capacity, and because plaintiff Haitian Centers Council, Inc. ("HCC") is a not-for-profit corporation organized and existing under the laws of the State of New York and has its principal place of business in Brooklyn, New York. Individual named plaintiff Yvrose Pierre is a resident of Brooklyn, N.Y. No real property is involved in this action.

   6. If the case is brought in state court, venue refers to the particular county within that state in which the suit should be brought. States have their own rules on venue.
   7. For a number of historical reasons, suits against federal agencies and officials prior to 1962 could generally only be brought in Washington, D.C. This situation was both inconvenient for plaintiffs and burdensome for the federal courts in the District of Columbia. As a result, Congress created specialized venue rules for suits against the government. *See* 14D CHARLES ALAN WRIGHT ET AL., FEDERAL PRACTICE & PROCEDURE § 3815 (3d ed. 2007).

9. Pleading a "Claim for Relief."   Now consider the Rule 8(a)(2) requirement that the complaint set forth "a short and plain statement of the claim showing that the pleader is entitled to relief." Under the Federal Rules, a legal claim is usually called a "claim for relief," although lawyers and judges also refer to a claim as a "cause of action" or a "theory of relief." So what does it mean to provide a statement of a claim showing that the pleader is entitled to relief? Essentially, the plaintiff must allege (that is, assert) in the complaint the circumstances that, if true, would entitle her under the law to the remedy she seeks.

For example, if the plaintiff seeks to recover for a tort, she must include in the complaint statements that, if they were eventually proved at trial, would establish that the defendant breached a duty to the plaintiff and caused the plaintiff damage as a result. This is often called alleging all of the "elements" of a claim. Can you identify all of the elements of the tort of negligence (duty, breach, causation in fact, proximate cause, damages) in Form 11 in the Appendix to the Federal Rules? If the plaintiff does not allege all of the elements of her claim—if, for example, she fails to allege that defendant's negligence was the cause of her harm—the defendant would be able to have the case dismissed. Specifically, the defendant would move to dismiss the case for "failure to state a claim upon which relief can be granted" under Rule 12(b)(6). (We will discuss Rule 12(b)(6) and motions to dismiss in more detail in Chapter Three.)

Even if the plaintiff pleads all of the elements of her claim, there is still the question of the level of detail required in a complaint. Assume the plaintiff simply asserts, "I was owed a duty of care by the defendant, which the defendant breached, causing me injury, and therefore I am entitled to relief." Is that sufficient? The answer is no; the plaintiff must include more detail than that, and failure to include a minimal level of detail necessary to put the defendant on notice as to what the plaintiff alleges took place and why she is entitled to relief would entitle the defendant to move for dismissal under Rule 12(b)(6). Rule 8 does not require much detail, however. Remember that in the model complaint in Form 11, the plaintiff alleges only that the "defendant negligently drove a motor vehicle against the plaintiff," the place and date of the accident, and the nature of the resulting damages. The information in those allegations is sufficient to put the defendant on notice of the grounds for the claim. Now examine the allegations in paragraphs 43 through 45 of the *McNary* complaint, reproduced previously. Do you think those paragraphs provide enough information to put the government on notice of the grounds of plaintiffs' First Amendment claim?

Although Rule 9 asks a plaintiff to provide additional factual detail when the plaintiff has alleged fraud or mistake,[8] the Supreme Court has said that it is impermissible for courts to require additional facts—that is, to impose a "heightened" pleading standard—in circumstances other than those mentioned in Rule 9. *See, e.g., Leatherman v. Tarrant County Narcotics Intelligence and Coordination Unit*, 507 U.S. 163 (1993) (rejecting heightened pleading standard in a civil rights suit against a municipality). For example, a court could not require a plaintiff who had filed a negligence complaint modeled on Form 11 to specify how the defendant was negligent—that is, that he drove too fast or had been driving while intoxicated.[9]

8. Mistake is a concept from contract law and essentially means an error in understanding facts, the meaning of contractual wording, or the law when entering into a contract.

9. The amount of factual detail courts can require in a complaint has been thrown into some doubt by a recent Supreme Court case called *Bell Atlantic v. Twombly*, 550 U.S. 544 (2007). In that case, the Court indicated that, at least for allegations of antitrust violations, the plaintiff must do more than make

10. *Choosing the Claims.* A simple lawsuit such as the negligence action mentioned earlier may state only a single claim. In a more complex case like *McNary*, the plaintiffs are likely to set forth several different claims, any of which might provide recovery based on counsel's preliminary understanding of the facts of the case. In *McNary*, for instance, the Yale team initially asserted seven claims, as the previous excerpts indicate. Furthermore, in some cases, the plaintiffs' claims evolve over the course of the lawsuit. In *McNary*, for example, as the students obtained more information about the detainees and their desires and circumstances, the lawsuit's focus changed. What began as a case about ensuring the Haitians had lawyers to represent them in their asylum hearings on Guantánamo developed into a case aimed at securing the release of everyone held at Camp Bulkeley.

Recall, however, that Lisa Daugaard and others on the team had always intended to go beyond the initial claim that the Haitians be granted access to lawyers; their aim from the outset was to free the refugees. *See STC*, pp. 58-59, 169. Thus, they saw the more modest claims made in the initial complaint as "wedge issues," meant merely to get the plaintiffs into court—after which the Yale team could seek the right moment to press for further relief. Why do you think Lisa wanted to proceed this way? Do you recall why Harold Koh resisted this strategy? What do you think might have happened had the Yale team asked on day one for everything the team ended up seeking at trial?

11. *Pleading "On Information and Belief."* The plaintiff must include enough information in her complaint to survive a motion to dismiss—but what happens if the plaintiff does not have all of the necessary information? What if it is information controlled by the opposing side? Consider the following paragraph from the *McNary* complaint.

> 31. On March 11, 1992, plaintiffs' counsel wrote defendant McNary and the Commanding Officer of the U.S. Naval Air Station, Guantanamo Bay, requesting access on behalf of plaintiff Haitian Service Organizations to Haitian citizens currently being held at the United States Naval Base on Guantanamo Bay and on Coast Guard cutters off Guantanamo, for the purpose of providing them legal counsel, advocacy, and representation. In particular, plaintiffs' counsel requested access to communicate with named plaintiffs Dr. Frantz Guerrier, Pascal Henry, Lauriton Guneau, Medilieu Sorel St. Fleur, Dieu Renel, Milot Baptiste, A. Iris Vilnor and with the leaders of the organization known as the Association of Haitian Political Exiles. Plaintiffs' counsel requested that plaintiff Haitian Service Organizations be given immediate access to these Haitian individuals on such terms and conditions as might be reasonable to the Government, before 9 a.m. Monday, March 16, 1992. As of that date and time, no response has been received by plaintiffs' counsel. On information and belief, defendants have denied the requests of all legal and advocacy groups seeking such access.

Notice that in the last sentence of this paragraph, the plaintiffs use a distinctive phrase: "on information and belief." This wording conveys to the court that the plaintiffs are alleging something they *believe* is true based on the information available to them but cannot be absolutely sure is true because they currently do not have enough information about the allegation. What about the assertion in paragraph 31 might the plaintiffs have been unsure about?

conclusory assertions and is required to include some factual detail showing that the plaintiff's claim is plausible. The effect of *Twombly* beyond antitrust cases remains unclear.

Why were the plaintiffs so careful to signal to the court that they were not absolutely sure of this particular assertion? Take a look at Rule 11(b)(3). By filing a complaint or any other signed document with the court, an attorney or unrepresented party warrants that the document's "factual contentions have evidentiary support or, if specifically so identified, will likely have evidentiary support after a reasonable opportunity for further investigation or discovery." Fed. R. Civ. P.11(b)(3). Pleading "on information and belief" conveys to the court that the pleader does not have personal knowledge of the fact asserted but that she is likely to have evidentiary support after an opportunity for further fact investigation. (Note that pleading "on information and belief" does not relieve the attorney of conducting a reasonable factual investigation and that the attorney must eventually obtain evidentiary support for statements alleged "on information and belief.") We will discuss Rule 11 in more detail in Chapter 4.

12. Fact Gathering and Client Communication. The information necessary to draft a complaint is often gathered through informal investigation—a vital component of litigation for several reasons. First, to make a reasonable assessment of a suit, an attorney must from the very start consider the evidence that will be required to prove the client's case at trial. Second, thorough preparation on the facts (and the law) helps anticipate and avoid possible problems later in the case. Third, as discussed in Chapter Four, Rule 11 requires that attorneys conduct an objectively reasonable investigation into the factual bases of their complaint before filing it with the court.

Informal investigation usually calls for interviewing the client and various witnesses, obtaining documentary and other evidence in possession of the client or cooperative third parties, and examining—depending upon the case—police reports, police records, medical reports, or other materials. Interviews are particularly valuable for learning the chronology and details of the dispute, the location of relevant documentary evidence, and the names of other parties and potential witnesses.

The inaccessibility of the team's clients in the *McNary* case not only made pre-filing investigation extremely difficult, it raised a thorny question: How could plaintiffs' counsel purport to file a complaint on behalf of clients they had never met? The answer has to do with a request for help that eventually made it into the hands of Michael Ratner. *See STC*, p. 50. Sometime in February 1992, several detained Haitians approached a Haitian-American priest, Father Jacques Fabré, whom the Justice Department had sent to Guantánamo to provide spiritual counseling to the Haitians. The Haitians asked Fabré for help, and he sent a fax to a Haitian organization in New York, repeating this request. The organization forwarded the fax to Ratner, who construed it as a request for legal representation.[10]

13. Requesting Relief. In their "prayer for relief"—the traditional phrase for the demand for relief required by Rule 8—the *McNary* plaintiffs requested several different forms of relief, as shown here.

---

10. Even when the Yale team was able to communicate with the Guantánamo detainees, the attorney-client relationship was complicated by language, culture, and other barriers, including different perceptions about the legal system (which many Haitians assumed was rigged). Such communication barriers, combined with restrictions on the detainees' ability to communicate with their lawyers and their lack of access to other resources, limited Yale's ability to engage in "client-centered lawyering," a term used to describe a variety of lawyering approaches that focus on client empowerment and decision making. *See* Katherine R. Kruse, *Fortress in the Sand: The Plural Values of Client-Centered Representation*, 12 CLINICAL L. REV. 369, 371-372 (2006). The interviews with Ronald Aubourg in Chapter Seven and Lisa Daugaard in Chapter Nine discuss this issue in more detail.

PRAYER FOR RELIEF

WHEREFORE, Plaintiffs and the members of the classes they represent pray for declaratory and injunctive relief as follows:

* * * *

(b) A declaratory judgment that the defendants' practices alleged above violate the terms of Executive Order 12324, the guidelines promulgated pursuant to the Executive Order, the interdiction agreement between the United States and Haiti, the Refugee Act of 1980, the Immigration and Nationality Act Sections 101(a)(43), 208 and 243(h), the Administrative Procedure Act, the United Nations Protocol Relating to Status of Refugees, the First and Fifth Amendments to the United States Constitution, customary international law, and other provisions of law;

(c) A declaratory judgment that the defendants' changes in practice violate the rulemaking requirements of the Administrative Procedure Act, and further declaring the actions taken or determinations made pursuant to defendants' recently instituted policies to be void;

(d) Setting aside the denial of asylum claims or the agency action "screening out" members of the plaintiffs' class as being arbitrary and capricious, not in accordance with law, and not in accordance with procedural requirements;

(e) Preliminary and permanent injunctive relief:

(i) Granting immediate access to plaintiff Haitian Service Organizations, their attorneys, employees, and members, to communicate with the Haitian plaintiffs detained at the Guantanamo Bay Naval Base and on Coast Guard cutters in order to advise these plaintiffs of their legal rights and options in the asylum process, as well as of the Organizations' interest in providing representation and assistance to them in furtherance of organizational goals;

(ii) Ordering defendants to ensure that plaintiff refugees are accorded their statutory and constitutional rights to communicate with counsel, so that they may have a full and fair opportunity to present the merits of their political asylum claims and to obtain advice about their legal options; and to render fair and regular determination of plaintiffs' asylum claims free from caprice and discrimination;

(iii) To refrain from sending back to Haiti those Haitians who have not been "screened in" as candidates for asylum until such time as procedures are implemented and followed which adequately protect and recognize the rights of these persons under the Executive Order, the INS guidelines promulgated pursuant thereto, the APA, and international law, as well as the privileges ordinarily afforded potential asylum applicants under the Refugee Act of 1980 and the Immigration and Nationality Act;

(iv) Ordering defendants to cease and desist immediately from conducting interviewing, screening, exclusion proceedings or asylum hearings on Guantanamo and to transport all "screened in" plaintiffs expeditiously to the United States to that they may be accorded asylum hearings with the full panoply of statutory rights.

(v) Ordering defendants to refrain from taking any action pursuant to policies instituted in violation of the rulemaking requirements of the Administrative Procedure Act unless and until such policies are properly promulgated pursuant to the A.P.A. and restoring all rights and privileges that plaintiffs and the classes named herein may have been denied while these policies were in effect;

(f) Such other and further relief as the Court may deem just and proper, including reasonable attorneys' fees and costs.

Respectfully submitted,

MICHAEL RATNER #3357
SUZANNE SHENDE
Center for Constitutional Rights
666 Broadway
New York, NY 10012
(212) 614-6464

HAROLD HONGJU KOH*
CARROLL D. LUCHT
Lowenstein International
Human Rights Clinic
Allard K. Lowenstein
International Human Rights Law
  Project
127 Wall Street
New Haven, CT 06520
(203) 432-4932

Note that the plaintiffs sought both an *injunction* and a *declaratory judgment.* Consider first the injunction, which is an "equitable," rather than a "legal," remedy. The explanation for this distinction lies in legal history. Centuries ago in England, there were several different types of courts of law—common law courts, civil law courts, ecclesiastical courts, and prerogative courts—each of which administered a different branch of the *lex terrae* or "law of the land." From the seventeenth century to the nineteenth century, however, two types of courts predominated: the civil law Court of Chancery, which decided cases "in equity," and the common law courts, which decided "suits at law." In civil (as opposed to criminal) cases, common law courts generally only had the authority to provide the legal remedy of money damages and were very rigid in their application of the law. For some civil plaintiffs, money was an insufficient remedy. These plaintiffs would file suit in the Court of Chancery, which was empowered to provide "equitable relief," such as the return of stolen property, the abatement of a public nuisance such as a polluting factory, or the removal of obstructions on the public highways or waterways.[11]

Historically part of the Chancery Court's power, a modern court's authority to issue equitable or injunctive relief means it can order a party to do or not to do something. There are several kinds of injunctions. By issuing a preliminary injunction or temporary restraining order, the court may, before reaching a final decision in a case, prohibit the defendant from engaging in conduct that harms the plaintiff until the case is decided. (We will discuss these forms of preliminary relief in more detail in Chapter Five.) A permanent injunction, on the other hand, is usually entered *after* the case has been finally decided. Review the prayer for relief. What do the plaintiffs want the judge to require the government to do? Would you have requested any additional relief? If so, what relief?

In contrast to an injunction, a declaratory judgment is simply a judicial declaration of the parties' respective rights. A relatively new form of relief in federal court, it was authorized in 1934 by a federal statute, the Declaratory Judgment Act. 28 U.S.C. §§ 2201-02. In *McNary*, the plaintiffs asked Judge Johnson to declare that the

---

11. For a more detailed discussion of the history of the courts of law and the Court of Chancery, see J.H. Baker, An Introduction to English Legal History (4th ed. 2002) and Frederick W. Maitland & Francis C. Montague, A Sketch of English Legal History (James Fairbanks Colby ed., 1915).

government had violated several statutes, constitutional provisions, and treaties. The availability of declaratory judgments is important because sometimes damages or injunctive relief are not available, but the plaintiff still wants to establish the correctness of his legal position. Take, for example, the interdiction agreement between the United States and Haiti mentioned by the plaintiffs in paragraph (b) of the prayer for relief. The students and the Haitians could not seek to enforce that agreement against the government, because it is a diplomatic arrangement between two *countries* and does not give individuals any right of enforcement. The Yale team, however, still thought it important that Judge Johnson declare that a violation of that agreement had occurred. Do you agree? Why or why not?

INTERVIEW
SARAH CLEVELAND ON RESEARCHING AND DRAFTING A COMPLAINT

As a third-year law student, you played an important role in drafting the *McNary* complaint. What factual research did the plaintiffs' team do for the complaint?

In drafting the complaint, we were trying to gather factual information regarding four main issues: (1) conditions in Haiti that were leading people to flee, to support the claim that bona fide refugees were at risk of being forcibly returned to a place where they would be in danger; (2) conditions on Guantánamo, including the percentage of people who were being screened-in and through what processes; (3) the evolving U.S. government policy toward the Haitians being interdicted and taken to Guantánamo; and (4) the character of the U.S. naval base on Guantánamo generally. The last of these issues was important to support the First Amendment claim that the exclusion of lawyers from the base constituted content-based discrimination, since non-lawyers were being allowed onto the base, and to support the claim that Guantánamo was not really "extraterritorial" and that U.S. constitutional and statutory law should apply there.

None of this information was easy to get. To obtain it, the plaintiffs' litigation team—both the students and the attorneys—was divided into groups that developed expertise in particular aspects of the litigation. For instance, one group of students, including me, tried to gather information from public sources regarding the government's conduct. We called the U.S. Coast Guard's public information line almost daily to obtain interdiction data, and using other public sources, we tried to monitor the percentage of Haitians who were being screened in. The number of Haitians reported as fleeing and interdicted always appeared to increase before a court hearing, as did the percentage of Haitians screened in at Guantánamo. This led us to believe the government was manipulating these numbers to support their case.* High numbers of Haitians fleeing supported the government's claim that the litigation was having a "magnet effect"—encouraging Haitians who were "merely" economic migrants, not bona fide refugees, to head for the United States. And high screen-in rates allowed the government to contend that it was applying fair processes on Guantánamo, lawyers were unnecessary there, and

---

* Paul Cappuccio, the Justice Department lawyer charged with oversight of the *McNary* case under the Bush administration, vigorously disputes this allegation.—Eds.

judicial intervention was not required. So obtaining these statistics was very important in the struggle for the sympathy of the court.

Another one of the many groups of students set out to learn as much as they could about Guantánamo from every imaginable public source, including U.S. military publications. I was part of this group as well. We discovered all manner of things about Guantánamo: Priests and a piano tuner had been allowed on the base, there was a McDonald's, and a little-known federal statute called the Slot Machine Act applied there. This last point was important because it suggested that federal law had force at Guantánamo. After all, if the Slot Machine Act applied, what about the Immigration and Nationality Act, the First Amendment, and the due process clause?

How did the fact that the Haitians were being held incommunicado affect the drafting of the complaint?

It severely hampered the pre-complaint fact-gathering effort. Because the *McNary* defendants were holding the Haitians incommunicado, we were able to obtain almost no information from the clients themselves. Indeed, even after we had names for the Haitian plaintiffs being detained on Guantánamo, we could not communicate with them. So we had to seek information through the circuitous channels, such as Father Jacques Fabré [*see* Note 12 above.] The result was that a number of paragraphs in the complaint allege facts "on information and belief," including many facts about the Guantánamo plaintiffs. This signaled to the court and the defendants that we had reason to believe that the allegations would prove true after a reasonable investigation, but we were unable to confirm them before filing the complaint.

Why did the team choose to draft such a detailed complaint? What messages were you trying to convey to the various audiences of the complaint? Why?

Detailed? The original working draft of the complaint was *much* longer. At some early point, Michael Barr and I were charged with preparing a detailed narrative from all the information our team had gathered, and the original (very rough) draft was a kitchen-sink recitation of that information. Fortunately, more experienced legal minds were responsible for honing it into a workable document.

Any complaint seeks to do more than just satisfy Rule 8, and in *McNary*, we faced a number of challenges that shaped how we framed the complaint. First, as noted above, we had very little direct information to go on. We therefore went to significant lengths to demonstrate that we had a soundly-researched case, and that there was a serious factual basis for our claims. That was critical because the complaint is the judge's first contact with the case, and it plays an important role in establishing the credibility of the attorneys involved and the legitimacy of the claims being asserted.

Second, *Baker* had been dismissed, so we needed to persuade the court immediately that our case was different enough from *Baker* that it should not be dismissed outright on grounds of res judicata. The complaint was crafted to anticipate the facially persuasive objections that the government would raise in a motion to dismiss.

Finally, the case was ultimately a story about very poor and disadvantaged people fleeing for their lives, and challenging the extraterritorial national security and immigration policy of the most powerful country in the world. We felt that persuading the court of the human plight of the clients and the basic unfairness of their treatment was the only way to get a level playing field in the case. It's also worth noting that in a public law litigation case such as *McNary*, with significant implications for public policy, the complaint needs to state a sympathetic case for the media and for the general public.

How did the team decide upon the claims that went into the complaint? And early on, what was your theory of the case?

As *Storming the Court* indicates, we conducted extensive legal research on various possible claims and framed the complaint around the most promising ones. Our primary focus in the complaint was free speech. It seemed legally quite sound and it was well supported by the fact that the government was barring lawyers but not others from Guantánamo. It was also a very compelling claim, politically speaking. Who can object to allowing lawyers and clients to speak to each other? Further, before we had clients on Guantánamo, it was a claim that could be asserted by the plaintiff legal services organizations in the United States.

The equal protection claim posed the greatest dilemma for the team. At the time, the differential U.S. policy toward Haitian and Cuban refugees was so stark that the Haitian policy seemed patently motivated by discrimination based on national origin. Yet in the immigration context, constitutional equal protection allows the government to discriminate based on nationality. So the legal claim was not a strong one.

Some members of the team—particularly Lisa Daugaard and Graham Boyd—felt passionately that the equal protection claim should be in the complaint because it captured the practical realities of the situation, even if it was infirm as a matter of legal doctrine. The lawyers on the team, particularly Harold, were reluctant to include a claim that was weak on the merits. The lawyers were concerned about establishing credibility with the court.

In the end, we included the claim but listed it last. And it did play an important role, by creating a vehicle through which the government's differential policy toward the Haitians could be raised and challenged, both in a court of law and in the court of public opinion. The claim appeared to have an impact on Judge Johnson, who commented early on that there was an "appearance" of discrimination in the government's policy, even if there was no discriminatory purpose. Ultimately, Judge Johnson never issued a ruling on the equal protection claim, but his decision on the Administrative Procedure Act claim in our favor had an equal-protection-like feel to it.

Drawing on the benefit of your experiences in *McNary* and beyond, what advice would you give to young lawyers drafting their first complaint?

Less is more. Young lawyers are much more likely to try to say everything they know in a complaint than more experienced lawyers. As a seasoned litigator once told me, "A complaint is a short and plain statement, not a novel." A complaint needs to be simple, flexible, and persuasive. The requirement of simplicity comes from Rule 8. But it also makes good sense. A judge (and her clerk) only has a certain amount of time to devote to your case. She does not want to have to read *Ulysses* in order to figure out what the claims are.

The requirement of flexibility comes from the realities of litigation. Litigation theories often change radically during the life of a case, as they did during *McNary*.

This happens for many reasons—litigants acquire new information, the defendant's position changes, earlier missteps in litigation strategy become apparent. The Federal rules anticipate the need for flexibility in pleading through amendment of the complaint under Rule 15, but the lawyers have to take advantage of that room to maneuver. The presence, or absence, of some flexibility in the joints has saved, or lost, many a case. In this regard, overpleading (pleading with too great specificity) can be more hazardous than underpleading, because it locks the litigant into a particular position.

As for being persuasive: The claims must be convincing not only to the court but to other constituencies in the broader social context. In *McNary*, we were making our case both to Judge Johnson and to the media and the general public. You also have another audience: your adversary. A well-drafted complaint, with the allegations simply and separately stated, helps prevent the defendant from responding with blanket denials that are contrary to Rule 8(b)(4). Allegations in the complaint that the defendant has no choice but to admit can be treated as established for purposes of the case, giving plaintiffs' counsel an opportunity to narrow and clarify the issues in a case at an early stage.

A final thought: Learn from others. I was shocked to discover this, but a complaint is rarely drafted from scratch. And of course it makes sense. Lawyers often use a pleading from a similar case as a model, if only to make sure that all the pleading requirements for the complaint are satisfied and the elements of the claims and the requirements for class claims, etc., are properly alleged.

An uncommon sight, most likely spring 1992: This Haitian sailboat somehow evaded the Coast Guard and made it all the way to Guantánamo—almost certainly by mistake, for the passengers were likely hoping to reach Florida. Photograph courtesy of Stephen Kinder.

14. Service of Process.   Lawyers cannot simply draft a complaint and file it with the court. They also must present it to the defendant through a procedure called service of process. This procedural requirement serves two functions: (1) It notifies the defendant that a lawsuit has been filed against him, and (2) it marks the court's assertion of personal jurisdiction over him. Rule 4 of the Federal Rules of Civil Procedure governs service of process. Rule 4 requires that the defendant be served with both the complaint and a simple document called the "summons," an example of which appears as Form 3 in the Appendix of Forms. *See* Fed. R. Civ. P. 4. Under Rule 4(a), the summons must be signed by the clerk of the court and bear the court's seal (an imprint from a fancy-looking stamp). In practice, the plaintiff generally obtains a blank civil summons form,[12] fills in the requisite information, and takes the form to the clerk's office to be signed and sealed before delivery (with the complaint) to the defendant.

Once prepared, the summons and complaint must be served in accordance with Rule 4. The rule specifies, for example, who may serve the summons and complaint and the manner in which service can be made on individuals and corporations. Rule 4 also allows for a procedure known as "waiver of service," according to which the defendant can waive the requirement of being served with a summons in exchange for a longer period of time to respond to the complaint. *See* Fed. R. Civ. P. 4(d). Waiver of service is not available in a suit against the United States. *See* Fed. R. Civ. P. 4(d)(1), 4(i). The rules regarding waiver of service are discussed in Note 9 of Chapter 3.

15. Amendments.   A plaintiff must limit her claims at trial to those she has stated in the complaint. This limitation presents a problem if the plaintiff's claims have evolved since the case was filed. In *McNary*, for instance, the original complaint did not mention the plaintiffs' central claim at trial—namely, that the Haitians on Guantánamo were being held indefinitely without charge and denied adequate medical care in violation of the due process clause. Accordingly, government lawyer Lauri Filppu sought to exclude evidence relating to medical care from the trial. *See STC*, p. 245. Filppu's basic argument was correct, and the rationale underlying the argument is an important one: The defendant may not have had sufficient notice of the new claim and judgment on that claim would violate the defendant's right to due process. How should the plaintiffs have responded to Filppu's argument? What steps could they have taken to avoid it? We consider both questions in the rest of this Note and the exercise that follows.

Under the Federal Rules, pleadings—such as complaints and answers—can be amended in certain circumstances. To amend a pleading simply means to change it, whether the change is large (adding a new claim or defense, new party, or new factual allegations) or small (correcting a typographical error). Rule 15 governs amendments of pleadings. In *McNary*, the court denied Filppu's motion to exclude evidence and allowed the plaintiffs to amend their complaint under Federal Rule 15. The following exercise will allow you to make arguments for and against allowing that amendment.

---

12. As of publication, the civil summons form for the Eastern District of New York was available at http://www.nyed.uscourts.gov/General_Information/Court_Forms/.

Class Exercise No. 1

Your professor will divide you into teams so that you can prepare this exercise before class. Half of the teams should prepare to play the attorneys for the *McNary* plaintiffs, and the other half should prepare to play the government attorneys. Plaintiffs' attorneys should prepare arguments supporting the amendment to add the claim based on denial of adequate medical care. Attorneys for the government should prepare arguments against allowing the amendment. Do not consider any other real or potential amendment. Remember, too, that you are *not* arguing the merits of the due process claim, but only whether the amendment meets the requirements of Rule 15.

You will need to carefully review Rule 15, which discusses both the *procedure* for seeking an amendment and the *standard* for when an amendment is allowed. The standard tells the plaintiffs what they must show in order to be allowed to amend the complaint. You may also want to review the complete versions of the original and amended complaints, which are available on the companion website.

For purposes of this exercise, you should assume that the motion to amend was made one month before trial and analyze it *only* under Rule 15(a).[13] In the real case, Tringali decided not to move to amend the complaint before trial because he was worried that the government would further delay the trial by requesting a continuance until the defendants had a chance to respond to the complaint. You should also assume that the defendants filed their answer within 60 days of service of the amended complaint (which occurred on March 17, 1992), as required by Rule 12 when the defendant is a government agency.[14]

Rule 15(a)(2) provides that leave to amend should be "freely" given "when justice so requires." Although this standard gives the court significant discretion in determining when an amendment should be allowed, the court will typically consider several factors in making this decision. Among other things, the court will consider (1) the prejudice to the defendant in allowing the amendment, (2) whether the amendment was unduly delayed or presented in bad faith, (3) whether the amendment would be futile or frivolous, (4) the hardship to the moving party if the amendment is denied, and (5) the burden that allowing the amendment would place on the judicial system. *See* 6 Charles Alan Wright et al. *Federal Practice and Procedure* § 1487 (2d ed. 1990). For the first part of the exercise, consider the principles we have examined in this chapter and the facts of the *McNary* case; make the best arguments you can and anticipate counter arguments by the other side; and support your arguments using the facts described in *Storming the Court* and this book.

---

13. Although Filppu's objection was raised prior to trial, the court treated it as if it had been raised during trial under Rule 15(b). This may have been because Filppu raised the objection close to trial and it concerned proposed evidence not relevant to the issues raised in the original complaint. *See* Fed. R. Civ. P. 15(b). For this exercise, however, disregard Rule 15(b) and analyze the motion only under Rule 15(a).

14. In the case, the defendants did not file an answer to the complaint until May 13, 1993—after the trial was over. This uncommon situation is explained in Note 9 of Chapter 3. As a result, the plaintiffs might have been allowed under Rule 15(a) to amend "as a matter of course" (that is, "as of right" or without having to seek leave from the court) up until trial began.

For the second part of the exercise, assume that the statute of limitations on the plaintiffs' due process claim had expired before they moved to amend their complaint. Now the situation is a bit more complicated because the plaintiffs must do more than just amend the complaint. Why? If the plaintiffs simply amended the complaint to add the due process claim, the defendants could move to dismiss on statute of limitations grounds. To get a new claim into the case after the statute of limitations has expired, the plaintiffs must both amend the complaint *and* ask the court to treat the claim *as if it had been included in the original complaint.* This is known as having the new claim "relate back" to the date the complaint was filed.[15]

Relation back is governed by Rule 15(c). Which provision of Rule 15(c) would apply to a motion by the plaintiffs to have the due process claim relate back to the filing of the original complaint? Which provision would have applied if they had sought to add a new party? Why do you think the requirements for adding a new party are more extensive than for adding a new claim?

---

15. "Relation back" is therefore only relevant when the statute of limitations has expired. If there were no statute of limitations problem, and assuming the claim had not previously been litigated, the plaintiff could simply bring a new lawsuit.

CHAPTER THREE

Responding to the Complaint

INTRODUCTION

Once a plaintiff has filed and served the complaint, our system of civil procedure requires the defendant to respond—indeed, if the defendant fails to respond, a default judgment may be entered against him. *See* Fed. R. Civ. P. 55. Under the Federal Rules, a defendant can respond to the complaint in one of two ways: by filing a motion to dismiss that raises certain defenses or by filing an answer. When the defendant files a motion to dismiss, he is not contesting the substance of the plaintiff's allegations in the complaint—that is, the factual assertions the plaintiff has made. Instead, he is arguing that the case should be dismissed because some other aspect of the lawsuit (such as personal or subject-matter jurisdiction) is in some way deficient.

The defendant's other option is to answer the complaint, identifying those factual allegations in the complaint that he disputes and setting the case up for discovery. *See* Chapters Six and Seven. The answer may also raise defenses, including those that might have been raised in a motion. There is good reason, however, to file a motion to dismiss before answering, for it gives the defendant the opportunity to get a decision from the court on a specific set of defenses before having to proceed any further with the case. If the defendant prevails on one or more of those defenses, then the case may be dismissed without the defendant ever having to file an answer (and, in some cases, without having to engage in discovery)—and that means saving time, energy, and lawyers' fees.

Motions to dismiss are governed by Rule 12, and answers are governed by Rule 8. This chapter will discuss how the government responded to the complaint in *McNary* under each of those rules, starting with its motion to dismiss.

RULE 12: RESPONDING BY MOTION

Under Rule 12(b), there are seven defenses that can be raised by motion before the defendant answers: (1) lack of subject-matter jurisdiction, (2) lack of personal jurisdiction, (3) improper venue, (4) insufficient process, (5) insufficient service of process, (6) failure to state a claim upon which relief can be granted, and (7) failure to join a party under Rule 19. By way of quick explanation, the first three of these defenses challenge whether the case belongs in the court in which it was brought.[1] The next two defenses challenge the way the papers that initiate the suit were prepared or presented to the defendant. The sixth defense we will discuss in this chapter. Finally, the seventh defense relates to the requirement in some instances that certain other parties be present before a case will be allowed to proceed. Although you may discuss some or all of these defenses in more detail in your civil procedure course, we will focus here on the motion made by the defendants in *McNary*—a motion to dismiss for failure to state a claim under Rule 12(b)(6). An excerpt from the motion to dismiss filed by the government appears below.

IN THE UNITED STATES DISTRICT COURT
FOR THE EASTERN DISTRICT OF NEW YORK

HAITIAN CENTERS COUNCIL, INC., et al.,)

                               Plaintiffs,   )

v.   ) Civil Action No.

GENE McNARY, Commissioner, et al.,   ) 92-1258 (Johnson, J)

                            Defendants.)
_____)

DEFENDANTS' MOTION TO DISMISS

INTRODUCTION

> A motion should always begin by stating the relief that the party seeks.

      Defendants hereby move the Court to dismiss the above-captioned case. Plaintiffs have no enforceable rights, lack standing and judicial intervention is otherwise barred for a number of reasons. The case should be dismissed for these reasons, and under Fed. R. Civ. P. 12(b)(6) for failure to state a claim upon which any relief can be granted.

---

1. As you will see, the government did not raise the defenses of lack of subject-matter jurisdiction (Fed. R. Civ. P. 12(b)(1)) or personal jurisdiction (Fed. R. Civ. P. 12(b)(2)). Subject-matter jurisdiction and personal jurisdiction are discussed in Notes 5 and 6 of Chapter Two. As described in more detail in those Notes, the government did not have a basis for contesting either subject-matter or personal jurisdiction in this case.

IN THE UNITED STATES DISTRICT COURT
FOR THE EASTERN DISTRICT OF NEW YORK

HAITIAN CENTERS COUNCIL, INC., et al.,   )
)
                         Plaintiffs,   )
)
              v.   ) Civil Action No.
)
GENE McNARY, Commissioner, et al.,   ) 92-1258 (Johnson, J)
)
                         Defendants.   )
_____)

DEFENDANTS' MOTION TO DISMISS

INTRODUCTION

Defendants hereby move the Court to dismiss the above-captioned case. Plaintiffs have no enforceable rights, lack
standing and judicial intervention is otherwise barred for a
number of reasons. The case should be dismissed for these
reasons, and under Fed. R. Civ. P. 12(b)(6) for failure to state
a claim upon which any relief can be granted.

For the reasons more fully set forth and supported in the
government's memorandum opposing plaintiffs' application for
preliminary injunctive relief, which is filed herewith and
incorporated herein by reference, plaintiffs' complaint should be
dismissed because none of plaintiffs' legal arguments have merit.

STATEMENT

On March 17, 1992, the plaintiffs filed their application
for preliminary relief, including a temporary restraining order
and a permanent injunction, supported by numerous declarations.
Thereafter, they filed a Complaint. On March 18, 1992, the Court

A reproduction of the first page of the government's motion to dismiss in McNary.

The motion to dismiss is the document that officially requests that the court take the action of dismissing the case. Most motions are one- or two-page documents that state the relief requested and, in a few short sentences, the grounds on which the request is based. This particular motion to dismiss is slightly longer than most and uncommon in that it contains an argument section. Legal arguments are generally reserved for a longer brief or memorandum (as it is sometimes called) that accompanies the motion. In this instance, the defendant's brief was 82 pages long.

This paragraph is the key to understanding the way that a motion to dismiss operates. Even though the government will no doubt contest many of the plaintiffs' factual allegations, the government is stating here that *even if all those allegations are assumed to be true, the government should still win the case based purely on the law.* We discuss this concept in Notes 1 and 2.

For the reasons more fully set forth and supported in the government's memorandum opposing plaintiffs' application for preliminary injunctive relief, which is filed herewith and incorporated herein by reference, plaintiffs' complaint should be dismissed because none of plaintiffs' legal arguments have merit.

STATEMENT

On March 17, 1992, the plaintiffs filed their application for preliminary relief, including a temporary restraining order and a permanent injunction, supported by numerous declarations. Thereafter, they filed a Complaint. On March 18, 1992, the Court directed the government to file its opposition to plaintiffs' application.

This motion seeks resolution of the case on the merits because, as a matter of law, the government is entitled to have the suit against it dismissed even if the factual allegations in plaintiffs' complaint are taken as true. The unwarranted intrusion and enormous burden placed upon Executive Branch efforts to respond to a crisis abroad by plaintiffs' misguided litigation, which substantially replicates claims that were decided in the government's favor in the United States Court of Appeals for the Eleventh Circuit in Haitian Refugee Center v. Baker, No. 91-6099, should be ended immediately if, as we respectfully submit, there is no role for plaintiffs or the Court to play in responding to this crisis.

ARGUMENT

The arguments and authorities that compel denial of injunctive relief also compel dismissal of this case on the merits. The government's memorandum examines each of the seven causes of action contained in the complaint. As to each, the government has demonstrated that, even when the factual averments of the complaint are deemed to be true, as they must for purposes of this motion, the plaintiffs are not entitled to the relief requested, nor any other relief.

Plaintiffs' causes based upon the First and Fifth Amendments are without merit. The First Amendment claims have been decided adversely to plaintiffs, both with respect to plaintiffs within this country and those abroad. See HRC v. Baker, 953 F.2d 1498 (11th Cir. 1992); Ukrainian-American Bar Ass'n. v. Baker, 893 F.2d 1374 (D.C.Cir.1990). The Fifth Amendment guarantee of due process has no application to aliens outside the United States. Landon v. Plasencia, 459 U.S. 21, 32 (1982).

Article 33, as incorporated by the Refugee Protocol, does not create enforceable rights. It applies only to refugees who have gained entry into the territory of a contracting State.

* * * *

The Immigration and Nationality Act provides no enforceable rights for aliens on the high seas.

* * * *

Neither the Executive Order nor the INS internal operating instructions creates any judicially enforceable rights.

* * * *

Plaintiffs cannot state a claim for relief under the Administrative Procedure Act.

* * * *

Judicial intervention is otherwise barred for a number of reasons.

* * * *

Second, with respect to plaintiffs here who were members of the class in <u>HRC v. Baker</u>, issues that were, or could have been litigated in that case, are barred by the doctrines of <u>res judicata</u> and collateral estoppel.

<u>CONCLUSION</u>

For the foregoing reasons, and the reasons set forth in the briefs incorporated herein by reference, plaintiffs' complaint should be dismissed with prejudice, and judgment should be entered in favor of the defendants.

The argument that refers to the *Baker* lawsuit is one of the most important arguments in the *McNary* case. From reading *Storming the Court*, do you recall the nature of this argument? We will discuss it both later in this chapter and then in detail in Chapter Ten.

Respectfully submitted,

STUART M. GERSON
Assistant Attorney General
Civil Division
STEVEN R. VALENTINE
Dep. Asst. Attorney General
Civil Division

ANDREW J. MALONEY
United States Attorney
U.S. Courthouse
225 Cadman Plaza East
Brooklyn, N.Y. 11201

[signature]
ROBERT L. BOMBAUGH
Director, Office of
Immigration Litigation

[signature]
SCOTT DUNN
Assistant U.S. Attorney

LAURI STEVEN FILPPU
ALLEN W. HAUSMAN
THOMAS W. HUSSEY
ALICE M. KING
CHARLES E. PAZAR
EMILY ANNE RADFORD
MICHELE Y.F. SARKO
NORAH ASCOLI SCHWARZ
KAREN FLETCHER TORSTENSON
MARK C. WALTERS
Attorneys
Office of Immigration Litigation
Department of Justice
P.O. Box 878, Ben Franklin Station
Washington, D.C. 20044
Tele: 202-501-7700
     FTS 241-7700

Dated: March 20, 1992

NOTES AND COMMENTS

1. The Basics of a Rule 12(b)(6) Motion.   It is crucial to understand that on a motion to dismiss under 12(b)(6), the court is *not deciding whether the plaintiff's claims are true.* By filing a 12(b)(6) motion, the defendant is saying to the court: Even if everything the plaintiff says is, in fact, true, there is no basis in the law for the plaintiff to recover. A very simple, intuitive example should help clarify things. Let's say a plaintiff absolutely hates blue bicycles . . . so he files a lawsuit against a defendant for the mere act of riding a blue bicycle down the street in an otherwise lawful manner. Your instinct should tell you that unless there's some special law against riding blue bicycles, this lawsuit is ridiculous. The way that the defendant deals with this meritless lawsuit under the Federal Rules is Rule 12(b)(6). Specifically, the defendant files a motion to dismiss for failure to state a claim on the ground that even if it's true that he rode a blue bicycle down the street, on those facts alone there is simply no legal theory that would authorize a recovery by the plaintiff. Make sense?

Now, in the *McNary* case, things were obviously a little more complicated. Begin by keeping this basic operational idea in mind. For purposes of deciding a motion to dismiss under Rule 12(b)(6), the court is guided by three basic principles. The court must (a) look *only* at the complaint and no other outside material,[2] (b) take everything the plaintiff says ("alleges") in the complaint as true, and (c) view all of plaintiff's allegations in the light most favorable to the plaintiff. Accordingly, as the motion to dismiss in *McNary* makes clear, the government was *not disputing* the facts recounted by the plaintiffs. Rather, it maintained that even if everything in the plaintiffs' complaint were true, the complaint would still be insufficient and the case should not be allowed to go forward.

2. Challenging the Sufficiency of the Complaint.   In deciding a 12(b)(6) motion to dismiss, a court will assess the sufficiency of the complaint against the requirements of Rule 8. That is, the court will try to determine whether the plaintiff has done what is required under Rule 8(a)—namely, to allege facts that, if true, would enable the plaintiff to recover. In that event, the plaintiff has, in the words of Rule 12(b)(6), stated "a claim upon which relief may be granted," and defendant's motion will be denied.

Generally, there are two different ways in which a plaintiff might fail to meet the requirements of Rule 8. First, the harm that the plaintiff alleges might not be one for which the law provides relief. You're already familiar with an example of this problem: the blue bicycle lawsuit. Even if it were true that the defendant rode a blue bicycle down the street, the law doesn't provide the plaintiff with a legal claim for such conduct. Second, the plaintiff might have a cognizable claim—in other words, the law does provide for recovery—but the plaintiff may not have alleged one or more of the *elements of the claim.* Take, for example, an action for negligence, which requires

---

2. In limited circumstances, courts may look at other documents if those documents are incorporated into the complaint through Rule 10.

the plaintiff to plead five elements: (1) a duty owed by the defendant to the plaintiff, (2) a breach of the duty (that is, negligent conduct), (3) causation, (4) proximate cause, and (5) damages. What happens if the plaintiff fails in his complaint to allege that the defendant was negligent? Even if all the facts in the complaint are assumed to be true, the complaint doesn't show that the plaintiff is entitled to relief because it doesn't contain an allegation of negligence.

Remember: The court is *not* trying to decide whether the defendant was or was not in fact negligent. All the plaintiff needs to do to survive a motion to dismiss under Rule 12(b)(6) is to include an allegation of negligence in her complaint.[3] This is often the most counterintuitive part of a 12(b)(6) motion. One naturally wants to delve into the merits of the case and ask whether there is support for the plaintiff's contentions. The time for that, however, is later—at the summary judgment and trial stages of the lawsuit. At this point in the case, the court's only job is to make sure that the allegation is *present* in the complaint—that the words themselves have been included within the four corners of the complaint—and the court will treat that allegation as if it had been proved for purposes of evaluating the motion to dismiss.

In its Rule 12(b)(6) motion challenging the sufficiency of the complaint in *McNary*, the government raised a number of arguments. Among other things, it maintained that the plaintiff organizations did not have a First Amendment right to communicate with their purported clients on Guantánamo. It also argued that the Haitian plaintiffs did not have any rights under the due process clause of the Fifth Amendment because they were located outside of the United States. Refer back to the two types of fatal flaws described earlier in this Note. From which type of flaw is the government claiming that the plaintiffs' complaint suffered?

On November 12, 1992, Judge Johnson issued a decision on the government's motion to dismiss. *Haitian Centers Council v. McNary*, 807 F. Supp. 928 (E.D.N.Y. 1992). In that decision, he denied the motion to dismiss the First and Fifth Amendment claims, holding that plaintiffs on Guantánamo *did* have rights under those provisions of the Constitution. Nevertheless, the court dismissed certain other claims that we have not examined here. See Note 9, later in this chapter, for a discussion of the timing of the Judge's November 12 decision.

3. Waiver. As noted in the introduction to this chapter, a defendant may choose to make a motion under Rule 12 before answering the complaint, and the *McNary* defendants did just that. If, however, the defendant does not have a good-faith basis for seeking dismissal of the complaint under Rule 12(b)(6) or any of the other provisions of Rule 12(b), such as lack of personal jurisdiction or improper venue, then her first response to the complaint will be an answer. Whether the defendant

---

3. Of course, it's not permissible for the plaintiff to concoct a false story and for her lawyer to draft and file a complaint based on that story. The allegations of the complaint must meet the requirements of Rule 11, as discussed in Chapter 4.

Haitian-American activists Johnny McCalla (left) and Ronald Aubourg on the ferry crossing Guantánamo Bay, February 6, 1993. McCalla, executive director of the National Coalition for Haitian Refugees ("NCHR"), and Aubourg, a staff member at NCHR, were among many non-lawyers who worked with the Yale team. Photographer unknown.

chooses to respond by motion or answer, however, it is absolutely crucial that she raise all of the Rule 12(b) defenses available to her in that first response.

Why? Certain defenses—specifically, the Rule 12(b)(2)-(5) defenses based on lack of personal jurisdiction, improper venue, insufficient process, and insufficient service of process—are waived if the defendant does not assert them in the first response to the complaint. *See* Fed. R. Civ. P. 12(h)(2). In other words, if the defendant doesn't present those defenses at the first opportunity, they are lost forever. The remaining defenses permitted under Rule 12—failure to state a claim (Rule 12(b)(6)), failure to join a required party (Rule 12(b)(7)), and lack of subject-matter jurisdiction (Rule 12(b)(1))—are *not* waived if they are not raised in this first response. In fact, a defendant may raise a defense based on failure to state a claim all the way until the end of trial—and a subject-matter jurisdiction defense *is never waived and can be raised at any time, including on appeal.* Rule 12 specifically provides that the court must dismiss the action if at any time the court finds it does not have subject-matter jurisdiction. *See* Fed. R. Civ. P. 12(h)(3).

There are some very good reasons for why these various defenses are treated so differently. Why do you think the defenses identified in Rule 12(b)(2)-(5) can be waived so easily? In contrast, why does Rule 12 preserve the defense of failure to state a claim through trial? Even more importantly, why do you think the defense of lack of subject-matter jurisdiction can never be waived?

RULE 8: RESPONDING BY ANSWER

Rule 8, which sets forth the requirements for a complaint, also provides the requirements for an answer. Drafting an answer is usually less demanding than drawing up a complaint because the defendant, in an answer, is generally required only to admit or deny the allegations made by the plaintiff. Nevertheless, a defense attorney may find it necessary to perform some of the same tasks undertaken by plaintiff's counsel in drafting the complaint, including legal research and a reasonable factual investigation. What follows is an excerpt from the answer filed by the government lawyers in *McNary* after their motion to dismiss was denied. For ease of reading, we have inserted and italicized the material from the amended complaint to which each paragraph of the answer is responding. (Note that an actual answer does not reproduce the allegations of the complaint.) As you read the answer, you should also take a look at the requirements of Rule 8(b) and (c), which are discussed in more detail later in this chapter.

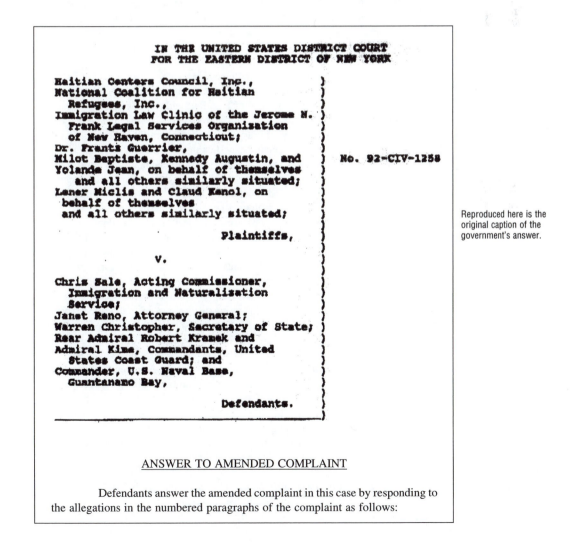

```
        IN THE UNITED STATES DISTRICT COURT
         FOR THE EASTERN DISTRICT OF NEW YORK

Haitian Centers Council, Inc.,           )
National Coalition for Haitian           )
  Refugees, Inc.,                        )
Immigration Law Clinic of the Jerome N.  )
  Frank Legal Services Organization      )
  of New Haven, Connecticut;             )
Dr. Frantz Guerrier,                     )
Milot Baptiste, Kennedy Augustin, and    )  No. 92-CIV-1258
Yolande Jean, on behalf of themselves    )
  and all others similarly situated;     )
Lener Miclis and Claud Kanol, on         )
  behalf of themselves                   )
  and all others similarly situated;     )
                                         )
                       Plaintiffs,       )
                                         )
             v.                          )
                                         )
Chris Sale, Acting Commissioner,         )
  Immigration and Naturalization         )
  Service;                               )
Janet Reno, Attorney General;            )
Warren Christopher, Secretary of State;  )
Rear Admiral Robert Kramek and           )
Admiral Kime, Commandants, United        )
  States Coast Guard; and                )
Commander, U.S. Naval Base,              )
  Guantanamo Bay,                        )
                                         )
                       Defendants.       )
```

Reproduced here is the original caption of the government's answer.

ANSWER TO AMENDED COMPLAINT

Defendants answer the amended complaint in this case by responding to the allegations in the numbered paragraphs of the complaint as follows:

PRELIMINARY STATEMENT

1. This is a complaint for declaratory and injunctive relief arising from defendants' illegal and arbitrary actions against Haitians and Haitian Service Organizations following the military coup that overthrew the government of Jean-Bertrand Aristide on September 30, 1991. Following the coup, many Haitians fled their country because of a well-founded fear of political persecution. Defendants have all but ignored those fears. Although binding domestic and international law mandates that refugees, such as the Haitian plaintiffs in this action, shall not be returned to countries where they face death and political persecution, defendants have interdicted numerous vessels on the high seas carrying the Haitian asylum seekers to freedom. Until May 24, 1992, defendants followed the practice of detaining those asylum seekers at Guantanamo Bay Naval Base and subjecting them to screening procedures nowhere mentioned in the Immigration and Nationality Act (INA). Refugees who were "screened out" after those screening procedures were then forcibly repatriated to Haiti. Many of those "screened-in" were ultimately transported to the United States to pursue their claims for asylum, in accordance with longstanding United States policy. But even after May 24, 1992, some of those who were "screened-in" have remained detained and for the most part uncounseled at Guantanamo for many months, based solely on their alleged medical status or that of their family members, even as they await further proceedings that may lead to their forced repatriation.

Note how the government lawyers proceed sentence by sentence in crafting their denials and admissions.

1. The first sentence of this paragraph characterizes plaintiffs' case and no answer is required. To the extent that an answer is required, defendants admit that a military coup overthrew the government of Jean-Bertrand Aristide and that September 30, 1991 is the day customarily cited as the day of the coup, but deny that defendants have acted illegally or arbitrarily. Defendants admit the allegation in the second sentence that following the coup many Haitians left their country. Defendants are without sufficient knowledge or information to form a belief as to the truth of the remaining allegations in the second sentence, which allegations are denied. Defendants deny the allegations in the third sentence. The allegations in the introductory clauses of the fourth sentence are assertions of law to which no response is necessary. To the extent that a response is deemed necessary, the assertions are denied. Defendants admit the allegation in the fourth sentence that they "have interdicted numerous vessels on the high seas" carrying Haitians. Defendants deny the remaining allegations in the fourth sentence. Defendants admit the allegations in the fifth sentence, except that defendants deny that Haitians were detained at Guantanamo, and that Haitians outside the United States can properly be described as "asylum seekers." Defendants aver, however, that migrants were not generally free to roam around the Base nor to travel to the United States. Regarding the sixth sentence, defendants admit that persons who are " 'screened out' [were] . . . forcibly repatriated to Haiti" if they were nationals of Haiti unless they were immediate relatives of Haitian nationals who were screened in. Defendants deny the remaining allegations contained within the sixth sentence. The allegations in the seventh sentence are denied, except that defendants admit that many screened-in Haitians have been transported to the United States. The eighth sentence is denied, except that defendants admit that some "screened-in" migrants have remained at the Guantanamo Bay Naval Base in Cuba, and that their medical status has been an important consideration in the government's actions respecting many of them.

This allegation refers to President Bush's May 24, 1992 executive order authorizing return of all interdicted Haitians directly to Haiti with no asylum screening interviews.

2. From May 1992 until the present time, defendants have failed to employ any screening procedure whatsoever to identify those Haitians on inter-dicted boats who face political persecution if they are returned to Haiti. All

Haitians on interdicted boats are summarily returned to Haiti without process of any kind. Defendants have forcibly repatriated a large number of "screened-in" refugee plaintiffs from Guantanamo without any determination that those Haitians are not bona fide political refugees. Many of these "screened-in" refugees would attempt to flee political persecution in Haiti again by boat, but for defendants' lawless policy, which cuts off their avenue of escape.

2. The first sentence of this paragraph is denied, except that defendants admit that Haitians interdicted after May 24, 1992, have not been screened. Defendants aver that the commanding officers of Coast Guard vessels involved in interdictions have the authority to provide protection to persons facing grave physical danger upon repatriation. The second sentence is denied, except that defendants admit that interdicted Haitian migrants currently are returned to Haiti without "credible fear" interviews, pursuant to Executive Order 12807. The third sentence is denied, except that defendants admit that they returned from Guantanamo to Haiti a limited number of "screened-in" migrants who tested HIV positive and who refused, after several requests, to participate in an interview to determine whether or not they had a well-founded fear of persecution, which is the standard for receiving refugee status under United States law, and that a small number of screened-in Haitians were inadvertently returned to Haiti in 1992. The fourth sentence is denied.

Consider how the government lawyers respond to the allegation regarding the President's direct return order. Why did they want to avoid admitting the allegation as drafted?

3. *Although the First Amendment protects the right of lawyers to associate with their clients, defendant officials have barred plaintiff legal and advocacy groups from counseling and representing Haitian refugees held within U.S. jurisdiction in connection with those refugees' claims for political asylum and to resist wrongful repatriation, based solely upon the content and viewpoint of the message those representatives would communicate. Defendants simultaneously have barred plaintiff Haitian refugees from communicating with their retained counsel with respect to those same claims, although defendants plan to adjudicate those claims in proceedings that may lead to their repatriation to death or serious injury. For months, defendants prohibited communication of any sort between plaintiff refugees and their retained counsel, and may at any time resume that prohibition.*

3. The first 14 words of the first sentence contain a legal conclusion to which no response is necessary. To the extent a response is necessary, the first 14 words of the sentence are denied. The remainder of the first sentence is denied. The second and third sentences are denied.

Note the precision with which the government responds. Such precision is necessary here to adequately put the plaintiff on notice of what allegations of the complaint the defendant contests. Note also that Rule 11(b)(4) requires attorneys to make a reasonable investigation into the basis of factual denials.

4. *Since the September coup, lower executive officials have acted arbitrarily and capriciously and in violation of unambiguous constitutional, statutory, presidential, and administrative mandates to coerce and detain plaintiff refugees and to diminish their right to resist forced repatriation to a brutal regime the United States Government has called illegitimate. In so doing, defendants have ignored binding international obligations that have been executed as United States law and which deny them discretion to return political refugees to a country where those refugees have a well-founded fear of political persecution. Finally, defendants impermissibly have applied these unauthorized, <u>ad hoc</u> procedures solely against Haitian refugees, based on their race and national origin.*

Why, in contrast to earlier paragraphs, did the government deny the entirety of paragraph 4 of the amended complaint?

4. This paragraph is denied.

* * * *

11. The individual named plaintiffs Dr. Frantz Guerrier and Milot Baptiste were held in detention at Guantanamo Bay Naval Base after being "screened in." They were subsequently involuntarily returned to Haiti without any determination by defendants that they lack bona fide asylum claims. While held at Guantanamo, they retained plaintiff Haitian Service Organizations to provide them with representation and advocacy, and they sought to exercise their procedural and other due process rights. These named plaintiffs also represent other similarly situated persons who were (a) detained within U.S. jurisdiction on Coast Guard cutters or at Guantanamo Bay Naval Base, (b) "screened in," and (c) involuntarily returned to Haiti without any determination that they lacked well-founded fears of persecution (the "repatriated screened-in plaintiffs"). On information and belief, this group numbers over 150. Although these Haitians were supposed to be brought to the United States and afforded full procedural safeguards, including the right to counsel, in pursuing their asylum claims, many of them languished at Guantanamo Bay for months on end before being forcibly repatriated, without being informed of their legal status or of their procedural rights. On information and belief, they again wish to flee political persecution, and would do so but for defendants' practice of summary repatriation.

11. Defendants deny the allegations in the first sentence, except to admit that plaintiffs Guerrier and Baptiste were screened-in at Guantanamo. Defendants aver that plaintiffs Guerrier and Baptiste were not free to travel to the United States nor to roam the Base at Guantanamo, but were not "detained." As to the second sentence, defendants admit that Guerrier and Baptiste were repatriated from Guantanamo without a determination as to the bona fides of their persecution claim, because they refused, after repeated entreaties, to participate in INS interview procedures designed to elicit information reflecting whether they possessed a well founded fear of persecution. Defendants aver that Guerrier and Baptiste waived any persecution claim they may have had. Defendants deny the remaining allegations in the second sentence. Defendants lack sufficient knowledge or information to form a belief as to the truth of the allegations contained within the third sentence respecting the retention of the Haitian Service Organizations, which allegations are denied. Defendants deny the allegations in the third sentence respecting the exercise or existence of procedural and due process rights at Guantanamo. Defendants lack sufficient knowledge or information to form a belief as to the truth of the allegations in the fourth sentence, which allegations are denied. The allegations in the fifth and sixth sentences are denied. Defendants lack sufficient knowledge or information to form a belief as to the truth of the allegations contained within the seventh sentence, which allegations are denied. Defendants aver that in-country refugee processing is available in Haiti and the Guerrier and Baptiste may apply for refugee status under that program.

An answer is also an opportunity for the defendant to present its side of the story, as the government does here by stating that Guerrier and Baptiste were returned only after they refused to participate in INS interview procedures "after repeated entreaties."

* * * *

30. Early in 1992, defendants began a new policy of medically testing "screened-in" Haitian refugees before they were physically transferred to the United States to pursue their asylum claims. Defendants have not subjected any other interdicted aliens to medical testing prior to their transfer to the United States. Defendants did not obtain the consent of the refugees before performing the medical tests, including blood tests. Days after the Supreme Court's denial of certiorari in the Florida litigation, defendants initiated a new policy of forcing some "screened-in" Haitian refugees to undergo multiple layers of review based on the refugees' alleged medical status, abandoning the prior practice of bringing such refugees directly to the United States for standard asylum adjudications. But for the preliminary injunction now entered in this case, defendants would be disposing of the political asylum claims of the "screened-in" Haitians who remain on Guantanamo, while denying them access to counsel, the opportunity to rebut and submit evidence and other procedural safeguards.

30. Defendants deny the allegations in this paragraph, but state that: medical testing of interdicted aliens generally did not occur prior to the recent Haitian crisis; HIV testing of Haitian migrants at Guantanamo began in response to concerns expressed by third countries when the United States sought the assistance of those third countries in establishing refugee camps for the Haitians; in a February 29, 1992 memorandum, the INS explained that many HIV+ Haitian aliens who were screened in were to be interviewed a second time to provide information about whether the aliens had a well-founded fear of persecution in order to inform a decision to be made about immigration parole and medical waivers; and defendants do not consider the statutory and regulatory provisions respecting asylum to extend to Guantanamo.

In this paragraph, the government admits those aspects of the allegations it is required to admit while recharacterizing the allegations in a light more favorable to its case. The averments in this paragraph also fore-shadow certain defenses the government raises later in its answer, including the inapplicability of U.S. law to Guantánamo.

* * * *

THIRD CLAIM FOR RELIEF

(Other Denial of Constitutional Due Process Rights)

61. The "screened-in" plaintiffs at Guantanamo repeat and reallege paragraphs 1 through 60 as though fully set forth herein.

This is plaintiffs' due process claim on indefinite detention and inadequate medical care.

62. Defendants have intercepted and indefinitely detained plaintiff refugees, who have committed no crime, under an extra-statutory legal regime without fixed or knowable procedures, timetables or standards for resolution of the detention, violating plaintiffs' right to be free of indefinite detention.

63. Plaintiff refugees have been, and at any time may be, arbitrarily subjected to beatings, incarceration and other punishments, without process of any sort, violating plaintiffs' right to be free of arbitrary punishment.

64. Plaintiff refugees have been subjected to interviews by INS asylum officers without the assistance of counsel, denying them a meaningful opportunity to present effectively their asylum claims, violating plaintiffs' right to present in an effective manner their claim for political asylum and for such claim not to be improperly denied.

65. Under defendants' policies challenged herein, plaintiff refugees have been and are denied the right to submit supplementary evidence, testimony and affidavits within thirty days after their asylum interview.

66. Under defendants' policies challenged herein, plaintiff refugees have been and are denied the right to a written Notice of Intent to Deny their claims to political asylum, stating the reasons for the intended denial, an assessment of the applicant's credibility, and information from sources other than those the applicant relied upon in reaching the negative determination.

67. Plaintiff refugees are denied the right to submit a response or rebuttal to a Notice of Intent to Deny.

68. Under defendants' policies challenged herein, plaintiff refugees have been and are denied the right to renew an application for political asylum to an immigration judge and to appeal an adverse determination to the Board of Immigration Appeals and to the federal courts.

69. Defendants have subjected and may at any time subject members of the plaintiff class to medical testing against their will, and have prescribed treatment for medical conditions notwithstanding plaintiff refugees' inability to consent or refuse consent to treatment on an informed basis due to inadequate counseling, violating plaintiffs' right to refuse medical testing and/or treatment.

70. Plaintiff refugees have been denied adequate medical care, by defendants' actions in failing to provide effective counseling regarding diagnosis and treatment of plaintiffs' medical conditions; in detaining members of the plaintiff class whose medical condition has so deteriorated that they cannot be properly cared for at facilities on Guantanamo; and in failing to provide specialist treatment for a number of medical problems suffered by plaintiff refugees, violating plaintiffs' right to adequate medical treatment while in defendants' custody.

71. By concentrating a large number of immune-suppressed individuals in a single detention facility, defendants have placed plaintiff refugees at needless risk of medical deterioration and disease infection, violating plaintiffs' right not to be confined in inherently unhealthful and life-threatening conditions.

* * * *

As you can see, when a defendant responds to allegations respecting a claim for relief, the usual approach is to deny almost everything.

61. Defendants reassert their preceding responses to plaintiffs' allegations in paragraphs 1 through 60 of their amended complaint.

62. The allegations in this paragraph are denied.

63. The allegations in this paragraph are denied.

64. Defendants admit that the INS has interviewed Haitian migrants without the assistance of counsel for the migrants. The remaining allegations in this paragraph are denied.

65–68. Defendants admit the allegations in these paragraphs, except that defendants deny that plaintiff Haitian migrants are "refugees," are involved in "asylum" interview processing or applications, and have the "rights" asserted under these paragraphs in the amended complaint.

69. The allegations in this paragraph are denied.

70. The allegations in this paragraph are denied.

71. The allegations in this paragraph are denied.

* * * *

The remainder of plaintiffs' complaint constitutes plaintiffs' prayer for relief to which no response is necessary. To the extent that a response is required, the prayer for relief is denied.

* * *

Any allegation of the complaint not expressly admitted is hereby denied.

Defendants deny that plaintiffs are entitled to the relief sought in the complaint or to any relief whatsoever.

* * *

In addition, defendants assert the following defenses:

FIRST AFFIRMATIVE DEFENSE

The amended complaint fails to state a claim upon which relief can he granted.

SECOND AFFIRMATIVE DEFENSE

Relief should be denied plaintiffs as an exercise of judicial discretion to withhold relief.

THIRD AFFIRMATIVE DEFENSE

The claims in the amended complaint are barred by the principles of res judicata and collateral estoppel.

FOURTH AFFIRMATIVE DEFENSE

The Court lacks jurisdiction over the claims in this lawsuit.

* * *

WHEREFORE, defendants request that the Court dismiss the complaint, grant defendants the cost of their suit, and grant defendants such other and further relief as the Court deems proper.

```
STUART SCHIFFER                          MARY JO WHITE
Acting Assistant Attorney                United States Attorney
  General
Civil Division

                                         ROBERT BEGLEITER
                                         Assistant United States
                                           Attorney

ROBERT L. BOMBAUGH
Director
Office of Immigration

[signature]                              [signature]
LAURI STEVEN FILPPU, Deputy              SCOTT DUNN
Office of Immigration Litigation         Spec. Assistant U.S. Attorney
DAVID J. KLINE                           One Pierrepont Plaza
CHARLES E. PAZAR                         Brooklyn, N.Y.  11201
ELLEN SUE SHAPIRO
ALICE M. KING
FRANCISCO ISGRO                          Telephone:  (718) 330-7180
Attorneys
Office of Immigration Litigation
Department of Justice
Box 878, Ben Franklin Station
Washington, D.C.  20044-0878

Telephone:  (202) 501-7700

ATTORNEYS FOR DEFENDANTS                 Dated:  May 13, 1993
```

NOTES AND COMMENTS

4. The Defendant's Response. In drafting an answer, a defendant has two main tasks under Rule 8(b)—to state his defenses and to respond to the allegations in the complaint. *See* Fed. R. Civ. P. 8(b)(1)(A), (B). As you can see from Rule 8(b), in responding to the plaintiff's allegations, the defendant must either admit or deny them. Just as the complaint must contain enough information to inform the defendant of the substance of the plaintiff's claims, the answer must inform the court and the plaintiff as to those parts of the plaintiff's contentions that the defendant disputes. Review carefully the allegations in paragraph 1 of the amended complaint and the government's responses in paragraph 1 of the answer to those allegations. What allegations did the government admit, and why? (Consider also Rule 11(b)(4) in answering this question.)

Counsel must be very careful about what is admitted. An admitted allegation is treated as an undisputed fact for purposes of summary judgment (a concept discussed at length in Chapter Eight) and trial. Further, when drafting the answer, a defendant must be vigilant about not overlooking an allegation. Failure to deny an allegation is treated as an admission. *See* Fed. R. Civ. P. 8(b)(6). (Keep in mind, however, that the defendant can amend the answer. *See* Fed. R. Civ. P. 15.)

Notice how the numbering of the paragraphs of the government's answer tracks the numbering of paragraphs of the amended complaint. This is good practice; it is easy for the court and the plaintiff's lawyers to determine what is admitted and denied— and it also ensures that defense counsel doesn't forget to respond to each allegation. Such numbering may also be required by local rule.[4]

---

4. In addition to the Federal Rules, each court can establish its own local rules. *See* Fed. R. Civ. P. 83. Judges also have the authority to set out their own rules for attorneys that appear before them. Each time you appear in a new court, you must be sure to familiarize yourself with these rules.

5. Denials.   Rule 8(b) sets out two types of denial. First, there is the explicit denial of an allegation. An example of such a denial can be found in paragraph 4 of the answer, set forth above. Second, if the defendant does not have enough information to form a belief about the truth of one of the plaintiff's allegations, he or she may say so and that statement will operate as a denial. *See* Fed. R. Civ. P. 8(b)(5); *see also* 5 *Federal Practice and Procedure* § 1262 (3d ed. 2004). An example can be found in the second sentence of the following paragraph of the answer (preceded by the relevant paragraph of the complaint).

---

23. *As a result of these grave conditions, thousands of Haitians have fled the brutality of the illegal Haitian regime. Thousands of refugees have fled to the Dominican Republic. Thousands more have set out in small boats that are often overloaded, unseaworthy, lacking basic safety equipment, and operated by inexperienced persons, braving the hazards of a prolonged journey over high seas in search of safety and freedom.*

23. Defendants deny the allegations in the first sentence except to admit that thousands of Haitians left Haiti in the last two months of 1991 and in 1992. With respect to the second sentence, defendants admit that Haitians have left Haiti for the Dominican Republic, but defendants lack sufficient information to admit or deny the remaining allegations contained in the second sentence, which allegations are denied. Defendants deny the allegations in the third sentence, but admit that thousands of Haitians have set out in small boats that are often overloaded, unseaworthy, lacking in basic safety equipment, and operated by inexperienced persons without due regard for the hazards of lengthy voyages on the high seas.

Can you determine which specific fact the government is denying in that sentence? Does it seem plausible to you that the government has insufficient information to form a belief as to this fact? Why or why not? Given the extensive statistics compiled by the State Department, do you think that the Department's Office of Caribbean Affairs might have some relevant information on this issue? How specific do you think the State Department's information would have to be before the government could no longer deny the allegation based on having insufficient information to form a belief as to the fact?

In a number of places in the answer, including paragraph 1, the government states that the plaintiffs' allegations "are assertions of law to which no response is necessary." Can you locate the provision in Rule 8 that authorizes the defendants to make that response? Trick question. In fact, there is no express authority in the Federal Rules for this form of denial. Nevertheless, it is widely used and has become generally accepted in pleading practice.

Rule 8(b)(3) also specifies the form of denials. A denial may be either general or specific. A general denial requires the defendant to deny *all* of the allegations of the complaint, including those upon which the court's jurisdiction depends. General denials are disfavored and rarely seen in practice today. Specific denials, such as those you have read in the excerpts from the government's answer, are directed only to specific allegations by the plaintiff.

The answer in *McNary* makes specific denials in two ways. In some places, the government just denies specific allegations, and in others, it denies the allegation generally and then says what is admitted. Both approaches are permitted under Rule 8(b)(3). Can you find examples of each in the excerpts reproduced previously?

6. Limits on Denials.   There are several provisions in Rule 8 that limit the extent to which a defendant may deny an allegation. For example, if the defendant intends to deny only part of an allegation, he must admit as true the rest of the allegation. *See* Fed. R. Civ. P. 8(b)(4). In addition, whatever their form, denials "must fairly respond to the substance of the allegation." Fed. R. Civ. P. 8(b)(2). This means that the defendant must respond, in good faith, to the substance of the claims the plaintiff makes in the complaint and avoid blanket or hyper-technical denials.

Consider these rules in light of the response in defendants' answer to paragraph 31 of the plaintiffs' amended complaint, reproduced together here.

> *31. Between April and June 1992, defendants forcibly repatriated at least 150 "screened-in" plaintiffs to Haiti against their will, either (a) as a result of error, (b) because a number of plaintiffs refused to submit to final asylum adjudications without counsel on Guantanamo, or (c) as a result of the inferior asylum processing system without procedural safeguards which defendants applied to those "screened-in" refugees who allegedly tested positive for HIV. Defendants repatriated many of these "screened-in" plaintiffs without ever determining that they lacked well-founded fears of persecution upon return to Haiti.*
>
> 31. Defendants admit that a small number of screened-in migrants were erroneously repatriated to Haiti, but aver that the vast majority of "screened-in" repatriated migrants included HIV positive individuals who refused, after several entreaties, to participate in a further interview to determine whether they possessed a "well-founded fear" of persecution in Haiti. Defendants further aver that it was these aliens' own refusal to participate in the further screening process which resulted in their repatriation "without [the INS] determining that they lacked well-founded fears of persecution upon return to Haiti." These aliens waived their opportunity for such a determination. The remaining allegations in this paragraph are denied.

There are certainly provisions of paragraph 31 of the amended complaint that the government could and should have denied, as it did. But the government could not deny the entirety of the paragraph, given that some of the allegations were undoubtedly true. For instance, the government could not deny that some individuals were mistakenly repatriated to Haiti. Such a denial would have violated Rules 8(b)(2) and 8(b)(4)—and potentially exposed the government to sanctions under Rule 11(b)(4), as well. (Rule 11 is discussed in Chapter Four.)

The government is not, however, limited to simply admitting the allegation and adopting the plaintiffs' characterization of the situation. As you can see, most of the paragraph consists of the government admitting what it must admit, but doing so in its own words (a strategy that the government used a number of times in the earlier excerpts of the answer, above). This approach enables the government to admit what is necessary but avoid being locked into the plaintiffs' description of the events in question.

Finally, consider the tenth sentence of paragraph 1 of the answer (reproduced previously), in which the government admits the allegations in the fifth sentence of paragraph 1 of the plaintiffs complaint (which begins, "Until May 24, 1992, defendants followed the practice . . . ") but denies that the Haitians were detained at Guantánamo. What precisely is the government denying here? Why? Is this denial consistent with the government's obligations under Rules 8(b)(2) and 11(b)(4)? Do you think the eleventh sentence of paragraph 1 of the answer (which begins, "Defendants aver, however, that migrants were not generally free . . . ") is sufficient to meet those obligations?

7. Affirmative Defenses.   The government's answer concludes with several affirmative defenses, which are authorized by Rule 8(c). In contrast to denials under Rule 8(b), which contradict the plaintiff's assertions, affirmative defenses under Rule 8(c) do not dispute the merits of the plaintiff's case. In essence, a defendant raising an affirmative defense is saying that even if the plaintiff is able to prove everything in the complaint, there is some other reason that plaintiff should not recover on his claim. *See* 5 *Federal Practice and Procedure* § 1270 (3d ed. 2004). The running of a statute of limitations is the classic affirmative defense. The argument is that even assuming everything the plaintiff says is true, and even assuming that the law would otherwise grant plaintiff a recovery, the defendant should still win because the period of time for asserting the claim has expired. The defendant bears the burden of proof on affirmative defenses, and failure to assert an affirmative defense generally results in waiver of the defense.

In *McNary*, the government's primary affirmative defense was res judicata (or "claim preclusion," as the doctrine is usually known today), which is one of 19 affirmative defenses expressly identified by Rule 8(c)(1). You should know from *Storming the Court* that res judicata is a doctrine according to which a plaintiff is only given "one bite at the apple"—the plaintiff can't sue twice for the same harm. The essence of the government's argument here is that everything raised in the *McNary* case was already raised and decided in the earlier case of *Haitian Refugee Center v. Baker. See STC*, pp. 37, 77. Res judicata is discussed in detail in Chapter Ten.

8. Counterclaims.   In addition to the denials authorized by Rule 8(b) and the affirmative defenses authorized by Rule 8(c), there is one other common response by the defendant to a complaint: the counterclaim. A counterclaim is an assertion by the defendant of a new claim against the plaintiff. Counterclaims are either compulsory or permissive. Compulsory counterclaims are counterclaims that arise out of the same transaction or occurrence as the original claim asserted by the plaintiff. *See* Fed. R. Civ. P. 13(a). An example of a compulsory counterclaim would be a claim by a defendant against a plaintiff in a suit arising from a car accident for injuries that the defendant suffered because of the plaintiff's negligence. In part for reasons of efficiency, such claims must be raised in the original lawsuit or they will be deemed waived. Permissive counterclaims include any other claim the defendant might have against the plaintiff. *See* Fed. R. Civ. P. 13(b). These may be raised by the defendant, but if they are not, the defendant may still bring them in a later lawsuit. *See id.* In *McNary*, the government defendants did not assert any counterclaims against the plaintiffs.[5]

9. Time to Respond.   The date by which the defendant must file an answer depends on several considerations. *See* Fed. R. Civ. P. 12(a). Generally, a defendant has 20 days to respond to the complaint with either a motion or an answer, but that time is increased to 60 days if the defendant waives the right to service of a summons under Rule 4(d). A defendant who waives service is waiving only formal service of the summons; the plaintiff is still required to provide the defendant with a copy of the complaint along with the request for the waiver. *See* Fed. R. Civ. P. 4(d)(1)(A). The defendant has the choice of either agreeing to the waiver or refusing (or ignoring) the request; if the defendant refuses to waive service, the plaintiff must serve the defendant under the normal procedures.

There are special rules for the government, however. First, under Rule 12(a)(2), the government is always entitled to 60 days to respond. The government is allowed additional time in part because at common law the sovereign enjoys certain advantages in litigation, and in part because of the more practical reason that attorneys representing the government must deal with a large bureaucracy in collecting facts and determining the legal position that the government will take in its response to the complaint. Further, waiver of service is not available in a lawsuit against the United States. *See* Fed. R. Civ. P. 4(i). Nor would the government necessarily have any incentive to waive service since it already is entitled to 60 days under the rules.

When a party must take action by a certain date, such as responding to a complaint, she may ask the court for an extension of the deadline if she has a good reason—what Rule 6(b) calls "good cause"—for making the request. Generally, it is good practice to ask the attorney on the other side for consent to the extension before requesting more time. It is common for counsel on both sides of a case to seek extensions during litigation. In *McNary*, although the government finally filed its answer nearly 14 *months* after the complaint was filed, this was not because it had requested an extension. Rather, the deadline for its answer was pushed back because of the complicated procedural maneuvers that occurred in the early stages of the case.

What happened? Initially, the government's decision to file a Rule 12(b)(6) motion to dismiss extended the time it had to answer to ten days after the motion was denied. *See* Fed. R. Civ. P. 12(a)(4)(A). An inexperienced observer might conclude that the government was therefore required to respond ten days after Judge Johnson granted Koh and the students access to Guantánamo Bay on March 27, 1992 in his temporary restraining order (TRO). A careful review of the court's decisions, however, reveals that neither in the TRO nor in the April 6, 1992 preliminary injunction order, reaffirming access to Guantánamo for plaintiffs' counsel, did Judge Johnson actually rule on the motion to dismiss. Indeed, the judge stated in his April 6 opinion that he had not heard full argument on the motion to dismiss and, by implication, was therefore not prepared to rule on it. *Haitian Centers Council v. McNary*, 1992 WL 155853,

---

5. In addition to a counterclaim, defendants can assert cross-claims against co-parties, *see* Fed. R. Civ. P. 13(g), as well as new claims against someone who is not a party to the case, at least in certain circumstances. *See* Fed. R. Civ. P. 14; *see also* Fed. R. Civ. P. 19(a)(2). None of these rules were at issue in *McNary*. The rules that govern the scope of a lawsuit—called "joinder" rules—are somewhat different when the defendant is the government. Although you may cover joinder in your civil procedure class, these rules were not at issue in *McNary* and will not be discussed here.

at *9 (E.D.N.Y., Apr. 6, 1992). The judge finally ruled on the government's motion to dismiss on November 12, 1992, ultimately dismissing two of plaintiffs' seven claims, but denying the motion as to the other five claims. *Haitian Centers Council v. McNary,* 807 F. Supp. 928 (E.D.N.Y., 1992).

Based on Rule 12(a)(4)(A), which gives the defendant ten days to file an answer after a Rule 12(b) motion is denied, the government's answer should have been due on November 26, 1992. (Why 14 days instead of ten? Because the period of time for responding was less than 11 days, weekends and legal holidays were excluded from the calculation of the deadline under Rule 6(a).) However, by November 1992, counsel for the Haitians and for the government had agreed to a continuance—a temporary suspension of all activity in the case—until President Clinton took office. When the case moved forward for trial, Judge Johnson allowed the plaintiffs to file an amended complaint, which they did on March 16, 1993. Under Rule 12(a)(2), the government was required to file an answer 60 days later. The government ultimately filed its answer on May 13, 1993—after the trial was over! This was an uncommon situation, to say the least.

After the defendant files his answer—which normally comes *much* earlier in the proceedings—the pleadings are generally "closed," meaning finished, although there are some exceptions that we will not address here. *See* Fed. R. Civ. P. 7. In pleading practice under the ancient writ system mentioned in Chapter Two, the parties engaged in multiple rounds of factual assertions to narrow the issues at stake. Although some narrowing of the issues occurs when the defendant identifies which issues are in dispute between the parties, the Federal Rules generally require the parties to use the discovery process to develop the facts of the case and sort out the evidence that bears on each claim. *See* Chapters Six and Seven.

CHAPTER FOUR

Rule 11

INTRODUCTION

Lawyers are expected to maintain the highest standards of honesty and integrity, and their conduct is regulated by several different sources of authority. For example, a lawyer's conduct can be regulated by state bar disciplinary boards and administrative bodies; in more egregious cases of misconduct, lawyers also can be subject to civil malpractice suits or even criminal prosecutions. Although the Federal Rules of Civil Procedure are primarily rules about how to litigate a civil action in federal court, several rules specifically regulate attorney conduct. The most important of these is Rule 11.

A Rule 11 motion asks the court to impose sanctions on the opposing party's attorney (or, in some cases, the opposing party) for presenting a document to the court for an improper purpose or without a sufficient basis in law or fact. A complaint, answer, motion, or other paper filed with the court may be subject to Rule 11 sanctions in three instances: (1) if it has been filed for an improper purpose, such as to harass the other side or unnecessarily delay the proceedings, (2) if the legal claims or arguments have no basis in law and there is no real argument for extending the law, or (3) if the factual allegations or denials of factual allegations have no evidentiary support or are unlikely to have evidentiary support after an opportunity for further investigation. *See* Fed. R. Civ. P. 11(b). Rule 11 also imposes a signature requirement on every document filed with the court.[1] By presenting a signed document to the court, a lawyer certifies that she has conducted a reasonable inquiry into the law and the facts, and that, to the best of her knowledge, the document she has signed does not suffer from any of the three defects listed above.

Finding oneself the target of a Rule 11 motion can be a nerve-wracking experience because the offending attorney or party may face sanctions if the court finds a violation of the rule. The sanction may be relatively minor, such as a reprimand by the court or an order that the offending attorney attend a continuing legal education

---

1. Rule 11 does not govern discovery requests, responses, and objections, which are not generally filed with the court. Rule 26(g) establishes the standards for attorney conduct with respect to discovery of documents; the standards are similar to those set out in Rule 11.

program. It can be considerably more severe, however—in some cases, extending to a financial sanction paid either to the court or to the opposing party for the costs, including attorneys' fees, of responding to the offending filing. *See* Fed. R. Civ. P. 11, Advisory Committee Notes for Subdivisions (b) and (c), 1993 Amendments. Legal malpractice policies are available to protect attorneys from crippling financial sanctions. Not surprisingly, almost every practicing litigator has such a policy. In the *McNary* case, Harold Koh was worried about the worst-case scenario: a financial sanction so great that it would bankrupt him. As you'll recall from the book, Koh's malpractice insurance situation was somewhat unclear. *See STC*, pp. 82-83. Nor was that his only concern: Even if a Rule 11 sanction is minor, a ruling that an attorney violated Rule 11 can injure that attorney's reputation with the court and in the legal community—and reputation is an important asset for an attorney.

The following are excerpts from the government's Rule 11 motion and accompanying brief. As you read the brief, first determine whether the government is attacking the Yale team's factual allegations or legal arguments. Second, try to identify the two interrelated arguments that the government makes under subheading A of the argument section of the government's brief. Can you summarize each argument in a sentence or two? (Note: As discussed in Note 2 in this chapter, Rule 11 has been amended since the *McNary* case, which is why the Rule 11 text quoted in the government's brief does not match the text in your copy of the Rules.)

**UNITED STATES DISTRICT COURT
FOR THE EASTERN DISTRICT OF NEW YORK**

HAITIAN CENTERS COUNCIL, INC., et al.,	)))	
Plaintiffs,	))	
v.	))	Civil Action No. 92-1258 (Johnson, J.)
GENE MC NARY, Commissioner, Immigration and Naturalization Service, et al.,	))))	
Defendants.	))	

MOTION FOR SANCTIONS

Pursuant to Rule 11 of the Federal Rules of Civil Procedure, defendants move for sanctions against plaintiffs and their attorneys on the grounds that plaintiffs' complaint is frivolous and that the filing of such pleading and the accompanying motion for injunctive relief violates the duties imposed by such rule.

In support of this motion, the Court is respectfully referred to the accompanying memorandum of points and authorities.

Respectfully submitted,

STUART M. GERSON
Assistant Attorney General
Civil Division
STEVEN R. VALENTINE
Deputy Asst. Attorney General
Civil Division

ANDREW J. MALONEY
United States Attorney

[signature]

ROBERT L. BOMBAUGH
Director, Office of
Immigration Litigation

[signature]

SCOTT A. DUNN
Asst. United States Attorney
U.S. Courthouse
225 Cadman Plaza East
Brooklyn, N.Y. 11201
718/330-7180

LAURI STEVEN FILPPU
ALLEN W. HAUSMAN
THOMAS W. HUSSEY
ALICE M. KING
CHARLES E. PAZAR
EMILY ANNE RADFORD

MICHELE Y.F. SARKO
NORAH ASCOLI SCHWARZ
KAREN FLETCHER TORSTENSON
MARK C. WALTERS
Attorneys
Office of Immigration Litigation
Department of Justice
P.O. Box 878, Ben Franklin Station
Washington, D.C. 20044
Tel: 202/501-7700
     FTS 241-7700

Dated: March 20, 1992

**UNITED STATES DISTRICT COURT
FOR THE EASTERN DISTRICT OF NEW YORK**

HAITIAN CENTERS COUNCIL, INC.,
  et al.,

                Plaintiffs,

     v.

GENE MC NARY, Commissioner,
  Immigration and Naturalization
  Service, et al.,

                Defendants.

Civil Action No.
92-1258 (Johnson, J.)

MEMORANDUM OF POINTS AND AUTHORITIES IN SUPPORT
OF DEFENDANTS' MOTION FOR SANCTIONS

PRELIMINARY STATEMENT

        Plaintiffs bring this action seeking to enjoin the repatriation of certain
Haitian nationals encountered by federal officers outside the United States, and to
modify the procedures by which defendants determine who among the interdicted
Haitians should be permitted to proceed to the United States to advance their

Notice that the defendants include a preliminary statement to remind the judge what the case is about. Federal judges have hundreds of cases on their dockets, and lawyers must be conscientious about reminding a judge about the basics of their case with almost every filing they make.

asylum claims.[1] Plaintiffs assert seven causes of action, including constitutional and statutory claims regarding their alleged interests in "access" to the interdicted Haitians for purposes of communications and counsel, violations of the Administrative Procedure Act, violations of international law, and denial of equal protection. Complaint, pp. 16-20. Plaintiffs raise these claims on behalf on all Haitians detained at Guantanamo Bay or elsewhere outside the United States, and all Haitians who have retained or in the future may retain "plaintiff Haitian Service Organizations."[2] Id., pp. 15-16.

> Here, the government is trying to make the claims in the *Baker* case seem as similar as possible to those in the *McNary* case. The aim is to lay the groundwork for the contention that *McNary* is barred by claim preclusion.

Last month the Supreme Court refused to stay and denied certiorari from a decision and judgment rejecting virtually identical challenges to the Haitian interdiction and repatriation program. In a suit brought by the "Haitian Refugee Center, Inc." to enjoin repatriation of Haitian nationals interdicted by federal officers on the high seas and to compel "access" by the Haitian Refugee Center ("HRC") to Haitians detained at Guantanamo or elsewhere outside the United States, plaintiffs asserted causes of action based on the same constitutional and statutory provisions and principles of international law raised by the present plaintiffs.[3] Haitian Refugee Center, Inc. v. Baker, 949 F.2d 1109 (11th Cir. 1991), cert. denied, 60 U.S.L.W. 2513 (U.S., February 24, 1992). The Eleventh Circuit Court of Appeals found that neither the First Amendment, nor the Immigration and Nationality Act and the Refugee Act, nor the Administrative Procedure Act, nor international law provides any basis for judicial intervention in the Haitian interdiction and repatriation program 949 F.2d at 1110-11. Although the appeal to the Eleventh Circuit was from the entry of a preliminary injunction, the appeals court not only vacated the injunction but also ordered the district court to dismiss each and all of the HRC claims for failure to state a claim upon which relief can be granted and directed that the mandate issue immediately. Id. Further demonstrating the total lack of merit in the claims asserted, the Supreme Court took the highly unusual action of entering a stay which removed the district court's injunctive bar to repatriation before the Eleventh Circuit ruled on the merits. Order of January 31, 1992, No. A-551 (Ex. 39). The Eleventh Circuit and the Supreme Court decisions have not been vacated, modified, or otherwise challenged, and defendants are aware of no case in which any court has recognized a cause of action on behalf of aliens outside the United States or by parties seeking "access" to such aliens. See Ukrainian-American Bar Ass'n v. Baker, 893 F.2d 1374 (D.C. Cir. 1990).

> The government's point here is that the Eleventh Circuit Court of Appeals took the uncommon step of issuing a final judgment in the case even though the federal district court had only made a preliminary ruling. The usual course would have been for the appellate court to reverse or affirm the preliminary ruling and then to return ("remand") the case to the district court to continue with proceedings until final judgment. The implication is that the appellate court was so sure that the case was without merit that it took the extraordinary step of dismissing the case before the district court even had a chance to reach a judgment of its own.

By separate papers, defendants have opposed plaintiffs' motion for injunctive relief and moved for dismissal of this action based, inter alia, on the conclusive and preclusive effect of the Haitian Refugee Center decision and judgment on the claims that plaintiffs raise to this Court. As shown in such

> Footnote 3 deals with the fact that both *Baker* and *McNary* were class actions—cases brought on behalf of many plaintiffs. The argument in this footnote is that the class of plaintiffs was very similar in each case, and therefore, that the judgment in *Baker* should preclude *McNary*. We will discuss this contention in Chapter Ten.

---

[1] For a more complete statement of the facts, the Court is respectfully referred to the memorandum and exhibits filed in support of defendants' accompanying motion to dismiss.

[2] "Haitian Service Organizations" does not appear as a party plaintiff in the caption but apparently includes the "Haitian Centers Council, Inc.", the "National Coalition for Haitian Refugees, Inc.", and the "Immigration Law Clinic of the Jerome N. Frank Legal Services Organization of New Haven." Complaint, p. 1. Plaintiffs offer no explanation regarding any relationship they may have with the Haitian Refugee Center, Inc.

[3] In Haitian Refugee Center the claims were asserted on behalf of all Haitians "detained or who in the future will be detained" at Guantanamo or elsewhere outside the United States. HRC Complaint, ¶ 62. Thus, there appears to be substantial overlap between the plaintiff class in Haitian Refugee Center and the presently proffered class. Compare HCC Complaint, ¶¶ 36-41.

opposition and motion, there is no basis in law for any of plaintiffs' asserted causes of action. Because the complaint and injunctive motion are frivolous and not warranted by existing law, defendants are entitled to sanctions under Rule 11 against plaintiffs and their attorneys.

ARGUMENT

PLAINTIFFS AND THEIR ATTORNEYS SHOULD BE
SANCTIONED FOR THEIR FRIVOLOUS ACTION

Rule 11 of the Federal Rules of Civil Procedure obligates the parties and their attorneys to assure that each pleading, motion, or other paper is

> well grounded in fact and is warranted by existing law or a good faith argument for the extension, modification, or reversal of existing law. . . .

Rule 11 further provides that,

> If a pleading, motion, or other paper is signed in violation of this rule, the court, upon motion or upon its own initiative, shall impose upon the person who signed it, a represented party, or both, an appropriate sanction, which may include an order to pay the other party or parties the amount of the reasonable expenses incurred because of the filing of the pleading, motion, or other paper, including a reasonable attorney's fee.

See Cooter & Gell v. Hartmarx Corp., — U.S. —, 110 S. Ct. 2447 (1990). Because it is clear that plaintiffs' assertions are contrary to law and that their complaint and motion offer nothing other than an attempt to reassert previously rejected claims, defendants are entitled to sanctions including the expense of defending this action.

A.   Plaintiffs' Complaint And Motion Violate Rule 11

Rule 11 requires that reasonable inquiry be made to assure that each claim brought before the Court is supported by existing law or by a good faith argument for a change in such law. However, application of the rule does not turn on the subjective good faith of the person submitting the pleading, motion, or paper, but involves an objective assessment of the submission under the pertinent law. Brasport, S.A. v. Hoechst Celanese Corp., 134 F.R.D. 45, 46-47 (S.D.N.Y. 1991). Where there is no chance of success and no reasonable argument can be made in support of the asserted position, the claim is frivolous and warrants sanctions. International Shipping Co., S.A. v. Hydra Offshore, Inc., 875 F.2d 388, 390 (2d Cir.), cert. denied, 110 S. Ct. 563 (1989); West Indian Sea Island Cotton Ass'n. Inc. v. Treadtex, Inc., 761 F. Supp. 1041, 1054-55 (S.D.N.Y. 1991).

It is clear that plaintiffs have no chance of success on any of their claims. At the time their complaint and motion were filed, no court had recognized any of their proffered causes of action and each of their claims had been examined and

---

Briefs usually contain a background section that lays out the relevant facts and procedural posture of the case, and an argument section that sets forth a party's legal arguments. As is the case here, the argument section generally begins by citing the key legal principles at issue.

Notice the words "good faith argument" for a change in the law. That was the standard in 1992. Today, the standard is that a litigant must present a "nonfrivolous argument" for extending the law or establishing new law.

As the government notes, attorney conduct is evaluated according to an objective, not a subjective, standard. What is relevant is what a reasonable attorney would have done, not whether the attorney in the specific case actually believes her research or arguments satisfied Rule 11's standards. See Note 3.

rejected by the Eleventh Circuit and the Supreme Court. See Borowski v. DePuy, Inc., 850 F.2d 297, 304-05 (7th Cir. 1988) ("ostrich-like" denial of dispositive authority warrants sanctions). This is not a matter of open issues or unsettled areas of the law. Compare Mareno v. Rowe, 910 F.2d 1043, 1047 (2d Cir. 1990), cert. denied, 111 S. Ct. 681 (1991), with Securities Industry Ass'n v. Clarke, 898 F.2d 318, 321-22 (2d Cir. 1990).

It is equally clear that no reasonable argument can be made in support of plaintiffs' position. Cf. Dennis v. Pan American World Airway, Inc., 746 F. Supp. 288, 291-92 (E.D.N.Y. 1990). Plaintiffs' demand for judicial intervention in the Haitian interdiction and repatriation program cannot be sustained without contradicting the judgment reached in Haitian Refugee Center, and such judgment cannot properly be ignored or circumvented. It is not enough for plaintiffs to assert that circumstances have changed since the Eleventh Circuit and Supreme Court examined the Haitian program. The judgment in Haitian Refugee Center held that there was no basis in law for claims against defendants' interdiction and repatriation of Haitian nationals. A change in facts cannot create a cause of action that as a matter of law does not exist.

The courts have recognized that Rule 11 sanctions may be appropriate where parties seek to raise successive or repetitious claims. Zaldivar v. City of Los Angeles, 780 F.2d 823, 830-32 (9th Cir. 1986); Cook v. Peter Kiewit Sons Co., 775 F.2d 1030, 1036 (9th cir. 1985), cert. denied, 476 U.S. 1183 (1986); Sealtite Corp. v. General Services Administration, 614 F. Supp. 352 (D. Col. 1985). Compare Stern v. Leucadia National Corp., 844 F.2d 997, 1005-06 (2d Cir.), cert. denied, 488 U.S. 852 (1988). This Court has imposed sanctions for bringing a complaint barred by collateral estoppel or res judicata. Neustein v. Orbach, 130 F.R.D. 12, 15-16 (E.D.N.Y. 1990). See also Truck Treads, Inc. v. Armstrong Rubber Co., 129 F.R.D. 143, 151-52 (W.D. Tex. 1988), aff'd as modified, 868 F.2d 1472 (5th Cir. 1989). However, Rule 11 is not limited to cases involving an identity of parties and suits; sanctions may be imposed for the re-assertion of claims previously rejected on similar facts where the proponent surely knew that the complaint had no hope of success. Damino v. Barrell, 702 F. Supp. 954, 957 (E.D.N.Y. 1988), aff'd, 875 F.2d 307 (2d Cir.), cert. denied, 110 S. Ct. 69 (1989); G & T Terminal Packaging Co., Inc. v. Consolidated Rail Corp., 719 F. Supp. 153 160-61 (S.D.N.Y. 1989). See also Peregoy v. Amoco Production Co., 929 F.2d 196, 197 (5th Cir. 1991), cert. denied, 112 S. Ct. 188 (1991). Moreover, pleadings that invite the Court to disregard controlling precedent or decisions by superior tribunals warrant sanctions. Howard v. Liberty Memorial Hospital, 752 F. Supp. 1074, 1080 (S.D. Ga. 1990); Thompson v. Sundholm, 726 F. Supp. 147, 150-51 (S.D. Tex. 1989).

Even if the present plaintiffs somehow can distinguish their case from that decided by the Eleventh Circuit and Supreme Court, the fact that they filed their complaint and motion without proper legal support and in the teeth of the previous decision and judgment is sufficient to warrant sanctions. Measured by the objective, competent attorney standards applied in this circuit, it was patently clear that plaintiffs' claims had absolutely no chance of success. See International Shipping Co., 875 F.2d at 390 (sanctions for failure to inquire as to jurisdiction). Plaintiffs' attempt to relitigate the HRC claims and issues is frivolous and violates Rule 11. Damino v. Barrell, supra.

The mention of "changed circumstances" refers to plaintiffs' attempt to avoid the application of claim preclusion on the ground that circumstances had changed since the *Baker* case was decided. *See* Chapter Ten, Note 4. The changed circumstances involved the government's issuance of the Rees Memorandum after the *Baker* decision, changing the INS interview procedures on Guantánamo. *See STC,* pp. 56-57.

B.   Defendants Are Entitled To Sanctions Awarding The
Reasonable Expenses Incurred Because Of The Filing
Of Plaintiffs' Complaint And Injunctive Motion

Where, as here, a pleading or motion violates Rule 11, sanctions must be imposed. O'Malley v. New York City Transit Authority, 896 F.2d 704, 709 (2d Cir. 1990); City of Yonkers v. Otis Elevator Co., 844 F.2d 42, 49 (2d Cir. 1988). It is immaterial that the offending submissions were made with good intentions or that the claims purportedly were raised toward a worthy objective. West Indian Sea Island Cotton Ass'n, 761 F. Supp. at 1055; see also Dreis & Krump Mfg. Co. v. International Ass'n of Machinists, etc., 802 F.2d 247, 255 (7th Cir. 1986) (passion for vindication no defense to Rule 11 sanctions). Defendants need not show injury or justification, for Rule 11 sanctions are mandatory and aimed toward curbing and deterring abuse of our legal system. See Business Guides, Inc. v. Chromatic Communications Enterprises, Inc., — U.S. —, 111 S. Ct. 922 (1991).

> Sanctions are no longer mandatory if the court finds a Rule 11 violation. *See* Note 2.

While sanctions are mandatory for violations of Rule 11, the courts retain discretion as to the extent of monetary and other relief to be awarded. See Anschutz Petroleum Marketing Corp. v. E.W. Saybolt & Co., 112 F.R.D. 355 (S.D.N.Y. 1986). Here, with little explanation and no justification, plaintiffs have burdened the Court and the government with virtually the same case that was so recently rejected by Eleventh Circuit and Supreme Court. Moreover, plaintiffs have disregarded the settled and substantial law reserving matters of foreign and immigration policy to the political branches of government (see, e.g., Kleindienst v. Mandel, 408 U.S. 753, 765-770 (1972)), willfully seeking to assert their claims before the wrong forum. See Saltany v. Reagan, 886 F.2d 438 (D.C. Cir. 1989), cert. denied, 110 S. Ct. 2172 (1990) (sanctions appropriate where attorney surely knew complaint challenging use of foreign bases to bomb Libya had no hope of success). Under these circumstances, plaintiffs and their attorneys should be ordered to pay the full costs and expenses of government's response to their complaint and motion, including reasonable attorneys' fees. See Neustein v. Orbach, 130 F.R.D. at 16; see also Becker v. NLRB, 678 F. Supp. 406 (E.D.N.Y. 1987).

While good faith may shield a party from the sanctions earned by his attorney (see Greenberg v. Hilton International Co., 870 F.2d 926, 934 (2d Cir. 1989)), at least as to the institutional plaintiffs in this case the present circumstances suggest no principled basis to draw such a distinction. See O'Malley v. New York City Transit Authority, 896 F.2d at 710. In accordance with applicable law, defendants ask for a judgment that plaintiffs and their attorneys, jointly and severally, are liable for the government's costs and reasonable attorneys' fees. See Damino v. Barrell, supra; Cedar Crest Health Center, Inc. v. Bowen, 129 F.R.D. 519, 527 (S.D. Ind. 1989). Plaintiffs should not be permitted to burden the courts or the public fisc with their continued dissatisfaction with the Haitian interdiction and repatriation program.

> Note that the government asks that the "institutional plaintiffs" (the Haitian refugee organizations and the immigration clinic at Yale) be held liable for the sanctions along with their attorneys. Can you find the provision of Rule 11 that authorizes such a ruling? Additional discussion on this issue appears in Note 7. The phrase "jointly and severally" liable means that the government would be able to collect the judgment from either the parties or the attorneys, or partially from both.

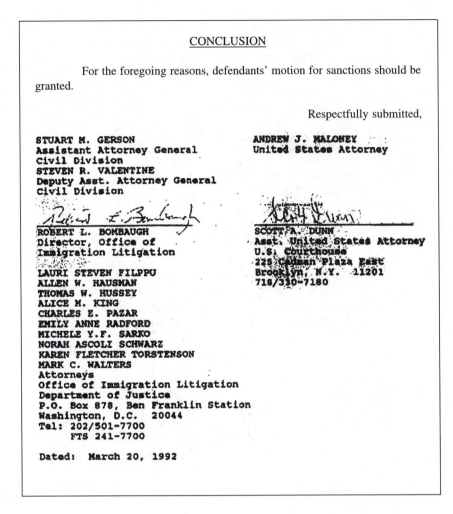

Within the bordered box:

CONCLUSION

For the foregoing reasons, defendants' motion for sanctions should be granted.

Respectfully submitted,

STUART M. GERSON
Assistant Attorney General
Civil Division
STEVEN R. VALENTINE
Deputy Asst. Attorney General
Civil Division

ANDREW J. MALONEY
United States Attorney

ROBERT L. BOMBAUGH
Director, Office of
Immigration Litigation

SCOTT A. DUNN
Asst. United States Attorney
U.S. Courthouse
225 Cadman Plaza East
Brooklyn, N.Y. 11201
718/330-7180

LAURI STEVEN FILPPU
ALLEN W. HAUSMAN
THOMAS W. HUSSEY
ALICE M. KING
CHARLES E. PAZAR
EMILY ANNE RADFORD
MICHELE Y.F. SARKO
NORAH ASCOLI SCHWARZ
KAREN FLETCHER TORSTENSON
MARK C. WALTERS
Attorneys
Office of Immigration Litigation
Department of Justice
P.O. Box 878, Ben Franklin Station
Washington, D.C. 20044
Tel: 202/501-7700
      FTS 241-7700

Dated: March 20, 1992

NOTES AND COMMENTS

1. The Government's Argument.   As you likely determined, the government focused on the Yale team's legal claims rather than the factual allegations. The Justice Department lawyers made two arguments in their request for Rule 11 sanctions, although they did not separate the two arguments all that clearly. The first argument was that if Judge Johnson examined the substance of plaintiffs' legal claims in any detail, he would conclude that those claims had absolutely no chance of success. The government's second argument was that it wasn't even necessary to examine the substance of the claims because they had all been litigated and decided in the earlier *Baker* case. Accordingly, the government argued, all of the plaintiffs' claims were barred under the doctrine of claim preclusion, also known as res judicata. We will explore claim preclusion in depth in Chapter Ten. As discussed in Chapter Ten, the Yale team raised several good arguments about why the claims in *McNary* were not barred—including that the *McNary* suit involved new claims and new parties that were not a part of the *Baker* litigation and that new circumstances had arisen after the *Baker* case had been decided.

2. Amendments to Rule 11.   Rule 11 has been substantially amended—twice, in fact: first in 1983 and then again in 1993.[2] Until 1983, Rule 11 was rarely used by litigants or courts, and the Advisory Committee evidently believed that the provision was not serving as a sufficient deterrent to frivolous litigation—at a time when some critics were making much of a perceived litigation explosion.[3] The 1983 amendments were intended to clarify both the standard of conduct for attorneys and the bounds of acceptable pleading, as well as to encourage greater use of sanctions. Toward this goal, the 1983 amendments made several significant changes, including making sanctions mandatory. If a court found a Rule 11 violation, it was *required* to sanction the offending attorney or party. This was the version of Rule 11 in place at the time *McNary* was filed. (Note the language under subheading B of the government's brief: "Where, as here, a pleading or motion violates Rule 11, sanctions must be imposed.")

As sometimes happens, however, the reforms proved to be too drastic. The 1983 amendments resulted in parties investing significant time and expense in filing and defending against Rule 11 motions, causing the courts to expend their limited resources dealing with Rule 11 litigation. (Such litigation is sometimes called "collateral" litigation because it generally does not address the merits of the dispute.) In response, the 1993 amendments—implemented the year after *McNary* was filed— made Rule 11 less severe. First, sanctions were again made discretionary, as they had been before the 1983 amendments. *See* Fed. R. Civ. P. 11(c)(1). Equally important, the 1993 amendments added the "safe harbor" provision of Rule 11(c)(2). This provision requires that a party intending to file a Rule 11 motion serve the opposing party with a copy of the motion at least 21 days before filing. If the responding party so chooses, it can correct or withdraw the allegedly offending document within the 21-day grace period. The addition of the safe harbor provision was intended to reduce the number of filings subject to Rule 11 litigation. It also addressed the concern that, under the prior version of the rule, a party's withdrawal of a pleading after being served with a Rule 11 motion could be construed as an admission that the filing was frivolous.

Lastly, note that Rule 11(c)(2) requires the withdrawal or correction of only "the challenged paper, claim, defense, contention, or denial." In other words, if the moving party's argument is that only one of the claims in a complaint is frivolous, the non-moving party may file an amended complaint without—or otherwise withdraw—the challenged claim. In *McNary*, however, because the government's motion was directed

---

2. The Supreme Court's power to promulgate and amend the Federal Rules of Civil Procedure is based on the Rules Enabling Act, which provides: "The Supreme Court shall have the power to prescribe general rules of practice and procedure and rules of evidence for cases in the United States district courts . . . ." 28 U.S.C. § 2072(a). The process of amending the Rules begins with the Judicial Conference, which is a policy-making body composed of judges that oversees the administration of the U.S. federal courts. After consideration by two different subcommittees and a period during which the public can comment on the proposed rules, the Judicial Conference considers amendments to the Federal Rules and transmits the amendments it proposes to the Supreme Court. The Supreme Court then transmits, by May 1 of the year in which the amendments are to take effect, its proposed changes to Congress. If Congress does not enact legislation to reject, modify, or defer the proposed changes, they take effect on December 1 of that year. *See* Federal Rulemaking: The Rulemaking Process—A Summary for the Bench and Bar, October 2007, available at http://www.uscourts.gov/rules/proceduresum.htm.

3. During the 1970s, the number of civil lawsuits filed in federal courts increased greatly, to the extent that commentators referred to a "litigation explosion." Some observers attributed responsibility for this increase in litigation partly to the liberal pleading requirements of the Federal Rules of Civil Procedure. *See* Carl Tobias, *Reconsidering Rule 11*, 46 U. Miami L. Rev. 855, 858-59 (1992).

at the entire lawsuit, the threat of potential sanctions likely would not have been avoided by anything less than withdrawing the entire complaint.

3. *The Objective Standard of Rule 11.* What is the nature of the certification that an attorney makes when she files a document with the court? The Rule 11 standard is an *objective* one: The attorney signing the document must have conducted an objectively reasonable legal and factual investigation before filing the document. A court ruling on a Rule 11 motion determines what a reasonable attorney would have done in similar circumstances prior to filing the document. The attorney will not avoid sanctions just because he may have acted in good faith. Put another way, a lawyer cannot avoid Rule 11 sanctions by relying on the "pure heart, empty head" defense of "Judge, I meant well when I researched and prepared that complaint, even if I had no clue about what I was doing."

If the initial investigation by the plaintiff's attorney does not provide support but there are indications that evidentiary support will be available after further investigation or discovery, the attorney can also indicate this in the complaint. (The defendant's attorney may do the same when drafting the answer to the complaint.) Although an attorney can state in the complaint (or answer) that factual allegations are "on information and belief"—that is, they are accurate to the best of the attorney's then-existing knowledge and belief—this does not relieve the attorney of his Rule 11 obligations. The attorney must still conduct an objectively reasonable inquiry into the facts of the case.

4. *Factual Investigation Under Rule 11.* The simplest way to explain Rule 11 is that lawyers must do their homework before going to court, both as to the legal theories on which they rely and as to the factual allegations they make. Unfortunately, some lawyers do not do the requisite homework, particularly when it comes to the facts. Indeed, failure to conduct sufficient factual investigation is probably the most common ground for Rule 11 sanctions. *See* Stephen C. Yeazell, *Civil Procedure* 359 (6th ed. 2004). Koh and the students did plenty of legal investigation before filing the *McNary* case. *See, e.g., STC*, pp. 36-41. What makes *McNary* so peculiar, however, is that when it came to factual investigation, they couldn't talk to their clients before filing the complaint, as discussed in the Sarah Cleveland interview in Chapter Two.

Remember that the standard of Rule 11 is based on the conduct of a reasonable attorney. Under this standard, what should constitute sufficient factual investigation in circumstances such as those presented in *McNary*? Specifically, which facts relating to the case should the team have been expected to verify before filing the complaint, and how could the team have verified them? As you may recall from Chapter 2 of *Storming the Court*, the students developed much of the factual background for the case using media sources, the Coast Guard's public affairs office, and Creole interpreters who had worked for the Justice Department on Guantánamo. Should that have been enough? What other sources might they have used? Keep in mind that in 1992, the Internet as we know it today did not exist.

5. *The Government's Strategy.* What do you think the government's strategy was in filing the Rule 11 motion? Paul Cappuccio and some of the other government lawyers truly believed that the Rule 11 motion was warranted. Koh, however, felt that the Justice Department was using Rule 11 to intimidate and harass Yale, and he saw the government's demand for a $10 million bond in the case as further evidence of such a

A four-star admiral from the Navy tours Camp Bulkeley sometime in 1992. His cap says CINCLANT, the acronym for Commander in Chief, United States Atlantic Command (this particular title no longer exists). The presence of such a high-ranking official at Bulkeley reveals how serious a concern the camp was to the Pentagon. Photograph courtesy of Stephen Kinder.

strategy.[4] Ironically, one aim of Rule 11 is to *deter* harassment. Given the potentially serious consequences of a Rule 11 motion, the possibility for abuse of the rule is obvious. Thus, the court may also impose Rule 11 sanctions on the party who *filed* the Rule 11 motion. In other words, a Rule 11 motion that is filed for an improper purpose (or otherwise violates Rule 11) can itself be subject to a Rule 11 motion. Indeed, this is exactly what happened in *McNary*: Harold Koh threatened to file his own Rule 11 motion against the government for bringing its Rule 11 motion.

Assume you are part of the government's litigation team and have been asked to decide whether to file the Rule 11 motion. Set aside for a moment the question of the strength of the government's legal argument in its motion (we'll discuss that in a moment). What are the *strategic* reasons for filing the motion? What impression would the motion convey to the judge? What message would the motion send to the plaintiffs' lawyers—and to the law students, who had almost no litigation experience?

6. The Plaintiffs' Response to the Government.   Now consider the plaintiffs' potential responses to the motion. The government's legal arguments attempted to broadly characterize the claims in both *Baker* and *McNary* so that it would be more likely that the court would find the new suit barred under principles of claim

4. A litigation bond is an amount of money that a court may require a party to put on reserve in order to continue with the lawsuit. It is usually sought in cases in which the plaintiff's claim may be questionable and the financial harm to the defendant as a result of defending the plaintiff's suit is considerable. The purpose of a bond is to ensure that there is money available to compensate the defendant for the costs of defending against a frivolous claim.

preclusion. There was a straightforward and simple appeal to the government's position, and Harold Koh knew there was some risk that a judge might latch onto that argument as a convenient way of dismissing an extremely controversial case. The plaintiffs, however, had several legal arguments as to why some, if not all, of their claims should go forward despite *Baker*. Among those arguments were that the *McNary* suit involved some parties not involved in the *Baker* case and that the government's interview processes had changed since the conclusion of the *Baker* litigation.

In addition, it seemed to Harold Koh that the government was overplaying its claim preclusion argument. Consider just one instance: The government asserts in the second paragraph under subheading A of its brief that "[a]t the time [plaintiffs'] complaint and motion were filed . . . each of their claims had been examined and rejected by the Eleventh Circuit and the Supreme Court." It is true that the Eleventh Circuit in *Baker* had rejected a number of the claims that were later raised in *McNary*. But it is *not* true that the Supreme Court had "examined and rejected" them. All the Supreme Court did was to refuse to hear the *Baker* case (the Court denied certiorari, or "cert," as lawyers say). It is a fundamental principle of federal practice that a denial of certiorari by the Supreme Court indicates *no position* by the Court on the merits of the case. (Media reports of Supreme Court cert denials routinely overlook this point.) On the other hand, there was support for the government's assertion: The Supreme Court did issue a stay of the district court's injunction against the repatriation of Haitian refugees in *Baker*, an unusual move that indicated the Court was sufficiently troubled by the district court's actions to intervene while *Baker* was pending before the Eleventh Circuit.

Given these considerations, think about the plaintiffs' strategy. Would you have filed a Rule 11 motion against the government had you been in Harold Koh's position? What might have been your reasons for doing so? What arguments might have counseled against filing the motion? Finally, evaluate the government's Rule 11 motion from Judge Johnson's perspective. The government's argument was based on plaintiffs' failure to adequately investigate the law; Rule 11(b)(2) provides the standard by which to evaluate the conduct of plaintiffs' counsel. In applying that standard, what information could help you determine whether the plaintiffs' attorneys conducted an objectively reasonable legal investigation into the legal basis of the motion? Now assume the government's motion had alleged an inadequate *factual* investigation by plaintiffs' counsel. In that event, which part of Rule 11(b) provides the standard for evaluating the motion, and what would you want to know before making your ruling?

Judge Johnson never ruled on the government's motion and the parties in *McNary* eventually reached an agreement to stop pursuing Rule 11 sanctions. Reproduced on the next page is the stipulation entered into by the parties regarding sanctions. As you can see, the government agreed to withdraw its motion for sanctions under Rule 11 and not pursue sanctions under any other authority. In return, the plaintiffs agreed not to seek sanctions for any of the defendants' conduct known to them prior to the stipulation. (The stipulation also was signed by Judge Johnson.) Was this a wise resolution of the issue? Why or why not?

7. Who Is Liable Under Rule 11?   Any attorney or pro se litigant (meaning an unrepresented party) who signs papers filed with the court is responsible for those filings under Rule 11. However, the signing attorney's law firm may be held liable as well, because the firm is thought to have a role in deciding whether to withdraw the

UNITED STATES DISTRICT COURT
FOR THE EASTERN DISTRICT OF NEW YORK

HAITIAN CENTERS COUNCIL, INC., et al.,	)
Plaintiffs,	)
v.	) Civil Action No.
	) 92-1258 (Johnson, J.)
GENE McNARY, Commissioner, Immigration	)
and Naturalization Service, et al.,	) STIPULATION AND
	) ORDER
Defendants.	)
	)

Based upon recent discussions between them, the parties have concluded that it is appropriate to resolve certain collateral matters without judicial determination. Therefore,

IT IS HEREBY STIPULATED AND AGREED, by and among the undersigned counsel for the parties, as follows:

1. Defendants withdraw with prejudice their motion dated March 20, 1992 for sanctions against plaintiffs and their attorneys for the filing in this action of both the complaint and the accompanying motion for injunctive relief, and will not seek sanctions against plaintiffs, or their attorneys, pursuant to Rule 11 of the Federal Rules of Civil Procedure, 28 U.S.C. § 1927 or any other statute or rule, for any conduct currently known to defendants, including without limitation the filing of any pleading or motion, undertaken before the date of this stipulation in connection with this action.

2. Plaintiffs will not seek sanctions against defendants or their attorneys, pursuant to Rule 11 of the Federal Rules of Civil Procedure, 28 U.S.C. § 1927 or any other statute or court rule, for the filing of defendants' sanctions motion dated March 20, 1992 or for any other conduct currently known to plaintiffs, including without limitation the filing of any pleading or motion, undertaken before the date of this stipulation in connection with this action.

3. All parties shall bear their own costs and expenses in relation to all aspects of the Rule 11 motion dated March 20, 1992, and this stipulation.

* * * *

contested filing during the 21-day safe-harbor period. *See* Advisory Committee Notes, 1993 amendments. Assume that the Yale team had been working under the current version of Rule 11. Given that liability can be imputed to other law firm members, should Michael Ratner have been on the hook here as well, even though he and Koh were not formal law partners? What about Joe Tringali and his law firm, Simpson, Thacher & Bartlett? What about the students? Remember, they had not yet passed the bar, so their names, if on the papers at all, would have been there only in a non-attorney capacity.

The court also has the power to impose sanctions on the party represented by the attorney who signed the papers, if it determines that the party "should be held accountable for [its] part in causing a violation." *See id.* In its Rule 11 brief, the government did not ask for the Haitians on Guantánamo to be held personally liable for the sanctions. Do you understand why? Instead, the government asked only that the "institutional plaintiffs" be held jointly and severally liable for the requested attorneys' fees. The two plaintiffs the government is referring to are Haitian Centers Council and the immigration clinic at Yale Law School, which is part of Yale University and its multibillion-dollar endowment. The government reasoned that sophisticated institutional plaintiffs should be held essentially to the same standard as a lawyer. Do you agree? While it was permissible under the 1983 version to hold parties accountable for any violation of Rule 11, Rule 11(c)(5)(A) now provides that a court may no longer impose *monetary* sanctions against a party (as opposed to a lawyer) for unwarranted *legal* claims and arguments. Unsupported *factual* allegations, however, can still lead to monetary sanctions against parties. Do you see the logic in this distinction?

8. The Sanction Imposed Under Rule 11.   Under the 1993 amendments, the sanction imposed "must be limited to what suffices to deter repetition of the conduct or comparable conduct by others similarly situated." Fed. R. Civ. P. 11(c)(4). Although the court may order the sanctioned party to compensate the moving party for harm "directly and unavoidably" incurred as a result of the Rule 11 violation, the Advisory Committee Notes to the 1993 amendments make clear that this sanction should be imposed only if necessary to deter the offending party or other parties from committing a similar violation. In other words, *it is not enough for the party seeking compensation to argue that he was harmed.* Rather, he must argue that requiring the offending party to compensate him for the harm caused by the violation is necessary to deter future offending behavior.

The court has significant discretion in determining what sanctions would best deter repetition of the conduct and can choose from monetary and nonmonetary penalties. In addition to requiring the sanctioned party to compensate the moving party for costs, for example, the court can also (or in the alternative) order the sanctioned party to pay a fee to the court. Would the government's requested sanction in *McNary* have been appropriate under the 1993 version of Rule 11? (You may want to review the Argument section of the government's brief in connection with this question.)

9. The Problem of Judge Shopping.   Think back to the filing of the complaint and the discussion of "judge shopping" in Chapter Two. Recall that under Rule 11, the lawyer responsible for any paper filed with the court must affirm that the filing is not being presented for any improper purpose. Should the Yale team's maneuvering to get a specific judge be considered an "improper purpose" under Rule 11? (Because a Rule 11 motion has to be related to a specific filing, in this instance the filing would be the motion for a temporary restraining order that Yale filed with Judge Eugene Nickerson in lieu of the required complaint.[5]) Recall how Judge Nickerson handled the situation. What other response might have been appropriate? *See* Advisory Committee Notes, 1993 amendments (suggesting that a wide variety of sanctions are available for violations of Rule 11).

10. Other Legal Authority Regulating Attorney Conduct.   Rule 11 is not the only legal authority that governs the conduct of lawyers. Federal courts have the inherent power to impose sanctions on parties who engage in bad faith conduct that is not covered by Rule 11. *See Chambers v. NASCO, Inc.,* 501 U.S. 32, 44

---

5. Plaintiffs' motion for a temporary restraining order is discussed in Chapter Five.

(1991). In addition, 28 U.S.C. § 1927 allows an award of costs, expenses, and attorneys' fees against any attorney who "multiplies the proceedings in any case unreasonably and vexatiously."

Outside the courtroom, the legal profession is largely self-regulated, which means that it is controlled not by the federal or state government but by legal professionals themselves. Typically, this regulation takes place through state bar associations, which are organizations that establish standards for and monitor competence and attorney conduct. The standards established by such organizations take a variety of forms, including bar passage requirements, ethics rules, and standards of competence, as well as regulations regarding advertising and interdisciplinary and ancillary business practices. Bar ethics and disciplinary rules are written and enforced on a state-by-state basis but in many instances they are modeled on the American Bar Association's Model Rules of Professional Conduct and its predecessor, the Model Code of Professional Responsibility. Violation of state bar association rules may lead to reprimand, censure, suspension, or disbarment.[6]

6. Lawyers are also regulated by state law, federal administrative law, and constitutional law. State law governs the profession through regulations that prohibit the unauthorized practice of law and govern malpractice claims. Federal administrative law provides rules for lawyers appearing before federal agencies such as the Securities and Exchange Commission and the Internal Revenue Service. Constitutional law also governs lawyer conduct. Attorney advertisements are a form of commercial speech protected by the First Amendment, and the Sixth Amendment protects the attorney-client privilege in the context of criminal prosecution.

CHAPTER FIVE

Preliminary Injunctive Relief

INTRODUCTION

Given the scope of material to be covered in an introductory civil procedure course, some topics inevitably receive only limited treatment. One such subject is preliminary injunctive relief. Although it sometimes isn't included on the menu for first-year students, preliminary injunctive relief is very important in the world of practice. The primary reason can be summed up in one word: speed. It can take a long time, sometimes many years, to obtain a final judgment. That won't be much help if your client wants to avoid an injury that may occur next week—or tomorrow.

Say, for instance, that several heirs to a historic Victorian home disagree about what to do with the building, and one of them announces he is going to begin wholesale renovations to turn it into a modern bed-and-breakfast—and brings in the construction crew to start tearing down walls. Or that a university wants to prevent protesters from blocking access to a campus building where a controversial public figure is scheduled to speak. Or that a group of law students wants to stop the United States government from forcibly returning Haitian refugees to Port-au-Prince, where they might face persecution. In each of these circumstances, the plaintiffs need a court to make a fast decision. A ruling months or years down the road won't do any good. The urgency of the plaintiffs' situation is reflected in the relief sought: an order that will prevent the harm from occurring, not compensatory damages for the plaintiffs' injuries after the fact.

The mechanisms available to plaintiffs in such situations are the preliminary injunction and the temporary restraining order (or TRO, as lawyers generally call it). See Fed. R. Civ. P. 65. Under Rule 65, a court can issue either a preliminary injunction or a TRO to immediately prevent a party from engaging in a particular course of conduct—in other words, well before the court makes a final determination on the merits of a case. TROs and preliminary injunctions have some similarities and some differences; in this chapter, we will go over the basics of both.

First, the similarities. Both a preliminary injunction and a TRO provide relief from an ongoing or anticipated harm, in contrast to so-called *retrospective* relief. Retrospective relief looks backward, aiming to rectify a wrong that took place in the past—money damages, say, for a breach of contract. Preliminary injunctions and TROs look to the present or the future, preventing a harm that is either ongoing or about to occur.[1] Two other important similarities: For obvious reasons, courts tend to decide motions for a TRO or a preliminary injunction quickly. In addition, both forms of relief—particularly the TRO—remain in place for only a limited period of time.

There are also a number of important differences between a TRO and a preliminary injunction. First, courts can issue a preliminary injunction only if the defendant has received notice of the proceeding and has had an opportunity to attend the hearing, *see* Fed. R. Civ. P. 65(a)(1), whereas a TRO may be issued without notice to the defendant, *see* Fed. R. Civ. P. 65(b)(1); 11A *Federal Practice and Procedure* § 2951 (2d ed. 1995). Because of this distinction, a plaintiff generally seeks a TRO only if the harm is *truly imminent*—so imminent that there may be no time for the defendant to be notified and the court to hold a hearing. (In practice, however, most judges prefer not to proceed without some kind of notice to the defendant if at all possible.) The pace surrounding a preliminary injunction is a little less frantic than for a TRO, as a preliminary injunction hearing may be scheduled days or perhaps a week or more in advance; in contrast, a TRO hearing might be held on the same day that the plaintiff files the motion.

A second key difference between a preliminary injunction and a TRO is that a TRO generally lasts for a much shorter period of time. Because a TRO affects the rights of a defendant without notice, it may remain in effect for only ten days, unless the court extends that time "for good cause." *See* Fed. R. Civ. P. 65(b)(2). In contrast, a preliminary injunction, entered after a defendant has had notice and an opportunity to be heard, may remain in place until the court issues a final judgment in the case. A third distinction between a TRO and a preliminary injunction is that the parties can appeal a district court's decision to issue (or refuse to issue) a preliminary injunction, *see* 28 U.S.C. § 1292(a)(1), but they *cannot* appeal the court's decision regarding a TRO.

Now that you understand the basic concepts of a TRO and a preliminary injunction, we will explore the roles they played in the *McNary* litigation.

THE TEMPORARY RESTRAINING ORDER

Recall, as set forth in Chapters 1 and 2 of *Storming the Court*, that Koh and the students initiated the case by filing an application for a TRO in the United States District Court for the Eastern District of New York. Federal court decisions on the requirements for a TRO vary slightly, and sometimes different courts within the same circuit may formulate the test differently. The formulation that Judge Johnson used focused on a single factor: that plaintiffs must show that they face immediate and irreparable injury. *See Haitian Centers Council, Inc. v. McNary*, 789 F. Supp. 541, 546-47 (E.D.N.Y. 1992). There was some debate between the parties as to whether this was the appropriate test, as most formulations are more rigorous, requiring that the court consider both the balance of hardships on the two parties (based on whether or not the TRO is granted)

---

1. Recall that money damages are one form of *legal* relief, while preliminary injunctions are a form of *equitable* relief. *See* Chapter Two, Note 13.

Courtroom sketch of Harold Koh and Solicitor General Kenneth Starr appearing before Judge Sterling Johnson, Jr., on May 28, 1992, during the second TRO hearing in McNary *(the direct return case). Sketch courtesy of Harold Koh. Courtroom artist unknown.*

and the likelihood that the plaintiff will succeed on the merits of the case. (Can you explain the importance of the latter requirement?) Because Judge Johnson focused almost exclusively on irreparable injury, however, that will be our focus in this section,[2] and we will review the hardship and likelihood of success elements in the preliminary injunction discussion later in this chapter.[3]

Irreparable injury refers to an injury that cannot be remedied after the fact by money damages. If the defendant could fully compensate the plaintiff for the injury at the conclusion of the suit, there would be no need for the court to take immediate action to prevent the injury from occurring. Other types of injuries cannot be remedied by money damages—for example, the destruction of an original artwork or a family heirloom. Such injuries are considered "irreparable."

---

2. Judge Johnson briefly addressed the other factors but asserted that "the court believes that the only factor that must be satisfied for a TRO is irreparable harm." *Haitian Centers Council, Inc. v. McNary*, 789 F. Supp. 541, 547 n.12 (E.D.N.Y. 1992).

3. You should also note that although Judge Johnson's decision reflects some disagreement about the appropriate test for a TRO, a number of more recent New York federal court decisions have concluded that the TRO test is identical to the test for entering a preliminary injunction, discussed below. *See, e.g., AIM Intern. Trading LLC v. Valcucine SpA*, 188 F. Supp. 2d 384, 386-87 (S.D.N.Y. 2002) (noting that in the Second Circuit, the "standard[s] for granting a temporary restraining order and a preliminary injunction . . . are identical. . . . [T]he movant must show: '(a) irreparable harm and (b) either (1) likelihood of success on the merits or (2) sufficiently serious questions going to the merits to make them a fair ground for litigation and a balance of hardships tipping decidedly toward the party requesting the preliminary relief' ") (quoting *Jackson Dairy, Inc. v. H.P. Hood & Sons, Inc.*, 596 F.2d 70, 72 (2d Cir. 1979)).

Put yourself in the position of the law students just starting to work on the case. How would you show that your clients would face irreparable injury if the TRO were not issued? Consider the basic advice that Michael Ratner gave Harold Koh just before he argued the TRO motion: "Harold, look. You've got the law down cold, but that's not what matters. Get to the point: These people are being sent back to Haiti even as we speak, and they could be tortured or killed. You just have to repeat that twenty different ways." *STC*, p. 69. Ratner was zeroing in on the most extreme form of irreparable harm that the Yale team could identify: the death of refugees who had been sent back to a place where they feared persecution. The Yale team believed that was the fate awaiting some of the Haitians were they returned to Haiti. How could you demonstrate this irreparable harm to the court? That is, what evidence would you introduce on this issue?

In most lawsuits, you would probably interview your client about the anticipated harm and file an affidavit[4] from your client detailing that harm. (Consider, for instance, the previous example about the Victorian home at risk of becoming a bed-and-breakfast. An heir who wants to preserve the home might file an affidavit that details its rare banister carvings, irreplaceable window treatments, and pristine parquet floors.) Things were not so simple in *McNary*. As you know, the students had no access to the Haitians at Guantánamo when they first considered filing a lawsuit on their behalf. Also, recall that the Yale team wanted to get into court as fast as possible, so there wasn't much time to gather evidence. As you ponder these challenges, consider the following excerpt from the brief that Koh and the students filed in support of their motion for a TRO.

A.   IRREPARABLE INJURY TO LIFE OR LIBERTY

Unless this Court acts, plaintiffs clearly demonstrate a likelihood of irreparable injury to life or liberty. The right to counsel exists for asylum, screening, and exclusion proceedings so that refugees who have a well-founded fear of political persecution will not be erroneously repatriated. According to the General Accounting Office, aliens are three times more likely to receive asylum in an exclusion or deportation hearing, and twice as likely to succeed in an affirmative asylum claim, when represented by counsel. Asylum: Uniform Application of Standards Uncertain—Few Denied Applicants Deported, Appendix I, G.A.O. (1987). Once granted access to their clients, plaintiff service organizations could inform Haitian plaintiff refugees of their rights, their options for alternative-country placement, and even the possibility that they have alternative grounds for entry into the United States (as returning aliens, immediate relatives, or the like).

As a result of defendants' actions, "screened-in" plaintiffs, "screened-out" plaintiffs, and plaintiff "Haitian Service Organization clients" all risk being forcibly repatriated to Haiti. Although deportation of aliens "is always a harsh measure, it is all the more replete with danger when the alien makes a claim that he or she will be subject to death or persecution if forced to return to his or her home country." INS v. Cardoza-Fonseca, 480 U.S. 421, 449 (1987).

---

4. An affidavit is a sworn statement of fact signed by the person making the statement (who is called the "affiant") and witnessed by a notary public, an officer with the power to administer oaths and authenticate documents. An affidavit begins with the caption of the case, followed by numbered paragraphs setting forth the affiant's factual assertions, the signature of the affidavit, and then the signature and seal of the notary public.

Despite defendants' callous assertion of a "lack of any credible evidence that "screened-out" Haitians who were returned to Haiti were harmed after they returned," Mem. Opp. at 76, the harms to repatriated Haitians are in fact well-documented.[28] Since the September coup, the Haitian regime has killed more than 1500 persons.[29] In a report issued on January 22, 1992, Amnesty International documented the fate that awaits the plaintiffs upon their forced return:

> Since October Amnesty International has continued to receive reports of grave human rights violations. Hundreds of people have been extrajudicially executed, or detained without warrant and tortured. Many others have been brutally beaten in the streets. . . . The military has systematically targeted President Aristide's political supporters. . . . Grassroots organizations, which had flourished during the seven months of President Aristide's government, have been virtually eradicated, their equipment and premises destroyed, and most of their activists in hiding. . . . Even children have not been spared the violence in Haiti. Thousands of people have been forced into hiding. . . . The fate of many of those arrested has not been clarified and there continue to be widespread reports of torture. Many of those tortured have sustained serious injuries but have been refused medical attention in custody, and at least four people have been tortured to death.

(Emphasis added). "Reinterdictees" report that Haitians who have already been returned to Haiti under the government's interdiction, screening and repatriation program have been hunted down and murdered.[30] See also Affidavit of Jocelyn McCalla (Exh. #3). If defendants' conduct goes unchecked, "screened-in," "screened-out," and "HSO client" plaintiffs who may be "screened-out" without counsel all face the quintessential irreparable harm: loss of life and liberty.

---

[28]The INS claims recently to have interviewed 309 repatriated refugees without encountering "any credible claims of persecution or reprisal after repatriation." See Becelia Dec. (Def. Exh. #). This claim is inherently incredible for two reasons. First, repatriated Haitians have no reason to tell true stories to the same INS officials who were responsible for sending them back to Haiti against their will. Second, many of the interviews were conducted in the presence of the Haitian Red Cross at Port-au-Prince, an entity that is not a member of the International Red Cross, that regularly obstructs the efforts of international human rights organizations to monitor events in Haiti, and that is known to cooperate with the present military regime in Haiti in the harassment of returnees. See McCalla Aff., at 11 (Exh. #3).

[29]Amnesty International, "The Human Rights Tragedy—Human Rights Violations Since the Coup" (Jan. 22, 1992).

[30]Contrary to the State Department's oft-recited position that there is "no evidence" that Haitians have suffered political persecution when returned, refugees who have fled, been repatriated, and fled again (hereinafter "re-interdicted" refugees) report "beatings, imprisonment, death threats." In December 1991, for example, the U.N. High Commissioner for Refugees reported that 73 people forcibly repatriated from Venezuela were immediately arrested and detained by the Haitian military. Affidavit of William G. O'Neill (Exh. #19) ("O'Neill aff.") at 5–6. Upon their return to Port au Prince, repatriated Haitians are interviewed, fingerprinted, and photographed before being allowed to leave the port area. N.Y. Times, Feb. 10, 1992. Many of them are pulled aside and required to give authorities their name and address. Miami Herald, Feb. 9, 1992. One "re-interdicted" Haitian related that two days after he was repatriated, "soldiers came looking for him at his mother's house . . . but were told he wasn't there;" he was later imprisoned and beaten along with more than 200 others repatriated with him from Guantanamo. That same day the returnee's cousin, who had also fled with him and been returned, was arrested and killed. later. N.Y. Times, Feb. 10, 1992. In a recent article, Time magazine reported that a Haitian youth named Marcelin was told, three days after he was repatriated from Guantanamo, "We'll come and kill you." Time, Feb. 17, 1992.

NOTES AND COMMENTS

1. Evidentiary Support for the TRO Request.   As you can see by reviewing their brief, plaintiffs' counsel relied on several sources of published information, including a Government Accounting Office (GAO) report, an Amnesty International report, and news articles from the *New York Times* and the *Miami Herald.*[5] They also relied on two affidavits—one by Jocelyn ("Johnny") McCalla, the executive director of a Haitian refugee advocacy organization, and one by William O'Neill, a human rights advocate who had recently visited Haiti. What do you think was the purpose of including these two different types of material—published sources and affidavits? Do they provide different kinds of support for the plaintiffs' case? How?

Now imagine yourself in the students' position. How might you have gathered all of this information? For the newspaper articles, the answer is fairly easy: a Westlaw or Lexis search in a current newspaper database, focusing on words like "Haiti," "refugee," "return," "returnee," "persecution," "harm," and "danger." As for the Amnesty International report and GAO report, the students had been getting advice from refugee experts and various human rights organizations, which helped lead them to this material.

The affidavits took a bit more work. True, the team already knew Johnny McCalla because his organization was one of the plaintiffs in *McNary*, and he was an expert on conditions in Haiti. (If they hadn't known McCalla, the students might well have had to cold-call human rights organizations and pro-Haitian groups, searching for someone with the necessary expertise who also had the time and inclination to file an affidavit in the case.) Even with the benefit of having McCalla involved, however, the team still had to: (1) interview him at length, (2) draft an affidavit based on the interview, (3) review the affidavit with McCalla to ensure its accuracy, and then (4) get the affidavit notarized—meaning that McCalla had to sign the statement in front of a notary public. The same process had to be repeated for the affidavit of human rights advocate William O'Neill, whom the team also knew because of his work in Haiti.

Does the evidence summarized in the earlier excerpt from the plaintiffs' brief persuade you that returnees faced irreparable harm in Haiti? Why or why not?

2. The Government's Evidence.   The plaintiffs' evidence was not the only information that Judge Johnson had before him on the issue of irreparable harm. Although the government had no time to assemble evidence before the hearing, Justice Department lawyers later submitted a brief in opposition to plaintiffs' motion for a TRO, and that brief disputed the Yale team's claims of irreparable harm.

The evidence submitted by the government included a March 20, 1992 declaration[6] by Joseph Becelia, Director of the Office of Caribbean Affairs at the State Department. Relying on that declaration, the government's brief states at page 79: "An INS team conducted 309 repatriate interviews in widely scattered locations throughout Haiti between March 4 [and March] 13, 1992. Ex. 118 [the Becelia Declaration]. The team encountered no credible claims of persecution or reprisal

---

5. Courts can take "judicial notice" of published newspaper accounts, which means that they can use the information in the account when rendering a decision.

6. A declaration is like an affidavit that has not been notarized—that is, the declarant has not sworn or affirmed in the presence of a public official that the statements contained in the declaration are true. Declarations can be used in place of affidavits in federal court so long as the declarant declares under penalty of perjury that what the declarant says is true. 28 U.S.C. § 1746.

after repatriation, even in La Gonave, the departure point for many Haitian interdic-tees."[7] Attached to Becelia's declaration were two telegrams from the American Embassy in Port-au-Prince. Read the Becelia Declaration and the attached telegrams carefully and then reconsider the arguments that Yale made in its brief, reproduced previously.

UNITED STATES DISTRICT COURT
EASTERN DISTRICT OF NEW YORK

```
-----------------------------------------------
Haitian Centers Council, et al.,              )
                            ,                 )
                                              )
        Plaintiffs,                           )
                                              )
                                              )            Case No.
vs.                                           )            92 Civ. 1258
                                              )            (Johnson, J.)
                                              )
Gene Mcnary, Commissioner, Immigration and    )
Naturalization Service, et al.,               )
                                              )
                                              )
        Defendants.                           )
-----------------------------------------------
```

DECLARATION OF JOSEPH F. BECELIA

1. I, Joseph F. Becelia, am the Director of the Office of Caribbean Affairs of the Department of State. I have held this position since August 1989.

2. I attach to this declaration a copy of telegram number 1077, unclassified, from the United States Embassy in Port au Prince, Haiti reporting on interviews with Haitian repatriates conducted by a team from the U.S. Immigration and Naturalization Service (INS) during the period March 3-14, 1992. The descriptive information in the telegram indicates it was transmitted on March 16, 1992 at 2:16 p.m. EST.

3. That telegram describes information obtained from interviews conducted in widely scattered locations in Haiti by a visiting INS team that contributed to the U.S. Embassy's on-going effort to monitor post-repatriation treatment of returnees. In addition to this INS monitoring team, embassy personnel have also been actively and consistently engaged in the monitoring effort and in reporting their findings to the Department of State by telegram. In this regard, a second telegram attached to this declaration, 92 Port au Prince 858, unclassified, transmitted on March 2, 1992 at 1:25 p.m. EST, contains another representative report transmitted to the Department by embassy teams monitoring repatriates.

4. The conclusion noted in paragraph 1 of Port au Prince 1077 that "The team encountered no credible claims of persecution or reprisal after repatriation" is what the embassy's monitoring teams have to date consistently reported to be true.

5. I believe that the descriptive information and assessments reported in the attached cables are credible.

---

7. Recall that La Gonave is the island from which Yvonne Pascal departed.

I declare under penalty of perjury that the foregoing is true and correct.

Executed in Washington, D.C.

March 20, 1992

Joseph F. Becelia

Attachments: 92 Port au Prince 01077 (UNCLASSIFIED)
                92 Port au Prince 858 (UNCLASSIFIED)

ROUTINE   ■■■■■■■■■■■■■■■■■■■■■   INCOMING
                         UNCLASSIFIED
                       EAP/L CARDS CENTER

PAGE 01   PORT A 01077 1619167   028415   S073786
INFO: LFO (01) LFOB (01) LARA (01) LPM (01) LFOO (01) LHRR (01)
-------------------- 16/21112 A3 DHP   (TOTAL COPIES: 006)
ACTION ARA-00

INFO LOG-00   AID-00 AMAD-01 CIAE-00 DODE-00 EB-00   HA-09
      H-01   INRE-00 INR-01   IO-19   LAB-04   L-00   ADS-00
      NSAE-00 NSCE-00 OIC-02   PA-02   PRS-01   P-01   RP-10
      SIL-00   SP-00   SR-00   SS-00   STR-20   TRSE-00 USIE-00
      /081K
                  -------------1B2E3D 1620572 /38
R 1619167 MAR 92
FM AMEMBASSY PORT AU PRINCE
TO SECSTATE WASHDC 6129
CCCDSEVEN MIAMI FL//OLE/AHO
COMDTCOGARD WASHDC//G-OLE
COMLANTAREA COGARD NEW YORK NY//A0// AI
COMNAVBASE GUANTANAMO BAY//OO
USINS WASHDC
USINS MIAMI FL
USINS DALLAS TX
INFO USCINCLANT NORFOLK VA
COGARD INTELCOORDCEN WASHINGTON DC
CJTF GTMO//J3
AMEMBASSY MEXICO

UNCLAS PORT AU PRINCE 01077

DEPT ALSO FOR ARA/DAS HRINAK
DEPT ALSO FOR ARA/CAR
INS/CO ALSO FOR HQRAP AND INTELLIGENCE - MS. MARZ
INS/DALLAS FOR REGIONAL INTELLIGENCE - GUNTHER WAGNER

GUANTANAMO ALSO FOR INS
AMEMBASSY MEXICO FOR DIDIR INS

E.O. 12356: N/A
TAGS: PHUM, PREF, HA
SUBJECT: MONITORING REPATRIATED BOAT PEOPLE: INS TEAM
-        COMPLETES MONITORING TRIP.

REF: PAP 1008 AND PREVIOUS

1. SUMMARY: AN INS TEAM CONDUCTED 309 REPATRIATE
INTERVIEWS IN WIDELY SCATTERED LOCATIONS THROUGHOUT HAITI
DURING THE PERIOD MARCH 4-13, INCLUDING THE FIRST
MONITORING TRIP TO THE ISLAND OF LA GONAVE. THE TEAM
ENCOUNTERED NO CREDIBLE CLAIMS OF PERSECUTION OR REPRISAL
AFTER REPATRIATION. END SUMMARY.

2. A VISITING TWO MAN INS TEAM, LED BY INS INTELLIGENCE
OFFICER GUNTHER WAGNER, INTERVIEWED 309 REPATRIATES
DURING THE PERIOD MARCH 4-13. THE REPATRIATED BOAT
PEOPLE WERE LOCATED IN PORT AU PRINCE, LEOGARE, GONAIVES,
-
CAP HAITIEN, CABARET, ARCANAIE AND LA GONAVE. THE INS
TEAM'S EXPERIENCE WAS SIMILAR TO THAT OF EMBASSY
MONITORS THUS FAR --- EXCEPTIONALLY FEW CLAIMS OF
PERSECUTION OR REPRISAL SINCE REPATRIATION AND NONE OF
THOSE CREDIBLE.

3. PARTICULARLY NOTEWORTHY WAS THE TEAM'S VISIT TO THE
ISLAND OF LA GONAVE MARCH 11, INCLUDING ANSE A GALET,
THE PRINCIPAL TOWN AND SITE OF THE ISLAND'S ARMY POST,

AND SECOND TOWN, ETROITS. LA GONAVE IS THE DEPARTURE
POINT FOR MANY BOAT PEOPLE. THE INS TEAM DEBRIEFED 67
REPATRIATES, AND A NUMBER OF OTHER PERSONS INCLUDING
THE LOCAL ARMY COMMANDER AND RESIDENT PRIEST. ALL
AGREE THERE HAVE BEEN NO KILLINGS OR VIOLENCE, BUT SOME
SHOOTING IN THE AIR. LA GONAVE HAS BEEN ONE OF THE

                         PORT A 01077 1619167   028415   S073786
QUIETEST SPOTS IN THE COUNTRY AFTER THE COUP AND
REMAINS VERY CALM. THE PRIEST HAD A POSTER OF ARISTIDE
PROMINENTLY DISPLAYED ON HIS FRONT DOOR. THE PRIEST
EXPRESSED NO FEAR OF THE MILITARY. THERE WERE NO
CLAIMS OF REPRISAL OR PERSECUTION. SOLDIERS DID
EXTRACT A $ 1-5 EMBARCATION FEE FROM DEPARTING BOAT
PEOPLE. DEPARTURES HAVE SLOWED NOW, EVIDENTLY BECAUSE
BOAT PEOPLE ARE BEING RETURNED TO HAITI IN LARGE
NUMBERS. WOULD-BE BOAT PEOPLE ARE SAID TO BE AWAITING
A "FAVORABLE LEGAL DEVELOPMENT" IN THE U.S., WHICH MANY
BELIEVE WILL BE FORTHCOMING IN THE NEAR FUTURE, BEFORE
THE NEXT LARGE EXODUS.

4. THE INS TEAM WILL BE MAKING A DETAILED REPORT OF
ITS FINDINGS THROUGH INS AND JUSTICE DEPARTMENT
CHANNELS. BASIC DATA CONCERNING REPATRIATES
INTERVIEWED BY INS IN HAITI ARE ENTERED INTO A MASTER
LIST COMPILED BY THE CONSULAR SECTION.

ADAMS

ROUTINE

|||||||||||||||||||||||
UNCLASSIFIED

INCOMING

DEPARTMENT OF STATE
ARA/NEA REARCS

PAGE 01 OF 02 PORT A 00858 00 OF 03 021831Z   036440   S006330   PORT A 00858 00 OF 03 021831Z   036440   S006330
ACTION: DJK (01)

INFO: HAFV (02) DCAR (01) DEP (01) CU (02) ARA (01) PPC (01)
       OAS (01) PPA (01) RJ (01) RSG (01) EX (01) PMD (01)
       --------------------- 02/2051Z A2 LK   (TOTAL COPIES: 015)
ACTION ARA-00

INFO LOG-00   AID-00   AMAD-01   CIAE-00   SJK-01   C-01   DODE-00
      DS-00   EB-00   KA-09   H-01   INRE-00 INR-01 IO-19
      LAB-04   L-03   ADS-00   M-01   NSAE-00 NSCE-00 OIC-02
      OMB-01   PA-02   PM-00   PRS-01   P-01   RP-10   SIL-00
      SNP-00   SP-00   SR-00   SS-00   STR-20   TRSE-00 T-01
      USIE-00 FMP-00   /089W
      --------------------157915 022037Z /40 38

R 021825Z MAR 92
FM AMEMBASSY PORT AU PRINCE
TO SECSTATE WASHDC 5956
CCGDSEVEN MIAMI FL//OLE/AMIO
COMDTCOGARD WASHDC//G-OLE
COMLANTAREA COGARD NEW YORK NY//AO//AI
COMNAVBASE GUANTANAMO BAY//00
USINS WASHDC
USINS MIAMI FL
USINS DALLAS TX
INFO USCINCLANT NORFOLK VA
COGARD INTELCOORDCEN WASHINGTON DC
CJTF GTMO//J3
AMEMBASSY MEXICO

UNCLAS PORT AU PRINCE 00858

DEPT ALSO FOR ARA/DAS HRINAK
DEPT ALSO FOR ARA/CAR
INS/CO ALSO FOR NCRAP AND INTELLIGENCE - MS. MARZ

INS/DALLAS FOR REGIONAL INTELLIGENCE - GUNTHER WAGNER
GUANTANAMO ALSO FOR INS
AMEMBASSY MEXICO FOR DIDIR INS

E.O. 12356: N/A
TAGS: PHUM, PREF, PREL, PGOV, ASEC, HA
SUBJECT: MONITORING REPATRIATED BOAT PEOPLE: SEVENTEEN
FURTHER INTERVIEWS AT RED CROSS, PORT AU PRINCE

REF. (A) PORT AU PRINCE 0749 (B) PORT AU PRINCE 704
1. SUMMARY. SEVENTEEN HAITIAN REPATRIATES WERE
INTERVIEWED DURING RED CROSS FOOD DISTRIBUTION IN PORT
AU PRINCE FRIDAY FEBRUARY 28. NONE OF THEM CLAIMED ANY
PERSECUTION OR HARASSMENT SINCE RETURNING TO HAITI.
FIFTEEN OPENLY ADMITTED THEY WERE ECONOMIC MIGRANTS,
BUT TWO SAID THAT THEY LEFT DUE TO THE GENERAL CLIMATE
OF VIOLENCE AND REPRESSION (ONE DEPARTED APRIL 1, 1992
-- WELL BEFORE THE SEPTEMBER 30 COUP), ALTHOUGH NEITHER
CHARACTERIZED HIMSELF AS A TARGET. WE PLAN TO CONDUCT
FURTHER INTERVIEWS OF REPATRIATES AT ANSE ROUGE WHEN
RED CROSS DISTRIBUTES FOOD THERE MARCH 5. TO DATE, INS
AND EMBASSY CONSULAR OFFICERS HAVE INTERVIEWED 196
HAITIAN REPATRIATES AND HAVE ENCOUNTERED ONLY ONE
COLORABLE CLAIM TO PERSECUTION, WHICH UPON
INVESTIGATION WAS FOUND TO BE UNSUBSTANTIATED. END
SUMMARY.

2. RESULTS OF THE SEVENTEEN INTERVIEWS: ALL SEVENTEEN
HAVE RETURNED TO HAITI WITHOUT SUFFERING ANY
HARASSMENT, ARRESTS OR OTHER PERSECUTION BY THE HAITIAN
AUTHORITIES. FIFTEEN ADMITTED THAT THEY WERE ECONOMIC

MIGRANTS, BUT TWO SAID THEY HAD FLED THE GENERAL
REPRESSION AND VIOLENCE WITHOUT SPECIFYING THAT THEY
WERE TARGETED INDIVIDUALLY.

- (A) TWO MIGRANTS STATED THAT THEY FLED GENERAL
VIOLENCE AND REPRESSION BUT HAVE ENCOUNTERED NO
PERSECUTION SINCE THEIR RETURN:

-      (1) RENOCK DORIVAL, TWENTY-THREE, AN
UNEMPLOYED WELDER, DEPARTED MARIANI ... APRIL 1, 1991
-- WELL BEFORE THE SEPTEMBER 30 COUP! HE SAID HE HAD
LEFT BECAUSE OF GENERAL VIOLENCE. HE WOULD LIKE TO
IMMIGRATE TO THE U.S.
-      (2) LOUIS NAUTIL PIERRE, THIRTY-ONE, GTMO
NO. 31865, CONSTRUCTION WORKER -- WHO WAS MORE THAN
FULLY EMPLOYED -- TOOK THE BOAT NOVEMBER 13, 1991. HE
SAID THAT CONDITIONS IN HIS NEIGHBORHOOD (A FEW BLOCKS
FROM THE CONSULAR SECTION ON MONSIGNOR GUILLOUX) WERE
UNSETTLED AT THAT TIME, INCLUDING DEMONSTRATIONS AND
SHOOTING. HE, HOWEVER, STATED HE WAS NOT A TARGET FOR
REPRESSION AND DID NOT PARTICIPATE IN THE
DEMONSTRATIONS. HE HAS NOT HAD ANY PROBLEMS WITH THE
AUTHORITIES, BUT COMMUTES TO SLEEP IN LEOGANE EVERY
NIGHT OUT OF FEELING OF QUOTE PANIC UNQUOTE. HE WILL
NOT GO BY BOAT AGAIN. HE AND HIS COUSIN LEFT IN SAME
BOAT, BUT HIS COUSIN -- WILLIO FILS -- WAS APPARENTLY
APPROVED AS A REFUGEE BUT MR. PIERRE HIMSELF WAS NOT.

- (B) FIFTEEN REPATRIATES TELL CONOFF THEY WERE
ECONOMIC MIGRANTS. THEY DEPARTED FOR ECONOMIC REASONS
AND SAID THEY HAD NOT BEEN HARASSED, ABUSED OR

OTHERWISE PERSECUTED BY THE POLICE OR OTHER HAITIAN
AUTHORITIES AFTER THEIR RETURN:

-      (1) JOSEPH SAM SIDORNE, 41 YEARS OLD,
CROIX DES MISSIONS NEAR THE CAPITAL CLAIMS TO BE A
HOUSEPAINTER AND VETERINARIAN. HE SAID HE PAID 160
HAITIAN DOLLARS FOR THE TRIP (THE BROKER ORIGINALLY
ASKED 300).

-      (2) JEAN SANON THERMIDOR, A 23 YEAR OLD
UNEMPLOYED PLUMBER FROM CABARET, DEPARTED BECAUSE QUOTE
I AM YOUNG. I CANNOT CONTINUE MY STUDIES, AND MY
PARENTS ARE POOR. I THEREFORE TOOK A CHANCE BY BOAT
SINCE I DO NOT HAVE ANY WORK HERE UNQUOTE.

-      (3) LEONE OSTIN LEDNIS, 22 YEARS,
UNEMPLOYED CONSTRUCTION SITE GUARD FROM THOMAZEAU NEAR
THE CAPITAL, DEPARTED BY BOAT QUOTE IN SEARCH OF A
BETTER LIFE UNQUOTE.
-      (4) ANUCLE JEUNE, 22, UNEMPLOYED, PESTEL,
TOLD CONOFF THAT HIS FRIEND OFFERED HIM THE CHANCE TO
TAKE THE BOAT.

-      (5) MARIE CARMEL CHERI, A 56 YEAR OLD
UNEMPLOYED MOTHER FROM PORT AU PRINCE, SAID SHE LEFT
BECAUSE QUOTE I HAD NO WORK, BUT I HAVE
RESPONSIBILITIES (FOR OTHERS, PRESUMABLY CHILDREN AND
GRANDCHILDREN) UNQUOTE.

-      (6) OHEL BELANCE, A 21 YEAR OLD FARMER
FROM PESTEL, SAID HE PAID SEVENTY HAITIAN DOLLARS

(ABOUT FORTY U.S. DOLLARS) TO SOMEONE NAMED ARNOLD (WHO
IS STILL IN GUANTANAMO) TO TAKE THE BOAT. ARNOLD
REPORTEDLY HAS A TRACK RECORD FOR SUCCESSFULLY PLACING
HIS CLIENTS ON THE FLORIDA SHORELINE. IN 1983 A GROUP
OF HIS PASSENGERS ARRIVED. MR. BELANCE DID NOT KNOW
ARNOLD'S LAST NAME.

-      (7) PATRICIA LAVAGUE, A 28 YEAR OLD
UNEMPLOYED WOMAN FROM PORT AU PRINCE, SAID SHE PAID

ROUTINE   UNCLASSIFIED   INCOMING

DEPARTMENT OF STATE
ARA/NEA REARCS

PAGE 02 OF 02 PORT A 00058 00 OF 03 0218312 036440   S006330   PORT A 00058 00 OF 03 0218312 036440   S006330
FIFTY HAITIAN DOLLARS (ABOUT THIRTY U.S. DOLLARS) TO   (E) 1 INTERVIEWED AT CONSULAR SECTION -- MICHELET
SOMEONE NAMED NENE. SHE LEFT IN SEARCH OF A BETTER   JOSEPH PIERRE, CHRISTIAN SCIENCE MONITOR TELEVISION
LIFE (QUOTE CHECHE LAVIE MIYO UNQUOTE).   NEWS INTEREST. THIS IS THE FIRST COLORABLE CLAIM TO
                                                                         POST-REPATRIATION PERSECUTION WE HAVE ENCOUNTERED SO
-        (8)   CENERITE CASSEUS, A 35 YEAR OLD   FAR, AND IT WAS FOUND TO BE UNSUBSTANTIATED (PORT AU
UNEMPLOYED CONSTRUCTION WORKER FROM LA GONAVE, SAID HE   PRINCE 0030).
PAID TWO HUNDRED HAITIAN DOLLARS (APPROXIMATELY ONE
HUNDRED TWENTY U.S. DOLLARS) TO THE UNNAMED OWNER OF   4. TRAVEL TO ANSE ROUGE TO INTERVIEW REPATRIATES AT
THE BOAT.   RED CROSS FOOD DISTRIBUTION MARCH 5.

-        (9)   CHAVANNE MONA, A 17 YEAR OLD UNEMPLOYED   THE RED CROSS PLANS TO DISTRIBUTE FOOD AT ANSE ROUGE
DRESSMAKER FROM LA GONAVE, STATED QUOTE SINCE I HAD NO   MARCH 5 AND EXPECTS MANY BOAT PERSONS FROM THE WESTERN
ONE TO HELP ME IN HAITI - BECAUSE MY FATHER DIED, MY   PART OF HAITI, A MAJOR MIGRANT EXPORT AREA OVER THE
FRIENDS ADVISED ME TO TAKE A CHANCE (BY BOAT) UNQUOTE.   YEARS. WE PLAN TO BE THERE PREPARED TO INTERVIEW AS
                                                                         MANY REPATRIATES AS DISCRETELY AS POSSIBLE TO DETERMINE
-        (10) VICTOR JEAN, A 39 YEAR FARMER FROM   IF ANY HAVE SUFFERED HARASSMENT SINCE THEIR RETURN.
MARIANI, LEFT FOR QUOTE LAVIE MIYO (A BETTER LIFE)
UNQUOTE. HE PAID 120 HAITIAN DOLLARS (ABOUT   ADAMS
SEVENTY-TWO US DOLLARS) TO MR. YVES JEAN, LA GONAVE,
FOR HIS TRAVEL.
-        (11) PETERSON NICOLAS, 19 YEARS, A STUDENT
IN MARTISSANT, DEPARTED FOR QUOTE LAVIE MIYO (A BETTER

LIFE) UNQUOTE. QUOTE I WAS NOT ABLE TO PAY FOR MY
SCHOOL, SO I TOOK THE BOAT TO RELIEVE MY PARENTS OF THE
BURDEN UNQUOTE.

-        (12) FRANCIA CHERY, TWENTY-EIGHT YEARS OLD,
UNEMPLOYED, MARIANI, ASKED FOR WHAT REASON SHE DEPARTED
BY BOAT, REPLIED QUOTE PROBLEMES ECONOMIQUES UNQUOTE.

-        (13) RONALD PREVIL, EIGHTEEN YEARS OLD,
CARREFOUR, A FISHERMAN, STATED THAT HE LEFT BECAUSE OF
QUOTE PROBLEMES ECONOMIQUES UNQUOTE.

-        (14) PATRICK LEGER, EIGHTEEN, MARTISSANT,
PAID 150 HAITIAN DOLLARS FOR THE BOAT TRIP (ABOUT
NINETY US DOLS) TO MR. GASPARD (FULL NAME UNKNOWN).
ASKED ABOUT ANY HARASSMENT OR PERSECUTION AFTER
REPATRIATION, HE RESPONDED THAT QUOTE NO ONE HAS STRUCK
ME, BUT I DO NOT FEEL AT EASE UNQUOTE.

-        (15) MAXISSAIRE ROSICLAIR, NINETEEN,
UNEMPLOYED WELDER, GRESSIER, SAID HE TRAVELED BY BOAT
WITH A GROUP OF FRIENDS.

3. 196 HAITIAN REPATRIATES INTERVIEWED: ONLY ONE
COLORABLE CLAIM TO PERSECUTION UPON RETURN --
UNSUBSTANTIATED.

THE EMBASSY AND INS HAVE INTERVIEWED A TOTAL OF 196
HAITIAN REPATRIATES AND REPORTED THE RESULTS AS FOLLOWS:

-        (A)   141 INTERVIEWED BY INS (FIFTY-ONE JOINTLY

WITH EMBASSY CONOFF - REFTEL B). INS SOUTHERN REGION
INTELLIGENCE OFFICER GUNTHER WAGNER HAS APPARENTLY SENT
HIS REPORT TO INS CENTRAL OFFICE. SEVERAL COLORABLE
CLAIMS TO PERSECUTION AFTER REPATRIATION WERE MADE
SEPARATELY TO CONOFF, BUT THEY WERE ULTIMATELY FOUND TO
BE WITHOUT MERIT.
-        (B)   23 INTERVIEWED IN PORT DE PAIX BY CONOFF
(REFTEL A).

-        (C)   14 INTERVIEWED DURING RED CROSS FOOD
DISTRIBUTION IN PORT AU PRINCE (SEPTEL IN PROCESS).

-        (D)   17 INTERVIEWED AT RED CROSS FOOD
DISTRIBUTION, PORT AU PRINCE (REPORTED IN THIS CABLE).

Note: The font size on these telegrams is very small and quite hard to read. This sort of problem appears from time to time when dealing with document review, although it has become less common with the advent of electronically stored information. If you have trouble reading the telegrams, you can do the same thing the students working on McNary might have done: Use a photocopier to make enlarged copies of the documents.

Which do you find more persuasive—the evidence presented by the plaintiffs or by the defendants? Why? How, if at all, do the arguments found in footnote 28 of the Yale brief reproduced previously affect your view? A leading treatise on civil procedure states: "[Several Supreme Court decisions on procedural due process indicate] that a court planning to issue a temporary restraining order must be particularly careful that the [moving party] has produced compelling evidence of the threatened irreparable injury . . . ." 11A *Federal Practice and Procedure* § 2951 (2d ed. 1995). In light of this, do you agree with the court's decision that the plaintiffs faced the requisite risk of irreparable harm?

3. *Notice to the Defendant.* As noted previously, a TRO is usually sought when the anticipated harm is so imminent that there may be no time to inform the defendant of the court proceeding. In *McNary*, however, notifying the defendant was not a problem. Remember that right before the TRO hearing, Michael Ratner simply walked into the U.S. Attorney's Office with a copy of the papers and told Assistant U.S. Attorney Bob Begleiter that plaintiffs were headed to court. *See STC*, p. 60. Given that notice was not an issue, might Koh and the students have filed a motion for a preliminary injunction instead? Why didn't they do so? (Keep in mind they would have had to file a complaint if they had sought a preliminary injunction. *See STC*, p. 48.)

4. *The Scope of Rule 65(b).* If you review Rule 65(b), you will notice that the rule seems to govern only restraining orders issued without notice *or* a hearing. In the *McNary* case, however, there was both notice *and* a hearing before Judge Johnson issued the TRO. Did his ruling go beyond the authority granted by Rule 65(b)? No. The courts have interpreted the rule to extend to cases where the defendant received notice and a hearing was held, but there was insufficient time for the parties to prepare adequately for the hearing. *See* 11A *Federal Practice and Procedure* § 2951 (2d ed. 1995). That was clearly the situation in *McNary*. Assistant U.S. Attorneys Bob Begleiter and Scott Dunn only had a few hours to prepare for the hearing before going into court.

5. *The TRO Itself.* So what does a TRO look like? The following are the last few paragraphs of Judge Johnson's opinion and order:[8]

For the foregoing reasons, it is hereby:

ORDERED, that sufficient reason having been shown therefore, pending the hearing for the plaintiffs' application for a preliminary injunction, pursuant to Federal Rule 65, defendants are temporarily restrained and enjoined from:

a) denying plaintiff service organizations access to their clients for the purpose of providing them legal counsel, advocacy, and representation;

b) interviewing, screening, or subjecting to exclusion or asylum proceedings any Haitian citizen currently being detained on Guantanamo, or in any other territory subject to U.S. jurisdiction (i) who has been screened in or who was screened in prior to the *Baker* litigation and has since been screened out and (ii) who is being denied or has been denied his or her right to communicate with counsel; and it is further

Note that the TRO will remain in effect only through the hearing on the application for a preliminary injunction.

---

8. *Haitian Centers Council, Inc. v. McNary*, 789 F. Supp. 541, 548 (E.D.N.Y. 1992).

Although discovery usually takes place after challenges to the pleadings, parties can sometimes engage in limited discovery early in the case on issues that must be resolved before the lawsuit can progress. Here, for example, plaintiffs' attorneys needed access to Guantánamo to gather evidence for the hearing on their preliminary injunction motion.

An order to show cause is an order for the party to appear in court and demonstrate ("show cause") why something should not be done. Practically speaking, such an order simply sets the date, time, and place for the next hearing.

> ORDERED that expedited discovery be granted thereby, in accordance with the following scheduling order:
>
> (i) defendants must produce documents for inspection and copying on or before March 31, 1992; and
>
> (ii) plaintiffs are granted leave to serve and depose Defendants on or before April 1, 1992 at 9:00 a.m.; and it is further
>
> ORDERED, that the defendants or their attorneys show cause before The Honorable Sterling Johnson, Jr., United States District Judge, at the United States Courthouse in the Eastern District of New York, 225 Cadman Plaza, Brooklyn, New York, in Courtroom 14 at 9:00 a.m. on April 1, 1992, why an order should not be entered granting Plaintiffs' request for Preliminary Injunction pursuant to Federal Rule of Civil Procedure 65 thereby in accordance with the terms of the TRO issued herein or as otherwise may be deemed just and proper.
>
> So ordered.

Note that the judge's open-ended order leaves much for the parties to work out through negotiation. For example, the judge did not say how many people should be granted access to Guantánamo to meet with the Haitians. In fact, the order does not expressly grant access to Guantánamo at all. The order grants the lawyers access to their *clients*, not to any particular geographical location. If, for instance, the government had decided to bring some of the Haitians to Miami to meet with the Yale team, the Justice Department might have been able to argue that there was no need to allow anyone from Yale on Guantánamo. Released late on a Friday, Judge Johnson's order produced fierce disagreement between the parties, and it took a Saturday afternoon telephone hearing with the judge to resolve several disputes about how the Yale team would take discovery.

6. *Taking Discovery After the TRO.*   The arguments between opposing counsel were just one small part of a four-day stretch of logistical nightmares for both sides. This brief period during the case illustrates an important point: Although law students spend most of law school discussing the development and nuances of doctrine, much of an actual lawsuit is devoted to administrative, organizational, and clerical work—often under time pressure. During this fast-track discovery phase in *McNary*, one team of lawyers, students, and interpreters went to Guantánamo to meet with the Haitian refugees; another team of lawyers and students went to Washington, D.C. to take depositions of government officials and review documents; yet another team went to Miami for depositions and to interview Haitians released from Guantánamo; and a fourth team worked in New Haven to assemble the evidence and research and write a brief. Consider everything that had to be planned, purchased, requested, and scheduled for all this to happen: dozens of plane tickets, overnight accommodations in three places, law firm conference rooms and court reporters for depositions, fax and photocopy machine access in Washington to send key government documents back to New Haven (remember: no Internet, no scanners, no PDFs)—and the list goes on. What should be clear is that a career in litigation requires a great deal of planning and organization.

7. *Some Considerations from the Government's Perspective.*   As you might expect, the Justice Department lawyers were deeply concerned when Judge Johnson issued the TRO. The order meant that the interview and repatriation process on

Guantánamo had to be temporarily suspended. Imagine the logistical problems this posed for a military and bureaucratic operation involving thousands of people. The Justice Department also had to deal with a flock of lawyers and students seeking access to government documents, State Department and immigration officials, and other sources. Finally, Paul Cappuccio in particular was concerned that Judge Johnson's order did not merely preserve the status quo (as a TRO is meant to do), but instead actually granted the plaintiffs part of the final relief they had requested—namely, the right to communicate with their clients. This aspect of the order, Cappuccio believed, would have been appropriate only at the *end* of the case, assuming that plaintiffs had won. Do you agree? Why or why not?

INTERVIEW
ROBERT BEGLEITER ON OPPOSING A REQUEST FOR EMERGENCY OR PRELIMINARY RELIEF

What are the biggest challenges a lawyer faces when opposing either a temporary restraining order application or a preliminary injunction motion?

There are different answers to how to handle a temporary restraining order (TRO) and a preliminary injunction (PI). If it's just a PI, and it begins, as most do, with an order to show cause [meaning the parties will have to file briefs and appear in court on a scheduled basis], then you're dealing with days, if not weeks, from when you have to appear at the hearing. That gives you some time.

If you're in the government, as I was, your first task is to figure out who's going to be serving as litigation counsel: the local United States Attorney's Office, Main Justice [in Washington], or sometimes, another agency that has its own counsel—for example, the Environmental Protection Agency. All you're really doing is figuring out who should be involved. Then you have to work out a schedule with the court, including reasonable deadlines, with the understanding that the other side is obviously in a hurry and it's important to them to have an early deadline.

In comparison to a PI, a TRO creates tremendous problems. The court can grant immediate relief to the plaintiff—in some instances, without any notice to the defendant. It's important that the lawyer seeking the TRO has ensured that there's been compliance with Rule 65, which requires some attempt at notice. So in the event that the judge *did* grant relief without notice to your side, your first line of defense is: Did opposing counsel meet the requirements of Rule 65(b)(1)(B)? That's the first issue. And in reality, it's rare that relief is granted without notice to the other side. Most judges feel really uncomfortable about issuing a TRO without the other party present, because they want to make sure they're not doing something crazy by accepting only one side's account of the facts.

Second, if you're part of the government—as I was during *McNary*—you've got to figure out what the position of the government is, and you've got to learn something about it in a hurry, usually in minutes. As an example, consider RU 486 [the pharmaceutical mifepristone, which can be used in small doses as an emergency contraceptive or "morning-after pill"]. At the time, it was prohibited in the United States, and it had been sent here from France and was in storage at JFK Airport. The plaintiff seeking a TRO, a woman who feared she might otherwise get pregnant, demanded that it be turned over to her immediately so she could take the drug.

I managed to reach a Department of Justice lawyer at the Civil Division who handled food and drug cases, and he filled me in on the FDA's position. I had to run over to court and argue to Judge Charles Sifton about why the plaintiff didn't need the drug and why banning RU 486 at the time was lawful, and I had to learn the arguments in a few minutes. I went in and argued it—and I lost. So the judge ordered the RU 486 turned over immediately.* I called up the Justice Department and they told me: Go get a stay at the court of appeals. I hurried to the court of appeals and wrote out the request in longhand and we went before a judge, and he granted the stay. The whole thing, from the moment I first got notice to the argument at the Second Circuit, took just three to four hours.

Another thing you worry about with the TRO is the posting of a bond [under Fed. R. Civ. P. 65(c)]—usually in cases that involve a lot of money. So, as in the *McNary* case, if litigants are going forward seeking a TRO, it can cost the government a lot of money if they get the TRO. You file a motion requesting that the judge require the other party to post the bond, and later, if the TRO was wrongfully granted, the bond covers the expenses that resulted from the TRO being granted.**

How do you do the legal research when you're defending a TRO?

You have no time to read the law, unless it's a single statute and it's really simple. Instead, you have to ask people who know about the law. In the government, we had different lawyers who were really experienced and knowledgeable in different areas of the law. You had to find them, and they would help you shape the argument you had to make. And you also have to hope that the judge will have some insight into the question. For example, Judge Johnson seemed to have a gut feeling about whether or not there should be lawyers on Guantánamo.

Of course, sometimes, the judge makes the decision on grounds that don't really have to do with the law. I remember one afternoon at 4:30 getting notice of a TRO request. A lawyer was asking a judge to prevent a plane from taking off because his client, an alien on board the plane, was being deported. And the judge looked at me and looked at the attorney for the alien and said, "It's too late. I'm not going to stop a plane from taking off from the airport." Later, I found out that the alien's case had gone all the way to the Supreme Court, and they'd refused to hear the case, so in the end this was really a meritless last-ditch effort, anyway.

You are now in private practice. How has that changed your responsibilities and approach with respect to defending against a TRO application/PI motion?

Since now I do mostly plaintiffs' work, I'm almost always in the position of requesting a TRO rather than defending against one. I follow the notice requirements of Rule 65 carefully and I make it a point to speak with the lawyer on the

---

* *See* Philip J. Hilts, *Judge Overturns Federal Seizure of Abortion Pill*, N.Y. TIMES (July 15, 1992), at A1.

** Recall that the government requested a bond in *McNary*, arguing that the costs of stopping the interviewing and repatriation process would run in the millions of dollars. Judge Johnson granted the bond request—but for only $5,000.—Eds.

other side and let him or her know what's going on. You have to be careful about this. Some lawyers like to be sneaky about Rule 65 notice and they don't really try to reach opposing counsel. That's not good practice, and as I said, judges are reluctant to grant relief if the other side isn't available.

Usually, the sophisticated lawyers who are seeking a TRO really do try to get a hold of you. And then we all try to work out a schedule so that it won't break our backs—a schedule that will give us a civilized amount of time to get things done. And that's not just for the sake of the defendants. Sometimes, the plaintiff's lawyers haven't had much time to put everything together. They might be going on nothing more than an outline when they get to court, and frankly, they'd like more time as much as you. So you work things out, and it gives everyone more time—and a bit of time for living, too.

What are the biggest mistakes a lawyer can make in defending against a request for emergency preliminary relief?

First, I'd say don't fight a judge on a TRO you know you're going to lose. I think back to when I was defending against two TROs regarding the military academies. The Army wanted to throw a cadet out of West Point and the Navy wanted to throw a midshipman out of the Naval Academy [in both instances, for bad behavior]. The cadet and the midshipman had each filed for a TRO to remain in school. As the defense counsel representing the government, I agreed to the TROs. The fact is, very few judges in such circumstances are going to let someone get tossed out of a service academy without a hearing. The question here for the government really was, Can we wait two to three weeks and have a preliminary injunction hearing where there can be a full hearing with a better developed record and more evidence? And the answer was, Yes, we could wait. Keeping these kids in school for two to three more weeks wasn't going to destroy the service academies, and the kids promised to behave in the meantime.

The second thing I'd say is: Don't make up facts. If you don't know something, don't guess at what it must be. You're far better off saying nothing than saying something that turns out not to be true and comes back to haunt you later. Then the judge wonders if you're careful as a lawyer and everything you say can become suspect. I once told the judge that a TRO applicant had been engaged in a "meretricious" relationship [i.e., one involving a prostitute]—because that's how the INS had described the situation. And the judge got very angry and demanded, "What are you saying?! What do you mean?!" I didn't have anything to back up what I was saying; I'd simply relied on the judgment of someone else at the INS, and it really made the judge mad.

After that, I was pretty careful about what I said in terms of the facts. I've always tried to avoid saying anything when I didn't know if it was 100 percent accurate.

What advice do you have for the young lawyer defending against a request for emergency preliminary relief?

If you're in the government, read the newspaper every day. Because very often, the issues you're going to face are in the public domain already. If you're

Robert Begleiter with his daughter in 1992. Photograph by Diana V. Lopez.

outside the government, make sure that you know the area of the law applicable to the TRO being requested. It's very hard to get up to speed on a new area of law, so like I said before, you talk to other people who know about that area. Finally: Don't exaggerate. It always gets you in trouble. And TROs are particularly fertile ground for exaggeration. The stakes are high. Emotions can run high. There's a lot of pressure. You're on weak ground when it comes to knowing the facts and the law, and you may tend to overstate things. Don't do it.

THE PRELIMINARY INJUNCTION

To recap, Judge Johnson issued the TRO on a Friday afternoon (March 27, 1992) and scheduled the preliminary injunction hearing for a Wednesday morning (April 1, 1992). *See STC*, pp. 88-89. In the days between the two, the Yale team had to gather as much evidence as it could to support its contention that the Haitians on Guantá-namo could suffer irreparable harm if they were returned to Haiti. A showing of "irreparable harm," however, is only one of several factors that courts consider when deciding whether to issue a preliminary injunction.

Generally speaking, courts weigh four factors in determining whether to grant a preliminary injunction: (1) the significance of the threat of irreparable harm to the plaintiff, (2) the balance between the hardship faced by the plaintiff (if the injunction is not issued) and the hardship faced by the defendant (if the injunction *is* issued), (3) the probability that the plaintiff will later succeed on the merits of the case, and (4) whether the injunction would serve the public interest. *Federal Practice and Procedure* §§ 2948, 2948.3 (2d ed. 1995). The plaintiff bears the burden of proof in this four-part inquiry.[9]

By way of a quick explanation, the first of these factors is similar to what the court must consider in weighing a motion for a TRO. The second factor ensures in part that the court takes into account the defendant's interests when deciding whether to issue the preliminary injunction. The third factor requires that the plaintiff show that there is a fairly good legal argument in his favor, although the plaintiff does *not* have to prove that he would actually win the case—that is an issue for trial. Nevertheless, focusing on the plaintiff's arguments on the merits makes sense: If the plaintiff were not likely to be successful at trial, there would be a greater risk that the defendant's interests would be harmed for no reason. Finally, the public interest factor allows the court to make a relatively open-ended policy inquiry. Not surprisingly, in almost every case involving a preliminary injunction motion, each party contends that *its* position is the one consistent with the public interest.

NOTES AND COMMENTS

8. Evidence of Irreparable Harm.   Irreparable harm was once again an issue at the preliminary injunction hearing. Recall that at the hearing itself, Harold Koh focused his discussion about irreparable harm on the story of Marie Zette. *See STC*, pp. 105-06. Koh asserted that Marie Zette was a Haitian woman who had a credible fear of persecution but had been mistakenly returned by the INS to Haiti, where she was supposedly killed. The government later put into serious question the accuracy of the Zette story. *See id.*, pp. 124-25. Do you think it was wise for Koh to rely so heavily on Marie Zette, given that the account of her death was supported only by a declaration submitted by an anonymous Haitian refugee interviewed by a law student? Before you answer, recall that Koh had very little concrete information to provide the court on the issue of persecution of repatriated refugees. At the time of the hearing, Koh's aim was to try to personalize the situation for the judge. Koh later said that with the benefit of hindsight, he would have tried to keep the focus on more general sources, such as the

---

9. As with a TRO standard, the precise formulation of the preliminary injunction standard varies from circuit to circuit. The Second Circuit's formulation, set forth in Note 3 earlier in the chapter, differs slightly from the basic standard set forth in the text—for instance, it does not expressly include a "public interest" factor—but is similar in application. *See Haitian Centers Council, Inc. v. McNary*, 969 F.2d 1326, 1338 (2d Cir. 1992). We stress these variations for a very practical purpose. In a traditional first-year course, it is often the case that you will learn one particular test for a preliminary injunction, only to discover when you start to practice that there is a little more confusion among the courts than you might have been led to expect. This sort of subtle variation across jurisdictions in even well-settled doctrines is not uncommon, and you should be aware of it—and always be sure to cite the precise formulation of the doctrine as articulated by the court before which you are arguing. For now, however, if you want to remember one test, it is best to know the four-factor test set out in the text above that cites FEDERAL PRACTICE AND PROCEDURE as authority. This is a widely adopted formulation for deciding whether to enter a preliminary injunction or a TRO.

Haitian man and toddler, Camp McCalla, probably spring 1992. Photograph courtesy of Stephen Kinder.

Amnesty International report (quoted in plaintiffs' TRO brief) that expressed broader concerns about returnees. Do you agree? Why or why not?

9. Challenging the Becelia Affidavit.   Another aspect of the Yale team's argument on irreparable harm is found in the team's preliminary injunction brief: an attack on the affidavit of State Department official Joseph Becelia. With student Michael Barr helping to formulate the questions, Simpson Thacher lawyer Joe Tringali took Becelia's deposition in Washington, D.C. on Monday, March 30, 1992—two days before the preliminary injunction hearing. Here is the portion of the plaintiffs' brief that tries to undercut the testimony he gave in his declaration. Before reading it, you may wish to review the Embassy telegrams, above, that are the subject of Becelia's declaration.

> When plaintiffs' counsel deposed Becelia . . . [his] prior declaration[] [was] thoroughly discredited. Becelia's testimony revealed that he had no first-hand knowledge of the investigations about which he was reporting and that his declaration had been at least triple hearsay. Even then, Becelia could not demonstrate that all 309 monitoring reports were in fact unsubstantiated . . . .[10]

Plaintiffs assert Becelia had no first-hand knowledge of the situation described in the Embassy telegrams. But couldn't a similar criticism also be leveled against the Haitian

___

10. Plaintiffs' Memorandum in Support of Their Motion for a Preliminary Injunction, April 1, 1992, at 15.

refugee who submitted the declaration about Marie Zette? Given the additional evidence submitted by the parties, how do you now see the irreparable harm issue? What would you have done if you were Judge Johnson? Does the fact that the possible harm in this case was so extreme, even if not clearly demonstrated, affect your decision?

   10. Hardship to the Defendants.   Now consider the government's perspective. As described previously, one of the four factors in the test for issuing a preliminary injunction involves a balancing of the hardships: the hardship faced by the plaintiff (if an injunction is not issued) balanced against the hardship faced by the defendant (if the injunction is issued). In their brief, Justice Department lawyers claimed that a preliminary injunction would impose a hardship on the government in many ways. Their central contention was that a continued freeze on repatriations would encourage more Haitians to flee their country—something that Paul Cappuccio and his co-counsel referred to as the "magnet effect." The resulting influx of refugees, the government claimed, would require a massive deployment of Coast Guard vessels and personnel in the Caribbean and military personnel on Guantánamo—at a potential cost of more than $665,000 per *day*. Justice Department lawyers also asserted that an injunction in the plaintiffs' favor would "injure[] the United States Government's flexibility in dealing with this international crisis" by making the United States vulnerable to "blackmailing"—specifically a threat by Haiti's "de facto authorities" to "encourage massive outmigration from Haiti."[11] What do you make of these arguments? How does this hardship balance against the hardship to the plaintiffs?

   After concluding that the screened-in plaintiffs could face torture or death if repatriated to Haiti, here is what Judge Johnson wrote about the balance of hardships in his order issuing the preliminary injunction:

> The Government argues that the issuance of a preliminary injunction will create a "magnet effect" drawing more Haitians to the high seas and will increase the Government's financial burden. After carefully weighing the hardships, I find that the balance tips decidedly in favor of the Plaintiffs. Moreover, I find that . . . any burden placed on the Government in permitting attorneys access to their clients for the purpose of interviewing would be minimal.

Haitian Centers Council, Inc. v. McNary, 1992 WL 155853, at *9 (E.D.N.Y. April 6, 1992). Do you agree with the court? Why or why not? In your view, is this a close call? Would you have expected the judge to provide more in-depth analysis of the issue? Would you have had to weigh the credibility of the assertions on each side? How would you do that?

   11. Appealing Judge Johnson's Ruling.   Earlier in this chapter we said the parties could not appeal the district court's decision on a TRO, but that they could appeal its decision regarding a preliminary injunction. These and other issues related to appeal will be discussed in Chapter Nine. For now, you should be aware of the general rule pursuant to 28 U.S.C. § 1291 that only *final* decisions of district courts are

---

11. Defendants' Memorandum in Opposition to Plaintiffs' Motion for Temporary Restraining Order and for Preliminary Injunctive Relief, and in Support of Defendants' Motion to Dismiss the Complaint, Mar. 20, 1992, at 80.

appealable; appeals of non-final decisions, which are only allowed in limited circum-stances, are known as interlocutory appeals. *See* 28 U.S.C. § 1292(a)(1). The Justice Department relied on Section 1292(a)(1) to appeal Judge Johnson's grant of the preliminary injunction motion. Simultaneously, Justice sought a *stay* of the preliminary injunction, meaning an order that would temporarily prevent the injunc-tion from taking effect. Chapter Nine also will address stay orders.

CHAPTER SIX

Discovery: Overview and Written Discovery

INTRODUCTION

As we have discussed, some suits are disposed of on a matter of law not relating to the merits—such as lack of personal jurisdiction or lack of subject-matter jurisdiction—or on a 12(b)(6) motion for failure to state a claim upon which relief may be granted. If a case survives those preliminary stages, however, the focus of the litigation moves away from the law and onto the facts. At this point, the parties enter one of the most potentially time-consuming and contentious phases of litigation: discovery. Discovery is a process that calls for each party to disclose witnesses, documents, and other materials based on requests by opposing counsel. It is the way our system of litigation works to develop and clarify the factual information that each side intends to rely on to make its case at trial. As you saw in *Storming the Court*, however—from the fight over the disclosure of the Camp Bulkeley surveillance videotapes to the tension permeating Yvonne Pascal's deposition—discovery is often anything but simple.

The aim of the discovery rules is to "make a trial less a game of blind man's bluff and more a fair contest with the basic issues and facts disclosed to the fullest extent practicable." *Rozier v. Ford Motor Co.*, 573 F.2d 1332, 1346 (5th Cir. 1978). In other words, the Federal Rules do not permit trial by surprise. To that end, the rules provide parties with the right to broad discovery, including a mandated exchange of several critical categories of information early in the discovery process. In theory, this pretrial "data swap" not only prevents parties from being ambushed in court, but also helps them form more accurate assessments of the case—and thus facilitates settlement.

Since the adoption of the Federal Rules in 1938, however, the drafters' idealistic view of the discovery process has been tempered by experience. Much of the problem stems from the fact that the discovery process is meant to be self-executing—that is, it is intended to occur outside of the courtroom and without judicial supervision. Unfortunately, this lack of supervision sometimes leads to considerable conflict between the parties—as well as abuse of the rules to harass, intimidate, or overwhelm the opposition. Concerns about the costs and abuse of the discovery process led to the revision of a number of discovery rules beginning in 1993, followed by additional revisions and modifications in 2000. Although those revisions will be explored in this chapter, it is important to keep in mind that the *McNary* case was litigated under the discovery rules as they existed in 1992.

Discovery is a sufficiently broad topic that we have divided discovery issues into two chapters. This chapter will provide an overview of the process and then examine written discovery. Depositions, which involve counsel questioning a party or witness under oath, will be discussed in the next chapter.

NOTES AND COMMENTS

1. Discovery and the Litigation Process.   Ordinarily, discovery takes place after the defendant has filed its response—either an answer or a motion to dismiss—to the complaint. Early in the discovery phase, counsel for the parties confer about a discovery plan and generally then meet with the judge. The parties must submit their discovery plan to the court, which subsequently issues a pretrial schedule. *See* Fed. R. Civ. P. 16, 26(f). The parties then have a limited period of time to complete discovery, after which one or both parties may move for summary judgment under Rule 56. Summary judgment, which is discussed in Chapter Eight, allows a judge to issue a final decision in the case before it goes to trial on the ground that there is no dispute about the facts that would otherwise have to be decided by a jury (or, in a bench trial, by the judge). If no party moves for summary judgment or the judge does not grant it, the parties must begin preparing for trial, including meeting with the court for a final pretrial conference. *See* Chapter Eight, Note 2.

The *McNary* case did not follow this typical pattern. As discussed in Chapter Five on preliminary injunctive relief, the trial court authorized a mini-discovery process at the very outset of the case, granting plaintiffs' temporary restraining order request and allowing plaintiffs' counsel to go to Guantánamo in search of evidence that the plaintiffs would face irreparable harm if returned to Haiti. Rulings permitting fact-finding at such an early stage are not that common. Recall, however, that in *McNary*, the Yale team could not have visited Guantánamo and met with their clients absent a judicial order permitting discovery before the preliminary injunction hearing.

2. Rule 26—Mandatory Disclosures.   Federal Rule of Civil Procedure 26 sets out a number of general rules governing the discovery process. Among other things, Rule 26 requires that the parties disclose certain information automatically; dictates the general scope of the information that each party is entitled to request from the other; provides for protective orders that put certain limits on discovery; lays out discovery procedures; and establishes a duty to supplement discovery responses. Review the current text of Rule 26(a)-(d) as you consider the discussion in Notes 2 through 5.

We start with the disclosures required by Rule 26(a)(1)(A). Generally, most information is exchanged in response to a request from the other side. This is in part why the process is self-executing—it is largely the parties who decide what information to ask for and how to respond to requests from the opposition. The current version of Rule 26(a)(1)(A), however, requires parties to disclose certain information automatically, without the need for discovery requests. At the start of discovery, each party must disclose the identity of certain witnesses, a description of some of the relevant documents by category and location, a computation of each category of damages, and information about any insurance policy the party has that might cover payment of the judgment. The purpose of the required disclosures rule was "to streamline discovery and thereby avoid the practice of serving multiple, boilerplate interrogatories and document requests, which themselves bring into play a concomitant set of delays and costs." *Tarlton v. Cumberland County Correctional Facility*, 192 F.R.D. 165, 168 (D.N.J. 2000). Furthermore, the rule prevents "a party from improperly withholding relevant documents on the grounds that the opposing party has not specifically asked for them." *Id.* The rule providing for this mandatory exchange of information was not in effect during the *McNary* litigation.

3. Rule 26—Scope of Discovery.   Rule 26(b)(1) governs the scope of discovery. The rule allows for discovery of any matter that is (1) "relevant to the claim or defense of any party" in the pending action and (2) not subject to privilege. This current version of the rule is the result of amendments to the Federal Rules in 2000. The prior version—in effect during *McNary*—was broader, providing for discovery of any matter "relevant to the *subject matter* involved in the pending action" (emphasis added).

It is difficult to precisely define the difference between the prior and the current standard, but the "relevant to the claim or defense" rule (the rule currently in effect) is intended to narrow the scope of discovery and to involve the court more actively in the management of discovery.[1] *See* 8 *Federal Practice and Procedure* § 2008 (2d ed. 1994 & Supp. 2008). Nevertheless, the rule remains very broad and errs on the side of encouraging production. The critical term in Rule 26(b)(1) is "relevant," which includes "any matter that bears on, or that reasonably could lead to other matters that could bear on, any issue that is or may be in the case." *Oil, Chemical & Atomic Workers Local Union No. 6-418, AFL-CIO v. N.L.R.B.*, 711 F.2d 348, 360 (D.C. Cir. 1983). Further, evidence need not be admissible at trial to be discoverable. Specifically, evidence that is relevant but inadmissible is nevertheless subject to discovery if it is "reasonably calculated to lead to the discovery of admissible evidence." Fed. R. Civ. P. 26(b)(1). For example, assume in a case about a car accident that one of the parties has a statement by a witness to the effect that while she was walking by the scene of the accident, she heard someone say that he saw the defendant drive through a red light. Under the hearsay rule discussed in Chapter Eight, this statement would not be admissible to prove that the defendant drove through the red light (and caused the accident). Nevertheless, the statement may be discoverable. Can you see how such a statement is both relevant and reasonably calculated to lead to the discovery of admissible evidence?

Despite the wide net cast by Rule 26(b)(1), discovery can be limited if it is unreasonably cumulative or duplicative or if "the burden or expense of the proposed discovery outweighs its likely benefit, considering the needs of the case, the amount

---

1. Under the current version of Rule 26(b)(1), it is possible for a party, upon a showing of good cause, to expand the scope of discovery to include matters relevant to the subject matter in the litigation.

in controversy, the parties' resources, the importance of the issues at stake in the action, and the importance of the discovery in resolving the issues." Fed. R. Civ. P. 26(b)(2)(C)(i), (iii). For example, if a plaintiff suing his former employer for wrongful termination sought to depose every company employee, including those with whom he never worked, that request certainly could be objected to on the ground that the burden would outweigh any benefit that might be obtained. Similarly, if the plaintiffs in *McNary* had demanded that they depose every single officer at Camp Bulkeley, the government could have objected that the depositions were unreasonably cumulative and perhaps unduly burdensome as well.[2]

    4. Rule 26—Privilege.   There are further limits to discovery. Under Rule 26(b)(1), a party may withhold information from discovery based on a valid assertion of privilege. The privileges most often asserted are: (1) the attorney-client privilege, which applies to all confidential communications between attorney and client in connection with legal representation or the process of obtaining legal representation; (2) the work-product privilege, set out in Rule 26(b)(3), which provides limited protection to trial-preparation and work-product materials (such as an attorney's notes drafted after interviewing a witness, *see Hickman v. Taylor*, 329 U.S. 495 (1947)); (3) the Fifth Amendment privilege against self-incrimination, which provides all persons—not just parties to the litigation—with a privilege against providing information that would tend to incriminate them; and (4) privileges that protect communications with spouses as well as physicians and certain other professionals.[3] A party withholding information based on a claim of privilege must produce a "privilege log"—a document that describes the withheld documents or information in a way that will enable other parties to evaluate the claim of privilege. *See* Fed. R. Civ. P. 26(b)(5). Can you explain the rationale behind each of the privileges set forth in this paragraph?

    5. Rule 26—Protective Orders and Motions to Compel.   If a party wishes to withhold information that the opposing party has requested on any ground other than privilege, he must seek a protective order from the court. Protective orders are designed to protect the parties and witnesses from "annoyance, embarrassment, oppression, or undue burden or expense." Fed. R. Civ. P. 26(c). A protective order can prohibit the requested discovery completely or limit it in specific ways, such as by keeping the information under court seal. Under Rule 26(c), the party or witness seeking a protective order must file a motion—ordinarily before the discovery is to occur—and certify that the moving party conferred or tried to confer with the opposing party to resolve the dispute without the court's involvement. A protective order is available upon a showing of good cause, and the

---

    2. The court may also limit discovery when the information sought "can be obtained from some other source that is more convenient, less burdensome, or less expensive," or when the requesting party has already had "ample opportunity to obtain the information by discovery in the action." Fed. R. Civ. P. 26(b)(2)(C)(i),(ii). Ordinarily a party seeking to limit discovery under Rule 26(b)(2) does so by seeking a protective order under Rule 26(c), as discussed in Note 5.

    3. This last set of privileges, along with the attorney-client privilege, depends on the law of the state where the case is being litigated.

decision to grant one is within the district court's discretion (meaning, essentially, that an appellate court is unlikely to overturn the ruling in the absence of clear error). Absent a protective order, the party can object to the request but must nonetheless produce the information in question.

During the deposition of one of the plaintiffs in *McNary*, the government asked a number of questions about the plaintiff's history of sexually transmitted diseases. As counsel for the plaintiffs, would you seek a protective order to prevent the government from asking these questions? On what basis? (Refer to Rule 26(c).) As counsel for the government at the deposition, how would you respond?

If a party refuses to comply with discovery requests without obtaining a protective order, the opposing party can file a motion to compel production under Rule 37(a). The moving party must make a good faith effort to confer with the other side and resolve the issue before filing the motion. *See* Fed. R. Civ. P. 37(a)(1). The party that prevails on the motion can require the losing party to pay the costs associated with making or defending against the motion. *See* Fed. R. Civ. P. 37(a)(5). Why do you think the rules provide for cost shifting in this situation? In addition, as described in Note 11, a party may be sanctioned under Rule 37 for failure to comply with a motion to compel or with other provisions of the discovery rules.

6. Discovery Methods.   The discovery rules provide for several methods of gathering information. As you review the methods set forth in the following notes and the discussion of depositions in the next chapter, consider the advantages and disadvantages of each type of discovery. Written discovery is one of the most commonly used methods of discovery and is governed primarily by Rules 33 and 34 of the Federal Rules of Civil Procedure. Depositions, which will be discussed in Chapter Seven, provide attorneys with an opportunity to directly question witnesses and parties under oath but can take significant time and resources. The conventional wisdom is that written discovery—obtaining information through document requests and written questions directed to the opposing party—is less expensive but also generally less informative than depositions. Do you agree? Why or why not? Do you think the conventional wisdom held true in the *McNary* litigation? Based on *Storming the Court*, what information do you believe was most helpful to the plaintiffs in preparing their case for trial? Why? How was it obtained?

7. Rule 34—Request for Production of Documents.   Rule 34 governs discovery of documents and other tangible items. This rule, like the rules pertaining to other discovery devices (such as Rule 33 for interrogatories and Rule 30 for depositions) is purely procedural. In other words, it does not govern the *scope* of discovery; scope is established by Rule 26, discussed previously. Rule 34 merely sets out *procedures* for obtaining access to documents and other items within the control of other parties.[4]

---

4. Rule 34 applies only to parties to the litigation. Documents and other tangible items may be obtained from a non-party pursuant to a subpoena authorized by Rule 45. A subpoena is "[a] writ commanding a person to appear before a court or other tribunal, subject to a penalty for failing to comply." BLACK'S LAW DICTIONARY 1467 (8th ed. 2004). The term derives from the Latin phrase *sub poena*, meaning "under a penalty."

The term *documents* is defined broadly in Rule 34(a) and includes all forms of electronically stored information. The rule covers not just pieces of paper, but also, for example, photographs, electronic copies of e-mails, files produced by word-processing, spreadsheet, or other programs, PDF files, MP3 and MPEG files, CDs, and old-fashioned tape cassettes and video recordings. The drafters of the Federal Rules and the courts have continually adapted the definition of "document" to accommodate technological developments that enable the recording and storage of electronic information.[5]

The mechanics of seeking documents and other tangible items under Rule 34 from a party are straightforward: Any party may serve document requests on any other party, who must then respond to those requests in writing within 30 days. The responding party must either produce or make available for inspection the requested documents or state objections as to why the discovery may not be had (say, because of a particular privilege). *See* Fed. R. Civ. P. 34(b).

8. Rule 34 in Practice.   Reproduced in this chapter are documents pertaining to some of the plaintiffs' early discovery requests and the government's responses to those requests. Consider the following questions as you review these documents.

a. In their motion for injunctive relief discussed in Chapter Five, the plaintiffs included requests for discovery, supported by, among other things, the affirmation of Harold Koh. Reproduced here are excerpts from this affirmation:

UNITED STATES DISTRICT COURT
FOR THE EASTERN DISTRICT OF NEW YORK

HAITIAN CENTERS COUNCIL, INC., et al.,   )
)
        Plaintiffs,   )   ————————
)
    v.   ) Civil Action No.
) 92-1258 (Johnson, J.)
GENE McNARY, Commissioner, Immigration   )
and Naturalization Service, et al.,   )
)
        Defendants.   )

---

5. On December 1, 2006, the Federal Rules were amended specifically to address issues related to the discovery of electronically stored information. Given the amount of material that is available in electronic form today and the number of formats in which this information may be stored, the potential burden and expense of electronic discovery, particularly in large cases, can be significant. One of the most important changes associated with the 2006 amendments was the requirement that the parties discuss the exchange of electronically stored information—such as whether electronic discovery will be sought and the forms in which electronic information should be produced—at their initial meeting to establish a discovery plan. *See* Fed. R. Civ. P. 26(f)(3)(C).

AFFIRMATION OF HAROLD HONGJU KOH

* * * *

Harold Hongju Koh, under penalty of perjury, hereby affirms:

1. I am one of the attorneys for the plaintiffs in the above-captioned case and make this affirmation in support of plaintiffs' order to show cause why expedited discovery should not be granted.

2. This Court's Temporary Restraining Order of March 27, 1992, afforded "screened-in" Haitians on Guantanamo access to counsel. Almost immediately, the rate at which defendant INS "screened-in" interdicted Haitians began to drop precipitously. According to figures supplied by State Department officials to Congressman Howard Berman, Haitians were being "screened-in" at a rate of 39 percent before April 1, 1992. The rate between April 1 and April 8, however, declined to 10 percent. Between April 8 and April 12, a mere 2 percent of interviewed Haitians were being "screened in." During those five days, defendants interviewed 1921 Haitians, but "screened in" only 48.

* * * *

7. Defendants' actions since April 1 thus constitute a deliberate effort to avoid the Court's preliminary injunction by eviscerating the certified class of "screened-in" plaintiffs who are subject to the protection of the Court's order. Defendants apparently seek to divest the Court of jurisdiction by completely eliminating the class of screened-in plaintiffs.

8. Pursuant to Rule 34(b), the plaintiffs request that the Court accept plaintiffs' proposed deposition schedule and allow ten days for defendants to respond to all document requests. The shorter time period is necessitated by the potential prejudice to the plaintiff class due to defendants' recent actions giving rise to this motion.

9. Pursuant to Local Rule 3(c)(4) of the Southern and Eastern Districts of New York, an order to show cause is necessary in the instant case because of the good and sufficient reasons that thousands of uncounseled Haitians, many of whom may have credible fears of persecution, have been repatriated to Haiti in the days following issuance of this Court's Temporary Restraining Order and Preliminary Injunction Order. See Wright & Miller, 1195 at n. 1. See also, Westhemco Ltd. v. New Hampshire, 82 F.R.D. 702, 705 n. 1 (S.D.N.Y. 1979). Any of these repatriated Haitians who had a credible fear of political persecution upon return to Haiti were members of the provisionally certified plaintiff class and would have remained under this Court's jurisdiction but for defendants' action of wrongfully repatriating them. The motivations for and extent of defendants' actions can best be known through granting expedited discovery.

10. No other request for this relief has been made to any other judge of this Court.

CONCLUSION

It is of deep concern to the plaintiffs that defendants' response to this Court's orders may be to screen out hundreds of refugees who have a credible fear of persecution. Such actions would foreclose the possibility that the protections this Court has ensured to the plaintiffs' class can extend to future screened-in refugees.

By effectively ceasing screening in Haitian refugees who may have a credible fear of persecution, the defendants are making final asylum determinations on the Coast Guard Cutters; they may be repatriating Haitians with a credible fear of persecution to face torture or death; and they have decided that such proceedings do not warrant the protection of counsel.

> All of these actions run contrary to this Court's Order of April 6 which assumed that no Haitian with a credible fear of persecution would be "screened out" and required that those "screened in" would be given protection of counsel before they could be sent back to Haiti.
>
>   Based on this new information, the possibility that defendants are circumventing the order of the Court, and the inherent powers of this Court to protect its ability to issue binding judgments, this Court should immediately grant the requested discovery.
>
> * * * *

Note the way in which the affirmation implicitly acknowledges the authority and general timing requirements of the rules and then explains why those requirements should not be followed here. What are the plaintiffs requesting and why? Should Judge Johnson have granted the expedited request for discovery? Why or why not?

b. Review the Plaintiffs' Second Request for Production of Documents, reproduced here:

UNITED STATES DISTRICT COURT
EASTERN DISTRICT OF NEW YORK

HAITIAN CENTERS COUNCIL, INC., et al.,   )
)
            Plaintiffs,   )
)
    v.   )   Civil Action No.
)   92-1258 (Johnson, J.)
GENE McNARY, Commissioner, Immigration   )
and Naturalization Service, et al.,   )
)
            Defendants.   )

PLAINTIFF'S SECOND REQUEST FOR PRODUCTION OF
DOCUMENTS

    PLEASE TAKE NOTICE that pursuant to Rule 34 of the Federal Rules of Civil Procedure, plaintiffs hereby request and demand that defendants produce and permit plaintiffs to inspect and copy the documents listed below commencing at 10:00 a.m. on the 17th of April, 1992, at such place as agreed to by counsel.

DEFINITIONS

    Plaintiffs incorporate the definitions from their First Request for Production of Documents as if set forth fully herein.

INSTRUCTIONS

Plaintiffs incorporate the definitions from their First Request for Production of Documents as if set forth fully herein.

DOCUMENTS TO BE PRODUCED

1. On the most expedited basis, all documents directing or otherwise relating or referring to the fact that the screened-in rate for Haitians should be, was, or is capped at a certain level or is, has been, or should be lowered.

2. On the most expedited basis, all documents dated after February 24, 1992 which refer or relate to country reports, situation reports, or the Resources Information Center, regarding Haiti or information on which defendants rely on or have relied on, in making screening determinations about Haitians.

3. On the most expedited basis, all documents dated after January 1, 1991 which refer or relate to State Department evaluations, including but not limited to evaluations written by officials and staff members of the Bureau of Human Rights and Humanitarian Affairs, that refer or relate to conditions in Haiti.

4. On an expedited basis, all documents dated after the filing of the complaint in this lawsuit on March 18, 1992 which refer or relate to United States government practices regarding the screening or interviewing of Haitians detained at Guantanamo Naval Base, on United States Coast Guard cutters, or elsewhere in territory subject to United States jurisdiction.

5. To the extent that defendants have failed to produce all the documents earlier requested by plaintiffs, plaintiffs renew their First Request for Production of Documents, and renew the request for documents set forth in Harold Hongju Koh's letter to Lauri Steven Filppu dated March 28, 1992 memorializing the major points of the status conference with Judge Sterling Johnson held on March 28, 1992.

6. All documents which refer or relate to lost records of Haitians.

7. All documents which refer or relate to computer errors, hardcopy errors, mistaken identification of refugees having been screened-in or screened-out.

8. All documents containing statements by defendants expressing the belief that repatriated Haitians would suffer or had suffered persecution on their return to Haiti.

9. All documents which refer or relate to investigations by defendants of persecution suffered by repatriated Haitians.

10. All interagency documents which refer or relate to the screening or re-screening process taking place on Guantanamo Bay or on Coast Guard cutters or elsewhere in territory subject to U.S. jurisdiction.

11. All documents which refer or relate to country conditions in Haiti relied upon by defendants in making screening and asylum determinations for Haitians since October 1991.

12. All documents which refer or relate to refusal or granting of access to lawyers to Guantanamo Bay Naval Base since October 1991.

13. All documents which refer or relate to changes in rates of Haitians being screened-in and screened-out.

14. All documents dated August-December 1981 which refer or relate to the U.S.-Haitian Agreement, Executive Order 12,324 establishing the Alien Migrant Interdiction Operation or the Haitian Migrant Interdiction Program or that program as otherwise referred to.

15. All documents which refer or relate to the interdiction of non-Haitians pursuant to Executive Order 12,324.

16. All Executive Agreements entered into pursuant to the President's directive in Executive Order 12,324.

17. All documents, not otherwise specifically called for above, which refer or relate to the allegations set forth in plaintiffs' complaint.

Dated: New York, New York
        April _16_, 1992

* * * *

Why are the plaintiffs requesting this information? Why do they include date limitations in their requests? Given what plaintiffs are trying to accomplish, what documents among those they are requesting would be most helpful to them?

Now imagine that you are the government attorney responsible for coordinating the collection of this information. Make the "to-do list" necessary to respond to this request—all the way down to the telephone calls you will have to make. For instance, how are you going to gather the information sought in request no. 3, regarding State Department evaluations of conditions in Haiti? (Writing down "Call State Department" isn't the answer. Who do you need to talk to at the State Department? How do you get to that person? What if he doesn't respond to your phone call or e-mail for two days?) Keep in mind that the person you are looking for might be busy with an important matter unrelated to your agenda. Then who do you call? How do you ask that person to help you? Remember, he or she is probably crushed with other work and may not be interested in hearing about some court order on a case that isn't a major concern for that person.

As the government attorney, do you think any of the requests call for the production of records that should be withheld on the grounds of privilege? Which requests, and why? (In answering this question, you should consult both Note 4 in this chapter and Note 12 in Chapter Seven on the deliberative process privilege.)

c. Now review the government's response to the Plaintiffs' Second Request for Production of Documents, reproduced here:

```
        IN THE UNITED STATES DISTRICT COURT
      FOR THE EASTERN DISTRICT OF NEW YORK


HAITIAN CENTERS COUNCIL, INC., et al.,   )
                                         )
              Plaintiffs,                )
                                         )
     v.                                  )      No. 92-CV-1258
                                         )
GENE MCNARY, COMMISSIONER,               )
IMMIGRATION AND NATURALIZATION SERVICE,  )
et al.,                                  )
                                         )
              Defendants.                )
_____)
```

DEFENDANTS' RESPONSE TO
PLAINTIFFS' SECOND REQUEST FOR PRODUCTION OF
DOCUMENTS

Pursuant to Rule 34 of the Federal Rules of Civil Procedure, defendants hereby make their written response to plaintiffs' second request for production of documents.

DISCOVERY PRODUCTION

On March 31, 1992, pursuant to an agreement between counsel, defendants provided plaintiffs access to all documents produced in Haitian Refugees Center, Inc. v. Baker, 949 F.2d 1109 (11th Cir. 1991), 953 F.2d 1498 (11th Cir. 1992), cert. denied, 112 S. Ct. 1245 (1992) ("HRC"). Counsel for plaintiffs identified documents they wanted copied, and copies of the documents were provided them that evening. Defendants also provided plaintiffs on March 31, 1992 under the terms of the stipulation and order signed on March 30, 1992, documents numbered 10,000 through 10,820 which had not been produced in the HRC litigation. Documents in this case numbered 10,000 and up were not produced in the HRC litigation.

On May 4, 1992, defendants produced documents numbered 10,813 through 14,001 and a draft log showing documents to which a privilege attaches ("Privilege Log") comprising 180 pages. This is a draft document subject to revision upon further review by defendants.

Counsel for plaintiffs were given an opportunity to review INS documents normally on file in Guantanamo on Tuesday, May 5, 1992, Wednesday, May 5, 1992 and Friday, May 8, 1992 at the Miami INS Asylum Office. On May 8, 1992, defendants produced pages numbered M1 through M794; on May 11, 1992, documents numbered M795 through M1,047; on May 13, 1992, documents numbered M1,048 through M1,335; and on May 15, 1992, documents numbered M1,336 through M1,890.

Why does the government spend the first several paragraphs recounting the status of production? This is not usual, and may reflect the government lawyers' effort to create a record showing their good faith in responding to plaintiffs' discovery requests in the event that plaintiffs file a motion to compel.

Note the description of the privilege log, discussed previously in Note 4. Consider the amount of time required to compile a privilege log of this length.

Parties responding to requests for documents can either send copies of the documents to the requesting party or provide the requesting party with the option of reviewing the documents at the location where they usually are kept.

Each document produced in litigation receives a unique number, called a Bates number, when it is produced to the other side. (The Bates Manufacturing Company invented an automatic numbering machine in the late 1800s.)

Consider the description here of the difficult circumstances the government says hindered its efforts to collect and copy the documents sought by the plaintiffs. Why does the government include this description? Note that Rule 26, as amended in 1993 and again in 2007, imposes a continuing obligation on parties to supplement their disclosures if they later learn that their earlier disclosures were incomplete or incorrect. *See* Fed. R. Civ. P. 26(e).

Defendants herewith produce the following items:

(1) Documents numbered 14,002 through 21,570;

(2) A draft log showing documents to which a privilege attaches ("Privilege Log") comprising 320 pages. This is a cumulative draft log, meaning that the draft log provided herewith incorporates the pages from the draft log produced on May 4, 1992. This is a draft document subject to revision upon further review by defendants.

Compliance with the requests for production involves the efforts of several Federal agencies in locating, copying, reviewing, and making available thousands of pages of documents from as far away as Guantanamo Bay, Cuba. Because of the sheer number of documents involved as well as the difficulty in coordinating efforts among the agencies and the Department of Justice, documents continue to be located and reviewed. Barring unforeseen developments, defendants intend to regularly produce documents responsive to plaintiffs' first and second requests for production of documents. Defendants also intend to regularly produce an updated version of the draft privilege log, as privileged documents are received from the client agencies, reviewed by Justice Department attorneys and added to the draft privilege log.

OBJECTIONS

Defendants do not waive any objection to any portion of any request for production by not setting it out at this time.

Defendants restate all objections previously stated in their response to plaintiffs' first request for production as though set out herein at length.

1. General Objection

Paragraph Four of the instructions contained in the First Request for Production states that in the event that any document called for in the request is destroyed, that document is to be identified by addressor, addressee, indicated or blind copies, date, subject matter, number of pages, attachments or appendices, all persons to whom distributed, shown or explained, date of destruction, persons authorizing destruction and persons destroying the document. Defendants object to this instruction as burdensome and not required by Rule or order of the Court. Documents are regularly destroyed in the normal course of business (for example, by the recipient of a teletype) and no record is kept of the destruction.

2. Specific Objections

a.   To the extent that ¶2 of the First Request for Production can be read to require production of all documents in the custody and control of the Guantanamo Joint Task Force (JTF), that relate to "any and all Haitians who have been detained at Guantanamo", and to the extent that ¶4 can be read to require production of all documents that refer or relate to Haitians who have been screened-in and are being held at Guantanamo, defendants object to such production as unduly burdensome.

b. To the extent that ¶¶ 2 and 4 of the First Request for Production can be read to require production of medical records in the custody and control of the JTF, defendants object to such production as unduly burdensome, not likely to lead to discoverable evidence, and not within the scope of the lawsuit. Approximately one-third of the JTF documents are medical files for Haitians at Guantanamo, screened-in or screened-out. Defendants object to the production of any medical records because plaintiffs have not provided signed releases for any such records.

c. To the extent that ¶¶ 2 and 4 of the First Request for Production can be read to require production of records of requisitions and other logistical matters, defendants object to such production. The JTF maintains several thousand pages of documents concerning the ordering of supplies and deployment of personnel to Guantanamo. While those documents may arguably "refer or relate" to detained Haitians at Guantanamo, the request for production is overbroad, and production of these JTF records will add nothing to the issues in the case, is unlikely to lead to discoverable evidence, and is not within the scope of the lawsuit. Defendants object to production of those documents.

What is the government's objection here? (Recall that JTF stands for Joint Task Force.) How would you respond to such an objection if you were counsel for the plaintiffs?

To comply with the request for production, Justice Department attorneys are working with JTF counsel to identify relevant documents, review them for assertion of appropriate privileges, and provide them to plaintiffs' counsel. Defendants will continue to produce copies of such documents.

d. To the extent that ¶¶ 2 and 4 of the First Request for Production can be read to require the production of desk blotters (including but not limited to reports of: criminal investigation, suspicious or potentially dangerous activities by migrants, and disturbances or violence within the camp) maintained by the Military Police at Guantanamo, defendants object to the production of such documents as irrelevant to the issues in the lawsuit and unlikely to lead to discoverable evidence. Further, the review of such reports and the redaction of privileged material from them would be burdensome. Defendants have not produced the desk blotters.

e. Paragraph 14 of the Second Request for Production requests production of all documents dated August-December 1981 which refer or relate to the U.S.-Haitian Agreement, Executive Order 12,234 establishing the Alien Migrant Interdiction Operation or the Haitian Migrant Interdiction Program or that program as otherwise referred to. Defendants object to production of documents under this paragraph. Plaintiffs have been given the opportunity to review the documents produced by defendants in Haitian Refugee Center v. Baker, 949 F.2d 1109 (11th Cir. 1991), 953 F.2d 1498 (11th Cir. 1992), cert. denied, 112 S. Ct. 1245 (1992). Plaintiffs identified numerous documents they wished to be copied, and were provided copies of the documents they identified. The material they reviewed contains 1981 documents pertaining to the AMIO.

* * * *

In its responses, the government lawyers both provided responsive documents and properly objected to certain instructions in the plaintiffs' requests. The government asserted that: (a) the production of certain categories of documents would be unduly burdensome, (b) certain other requests were overbroad, and (c) production of some requested records was "unlikely to lead to discoverable evidence" and was "not within the scope of the lawsuit." *See* Fed. R. Civ. P. 26(b)(1). Which objections do you agree with? Why? If the government thought these requests were objectionable, why did it not seek a protective order?

d. Ultimately, the government filed at least *18* separate responses (meaning 18 collections of documents) to the plaintiffs' requests for the production of documents. Filing multiple consecutive responses (as opposed to just one response with all of the requested documents) is not common and reflects yet another unusual aspect of the *McNary* case. What in particular might have led defense counsel to produce documents in waves like this? Among other possible explanations, the government had to search for records on Guantánamo, and the personnel there had almost certainly *not* been storing records with the possibility of litigation in mind.

To consider just one aspect of gathering records on Guantánamo, recall that for the first several months after the military coup in Haiti, the INS, military, and Coast Guard were simply struggling to keep up with the influx of Haitians. They were transporting, housing, feeding, and interviewing thousands of non–English-speaking refugees in a chaotic, windy, outdoor environment, with inadequate office space and data storage facilities. Recordkeeping was bound to be a problem—and it was. Given the circumstances, perhaps the large number of updated responses from the government should come as no surprise.

Haitian children playing at Camp Bulkeley, fall 1992. Photograph courtesy of Stephen Kinder.

The government's many responses might also have reflected a strategic attempt to *appear* diligent in responding to the plaintiffs' discovery requests. The plaintiffs' lawyers often sparred with government counsel over the delays involved in the production of documents in pretrial discovery. The Yale team viewed the delays as an effort to impede its investigation into the conditions on Guantánamo and to postpone the trial. From Yale's perspective, the delays were especially galling given their perception of the disparity in resources between the plaintiffs and the government and the fact that the government controlled plaintiffs' counsel's access to their clients. The government lawyers rejected this characterization of their actions. They saw the plaintiffs' case as a legally untenable, resource-draining attempt to interfere with an extremely complicated situation on Guantánamo, and the government lawyers insisted they were doing the best they could to comply with their discovery obligations. In this regard, you may wish to review Lauri Filppu's request to postpone the trial and Joe Tringali's response. *See STC*, pp. 155-56.

9. *Rule 33—Interrogatories.*   Rule 33 governs the process of obtaining information through written questions, known as "interrogatories." The procedures for serving and answering interrogatories are similar to the procedures for document requests. The party seeking information serves the interrogatories and the party receiving them has 30 days to respond. Typically, the response will include written answers to the questions, along with objections, such as an objection that the question seeks information unlikely to lead to discoverable evidence. Fed. R. Civ. P. 26(b)(1). Note that although it is common for the attorney to draft the responses, the *party* must sign the answers to the interrogatories (*see* Fed. R. Civ. P. 33(b)(2))—and good practice calls for the attorney to review the responses with the client. The current version of the rule, adopted in 2000, limits the number of interrogatories to 25, although a party may seek the court's permission to serve more. Parties cannot serve interrogatories on non-parties.

10. *Rule 33 in Practice.*   At the time of the *McNary* litigation, there was no limit on the number of interrogatories that a party could serve on another party. Below is one of the sets of interrogatories that the government served on the plaintiffs.

IN THE UNITED STATES DISTRICT COURT
FOR THE EASTERN DISTRICT OF NEW YORK

HAITIAN CENTERS COUNCIL, INC., et al.,   )
)
              Plaintiffs,   )
)
       v.   )   No. 92-CV-1258
)
GENE MCNARY, COMMISSIONER,   )
IMMIGRATION AND NATURALIZATION SERVICE,)
et al.,   )
)
              Defendants.   )
)

DEFENDANTS' THIRD SET OF INTERROGATORIES

DEFENDANTS Gene McNary, Commissioner Immigration and Naturalization Service, et al., submit to plaintiffs the following interrogatories, which are to be answered separately and fully in writing under oath in accordance with the procedures specified in Fed. R. Civ. P. 33. Unless otherwise indicated, all information is required as of the date of the answers, and these interrogatories are deemed to be continuing to the full extent allowed by law. By propounding these interrogatories, defendants do not waive any objections they may have to relevance or materiality of any of plaintiffs' evidence.

DEFINITIONS

As used herein:

Today, the definition of "document" should also include various forms of electronically stored information.

I. The term "document" means any written or graphic matter or other means of preserving thought or expression, including, but not limited to, correspondence, contracts, memoranda, handwritten notes, applications, medical records, x-rays, leases, notebooks, books, brochures, studies, surveys, graphs, charts, calculations, analyses, drawings, reports, bills, invoices, checks, check stubs, clippings, computer printouts, tape recordings, photographs, videotapes, microfilm, transcripts, diary entries, desk calendar entries, appointment books, telephone message slips, telephone logs and expense reports, whether originals, copies or drafts, however produced or reproduced. Any copy of a document which contains information or markings not contained on the original of the document should be considered a separate document.

"Plaintiffs' Guantanamo travel contingent" includes all attorneys, law students, translators or interpreters, medical personnel, representatives of plaintiffs, and any other person travelling to Guantanamo Bay, Cuba, as part of any of plaintiffs' groups that have gone to Guantanamo since March 15, 1992.

II. The term "identify" when used in reference to a natural person means to:

(A) State his/her full name and title;

(B) State his/her present or last known business and residential address and telephone number at each address;

III. The term "identify" when used in reference to a document means to

(A) state the date of preparation, author, title, subject matter, and type of document. If the document cannot be identified in this manner, state some other means of distinguishing the document; and

(B) state whether you are in possession or control of the document, and, if not, state the name, address and telephone number of each person who has the original or a copy of the document.

See also "Uniform Definitions in Discovery Request," Rule 47 of the Joint Civil Rules of the Southern and Eastern Districts of New York, which were adopted by this Court on December 22, 1987 and deemed incorporated by reference into all discovery requests.

INSTRUCTIONS

I. If you cannot answer any interrogatory in full after exercising due diligence to secure the information to do so, answer the interrogatory to the extent possible, explain any inability to answer, and state the information presently available to you concerning the unanswered portion.

II. If you elect to produce any document in response to one or more of these interrogatories, indicate to which interrogatory or part thereof the document responds.

III. Each interrogatory should be construed so as to make the interrogatory inclusive rather than exclusive. Thus, words importing the singular shall include the plural; words importing the plural shall include the singular; words importing the masculine gender may be applied to females; and words importing the feminine gender may be applied to males; "and" and "or" shall be construed conjunctively or disjunctively as necessary to make the interrogatory inclusive.

> Interrogatories and document requests often include provisions regarding their interpretation to limit the ability of the opposing party to avoid disclosure through an overly narrow interpretation of the request.

IV. If you refuse to answer an interrogatory, state in detail the basis for your refusal. See Standing Orders of the Court on Effective Discovery In Civil Cases Rule 21(b), Eastern District of New York.

INTERROGATORIES

The interrogatories in the instant request correspond to the simultaneously-served Defendants' Second Request for Production of Documents. As to the documents demanded in that request, provide the following information.

1. As to plaintiffs' witness Nanaj (or "Ninaj") Raoul,

   (a) identify all documents which the witness will use, refer to, or rely on at trial, and

   (b) identify all other documents relating to the proposed testimony of this witness.

> Parties often use interrogatories to request identification of trial witnesses and documents, although such requests can be duplicative of the pretrial disclosures required by Rule 26(a)(3). It can be helpful, however, to ask for other documents relating to the witness's testimony that the opposing party does not intend to use at trial. These other documents may not necessarily be disclosed pursuant to Rule 26(a)(3) but may nevertheless shed additional light on the opposing party's case.

2. As to plaintiffs' witness Stephen Roos,

   (a) identify all documents which the witness will use, refer to, or rely on at trial, and

   (b) identify all other documents relating to the proposed testimony of this witness.

3. As to plaintiffs' witness Paul Wickham Schmidt,

   (a) identify all documents which the witness will use, refer to, or rely on at trial, and

   (b) identify all other documents relating to the proposed testimony of this witness.

> As noted previously, parties are currently limited to 25 interrogatories. For purposes of this limitation, each "discrete subpart" is considered a separate interrogatory. Fed. R. Civ. P. 33(a)(1). This prevents parties from avoiding the limit by relying heavily on subparts. Subparts (a) and (b) in interrogatories 1-3, however, are so related that the government could have argued that, together, the two subparts should in each instance be considered only one interrogatory.

* * * *

Defendants served these interrogatories in February 1993. What might have led them to seek the information identified in interrogatories nos.19-21? *See STC*, pp. 191-94. Recall that Harold Koh, Michael Ratner, Lucas Guttentag, and Ronald Aubourg visited Haiti in January 1993 to investigate conditions there. Defendants evidently knew about the visit and wanted copies of any pictures, audiotapes or videotapes that the group had taken, made, or obtained while in Haiti. How is this material relevant to the *McNary* case? Might it have played a different role in February 1993 than in March 1992? How?

19. State whether plaintiffs, or their attorneys or agents, made any still photographs of any Haitian or other foreign national, or of any United States Government employee or other United States citizen, or of any other person or thing in or around Haiti. If the answer to this Interrogatory is "yes",

(a) identify the photograph(s),

(b) identify any person(s) who created, developed, or otherwise prepared the photograph(s), and

(c) identify any person(s) who viewed the photograph(s).

20. State whether plaintiffs, or their attorneys or agents, are in possession of any video or tape recording of any Haitian or other foreign national, or of any United States Government employee or other United States citizen, or of any other person or thing in or around Haiti not otherwise produced by defendants in response to discovery requests. If the answer to this Interrogatory is "yes",

(a) identify the video or tape recording(s),

(b) identify any person(s) who created, edited, otherwise prepared the video or tape recording(s), and

(c) identify any person(s) who viewed or listened to the video or tape recording(s).

How is Interrogatory no. 21 different from no. 19? Consider this: What if someone in Hinche (*see STC*, p. 193) had given Koh a photograph of a dead Aristide supporter? Would plaintiffs have been required to produce that photograph in response to no. 19? Note that these interrogatories were necessary in order to get certain information about each photograph or other item from Haiti that the plaintiffs produced to the defendants. By framing this as an interrogatory instead of a document request, the government was able to ask for information about each photograph or other item from Haiti that the plaintiffs produced to the defendants.

21. State whether plaintiffs, or their attorneys or agents, are in possession of any still photographs of any Haitian or other foreign national, or of any United States Government employee or other United States citizen, or of any other person or thing in or around Haiti not otherwise produced by defendants in response to discovery requests. If the answer to this Interrogatory is "yes",

(a) identify the photograph(s),

(b) identify any person(s) who created, developed, or otherwise prepared the photograph(s), and

(c) identify any person(s) who viewed the photograph(s).

* * * *

Review the definitions and instructions at the beginning of the Defendants' Third Set of Interrogatories. As you can see, the term *document* is defined broadly and the term *identify* is defined with demanding precision. If you were a member of the Yale team, would you object to any aspect of these definitions? The government has also provided specific instructions on what steps the plaintiffs are to take in connection with answering the interrogatories. Would you object to any aspect of the instructions? Note that both the definitions and the instructions include references to the Local Rules for the Eastern District of New York.

Review Interrogatories 1 through 3. Note that these interrogatories were served with less than a month to go before trial. As it turned out, the parties ultimately agreed to provide the requested information through an exchange of witness summaries, making these interrogatories unnecessary. Why might it be unlikely to see such interrogatories at the outset of discovery?

Neither plaintiffs nor defendants in *McNary* made much use of interrogatories. Interrogatories can be helpful in obtaining certain types of information but generally have limited value as a discovery device. That is because the answering party has time to craft a response, is not present to be evaluated for credibility, and is not available for immediate follow-up questions. Interrogatories are best used to require a party to state its contentions—that is, its principal arguments—in the case, to obtain technical or statistical data, and to learn the identity and location of persons with knowledge about the case. In *McNary*, the plaintiffs and the government already were well versed in many of the contentions of the other side because of the extensive litigation over the plaintiffs' initial request for injunctive relief. And the use of other discovery devices—requests for the production of documents and depositions—may have made extensive use of interrogatories unnecessary for obtaining data or learning the identity of witnesses. (In Interrogatories 19 through 21, the government asks questions that amount to requests for the production of certain documents.)

11. Sanctions.   Earlier, we emphasized the self-executing nature of the discovery rules. What happens when a party does not comply with the rules? Rule 37 authorizes the court to impose sanctions on the non-compliant party. Generally, a party seeking sanctions must first obtain an order compelling discovery under Rule 37(a). If the opposing party refuses to comply with the order, the party seeking the discovery may then move, under Rule 37(b), for sanctions. In situations involving a party's complete failure to participate in the discovery process—for example, a party's failure to attend his or her own deposition—sanctions are available without seeking an order compelling discovery. *See* Fed. R. Civ. P. 37(d).

The court may impose a variety of sanctions, ranging from an order that deems certain facts to be established against the non-complying party to entry of judgment against the non-complying party. *See* Fed. R. Civ. P. 37(b)(2). In *McNary*, the parties' conduct during the discovery process largely did not give rise to conduct worthy of sanctions under Rule 37. Can you think of any instances discussed in *Storming the Court* that might have been sanctionable?

CHAPTER SEVEN

Discovery: Depositions

INTRODUCTION

Written discovery, as detailed in Chapter Six, essentially involves the parties—with plenty of help from their attorneys—exchanging pieces of paper and electronic files. Depositions are a much more dynamic process: attorneys questioning parties or witnesses under oath. Deponents (the people who are being deposed) must respond to all manner of questions on the spot, often revealing information they would rather not. As a result, depositions can be a particularly valuable form of discovery, enabling lawyers to learn important new information about the case and to pin down testimony that they can use to their advantage during cross-examination at trial.

At the same time, depositions can be quite expensive. There are attorneys' fees for the lawyers taking and defending the deposition. A court reporter must be paid to transcribe the deposition. Travel expenses for the lawyers and deponents can add up, as well. Nevertheless, any attorney will be quick to say that depositions are an indispensable discovery tool, and even the most basic preparation of a case requires the taking of one or more depositions. This chapter will explore the deposition process using excerpts from the depositions of Colonel Stephen Kinder of the United States Army and plaintiff Yvonne Pascal.

NOTES AND COMMENTS

1. Rule 30—The Basics. Rule 30 governs the procedures for scheduling, taking, and defending depositions. Under the current version of Rule 30, each side is entitled to only 10 depositions. Fed. R. Civ. P. 30(a)(2)(A)(i). In addition, the length of a deposition is limited to "1 day of 7 hours." Fed. R. Civ. P. 30(d)(1). These limits may be modified by agreement or court order.

Depositions, like discovery generally, are self-executing, meaning that a party need not seek the court's permission to depose a witness except in limited circumstances not relevant here. *See* Fed. R. Civ. P. 30(a)(1), (2). To schedule a deposition, Rule 30(b)(1) requires that a party provide "reasonable written notice" to all of the other parties in the case, stating the time and place of the deposition. The deponent may be required to produce documents at the deposition. Fed. R. Civ. P. 30(b)(2). Unless otherwise agreed by the parties, the deposition must be conducted before an officer designated under Rule 28—generally, an officer authorized by law to administer oaths. Traditionally, this is a court reporter, who swears in the deponent and transcribes the deposition as it takes place using a special stenographic machine. A deposition may also be taped with audio or audiovisual equipment. Fed. R. Civ. P. 30(b)(3)(A).

2. Deposition Mechanics.   A deposition shares some similarities with the examination of witnesses at trial. The attorney conducting the deposition asks questions of the deponent, while the opposing attorney—who "defends" the deposition—listens and, where appropriate, objects to the questions.[1] The opposing attorney then has the right to ask follow-up or clarifying questions of the witness she is defending. Despite these similarities, a deposition serves very different purposes than a witness examination at trial. Trial is not the time for lawyers to uncover the facts behind the parties' allegations; the lawyers should already know those facts cold. Rather, as we will discuss in Chapter Eight, the purpose of examining a witness at trial is to provide testimony necessary to prove the party's case to the jury or judge and to challenge the other side's position.

In contrast, the purpose of the deposition is to do the investigative work necessary to prepare for trial: to find out what the parties and witnesses know about the events that gave rise to the case. During a deposition, an attorney will generally ask a great deal about the witness's role in, and understandings and recollections of, those events. The attorney will also probe the accuracy of the witness's perceptions and memory and try to assess the witness's credibility and persuasiveness. In addition, the attorney may ask the witness to identify individuals and documents that might provide additional information relevant to the case—potentially leading to more depositions. Finally, and of great importance, an attorney will aim to force parties and witnesses to commit to a particular version of the events in dispute in a case, thus preventing them from trying to change their story once in court.

3. Using Deposition Testimony at Trial.   Generally, witnesses must appear at trial to give their testimony. A witness's deposition can be used at trial in lieu of his or her live testimony in court only in limited circumstances.[2] The deposition testimony of a *party*, however, constitutes what is known as an "admission" and is admissible at trial for any purpose. *See* Fed. R. Civ. P. 32(a)(3); *see also* Fed. R. Civ. P. 32(a)(1). This rule illustrates another important purpose of a deposition—to elicit admissions from the opposing party that undermine the opposing party's case.

Further, in the case of both parties and witnesses, deposition testimony can be used to "impeach"—challenge or discredit—the party or witness's trial testimony. Fed. R. Civ. P. 32(a)(2). For example, in an auto accident case, assume that a witness says in her deposition that she couldn't remember whether the traffic light was red or green for the plaintiff at the time of the accident. In court, however, she claims that the light was green for the plaintiff. In that event, defense counsel could introduce the witness's deposition testimony to impeach her credibility regarding her recollection of the color of the light.

---

1. Objections are discussed in Note 8.
2. Deposition testimony generally cannot be used at trial for several reasons, including the fact that it may constitute hearsay, which is discussed in Note 14 of Chapter Eight.

Finally, depositions can also be introduced in lieu of live testimony when the witness would be "unavailable" to testify at trial—that is, unable to attend because of illness, death, distance, or other specified reasons. Fed. R. Civ. P. 32(a)(4). In these circumstances, it is important to preserve the witness's testimony under oath for use at trial. This was the situation faced by the Yale team. Because the government would not allow the plaintiffs to enter the United States, they could not testify at trial. Their testimony therefore had to be preserved via deposition so that it could be read into the record during the trial.

Deposing one's own witness is relatively uncommon; a party generally deposes only the opposing party and his witnesses. (Can you explain why?) Depositions taken of the opposing party or his witnesses—the most common type of deposition—will generally resemble cross-examinations. Where, however, parties depose their own witnesses to preserve that testimony at trial, the deposition will be much more like a direct examination, with the attorney seeking to elicit favorable rather than damaging testimony. This was the case in Yvonne Pascal's deposition, where law student Veronique Sanchez conducted the deposition with the aim of enabling Pascal to tell her story in the most favorable light possible. Government lawyer Lauri Filppu then conducted the cross-examination with the aim of undermining Pascal's position. (Recall that there was no redirect examination by Sanchez or recross by Filppu because Yvonne Pascal fell ill at the conclusion of Filppu's cross-examination of her. *See STC*, p. 222.)

4. The Timing of Depositions.   Depositions can be taken at any point during the discovery process, and the timing of a deposition depends on the purpose for which the information is sought. Most depositions are taken later in the discovery process, after an attorney has gathered information through requests for documents and interrogatories. Can you explain why this might be so? Sometimes, however, it can be useful to take a deposition in the early stages of discovery. An early deposition can help establish the opposing party's version of the facts or provide information helpful for conducting additional discovery, such as the location of electronically stored information.

5. Noticing Depositions.   Depositions are generally initiated by sending a notice to the party to be deposed, a process that is called "noticing" a deposition. The notice contains the time and place of the deposition. The plaintiffs' notice for the deposition of a number of government officials, below, is an example.

**UNITED STATES DISTRICT COURT
EASTERN DISTRICT OF NEW YORK**

- x

Haitian Centers Council, Inc., et. al.

:

         Plaintiffs,

:   **NOTICE TO TAKE**

vs.   **DEPOSITIONS UPON**

:   **ORAL EXAMINATION**

Gene McNary, Commissioner, Immigration
and Naturalization Service, et. al.,   :   **92 Civ. 1258**
                                         (Johnson, J.)

         Defendants.   :

- x

SIRS:

PLEASE TAKE NOTICE, that plaintiffs, Haitian Centers Council, et. al., will take the depositions upon oral examination of the defendants and plaintiffs, before a notary public duly authorized to administer oaths and take testimony, at Guantanamo Bay Naval Base, Miami, Florida, Washington, D.C. or wherever they may reside, at the times and dates set forth below:

Deponent	Time and Date
Scott Busby	10:00 a.m., April 20, 1992
Tina McCoy	2:00 p.m., April 20, 1992
Gregg Beyer	10:00 a.m., April 21, 1992
Donna Hrinak	2:00 p.m., April 21, 1992
Gunter Wagner	10:00 a.m., April 22, 1992
James McClean	2:00 p.m., April 22, 1992
Brunson McKinley	9:00 a.m., April 24, 1992
The military officer best in a position to have knowledge of any directive from military or national security personel regarding screen-in rates or procedures	3:00 p.m., April 24,1992
Gene McNary	10:00 a.m., April 27, 28, 1992

PLEASE TAKE FURTHER NOTICE, that the aforesaid depositions will continue from day to day until completed. You are invited to attend and cross-examine.

Dated: New Haven, Connecticut
    April 16, 1992

LOWENSTEIN INTERNATIONAL HUMAN RIGHTS CLINIC

By: _Harold H. Koh_
    Harold Hongju Koh

Yale Law School
127 Wall St.
New Haven, CT 06520

(203) 432-4932

Attorneys for Plaintiffs
    Haitian Centers Council, Inc., et. al.

To: United States Attorney for the
      Eastern District of New York
      Attorneys for Defendants
      Cadman Plaza East
      Brooklyn, NY 11210

When the person to be deposed is not a party to the litigation, the attorney seeking the deposition can, if necessary, compel the deponent's attendance by subpoena under Rule 45. In the case of a non-party, the subpoena can also specify that the deponent is to bring certain documents to the deposition. *See* Fed. R. Civ. P. 45(a)(1)(C). This is called a subpoena *duces tecum* (meaning "bring with you under penalty of punishment" in Latin). By contrast, an attorney can ask that a *party* bring documents to a deposition by sending a request for production of documents under Rule 34 with the deposition notice.

6. Rule 30(b)(6) Depositions.   Rule 30 provides a special procedure for deposing organizations, including government agencies. Why? Put yourselves in the position of the Yale team. You are suing the Immigration and Naturalization Service. Suppose you wanted to question the INS about the decisions the agency made in establishing its refugee screening procedures, but you do not know whom within the organization to depose. What would you do? You would rely on Rule 30(b)(6), which puts the onus on the organization to choose the person who will testify on its behalf. Under Rule 30(b)(6), a party may name the entity in the deposition notice and describe the subjects about which she seeks to depose the entity. The organization must then "designate," meaning identify, one or more individuals who are knowledgeable about those subjects. These people are called "30(b)(6)" witnesses.

Because the Yale team knew the identity of most of the individuals it wanted to depose, it did not make much use of Rule 30(b)(6). On the deposition notice reproduced earlier, the plaintiffs did include one 30(b)(6) notice, when they sought to depose the "military officer best in a position to have knowledge of any directive from military or national security personnel regarding screen-in rates or procedures."

7. The Deposition of Yvonne Pascal.   Yvonne Pascal's deposition was taken in February 1993, some weeks after the hunger strike had begun. *See STC,* pp. 220-22. With the help of an interpreter, Pascal testified before the lawyers and a court reporter in a trailer near the dirt soccer field where she had camped out for the strike. As you read, keep in mind that Pascal was answering in Creole, and the interpreter was then translating her answers into somewhat stilted English. We will first consider part of her direct examination by Veronique Sanchez and then part of her cross-examination by Lauri Filppu.

a. Direct Examination.   As discussed previously, Yvonne Pascal's deposition was uncommon because she was deposed by her own attorney to preserve her testimony for trial. Compare the emotionally charged account of the deposition in *Storming the Court* to the deposition transcript below. Note how a transcript can fail to convey much of what is actually happening during a deposition, from a simple hand gesture to shouting and crying. To capture such matters, the lawyer conducting the examination might go so far as to say something such as, "Let the record reflect that the witness is shaking his fist at the questioning attorney."

```
 1                    UNITED STATES DISTRICT COURT
                      EASTERN DISTRICT OF NEW YORK
 2
                           Case No. 92-CV-1258
 3
        HAITIAN CENTERS COUNCIL, INC.,     )
 4      et al.,                            )
                                           )
 5                           Plaintiff,    )
                                           )
 6      vs.                                )
                                           )
 7      GENE McNARY, COMMISSIONER,         )
        I.N.S., et al.,                    )
 8                                         )
                             Defendants.   )  COPY
 9      _____)

10

11                                   Camp Bulkeley
                                     Guantanamo Bay, Cuba
12                                   February 21, 1993
                                     6:45 p.m. - 9:00 p.m.
13

14

15

16                    DEPOSITION OF YVONNE PASCAL

17

18              Taken before Mia Sohn, Notary Public

19      in and for the State of Florida at Large, pursuant

20      to Notice of Taking Deposition filed in the above

21      cause.

22                      - - - - - - -

23

24

25
```

Mia Sohn was the court reporter and was responsible both for swearing in the deponent and transcribing the deposition.

This is the name of the court reporting firm that employs Mia Sohn.

JACK BESONER & ASSOCIATES
1499 West Palmetto Park Road, Suite 216
Boca Raton, FL 33486 (407) 750-8505 Fax: (407) 750-8507

```
 1       APPEARANCES:

 2


 3            ON BEHALF OF THE PLAINTIFF:


 4

              NATIONAL REFUGEE RIGHTS PROJECT
 5            San Francisco Lawyers'
              Committee for Urban Affairs
 6            301 Mission Street, Suite 400
              San Francisco, California 94105
 7            BY:  Robert Rubin, Esq.
                        and
 8                  Veronique Sanchez, Law Student

 9            ON BEHALF OF THE DEFENDANTS:


10            OFFICE OF IMMIGRATION LITIGATION
              Department of Justice
11            Patrick Henry Building, Room 8132
              601 "D" Street, N.W.
12            Washington, D.C. 20004
              BY:  Lauri Steven Filppu, Esq.
13                      and
                    William J. Howard, Esq.

14
              ALSO PRESENT:
15
              Ginette Cesar, Interpreter
16            Major Kevin Hart, U.S. Army
              Alix Perrault, Interpreter
17


18                  - - - - - - -


19                  I N D E X

20       Witness       Direct  Cross  Redirect  Recross
         Yvonne Pascal    3      32      - -       - -
21


22                  E X H I B I T S
         For Plaintiff:
23           #1,    Page 29,    Line 23

24


25
```

Ginette Cesar was the interpreter for the Yale team. Why do you think the government brought its own interpreter, Alix Perrault?

Almost every deposition begins with the lawyer asking the deponent to state her name, date of birth, residence, and occupation. On occasion, a lawyer will instead ambush a hostile deponent at the outset with a substantive question about the case that the deponent wasn't expecting. This was the deposition of a party by the party's own lawyer, however, and Yvonne Pascal already knew essentially all the questions Veronique Sanchez was going to ask her and in what order.

1   (Thereupon, Ginette Cesar was sworn to act as

2   interpreter during the taking of the deposition.)

3   Thereupon:

4   YVONNE PASCAL

5   was called as a witness by the Plaintiff, and

6   after being first duly sworn, was examined and

7   testified under oath as follows:

8   DIRECT EXAMINATION

9   BY MS. SANCHEZ:

10   Q. Please state your name for the Record.

11   A. Yes. My name is Yvonne Pascal.

12   Q. And Miss Pascal, what is your birthday?

13   A. I was born on January 13, 1964.

14   Q. How old are you?

15   A. Now I'm 29 years old.

16   Q. Miss Pascal, why did you leave Haiti?

17   A. I left Haiti because I had political

18   problems.

19   Q. What kind of political problems?

20   A. The political problems that I had was

21   that I was a member of K.I.D. which works with

22   Evans Paul in F.N.C.D. which is also affiliated to

23   K.I.D. I'm a typist for K.I.D.

24   Q. Miss Pascal, could you spell out the name

25   of the organizations that you are describing?

```
 1      A. K.I.D. means Konfederasyon Unite

 2   Demokrasy. Confederation for Unity and

 3   Democracy.

 4      Q. Please continue.

 5      A. F.N.C.D. means Front National Pour le

 6   Changement et la Democratie, National Front For

 7   Changes in Democracy.

 8      Q. And what, again, was your involvement

 9   with these organizations?

10      A. In these organizations, I used to type

11   papers for K.I.D. After the coup, Aristide's

12   coup,—

13      Should I go on?

14      Q. Yes.

15      A. My husband, whose name is Antenor

16   Joseph, he became the spokesperson for K.I.D.

17   after Evans Paul became the mayor of

18   Port-au-Prince. After they arrested Evans after

19   the coup, they arrested my husband. My husband

20   went into hiding at a place called Carrefour

21   Feuille. I used to go see him. Even though he

22   was in hiding, we were still mobilizing the

23   people.

24      Q. Miss Pascal, why was your husband in

25   hiding?
```

A line like "please continue" isn't ideal—technically, it is not even a question—but Sanchez is simply trying to get Yvonne Pascal to tell her story. Sanchez might have said, "And what does F.N.C.D. stand for?" Still, Sanchez was doing a pretty good job—this was the first deposition she'd ever taken!

Sanchez may have been about to interrupt Pascal to ask a follow-up question here. Notice how much is left unclear when all one has is a record of the words said, without any indication of tone of voice, cadence, and so forth.

There are actually many follow-up questions that Sanchez could have asked to flesh out Pascal's testimony here. Can you think of some of them? To her credit, Sanchez did focus on the most important question of all: Why was Pascal's husband in hiding? But notice what happens next . . .

Pascal's answer here isn't enough. The follow-up question should be: Why would your husband, Antenor, have to be in hiding because of this job? A lawyer should follow up until she gets the most important testimony on any given issue. Here, that testimony is that Pascal's husband was in hiding because he feared for his life based on his political activities. That establishes that he is a potential refugee, and it sets the stage for Pascal's argument that she, too, was afraid for her life because of her own political activities alongside Antenor—and because she was married to him.

The story behind Pascal's "nickname" was omitted from *Storming the Court* but may explain what is happening at this point in the deposition. Yvonne Pascal had a different name when she was born, which she refers to here as her "nickname," and which we have redacted to protect Pascal's privacy. When Pascal fled Port-au-Prince, she adopted a pseudonym and ceased using her birth name to help avoid recognition by any Haitian official. Pascal has been using her pseudonym ever since; when writing *Storming the Court*, Brandt Goldstein created the name "Yvonne Pascal" at Pascal's request to disguise both her birth name and the pseudonym she has been living under since she fled Haiti.

1   A. Because he had taken over Evans' job as

2 the spokesperson for K.I.D.

3   Q. Please continue.

4   A. We were still trying to mobilize the

5 people. I was typing flyers to distribute to the

6 people in all the neighborhoods. I used to go to

7 Cite Soleil with somebody who was affiliated with

8 us. His name is Fritz Desrosiers.

9   While my husband was in hiding in

10 Carrefour Feuille, I went to my mother's house in

11 Cite Soleil. I used to bring—I used to give

12 the flyers to Fritz Desrosiers, and they found

13 that out, so they arrested him and they killed

14 him.

15   Around my mother's neighborhood, they

16 were giving out—they were distributing flyers,

17 also, but in that same neighborhood, there's a

18 military man named Pierre Richard. He went around

19 and talked to the people, so they came and looked

20 for me. They didn't know exactly where I lived.

21 It was a kid named Dieufete, they took him to my

22 house.

23   I have a nickname which is [REDACTED].

24 They said, "Is this where [REDACTED] lives", and my

25 mother said, "I don't know anybody named

```
 1    REDACTED."

 2          They went inside the house, inside my

 3    mother's house. They arrested me. They

 4    handcuffed me. It was on April 27, 1992. They

 5    had a car waiting for them on the streets. They

 6    beat me a lot.

 7          When I got to the car, they pushed me

 8    inside the car, then they took me to Recherche

 9    Criminel. When I got to Recherche—

10    Q. Miss Pascal, what is Recherche Criminel?

11    A. Recherche Criminel is the place where

12    they take you and they beat you a lot. They

13    practically kill you so that they can say that you

14    are a political person, that you are a criminal.

15    Q. What happened when you were taken

16    there?

17    A. When I got there, they took me up to

18    the person who had given the order of arrest, the

19    person in charge.

20    Q. Do you remember his name?

21    A. No.

22          When I got to the person in charge, the

23    commander, he said to me, "Are you the person who

24    is giving problems in Cite Soleil? Evans and

25    Antenor are both in hiding."
```

1   I said that I didn't know where the

2   people were.

3   One had hit me with a rifle in my

4   waist.

5   Q. Who hit you with the rifle?

6   A. The military who was standing next to

7   the commander.

8   Q. And then what happened?

9   A. After he hit me with the rifle, the

10   commander said not to hit me anymore, but I was

11   three months pregnant, and he was asking me if I'm

12   not going to tell them where the people were. I

13   said I didn't know anything.

14   One of them was smoking near the

15   commander. In order for me to talk, he would turn

16   over the cigarette in my arm (indicating).

17   MS. SANCHEZ: Let the Record reflect

18   that the witness is pointing to a scar on her

19   arm.

20   BY MS. SANCHEZ:

21   Q. Please continue.

22   A. Then the baby was aborted. I lost the

23   baby. I spent two days in Recherche Criminel,

24   then they took me to the military hospital where I

25   spent three days.

Notice the problem with this translation. The soldier actually pressed the lit cigarette into Pascal's arm. An experienced lawyer would have clarified this.

Sanchez was quick enough to remember that she had to make clear for the record what was happening here. Pascal showed a cigarette burn scar on her arm to Sanchez but that would not have appeared in the deposition transcript without Sanchez explaining for the record what Pascal was doing.

1   While I was in the hospital—

2   I have a friend of my brother's who is

3   also a military person. He went and spoke to

4   people, and that way I was released. I was

5   released provisionally, because they said that

6   they know since they have arrested me, my husband

7   would find a way to come to my mother's house to

8   see me.

9   Q. Miss Pascal, what is your brother's

10   name?

11   A. [REDACTED].

12   Q. Okay. Please continue.

13   A. I was released provisionally, but they

14   sent people to post around my house. They put my

15   house in surveillance.

16   I had a friend whose name is also

17   Yvonne. She told me that she saw the military

18   walking around; "They were pacing. They were

19   watching you."

20   She told me to leave the neighborhood.

21   Q. Where were you at this time?

22   A. I had fled. I went to Baraderes to her

23   uncle's house.

24   Q. What is the uncle's name?

25   A. Pascal.

```
 1        Q. Is there a surname?

 2        A. First name [REDACTED], last name Pascal, just

 3    like mine.

 4        Q. What happened when you were at the

 5    uncle's house?

 6        A. When I got to my uncle's house, things

 7    were the same, because the section chief was

 8    always questioning people who were just arriving

 9    to this part of town. He told a friend who was

10    leaving to take me with him.

11        Q. What friend?

12        A. A friend of my uncle's. I don't know

13    his name.

14        Q. So who told the friend?

15        A. My uncle.

16        Q. Please continue.

17        A. I spent ten days in the countryside.

18    The trip was organized for the 12th. I spent the

19    13th at sea. I arrived on the 14th.

20        Q. Miss Pascal, why did you decide to get on

21    a boat to leave Haiti?

22        A. Because if I didn't flee, they would

23    have killed me.

24                    * * * *

25
```

As should be evident from the above excerpt, taking a deposition is not easy. Veronique was merely trying to elicit the basic facts of Yvonne Pascal's story, and even though Pascal is smart, focused, and articulate, many questions remain about exactly what happened to her and why. In the end, these uncertainties were not important as a *legal* matter for trial, because Pascal had already been screened in, and the trial was focused on indefinite detention and lack of medical care, *not* the refugee status of the Bulkeley Haitians. By contrast, if this examination had taken place during an asylum hearing, Sanchez would have to have been much more careful about covering the details of Pascal's persecution. Had that been the context, what are some of the follow-up questions you might have asked Pascal in order to develop and clarify her story? For purposes of the *McNary* trial, the testimony Sanchez did elicit, though not central to plaintiffs' claims, was still very important. Can you explain why?

One of the most important things that a lawyer must do is make sure that deposition testimony is clear. Unclear testimony can create all manner of problems, from questions about the witness's credibility or accuracy of perception to arguments by the opposition that the witness's testimony doesn't support the claim or defense to which it supposedly relates. Clarity was all the more crucial in Pascal's deposition, since she was not going to be present at trial to clarify her answers. In that regard, consider the following excerpt of Pascal's deposition and how Veronique Sanchez handled some confusion about a medical word. Pascal is testifying about her agreement to have a birth control injection, based on the misunderstanding that it would help treat her HIV infection.

---

* * * *

22   Q. So you eventually decided to take the

23   shot; is that right?

24   A. Yes, because I was told that it would

25   be good for T-cell and also for my health as I

1   depend on them.

2   Q. But you were aware that this was a

3   method of birth control?

4   A. Do you mean for my health, to control

5   my health?

6   Q. To prevent you from getting pregnant.

7   A. I didn't know that. I thought more

8   about my health, the fact that the T-cell was

9   low.

10   Q. Were you told of any possible side

11   effects from taking this shot?

12   A. If they had told me about the side

13   effects, there was no way I would have taken it.

14   Q. Miss Pascal, you said that you had

15   decided to take these shots because it was good

16   for your T-cell count, it was good for your

17   health.

18   Were you aware that it was also a

19   method of birth control?

20   A. Yes. They said that the T-cell count

21   was low, that the shots would help and it would

22   prevent us from getting pregnant.

23   Q. Miss Pascal, after you received this

24   shot, did you have any side effects?

25   A. Yes.

1   Q. What were they?

2   A. Well, the first month I got it was the

3   month of September. I spent the whole month

4   bleeding. After September, there was October and

5   November. I didn't have it anymore, but I always

6   feel pain in my belly and my head always aches.

7   When I went back to the hospital, they

8   told me they were going to have a PAP, meaning a

9   pelvic examination.

10   Every time I went for the pain in my

11   belly, they gave me Tylenol.

12   Q. Miss Pascal, when did they tell you at

13   the hospital that they were going to give you a

14   pelvic exam?

15   A. In January.

16   Q. Was that after you had been examined by

17   the doctor that the lawyers had brought on their

18   trip, Doctor Jean-Baptiste?

19   A. The doctors that my lawyers brought

20   went to the hospital and asked that I be given the

21   pelvic examination.

22   MS. SANCHEZ: Just for the Record,

23   earlier, Ginette, you said, "pop".

24   Can you clarify what that is for the

25   Record?

1   THE INTERPRETER: Well, that's what she

2   said.

3   MS. SANCHEZ: And it was referring to a

```
 4     PAP smear?

 5         THE INTERPRETER: She used the word

 6   pop.

 7         MS. SANCHEZ: I was just trying to

 8   distinguish PAP, P-A-P, from pop, p-o-p, for the

 9   Record.

10         THE INTERPRETER: PAP, P-A-P.

11         MS. SANCHEZ: Thank you.

                           * * * *
```

A Pap test or Pap smear, as you may know, is a test for cancerous or pre-cancerous cells in the cervix. Although this testimony was not crucial to the case, it is a valuable example of how to clarify testimony for the record. Notice how Sanchez stopped herself, spoke directly to the interpreter, and asked for clarification about "pop." (Pascal would have pronounced "Pap" as "pop" because of her French-Creole accent.) In the exchange that follows, the interpreter actually sounds a little annoyed and defensive, but Sanchez calmly makes sure she has the clarification on the record and proceeds. This is impressive lawyering, given Sanchez's lack of experience.

INTERVIEW
RONALD AUBOURG ON LANGUAGE AND CULTURAL BARRIERS IN LAWYER-CLIENT RELATIONSHIPS

How did the English-Creole language divide affect lawyer-client communication in the *McNary* case?

As in any attempt to communicate, both parties must be willing and able to understand both each other and the context in which the conversation is taking place. In the *McNary* case, the lawyers were at a real disadvantage in trying to communicate with their clients. Most of the lawyers did not speak French or Creole, and most of the Haitians did not speak English. On top of this obvious language divide, the Haitians were unjustly incarcerated, angry, and impatient. They were interested in hearing about only one thing: their release. Given these circumstances, the Haitians were not all that receptive to what the lawyers wanted to say, whether that message was delivered in English, French, or Creole.

Now as it turned out, there were two or three Haitians in Camp Bulkeley who spoke very good English. Initially, at least, they were responsible for some of the communication with the lawyers. The problem was that the rest of the camp population didn't have much faith in what those two or three Haitians were speaking about with the lawyers. As with so many other aspects of this situation, it was a matter of trust.

That's why interpreters like me—fluent in English, French, and Creole—were able to fill a role. I asked the lawyers to be patient and let me act as a representative for the litigation team, at least initially. I thought if I could relate to our clients in my own way to start, it would help. I told the Haitians about my own story as an immigrant from Haiti and the fact that I had family in both Haiti and the United States, and I think that helped.

At the same time, when things began to go more smoothly, I needed to assume a more traditional role as an interpreter. What sometimes happens is that the lawyer and client will both look at the interpreter instead of each other. That's a barrier to communication that you want to avoid. If that happens, the interpreter needs to help lawyer and client to look at each other so that they can communicate non-verbally. Otherwise, a lot gets lost: facial expressions, hand gestures, all sorts of things.

The interpreter also helps in this process of direct communication by careful use of pronouns. What I mean is that an inexperienced interpreter might translate a client saying "I want to go to the store" as "He says he wants to go to the store." Instead, the translator should say exactly what the client said: "I want to go to the store." Otherwise, what happens is that the lawyer might say, "Ask him what store he wants to visit"—when the lawyer *should* say, "What store do you want to visit?" Otherwise, we're back to the situation where lawyer and client are both looking at the interpreter and not each other.

How, if at all, did differences between Haitian and American culture affect communication and the development of trust between the lawyers and the Haitians?

Cultural issues are very important in any relationship, and it was no different in this relationship. From the very beginning, the lawyers working for the Haitians were viewed as "officials"—and in Haitian culture, "officials" are not viewed with admiration or respect; they are reviled. Remember that it was not long ago that Haitians broke away from a repressive government—the country was a dictatorship until the 1990s—and the instruments of repression were government officials and the military. Given that historical context, it wasn't easy to develop trust between lawyers and clients.

Another factor played into the issue of trust. Before the lawyers and students from Yale visited Guantánamo, representatives of many other entities, such as the United Nations High Commissioner for Refugees, had visited the Haitians and made many promises: We'll fight for you, we'll get you out of here, etc., etc. Well, those promises were never kept. So when the legal team from Yale arrived on Guantánamo and announced they were there to help, the Haitians simply didn't believe it.

At the outset, they dismissed the legal team altogether, and many of the Haitians remained hostile to the legal team for months afterwards. Rather than being thankful, the Haitians started out by asking pointed, even angry, questions of the lawyers: "We didn't hire you; why are you representing us?" "Why would you do this?" "What's in it for you?" And so on. Ultimately, the Haitians only wanted to hear the lawyers' answers to the questions, "How and when we will be getting out of here?"

I think it really helped to establish trust when I broke military security rules on Guantánamo and secretly accompanied the Haitians back to Camp Bulkeley [*See STC*, pp. 167-68—Eds.]. I had to take this chance, as I believed the Haitians would not cooperate with the legal team until they saw one of us take some kind of real risk—and I would have been in serious trouble had I been caught. The time I spent at Bulkeley allowed me to see firsthand the disgusting conditions they were living in, to really experience what they were going through. After that bold move, the Haitians seemed assured that we were there to help them, and they began to cooperate with us.

Did the Haitians' medical status complicate your efforts in any way?

Yes, very much so. When the lawyers began to discuss medical issues, they undermined whatever fragile understanding had begun to develop with the Haitians. The mood changed. They started booing and shouting at the lawyers and even the Haitian-American doctors with the lawyers. The health issue was important for the legal team, of course, but it was a non-issue for the Haitians—at least initially. In their view, the lawyers were simply joining the American military and the United States government in accusing them of being infected with HIV/AIDS.

The Haitians had a very difficult time believing this was possible. Their rationale was: "If we're sick, why are we being kept in these unsanitary conditions?" It seemed instead a false pretense for keeping them imprisoned. What the Haitians wanted to hear was not, "We're here to help," or "We think you might be sick." They wanted to know: *How can you help us get out of here?*

I should add that even when it came to the discussion of an exit strategy, the Haitians had a different view of things than the lawyers did. The Haitians had in mind a political strategy, which first took the form of organizing and demonstrating and later escalated to a hunger strike. Many (though not all) of the lawyers were thinking largely in terms of a legal strategy and how to win the Haitians' freedom in a courtroom. In the end, of course, both strategies were used, and both helped to close Camp Bulkeley.

In your experience, what are the most common mistakes lawyers make when working with translators?

I think that when dealing with interpreters, there are any number of inherent challenges at play, such as professional, cultural, political, and gender-based issues, to name just a few. Professionally, what's most important to understand is that just because an interpreter speaks the language does not mean that the person can effectively interpret your client's story. You must be aware of the interpreter's capacity to really convey the meaning of what the person is saying, and this is particularly true in an asylum case.

For instance, you should know the interpreter's political outlook as it relates to the country where the asylum seeker is coming from. An interpreter may be politically biased, either for or against the views of the client, and that can influence the lawyer's evaluation of a case. Ninaj Raoul* reported to me that when the Haitians were being interviewed on Guantánamo, a couple of interpreters were

---

*A Haitian-American activist who initially served as an interpreter for the Department of Justice on Guantánamo but quit and ended up working with the Yale team.—Eds.

providing their own political spin on what the interviewees were saying to the government officials conducting these interviews. That's not appropriate. So a lawyer needs to be sure that the interpreter he or she is working with can be neutral in relating the asylum seeker's story.

Also, to understand the cultural aspects of a client's story, it's valuable for the interpreter to hail from the same country as your client. But that does not always mean that they share similar cultural values. For example the interpreter may be fluent in both English and the client's language, but what if the interpreter has spent most of his or her life in the U.S.? In that case, the interpreter may not espouse your client's native cultural values—and might even be hostile to them. Obviously, this can affect the way the interpreter works.

The issue of gender must also be taken into consideration. Particularly with respect to certain cultures, there are specific situations where it may be best for a woman to interpret for a female client and for a man to interpret for a male client, as there are issues that they could be very uncomfortable speaking about in front of the opposite sex.

Finally, I think it's important for the lawyer to stay present in the conversation with the client as much as possible during a meeting, and not to engage in too much extra back-and-forth with the interpreter in English while the client looks on. I've had to deal with this problem in the past. It makes clients uncomfortable and they can begin to lose trust in the lawyer and interpreter because they don't know what's going on. If the lawyer needs to clarify something with the interpreter now and again, that's fine. But save longer conversations for later, when the lawyer and interpreter are alone.

More generally, what advice do you have for attorneys representing clients from a different country or different culture and who speak a different language?

I think the most important rule of thumb is to tell the client, in honest, straightforward terms, the situation they are facing and what can—and cannot—be done about it through the American legal system. However, one also has to be keenly aware of cultural issues, such as the fact that Haitians do not always look one another in the eye the way Americans do. (In Haiti, looking someone in the eye can be a sign of disrespect, while in America, people often think it means you're avoiding something or even being dishonest.) Further, while it's sometimes inevitable, try not to get too emotionally involved. You don't want to exaggerate what you'll be able to do or what you think the possible outcome of the case might be. Finally, reach out to people who can advise you about issues that you may confront with your clients, such as the complicated political situation in their homeland. You can read all you want on the Internet, but at some point, you need to talk directly with people from a particular country or culture who can help you really understand what's going on.

b. Cross-Examination. For Yvonne Pascal's testimony to be admissible at trial, the government had to have an opportunity to challenge that testimony through cross-examination. Before we go over some excerpts from the cross, think about the big picture for a moment. Assume you are government lawyer Lauri Filppu. What goals would you have for your cross-examination of Pascal? What basic lines of questioning would you follow to achieve those goals?

Turning to the transcript of the cross-examination, consider first the following excerpt, in which Filppu questions Pascal about the possibility that she might be resettled somewhere other than the United States.

* * * *

8   BY MR. FILPPU:

9   Q. Miss Pascal, you testified that when you

10   left Haiti, you had no specific destination.

11   Is it currently your intention to go to

12   the United States?

13   A. Evidently I did not have a destination,

14   but since the Americans picked me up from the sea,

15   I suppose that they have a place for them to put

16   me.

17   Q. Would you be willing to go back to

18   Haiti?

19   A. As long as there is democracy at home,

20   I will go back.

21   Q. Would you be willing to stay at

22   Guantanamo until there is democracy in Haiti?

23   A. The reason why I couldn't stay in

24   Guantanamo until there is democracy is because I

25   will die here before there is democracy.

1   Q. Is that because you expect to die on

2   the hunger strike?

3   A. Mistreatments is one of the problems.

4   That is why we started the hunger strike, so that

5   this body can get spoiled and then the soul can go

6   to God.

7   Q. What is the mistreatment that you speak

Filppu is an experienced attorney, but he gets off track by asking this question. To be sure, there was a reason to ask this question. (What was the reason?) But was this the right time to ask it? Pascal seems to take the question as an opportunity to start venting at him. Notice what Filppu has to do at line 14, on the next page, to refocus things.

8   of?

9   A. We are sick. They say that we are

10   sick, but look at the treatments that are given to

11   us as sick people. We have HIV and the type of

12   medication that is given to us, we will die before

13   we can be treated.

14   Q. I'll get back to those issues in a

15   moment, but let's return to the question of your

16   desires to leave Guantanamo.

17   If the opportunity were available,

18   would you be willing to go to a refugee camp in a

19   third country?

20   A. If I were given the opportunity, why

21   exactly would they send me to a camp?

22   Q. I know it may be difficult for you to

23   understand why you might be sent to another camp,

24   but what I'm trying to find out is whether you

25   have any objection to living in another refugee

1   camp in another country, for example, such as

2   Venezuela or the Dominican Republic or Honduras or

3   any other country in the region that might be

4   willing to accept you.

5   MR. RUBIN: Objection. Improper

Objections are discussed
in Note 8.

6   hypothetical. No foundation as to whether any of

7   those countries would offer resettlement to Miss

8   Pascal.

```
 9    BY MR. FILPPU:

10        Q. I would appreciate an answer, however.

11        A. Now, why would they send me to another

12    refugee camp?

13            It's like taking me from one

14    concentration camp and putting me in another

15    concentration camp.

                              * * * *
```

What do you think Filppu was hoping to achieve by asking whether Pascal would return to Haiti or be willing to resettle in a third country? Do you think he succeeded? Do you think it was worth asking these questions? Why or why not? How might this line of questioning fit into an overall cross-examination strategy?

Now consider Filppu's cross-examination of Pascal regarding the asylum hearings on Guantánamo. (The term "block leader" in this excerpt refers to Pascal's leadership role in the camp.)

```
                              * * * *

20        Q. Yesterday you indicated that you would

21    like a lawyer if you were to have a second

22    interview.

23            Do you want a second interview?

24        A. Yes, with my lawyer I would want to do

25    it.

 1        Q. As a block leader, do you know whether

 2    other Haitians want a second interview?

 3        A. Yes. It depends upon whether they can

 4    go with their lawyers or not.
```

5   Q. As a block leader, do you know whether

6   there are Haitians who want to go to the United

7   States without a second interview?

8   A. Well, I believe that in order for them

9   to apply for political asylum, they need to have

10   their lawyers with them to do it.

11   Q. Yesterday you told me that when you

12   first arrived at Guantanamo, you told your story

13   to the Immigration Service about why you left

14   Haiti.

15   You didn't have a lawyer with you at

16   that time, did you?

17   A. No, I didn't have a lawyer with me.

18   Q. You could tell your same story to the

19   Immigration Service again without counsel there a

20   second interview, couldn't you?

21   MR. RUBIN: Objection. Argumentative.

22   THE WITNESS: To tell the same story

23   again?

24   BY MR. FILPPU:

25   Q. Yes, the story that you told

1   Immigration and that you told last night.

2   A. Yes.

                    * * * *

What was Filppu trying to accomplish with this line of questioning? Specifically, what purpose might Pascal's answer at the very end of this excerpt serve for Filppu at trial? Do you think that answer would have any real impact on Judge Johnson's ultimate decision in the case? In that regard, keep in mind two points. First, although access to lawyers during asylum hearings on Guantánamo was an important issue early on in the case, it was not central to the trial. Second, the question of whether aliens on Guantánamo have the right to counsel under either the Immigration and Nationality Act or the due process clause was a *pure question of law*. In that light, does Pascal's answer to Filppu's question even matter?

In the end, Filppu's cross-examination covered a lot of ground, but he asked only a few questions about each topic, and almost none of Pascal's testimony on cross was read at trial. Do you think there was much to be gained by a cross-examination of Pascal? What questions might you have asked in a cross-examination in anticipation of reading her answers into the record at trial? (Keep in mind that you are limited in your cross to the scope of questioning on direct, so base your answer on the excerpts of the direct examination you have seen above.) How do you think the answers to your questions would help the government at trial?

8. *Objections During a Deposition.*   Objections are a critical aspect of depositions. During the deposition, the defending attorney can make many of the same objections that she could make at trial. It is particularly important to make objections that relate to the form of the question posed—the way in which the question is asked. Why? Such objections are waived if not raised during the deposition. Other defects, such as lack of relevance, generally are not waived. *See* Fed. R. Civ. P. 32(d)(3)(A), (B). The rationale for distinguishing between objections as to form and other objections is that questions that are objectionable as to form can be "cured," or corrected, during the deposition. The law thus provides an incentive for attorneys to raise these objections at the time and for the questioning attorney to immediately rephrase the question and then ask it again.

Objections as to form include objections that the question is vague, compound, or argumentative. Here is a capsule summary of each objection:

- A question might be vague if it does not provide the deponent with enough information about what is being asked. Consider, for example, if a deponent is asked, "How large is Camp Bulkeley?" The problem here is that the deponent might not understand whether the question relates to physical size or population.
- Compound questions are multiple questions combined into one. Here is an example of a compound question: "Were you taken to Camp McCalla in March and Camp Bulkeley in June?" If the deponent answers "no" to this question, it is not clear what she means.
- Argumentative questions state a conclusion as part of the question, such as: "You have no medical training, so how do you know what caused the medical problems of other women in Camp Bulkeley?"

Finally, the objection "asked and answered" is not an objection as to form. Rather the objection is based upon the fact that—as it suggests—the attorney has already asked and the witness has already answered the question.

9. *Objections During Yvonne Pascal's Deposition.*   A number of the aforementioned objections were made during Pascal's deposition. Consider Filppu's cross-examination with respect to her testimony on direct that other women had complained about side-effects from birth control shots they had received. (Note that attorney Robert Rubin, rather than Veronique Sanchez, defended Pascal on cross.)

---

* * * *

11   Q. Miss Pascal, what medical training have

12   you had?

13   A. I have no medical training. The only

14   thing is that they say that I had low T-cell count

15   and they were giving me AZT.

16   Q. During your Direct Examination, you

17   indicated that there were other women who have had

18   problems because of shots they have received; is

19   that not correct?

20   A. The other women complained to their

21   lawyers about the shots.

22   Q. You've just told me you have had no

23   medical training. Therefore, you have no medical

24   basis for making a judgment as to why any other

25   woman may be experiencing problems; isn't that

1   true?

2   MR. RUBIN: Objection. Argumentative.

3   I'm going to object to this line of questioning

4   and there may be a point at which I'm going to

5   instruct the witness not to answer.

6   THE WITNESS: It is not like that. It

7   is just that I went to my lawyers and complained

8   and so did everybody else. They went to the

9   lawyers and complained.

```
10    BY MR. FILPPU:

11        Q. But it's true that you don't have

12    medical knowledge to know why other women may be

13    experiencing problems?

14          MR. RUBIN: Objection. Asked and

15    answered. Argumentative.

16          Counsel, there's a short stick on this,

17    I promise you. You've now asked the same question

18    three times.

19          If you want to make a legal argument,

20    make it, but don't make it to her.

21          If you want to elicit testimony, that's

22    fine.

23    BY MR. FILPPU:

24        Q. (To the Interpreter) Please ask the

25    question.

 1        A. I'm not a doctor, but I had to ask

 2    questions to find out what I could do. I'm not a

 3    doctor, and if they had told me, I would have

 4    never taken it.
                        * * * *
```

Why did Filppu ask Pascal if she had medical training? Do you agree with Rubin's objections? What does Rubin mean when he says, "If you want to make a legal argument, make it, but don't make it to her. If you want to elicit testimony, that's fine"? Next consider the objection that Rubin made during Pascal's testimony about having a lawyer at her asylum hearing, reproduced earlier in the second excerpt from the cross-examination of Pascal. Do you agree with his assertion that the question was argumentative? Why or why not? We will continue to explore the role of objections during the discussion of Colonel Stephen Kinder's deposition.

10. The Deposition of Col. Stephen Kinder.   Colonel Stephen Kinder was the Joint Task Force Commander charged with guarding the Haitians at Guantánamo Bay from early September 1992 through early December 1992. As described in *Storming the Court*, Kinder worked hard to establish trust with the Haitian refugees and to make the camp a more pleasant place to live. One of the Yale team's primary objectives in deposing Kinder was to gather information about the conditions at Camp Bulkeley and, specifically, the changes that Kinder instituted. Review the excerpt below, in which Tringali begins to ask Kinder about the conditions on Guantánamo, and David Kline, the attorney representing the government at Kinder's deposition, lodges an objection.

<pre>
                          * * * *
   1   Kinder

   6   A. As a commander of the task force, I

   7   was responsible for providing temporary

   8   humanitarian relief for the Haitian immigrants

   9   that were at Guantanamo Bay.

  10   Q. When you arrived in mid-September,

  11   sir, during your tenure there did you make any

  12   changes in what had been the preexisting

  13   arrangements for the Haitians held in Guantanamo?

  14   A. Yes, I did.

  15   MR. KLINE: I am going to

  16   object to this. I'm not going to direct

  17   the witness not to answer questions about

  18   camp conditions, but I wish to make a

  19   continuing objection to relevance to camp

  20   conditions in this lawsuit.

  21   Q. And, Colonel, can you tell us what

  22   changes you implemented?

  23   A. Yes, I can.
</pre>

Now consider the portion of Kinder's deposition in which he discusses changes he implemented with respect to Camp VII, the segregation camp where detainees who had allegedly engaged in some form of misconduct were held.

```
                            * * * *
     1                      Kinder

     5       Q. And could you tell me what Camp 7

     6   was?

     7       A. Camp 7 was a segregation facility

     8   that was used to house personnel that [***] either

     9   committed some kind of misconduct or were

    10   troublemakers in the camp.

    11       Q. When you say personnel you're

    12   referring to the Haitains?

    13       A. That's correct.

    14       Q. And do you know who determines

    15   whether or not a particular Haitain should be

    16   confined to Camp 7?

    17       A. The way the procedures were, an

    18   incident would happen, it would be evaluated by

    19   the military police there, a recommendation would

    20   be made to the joint task force commander and he

    21   would make the final decision.

    22       Q. And do you know whether there was

    23   any right to review of that decision at the

    24   request of a Haitain?

    25           MR. KLINE: I am going to
```

```
 1                        Kinder

 2        object to this as irrelevant. I am not

 3        going instruct the witness not to answer,

 4        but I wish this to be a continuing

 5        objection also.

 6        A. Well, there were procedures for the

 7     reevaluation of anybody that was in there. I

 8     don't think it was, you know, I think that the

 9     mechanism was there. I don't know because I

10     didn't have to use that mechanism.

                         * * * *

 1

24        Q. And did you make any changes to the

25     operation of Camp 7 during your tenure there, [sir]?

 1                        Kinder

 2

 3        A. Yes, I felt that

 4     [***there] was an opportunity to relook

 5     the need for Camp 7.

 6        Q. And what did you do as a result of

 7     your looking at Camp 7?

 8        A. I interviewed each individual that

 9     was there, talked to them, talked to the military

10     leaders that were there before me, made a

11     personal agreement with each one, and released

12     them the next day. Except for three, one was in
```

```
13    a medical-hold facility because he had attempted

14    suicide, the other two I wanted to evaluate a

15    little longer.

16        Q. Did you ultimately release the other

17    two as well?

18        A. I moved those other two into a

19    different area, right away as well. That was

20    because there was only a couple of them, there

21    was some other buildings that they could move

22    into that was separate from the rest of the camp.

23        Q. And for the remainder of your

24    tenure, sir, did Camp 7 not operate?

25        A. Camp 7 was taken down, three days


1                            Kinder

2     after I arrived. Completely struck.
```

Why did Kline object to questions about camp conditions as irrelevant? Why did Tringali want to elicit this testimony about Camp VII from Colonel Kinder? Kline is not required during the deposition to explain the reasoning behind his objection, but he *would* be required to explain his reasoning to the court if he did not want the testimony to be admitted into evidence at trial. What arguments should Kline make to the court to support his objection on the ground of relevance? How should Tringali respond?

11. Depositions by Telephone.   The Yale team also encountered difficulties in getting the government to make certain witnesses available for depositions. For instance, Yale found it impossible to get access to military personnel for depositions. The government would not allow Kinder to appear in person for a deposition, and Tringali had to fight simply to depose him by telephone. *See STC*, p. 264. Rule 30(b)(4) allows depositions to be taken over the telephone either by order of the court or stipulation of the parties. Do you think the plaintiffs' lawyers were at a disadvantage by not being in the room with Kinder while asking him questions? What might Tringali have missed by having to conduct the deposition by telephone?

12. Deliberative Process Privilege.   In addition to those privileges set out in Chapter Six, the U.S. government enjoys certain privileges unavailable to private

Colonel Stephen Kinder at Guantánamo Bay, autumn 1992. Photograph courtesy of Stephen Kinder.

parties in civil litigation. Most pertinent to the *McNary* case was the "deliberative process" privilege, asserted by counsel for the government during the deposition of Colonel Kinder. The deliberative process privilege protects from disclosure the internal recommendations, opinions, and advice expressed by government officials about a pending decision before a final decision on the matter is reached. Before reading further, what do you think the rationales for this privilege might be?

First, by privileging deliberative processes, the law ensures that government officials feel free to debate alternatives, no matter how unorthodox or controversial. This freedom can improve the quality of decision-making. Second, the privilege prevents confusion among members of the public that might result if, as a result of discovery, preliminary recommendations or opinions were released before government officials had reached a final decision. Third, the privilege protects public officials by ensuring that they are judged on the basis of the decision reached, not the options they considered. *See Russell v. Department of the Air Force*, 682 F.2d 1045, 1048 (D.C. Cir. 1982). Deliberative process is a qualified privilege, which means that the government can in some circumstances be required to produce the information sought. In evaluating an assertion of deliberate process privilege, the district court must balance the requesting party's need for the information against the government's interest in protecting the confidentiality of its decision-making process. *See Dudman Communications Corp. v. Department of Air Force*, 815 F.2d 1565, 1567-69 (D.C. Cir. 1987).

The government objected to a number of Tringali's questions to Colonel Kinder on the grounds that Kinder's answer would reveal such predecisional recommendations. Read the following excerpts from the deposition of Kinder in light of the three principal policy reasons for having a deliberative process privilege.

```
                              * * * *
   1                          Kinder

  16       Q. Did you during your tenure at Camp

  17   Bulkeley ever request parole for medical reasons

  18   for any of the Haitians refugees?

  19               MR. KLINE: Objection, calls

  20          for a deliberative processes. I direct

  21          the witness not to answer.

                              * * * *
   1

  15       Q. Was there any—did you express any

  16   concern that the continued operation of Camp

  17   Bulkeley was in any way detrimental to the

  18   military?

  19                  MR. KLINE: I am going to

  20          object here.

  21          It appears that the question is

  22          delving into recommendations, deliberation

  23          and opinions that were made to Colonel

  24          Kinder's superiors. I will direct him

  25          that he can answer the question, if

   1

   2   disclosure of the answer does not disclose

   3   recommendations, deliberations and

   4   opinions in a pre-decisional posture.
```

Consider Tringali's first question regarding whether Kinder had requested medical parole for the Haitian refugees. Why would an answer to that question reveal information protected by the deliberative process privilege? Now consider Tringali's second question: whether Kinder expressed concern that the operation of Camp Bulkeley was detrimental to the military. Why would an answer reveal pre-decisional deliberations? Finally, would preventing Kinder from answering these questions serve the purposes of the privilege as described above? Why or why not?

13. Instructions Not to Answer.   You may have noticed that although Kline objected to the questions about camp conditions in the earlier excerpt, Tringali continued to question Kinder and Kinder continued to answer. Contrast that with the excerpt in which Kline instructed Kinder not to answer questions that might reveal pre-decisional deliberations. As a general rule, if the attorney for the deponent objects to the question posed, the deponent nonetheless has to answer. The judge will later rule on the objection, deciding whether the testimony elicited after the objection is admissible as evidence at trial. Under Rule 30(c)(2), however, an attorney may instruct a deponent not to answer if answering would violate either a court order or a privilege—such as the deliberative process privilege just discussed. In addition, an attorney may instruct a deponent not to answer in connection with a motion to terminate or limit the deposition under Rule 30(d)(3). Such a motion may be made on the ground that the deposition is being conducted in bad faith or in a way that "annoys, embarrasses, or oppresses the deponent or party." Fed. R. Civ. P. 30(d)(3). Why do you think deponents are required to answer questions that might not be permitted at trial? And what are the reasons for the exceptions to this rule?

Tringali disagreed with Kline's instruction to Kinder not to answer the question of whether Kinder ever had requested that any of the Haitian refugees be paroled (released into the United States) for medical reasons. In fact, Tringali threatened to call Judge Johnson at the end of the deposition to get a ruling forcing Kinder to answer the question. Here is the relevant portion of Tringali's response to Kline's instruction:

```
                         * * * *
 1                      Kinder

22             MR. TRINGALI: Dave, that is

23        not deliberative process. And, if you're

24        going to object and instruct him not

25        answer, we'll be on the phone to Judge

 1

 2     Johnson.

 3                MR. KLINE: Deliberative

 4        processes is the calling for

 5        recommendation deliberation and opinions
```

6   in a pre-decisional posture. It is most

7   assuredly calling for an answer that

8   involves the deliberative processes.

9   MR. TRINGALI: I will tell you

10   that when we finish today, I'll call Judge

11   Johnson, if we can get Judge Johnson,

12   we'll get Judge Johnson at the conclusion

13   of this and have him make a decision, but

14   the idea that you can deny us to know

15   whether or not the military on Guantanamo

16   was seeking the evacuation of people,

17   because they couldn't be adequately cared

18   for on Guantanamo and you're going to

19   claim that we can't know about that

20   because that's deliberative process, is an

21   outrage.

22   Q. Colonel Kinder, let me ask, did the

23 military—

24   MR. KLINE: Joseph, I am going

25   to suggest that the answer to that

1

2   question calls for privileged information

3   and because the answer to that question

4   calls for privileged information, I

5   instructed the witness not to answer.

```
 6              MR. TRINGALI: That's fine,

 7          and I've told you what I am going to do.

 8          Q. Colonel Kinder, during your tenure

 9      on Guantanamo, did the military doctors ever tell

10      you that they did not believe they could

11      adequately treat any Haitians refugee at Camp

12      Bulkeley?

13          A. Yes. That's correct. There was a

14      case where there was a couple of individuals that

15      had eye problems, that we even brought a

16      specialist in that could not correct there at

17      Guantanamo Bay. Required him to be sent to the

18      United States for some specialized care and we—

19      that was recommended to me, to have those folks

20      given additional medical care that we could not

21      provide at Guantanamo Bay.

22              MR. KLINE: I am going to

23          instruct the witness not to answer

24          questions by disclosing recommendations,

25          deliberations and opinions in a

 1

 2      pre-decisional posture.
```

It appears that Tringali ultimately did not bring this dispute to the judge. Why might he not have done so?

14. Competency of Testimony.   As you will learn in Chapter Eight, a trial witness's testimony must be "competent." For nonexpert witnesses, this means that their testimony must be based on their personal knowledge. Different rules apply to expert witnesses; because of their credentials, they can offer opinions on matters outside of their personal knowledge. Consider this rule in light of the following excerpt from Kinder's deposition.

```
                            * * * *
1                          Kinder

9          Q. Did you find during your tenure

10     there, sir, that the Haitians, any of the

11     Haitians were depressed?

12          A. With regard to being confined to

13     Camp Bulkeley?

14              MR. KLINE: I object. This

15         witness is not qualified to issue medical

16         opinions about depression or not of

17         Haitians.

18              MR.TRINGALI: I am not

19         asking, sir, for your medical opinion,

20         when I use the term depressed, I'm not

21         asking for you to make a clinical

22         diagnosis.

23          Q. I'm asking you have you ever

24     described the Haitians on Guantanamo as being

25     depressed?

1                          Kinder

2          A. Yes, I did.

3          Q. What was that based on, sir?

4          A. Again, when I first arrived, they
```

```
 5     were—I wouldn't say the word hostile, but they

 6     were very uptight about their situation, and what

 7     was going to happen.

 8             And, every once in a while, they

 9     would, individuals if not groups, would lapse

10     into that same feeling of hopelessness because

11     the court case was going too slow, or the

12     procedures were going too slow or whatever it

13     might be.

14             They kept looking at milestones,

15     like they looked at the presidential election as

16     a milestone and then they looked at something

17     else and in between those milestones there was a

18     period of time where individuals were depressed.
```

Kline's objection here is that Kinder does not have the medical credentials necessary to offer an opinion on whether the Haitians were depressed. Notice how Tringali then rephrases his question. Why isn't the rephrased question subject to the same objection?

15. Concluding the Deposition.   After a deposition is concluded, a transcript of the deposition will be sent to the parties for their review. The deponent is permitted to make changes to her deposition testimony, such as substituting a word that the court reporter mis-transcribed (e.g., "Bulkeley" in place of "Buckley") or clarifying something that was confused in the original testimony. For the deponent to make such changes, attorneys must reserve the right to read and sign the transcript before the end of the deposition. *See* Fed. R. Civ. P. 30(e). The original transcribed material is not deleted but remains part of the transcript; the changes are simply appended to the original with the deponent's explanation of why the change was necessary.

Harold Koh and Reverend Jesse Jackson arrive at Guantánamo Bay, February 1993. Photograph courtesy of Harold Koh. Photographer unknown.

CHAPTER EIGHT

Summary Judgment and Trial

INTRODUCTION

Once discovery is completed, a case will typically take one of two paths toward resolution—a motion for summary judgment under Fed. R. Civ. P. 56 or preparation for trial—and sometimes both.[1] Even people who have never been to law school are familiar with the trial process. We are bombarded with accounts and portrayals of dramatic courtroom showdowns in the media and popular culture, and more than a few people have decided to go to law school after watching a stirring courtroom summation in movie. Indeed, one of the reasons Brandt Goldstein thought the *McNary* case might make a good book for the general reader was because it ended with the trial to release Yvonne Pascal—a high-stakes battle for the freedom of a democracy activist and young mother.

The summary judgment stage of litigation, which precedes trial, is considerably less dramatic but plays a crucial role in our system of civil procedure. Summary judgment enables a judge to decide a case without going to trial. To understand the concept of summary judgment and its relation to trial, begin by recalling that there are two aspects to adjudication of legal disputes: the finding of facts and the application of law to those facts. It is the task of the judge to decide the law and the task of either the jury (in a jury trial) or the judge (in a "bench" trial) to decide the facts. A trial is necessary *only if the parties genuinely dispute material issues of fact.* That is, the purpose of trial is to resolve factual disputes, with each side attempting to convince the fact-finder to believe its particular account of what happened. Once the fact-finder has reached a decision about the facts, the law can then be applied to those facts to produce a final decision. That decision, as you probably know, is called the *verdict*—a word that derives from the Latin for "true" and "speech."

Now, how does summary judgment figure into this picture? If the parties do not dispute the facts, or if they dispute the facts but one or both cannot produce evidence to support their claims about those factual disputes, then there is no reason for trial.

---

1. There is, of course, a very common third path towards resolution: After discovery, when the parties have a much stronger sense of the strength of their respective cases, a case may settle.

In other words, if the parties do not have a genuine disagreement about (or evidence to support their disagreement about) the material facts—the facts that would make a difference in the outcome of the case—then *the judge may decide the case herself by applying the law to the undisputed facts.* The process of deciding a case in this manner is known as summary judgment. Rule 56 sets forth the procedures for moving for summary judgment and the standard to be applied in deciding a case on summary judgment.

This chapter will introduce you to both summary judgment and the trial process. The summary judgment section of the chapter is relatively brief because neither party in *McNary* moved for summary judgment, although as explained later, such a motion would have been possible. After summary judgment, we will move on to an exploration of trial, discussing trial planning and organization, the phases of a trial, and the ways in which a trial is resolved—or in some circumstances, simply cut short. To illustrate various aspects of trial practice, we include excerpts from the trial transcript, which make for some of the most interesting reading in the case.

SUMMARY JUDGMENT—NOTES AND COMMENTS

1. The Basic Concept.   As just explained, summary judgment is a procedural mechanism that enables a court to resolve a case without trial when there are no disputed material facts in the case. To understand how summary judgment functions, contrast summary judgment with a motion to dismiss under Rule 12(b)(6). In evaluating a motion to dismiss under Rule 12(b)(6), the facts as alleged by the plaintiff *are assumed to be true.* The only question is whether the plaintiff has made factual allegations which, if true, would establish the elements of his claim. If a plaintiff, when suing on a simple negligence claim arising out of a car accident, pleads all the elements of the claim—duty, breach, causation, proximate cause, and damages—he can survive a motion to dismiss, whether or not the allegations that he sets forth ultimately turn out to be true. The court never looks beyond the complaint to ask whether the alleged facts are actually true. (The parties will have a chance during discovery to investigate whether the allegations in the complaint and the affirmative defenses in the answer actually have some factual support.)

In contrast to a Rule 12(b)(6) motion, a court ruling on a summary judgment motion will consider the actual facts in the case. Summary judgment generally (although not always) takes place *after* the parties have had an opportunity during discovery to investigate and test the allegations of the other side. At this point, depositions, documents, interrogatory answers, and other information produced during the discovery process have fleshed out the facts of the case. The question at the summary judgment stage, as set forth in Rule 56(c), is whether, in light of the evidence presented to the court, "there is no genuine issue as to any material fact and . . . the movant is entitled to judgment as a matter of law."

The phrase "no genuine issue as to any material fact" is the key to summary judgment. It means that there is no dispute about the material facts that would need to be resolved at trial. There are several ways in which a case might lack a genuine issue as to any material fact. For example, there are situations in which the parties might agree on the facts and simply disagree about the law or how that law is to be applied to those facts. Consider the Yale team's challenge to the Bush administration's direct return policy in *McNary*. The parties agreed on the facts of the interdiction process. The government did not dispute the plaintiffs' allegations that under orders from the president, the Coast Guard was intercepting Haitian boats and sending the Haitians aboard straight back to Port-au-Prince. The only dispute between the parties was a legal one: whether federal and international law permitted the United States to intercept Haitian refugees in international waters and return them to Haiti to face possible persecution. *See STC*, p. 224. The single issue before the court was how to interpret the law and apply it to the undisputed facts. That issue came before the court as a request for a preliminary injunction—a request for temporary relief—but it was also an issue that would have been appropriate for resolution on summary judgment, producing a final decision in the case.

Summary judgment is also appropriate when the party with the burden of proof on a claim is unable to produce evidence with respect to one or more element of the claim. If the plaintiff does not have any evidence to support his allegations regarding a material fact in the case, there is "no genuine issue as to any material fact" to be decided at trial. As an example, consider a negligence case based on an auto accident. Assume that discovery has been taken and the plaintiff was unable to produce any evidence that the defendant breached her duty of care to the plaintiff. Specifically, there is no evidence to support the plaintiff's initial allegation that the defendant ignored a stop sign at an intersection or was otherwise driving in a negligent manner. In this instance, there is no *genuine issue* of material fact as to the element of negligence: No jury or judge could find that the defendant breached his duty of care because there is simply no evidence on the matter. As a consequence, the court will enter summary judgment for the defendant.

What is critical to understand is that on summary judgment, the court *does not weigh the evidence or assess its credibility*. Rather, the court decides whether there is a *dispute* about a material issue of fact requiring that the case go to trial, where the factfinder then must resolve the conflict in the evidence and make factual findings. Put another way, it is not up to the court to decide, on summary judgment, whose evidence is more persuasive. As long as there is a genuine dispute between the parties about what happened, with supporting evidence, there is an issue for trial and summary judgment must be denied.

2. *The Basic Procedure.* There are two procedural issues critical to the summary judgment process—the first relates to the respective burdens, or responsibilities, of the parties, and the second relates to the evidence used to meet those burdens. First, in bringing a summary judgment motion, the moving party has the initial burden, or responsibility, of pointing to the absence of a genuine issue as to any material fact in the case.[2] The burden then shifts to the non-moving party, who must produce evidence that "set[s] out specific facts showing a genuine issue for trial." Fed. R. Civ. P. 56(e)(2). At this point, the court must determine whether there is a genuine issue of material fact. If there is none—if there is no real conflict in the evidence—the court will decide the law and enter summary judgment for the moving party. If a genuine dispute of

---

2. The moving party can, but is not required to, come forward with evidence to support this assertion. *Celotex Corp. v. Catrett*, 477 U.S. 317 (1986).

material fact does exist, however, the court will deny the summary judgment motion and the case will go to trial.

Second, the evidence that the court may consider on a summary judgment motion includes "the discovery and disclosure materials on file, and any affidavits" submitted. Fed. R. Civ. P. 56(c).[3] The court can therefore consider deposition testimony, interrogatory responses, and other evidence obtained through discovery, along with sworn affidavits by parties and witnesses. Further, the evidence submitted by the parties must be admissible or indicate the existence of admissible evidence that could be used at trial. This makes intuitive sense, because if a party has no admissible evidence on an element of her case, there is no need to have a trial and the judge can enter judgment. That is why affidavits must be "on personal knowledge, set out facts that would be admissible in evidence, and show that the affiant is competent to testify on the matters stated." Fed. R. Civ. P. 56 (e)(1). The affidavit demonstrates that there is a witness who will testify at trial and provides an overview of that witness's testimony.

3. Material Facts.   The summary judgment standard requires that there be no genuine issue of *material* fact, and it is important to fully understand what this means. The "material" criterion is simple enough: A material fact is "one that might affect the outcome of the case under the governing law." Richard D. Freer, *Introduction to Civil Procedure* 429 (2006). "Factual disputes that are irrelevant or unnecessary will not be counted." *Anderson v. Liberty Lobby*, 477 U.S. 242, 248 (1986). Materality is thus a relative concept—a fact that is material in one case might not be material in another. It depends on whether resolution of that particular factual dispute will affect the outcome of the case.

For instance, in the auto accident negligence case discussed above, imagine that the plaintiff does not submit any evidence about the defendant's alleged negligence, but instead submits considerable evidence about the injuries she suffered. Even though the plaintiff is required to establish that she was harmed by the defendant's negligence, any dispute between the parties regarding damages is irrelevant if the plaintiff has no evidence that the defendant was negligent. In this situation, the issue of damages is not *material* because its resolution would not affect the outcome of the case—absent a finding of negligence, the plaintiff will lose regardless of whether she shows she was injured. Conversely, imagine that the plaintiff has evidence that the defendant was negligent but does not have any evidence that she was damaged. Now, the issue of damages is in fact material because it affects the outcome of the case.

4. Genuine Issue.   The question of what constitutes sufficient evidence to create a *genuine issue* of material fact is a little more challenging. The Supreme Court tried to clarify what is meant by a "genuine issue" when it decided a trilogy of cases on the same day in 1986.[4] In one of those cases, the court explained that "[t]he mere existence of a

---

3. Rule 56(c) also states that the court may consider the pleadings in making its determination, but this is a bit confusing. Pleadings are not evidence and a party cannot rely on a pleading to create a genuine issue of material fact, *see* Fed. R. Civ. P. 56(e)(2).

4. *See Anderson v. Liberty Lobby*, 477 U.S. 242 (1986); *Celotex, supra* note 2; *Matsushita Electric Industrial Co. v. Zenith Radio Corp.*, 475 U.S. 574 (1986). These three cases are generally viewed as encouraging the lower courts to grant summary judgment more frequently than had previously been the case. As Professor Richard Freer puts it, the message was, "Loosen up and grant summary judgment more readily." RICHARD D. FREER, INTRODUCTION TO CIVIL PROCEDURE 429 (2006).

scintilla of evidence in support of the plaintiff's position will be insufficient; there must be evidence on which the jury could reasonably find for the plaintiff." *Anderson*, 477 U.S. at 252. In other words, there has to be sufficient evidence such that a *reasonable jury* could find in favor of the nonmoving party. If the evidence presented by the plaintiff is so minimal that no reasonable jury could possibly find in her favor, the judge can properly enter summary judgment against her.

This requirement does *not* mean, however, that the judge should weigh the evidence on a motion for summary judgment. To illustrate this point, let's return to the car accident case yet again. Assume that the only evidence the plaintiff produces in response to the defendant's summary judgment motion is her own affidavit swearing that the defendant ran a stop sign. Even if the court does not find the evidence submitted by the nonmoving party particularly persuasive, it must nonetheless deny the motion for summary judgment. The plaintiff's affidavit is far more than a "scintilla" of evidence in her favor, and it will be the job of the jury or judge at trial to weigh the respective evidence and assess the credibility and perceptive accuracy of the witnesses on both sides.[5]

5. Summary Judgment in McNary.   Neither party in the *McNary* case filed a motion for summary judgment, but in retrospect, it seems that the plaintiffs might have been able to move for summary judgment on their claim that the Haitians were being denied adequate medical care in violation of the due process clause.[6] As construed by the court in *McNary*, that claim can be understood as having three elements: (1) the plaintiffs were being detained by the government, (2) the plaintiffs were in need of medical care, and (3) government officials denied adequate care to the plaintiffs, such as by being deliberately indifferent to the plaintiffs' medical needs. *Haitian Centers Council, Inc. v. McNary*, 823 F. Supp. 1028, 1043-44 (E.D.N.Y. 1992).[7]

The government would likely have had a difficult time contesting the first element (although in its answer, the government actually refused to admit that it was "detaining" the Haitians, presumably on the ground that they were free to return to Haiti). The government would not have been able to contest the second element, particularly regarding Haitians who were suffering from full-blown AIDS. Everyone agreed they were in need of medical care. Therefore, the essential issue on a summary judgment motion would have been the third element of the claim: whether the government was being deliberately indifferent to the Haitians' medical needs.

As described in *Storming the Court*, a member of the U.S. military had testified at the preliminary injunction hearing before Judge Johnson that the Haitians were receiving medical care that met "U.S. standards." *STC*, p. 245. Although government lawyer

5. In determining whether there is sufficient evidence for a reasonable jury to find on behalf of the nonmoving party, a court evaluates the evidence to determine whether it meets the minimum threshold amount necessary to create a reasonable dispute about the facts. *Matsushita*, 475 U.S. at 593. This resembles a judicial weighing of the evidence.

6. This would have been a motion for *partial* summary judgment, which is permitted by Rule 56(a). A motion for partial summary judgment may either be directed at one or more of the claims at issue or at part of a single claim—for instance, the liability causation aspect of a negligence claim, with the damages element of the claim to be determined at trial because there is a genuine issue of fact as to damages.

7. Purely as a matter of law, the plaintiffs also had to persuade the court that the due process clause of the Constitution applies at Guantánamo Bay. Because this determination was a matter of law—not fact—it did not give rise to a genuine issue of material fact at the summary judgment stage and was not the subject of testimony at the trial.

Young men waiting at Camp McCalla, most likely spring 1992. Photograph courtesy of Stephen Kinder.

Lauri Filppu also made a similar claim to the judge at a pretrial hearing, it was not clear when trial began that this claim was supported by the deposition testimony of any of the government physicians Filppu had named as witnesses. *Id.*

At trial, however, something remarkable happened. As you will recall, after the Yale team had presented its evidence on the lack of proper medical care, government lawyer Bob Begleiter announced to the court that the government would not contest the plaintiffs' factual contentions as to medical care, at least at they related to people who were suffering from full-blown AIDS. *Id.*, p. 266. As described in *Storming the Court*, which relies in part on the trial transcript:

> [Bob Begleiter said,] "These [government] doctors will also testify that the medical facilities at Guantánamo are not presently sufficient to provide treatment for AIDS patients under the medical care standard applicable within the United States itself."
>
> There was a long pause.
>
> "You're saying," [Judge] Johnson asked, "people who have T cells under two hundred, they cannot receive adequate treatment at Guantánamo?"
>
> "I'm saying that doctors will testify and say that presently, they could not receive sufficient treatment at Guantánamo Bay Naval Base."
>
> Johnson cocked his head. *"Is that the same thing plaintiffs are saying?"*
>
> Tringali, unsure of what Begleiter was doing, got to his feet. *"Yes, Your Honor,"* he said. *"It is."*

Id., pp. 266-267 (emphasis added).

What Begleiter was conceding here is that *there was no genuine issue of material fact* as to the plaintiffs' claim about inadequate medical care. Not surprisingly, Judge Johnson's final order relies on Begleiter's admission as part of the ruling that the government, in violation of the due process clause, was deliberately indifferent to the medical needs of those plaintiffs who had full-blown AIDS. *McNary*, 823 F. Supp. at 1045. Given this set of circumstances, one might ask: Why did the plaintiffs not move before trial for summary judgment on the inadequate medical care claim?

The answer is twofold. First, Bob Begleiter's representation to the court during trial was a highly unusual event, and not something that the plaintiffs could have anticipated. It is rare for a party to announce at trial that it will not contest a factual allegation that it had contested prior to trial. (Hence the long pause after Begleiter spoke. Neither Judge Johnson nor plaintiffs' counsel were able to believe what they were hearing.)

Second, the plaintiffs could not have moved for summary judgment on the inadequate medical care claim because when trial began, *that claim still was not in the complaint.* It was only added through an amendment to the complaint during trial, although Judge Johnson allowed the plaintiffs to present evidence on the claim at trial. *See* Chapter Two, Note 15.

6. *Judgment as a Matter of Law.* During a jury trial, a party can move for what is known as *judgment as a matter of law* pursuant to Rule 50(a).[8] Under Rule 50(a), either party may move at trial for judgment as a matter of law on a claim once the other party "has been fully heard on [the] issue." Fed. R. Civ. P. 50(a)(1). This procedure is akin to a motion for summary judgment that is made during, rather than before, trial. The moving party is asserting that, based on the evidence put forth at trial, "a reasonable jury would not have a legally sufficient evidentiary basis to find for the party on that issue." *Id.* In essence, a motion for judgment as a matter of law is another way of contending that trial has revealed there to be no genuine issue of material fact on a particular issue and the case therefore does not need to be decided by the jury.[9]

Although Rule 50 applies only to jury trials and *McNary* was a bench trial, the *McNary* plaintiffs could have moved for a judgment on partial findings under Rule 52(c), which is roughly equivalent to a motion for a judgment as a matter of law. *See* Fed. R. Civ. P. 52(c). Given how unequivocal Bob Begleiter was in his exchange with Judge Johnson, why did the plaintiffs not make such a motion? There are two reasons. The first is the same reason they did not move for summary judgment earlier: They had yet to amend their complaint to include the due process claim for inadequate medical care. Second, although a motion for judgment as a matter of law prevents the case from being submitted to the jury, a motion for judgment on partial findings does not alter the trajectory of a bench trial that significantly—whether the motion is granted or denied, it is the judge who decides the issue at hand.

---

8. This motion used to be known in the federal courts as a motion for a directed verdict. Many state courts (and some federal courts) still use the directed verdict terminology.

9. A similar motion available to either party in a jury trial at a later stage in the proceedings is a Rule 50(b) renewed motion for judgment as a matter of law, once known as a motion for judgment notwithstanding the verdict. In this instance, the motion is made *after* the jury has returned the verdict, with the losing party contending that there was insufficient evidence for a reasonable jury to find in favor of the winning party. (A party must make a Rule 50(a) motion at the close of the evidence before the case is submitted to the jury in order to "renew" it as a Rule 50(b) motion for judgment as a matter of law.) This might seem to contravene the right to a jury trial under the Seventh Amendment (indeed, the same might be said for summary judgment and a motion for judgment as a matter of law). But there is no absolute right under the Seventh Amendment to a jury trial in a civil case. (By contrast, there is an absolute right under the Sixth Amendment to a jury trial in a criminal case.)

TRIAL—NOTES AND COMMENTS

7. Introduction—Trial or Settlement?   If neither party files a motion for summary judgment or the judge refuses to grant the motion, the case then proceeds to trial. Trial is not the final chapter of litigation, but it often feels like the climax of the process. Indeed, it's not surprising that Lisa Daugaard felt like she was in a movie as she watched Joe Tringali rise to give plaintiffs' opening statement at trial on that chilly 1992 March morning in Brooklyn. But the human-interest story at the heart of the *McNary* trial shouldn't eclipse a broader point: Trial in civil litigation is rare. In fact, recent statistics show the civil trial rate hovering somewhere between two and four percent—one in every 25 to 50 suits filed in federal court.[10] The vast majority of cases end before trial in one of two ways. According to one study, for instance, about 30 percent of cases are disposed of by the court through procedural mechanisms such as dismissal under Rule 12(b)(6) or summary judgment under Rule 56.[11]

All other cases that don't go to trial are settled by the parties. Most observers see settlement as highly desirable because it saves the parties and the judicial system time, money, and energy.[12] Courts routinely encourage settlement, and, in recent years, parties have increasingly turned to the alternative dispute resolution methods of arbitration and mediation to help them resolve a dispute before trial or even instead of filing a lawsuit. When other methods of resolving a dispute aren't possible, however, the last resort is trial—clearly the direction that *McNary* was headed, as Koh and Mike Wishnie recognized after their meeting with Justice Department official Michael Cardozo. Cardozo, you'll recall, told them that President Clinton "could weather dead HIV-positive Haitians on Guantánamo better than the political fallout of letting them in the U.S." *STC*, p. 214.

In keeping with the public perceptions of trials in our legal system, the *McNary* case produced some remarkably dramatic moments, although long stretches of the trial were relatively mundane. The truth is that the vast majority of courtroom trial work does not involve opposing lawyers shouting at one another or an attorney exposing a lying witness to a chorus of gasps from the gallery. Far more often, it's day after day (or week after week) of counsel on both sides seeking to make their respective cases by methodically entering evidence into the record—primarily testimony or documents— that supports their legal claims or defenses, while the other side tries to blunt the force of that evidence through objections and cross-examination. The focus is on evidence because, as discussed in the summary judgment section of this chapter, the point of a trial is to *resolve the factual disputes between the parties.* Up until this point, any resolution of the case (outside of settlement) will have been the result of the judge deciding questions of law or, in the case of summary judgment, determining that there was no material factual dispute between the parties sufficient to merit a trial.

10. Administrative Office of the United States Courts, 2007 Annual Report of the Director: Judicial Business of the United States Courts 169 (2008) (for the 12-month period ending September 30, 2007, 4.1 percent of all federal cases ended in trial); Administrative Office of the United States Courts, Federal Judicial Caseload Statistics 52 (2007) (for the 12-month period ending March 31, 2007, 1.4% of all federal civil cases ended in trial).

11. Stephen C. Yeazell, Civil Procedure 474 (7th ed. 2008).

12. There is vocal minority of academics and practicing lawyers who disagree that settlement is a desirable tool for resolving legal disputes. For the classic formulation of this view, see Owen Fiss, *Against Settlement*, 93 Yale L.J. 1073 (1984).

8. Trial Preparation.   Although trial itself can be exceedingly demanding and stressful, most of the work of a trial actually occurs in the weeks before it begins—the trial preparation phase, which lawyers call "trial prep." During this period, members of the trial team spend most of their time preparing and organizing the evidence they will present at trial around their theory of the case—the story they will tell the judge or jury about what happened and why, and who should bear responsibility for the harm that resulted.

In the *McNary* case, for example, the story that Tringali and the Yale team wanted to tell at trial centered on the plight of the Haitian refugees detained on Guantánamo. Recall that after the Clinton administration refused to parole the refugees into the United States, Tringali and the team realized they needed to seek unconditional release for the Haitians. To achieve this goal, they aimed to demonstrate that the conditions of confinement violated due process. They hoped to do so by showing that the medical care at Camp Bulkeley was inadequate and that the government knew this but didn't care. Plaintiffs' counsel also set out to show that the camp itself was a miserable and unsafe place to live, even though this was not an element of their medical care due process claim. Why, then, do you think they chose to present this issue?

Trial prep also involves ensuring that the evidence is sufficient to establish each of the elements as to which the team will bear the burden of proof and preparing organizational aids to guide the litigation team at trial. Part and parcel of this work are the tasks of drafting direct and cross-examination questions, rehearsing opening statements and closing arguments, and many other matters. During trial preparation, the team will also prepare witnesses to testify on the stand. It is both appropriate and expected that attorneys will meet with their witnesses to talk about what to expect during a deposition or trial and to practice their direct examination and responses to questions likely to be asked on cross-examination. Recall, for instance, that Robert Rubin counseled Yvonne Pascal in advance of her deposition and that ACLU lawyer Lucas Guttentag spoke with Yannick Mondesir about her testimony before trial. *See STC*, pp. 219-20, 243.

9. Pretrial Conference.   In advance of trial, the court will also schedule a final pretrial conference. *See* Fed. R. Civ. P. 16. At that conference, the court may discuss a variety of matters with the parties, including the expected duration of the trial, withdrawal of insignificant claims and defenses, elimination of duplicative evidence, and stipulations (agreements) as to undisputed facts. Courts generally seek reasonable ways to streamline the trial, and they will also usually encourage the parties to revisit the possibility of settlement. In fact, it's not uncommon for parties "to settle on the courthouse steps" when confronting the disquieting prospect that no matter how strong one's case, there is no assurance about the outcome at trial.

10. Jury Trial or Bench Trial?   Cases can be tried before either a jury or a judge. In a jury trial, the jury is responsible for finding the facts. The judge will explain to the jurors the law they must apply in reaching a verdict. In a bench trial, a case tried before a judge, the judge will both find the facts and apply the law to those facts.

A jury trial starts with the selection of the jury. In this process, a group of possible jurors is directed to appear at the courthouse at a certain date and time, and the judge and the attorneys then have an opportunity to question them about a variety of issues. *See* Fed. R. Civ. P. 47(a). This process is known as "voir dire." Voir dire allows potential jurors to be dismissed two different ways. They can be dismissed "for cause" if it objectively appears that they would not be able to decide the case fairly—for example, if they were related to one of the parties or lawyers in the case. A certain number of jurors may also be excused without explanation by attorneys for each side. These are called "peremptory" challenges.[13]

The trial in *McNary* was a bench trial. Why? Because the plaintiffs in *McNary* essentially were suing the United States, they were not entitled to a jury trial. *See* 28 U.S.C. § 2402. Even if *McNary* had been a lawsuit between private parties, there nevertheless would not have been a jury trial. Although the right to a jury trial is protected by the Seventh Amendment and Fed. R. Civ. P. 38, this right does not extend to plaintiffs who seek only injunctive relief. This is because the Seventh Amendment does not *create* a right to a jury, but only "*preserve[s]*" the historical English right to a jury that existed in 1791, when the Seventh Amendment took effect along with the rest of the Bill of Rights. Historically, plaintiffs in equity suits—litigants seeking only equitable remedies such as injunctions or specific performance—did not have the right to have their cases tried by a jury. Jack H. Friedenthal et al., *Civil Procedure* 520-22 (4th ed. 2005). In any event, it is likely that plaintiffs' counsel would have sought a bench trial even had they been entitled to ask for a jury. This might be somewhat surprising; plaintiffs' lawyers often prefer to try their case to a jury. Why might that usually be the case? Despite this general tendency, the lack of a jury trial in *McNary* did not concern plaintiffs' counsel. Why?

11. The Phases of a Trial.   Although trial procedures differ by jurisdiction, all trials follow essentially the same basic progression. First, the plaintiff puts forth the evidence that she contends supports her arguments, while the defendant tries to discredit or contradict that evidence. Then the defendant is afforded the opportunity to put forth the evidence that he contends supports his arguments, with the plaintiff seeking to discredit or contradict that evidence. In a bit more detail, the roadmap of a trial looks roughly as follows:

- Opening statements by both sides (occasionally, defense attorneys will wait until they present their case to deliver an opening statement)
- Plaintiff's case-in-chief
- In a jury trial, a motion under Rule 50(a) for judgment as a matter of law, if any (at this stage, such a motion could be filed only by the defendant, who would claim that the plaintiff had not established one or more elements of his case)
- Defendant's case-in-chief
- Plaintiff's rebuttal, if any (sometimes followed by a surrebuttal by the defendant)
- In a jury trial, a motion under Rule 50(a) for judgment as a matter of law, if any (at this stage, it is possible that either or both sides might file such a motion)
- Closing arguments by both sides
- Jury instructions and deliberations (if the trial is by jury)
- Announcement of verdict and entry of judgment
- Post-judgment motions, such as a Rule 50(b) renewed motion for judgment as a matter of law

---

13. Attorneys cannot exercise peremptory challenges based solely on discriminatory grounds, such as race or gender. *See Snyder v. Louisiana*, 128 S. Ct. 1203 (2008); *J.E.B. v. Alabama*, 511 U.S. 127 (1994); *Edmonson v. Leesville Concrete Co.*, 500 U.S. 614 (1991); *Batson v. Kentucky*, 476 U.S. 79 (1986).

During the plaintiff's case, she will call witnesses and introduce evidence, and the defendant will cross-examine the plaintiff's witnesses and make objections. *See* Note 14. At the end of the plaintiff's presentation of her case, she will "rest," meaning she has no further evidence to introduce. It will then be the defendant's turn to present evidence, with the plaintiff making objections and cross-examining the defendant's witnesses. The defendant will then rest. After the defendant's case, the plaintiff may have an opportunity to call additional witnesses and introduce additional evidence in response. This stage is called rebuttal and is limited to responding to issues raised in the defendant's case.

Defendants often have less to do when they present their case. Although the plaintiff bears the burden of proof as to her claims, the defendant generally bears that burden only with respect to the affirmative defenses he has asserted, and he is *required* to submit evidence only regarding those affirmative defenses. Often, however, defendants choose to challenge the plaintiff's evidence by submitting evidence on issues as to which they do not bear the burden of proof. Consider, for instance, a breach of contract case. If the plaintiff testifies that the contract was signed by both parties, the defendant may put a witness on the stand—perhaps the defendant himself—to testify that he didn't sign the contract.

INTERVIEW
JUDGE STERLING JOHNSON, JR.
ON MANAGING A CIVIL TRIAL

How would you describe your courtroom management style?

I try to be fast and efficient. I separate the wheat from the chaff. My approach is influenced by the time I practiced as a prosecutor in state court in New York City. There were tens of thousands of cases, so judges, prosecutors, and defense counsel had to move. The federal prosecutors used to complain about their workload, but my caseload was many times greater than theirs. I remember arraignment in state criminal court, when the judge notifies the defendant of the charges against him, and makes sure he has an attorney and sets bail. It took those state judges just five minutes to take care of that. The point was, "Move the case, move the case."

This does not mean that, as a judge, I'm going to prevent someone from being heard or let an important issue go unaired. But it does mean that I want to get at the core of things. For instance, during cross-examination, I may sustain objectionable questions without even hearing an objection [as happened at times in the *McNary* case]. I won't necessarily hear an objection, but I'll already have said, "Sustained." The point is, stick by the rules and move along.

What are your biggest concerns in managing a civil trial?

The answer to this question boils down to one simple word: control. If I do not establish control, there will be chaos. Lawyers sometimes have a habit of getting off course and not focusing on the issues as they have been set out in the pretrial order. So from the start, I demand basically three things: punctuality, preparation, and professionalism. First, a 9:30 a.m. calendar call [when proceedings begin] means 9:30 a.m. If I have to, I tell the parties, "If you are on time, you are late. If you are early, you are on time." This lecture usually has the desired effect. Second, there is no excuse for being unprepared. Such conduct by an attorney reflects unfavorably on the client. Do your homework; know the issues and the law; have your case ready. Third, although litigants have opposing views that they must advocate, they can disagree without being disagreeable. Some lawyers take litigation too personally and can get carried away. If I have to, I'll issue a warning to counsel—sometimes a stern one—to ensure civility in my courtroom.

Why do you manage a trial the way that you do?

I am a product of my background and experiences. I have 12 years in law enforcement, 20 years as a state and federal prosecutor, and more than 17 years on the bench. The practices and procedures that I learned in the past are useful to me today as a judge. I've already described how practicing in state court affected me. My time working as a federal prosecutor also had an important influence on me. I practiced before some extraordinary federal judges, such as Judge Edward Weinfeld [1901-1988; appointed to the bench by President Harry S Truman]. He would not let you get bogged down in trivial things. He wanted to get to the core of the case. His approach had a strong impact on me.

As for my time in law enforcement: I learned that everyone has a role to play, and you have to stay within the bounds of that role. For instance, the role of a witness is to be a witness—nothing more, nothing less. Based on my experience, some law enforcement officers don't see it that way; when they testify in court, some of them think it's their job to convict the defendant. That's not their job. A law enforcement officer isn't there to testify to convict, but to say what he or she saw and/or did. Awareness of this type of issue has made me attuned to witness bias not just in criminal cases, but in civil cases as well.

How did the *McNary* case differ from a typical civil trial? Did that influence your management of the case in any way?

McNary was not a typical civil case—it was a media event. There were complex constitutional and administrative law issues. There were international human rights issues. There was the *Baker* case from the Eleventh Circuit, which, according to the government, barred *McNary*. There were the heavyweights from the Justice Department. The case was so important to the government that the Solicitor General of the United States came to the Eastern District to argue that the court should dismiss the case. I was a brand-new judge, and while I had an extensive criminal background, I had little civil experience.

McNary reinforced my belief that in every case, the court must always keep control. The first day of proceedings, as described in *Storming the Court,* the government lawyers announced that Ken Starr was coming up from Washington to argue the case. I took that as a challenge—not in what the government attorneys were saying, but in how they said it. That's when I told them I was from Bed-Stuy and would not be intimidated. I wanted to make it clear they would not be taking control of the courtroom. The government is not entitled to greater consideration than any other party—or to any less consideration. All parties stand as equals at the bar of justice. I work very hard to make sure of that, and in *McNary*, I needed to send a strong reminder to the government that I was not going to give them any special deference.

I do what I think is the right thing to do under the law. The Second Circuit might reverse me, but they make mistakes. So does the Supreme Court. I recently read a list of the ten worst Supreme Court opinions in history. Think of *Plessy v. Ferguson* [163 U.S. 537 (1896), approving separate but equal accommodations]. I have a mirror in my desk drawer at work. I look at myself at the end of the day. If I look in the mirror and I'm not ashamed at what I see, then I've done a good job.

12. The Opening Statement. The opening statement gives the jury its first impression of the case and provides an important opportunity for counsel on both sides to frame the issues. (Note that it is *not* called an opening argument.) Contrary to what we often see in movies or television, this is not the time for the attorney to argue the case—that is, to draw inferences from the evidence and ask the fact-finder to reach certain conclusions. Instead, as you can see from Joe Tringali's opening statement, reproduced below, attorneys try to lay out what they maintain that the evidence will prove. You will also notice that Tringali emphasizes the plaintiffs' story, or theory, of the case: that the Haitian refugees had been arbitrarily detained in substandard conditions in violation of their constitutional rights.

```
                        Tringali/opening

                           *  *  *  *

  4         MR. TRINGALI: Almost one year ago we first came

  5    before your Honor. At that time defendants urged the Court

  6    to be deaf, dumb and blind to the suffering of the Haitians

  7    held on Guantanamo. They invited you to give them

  8    unfettered discretion to hold the Haitians however long and

  9    in whatever conditions they saw fit. You declined their

 10    invitation, and the Second Circuit did as well.

 17                         *  *  *  *

 18         MR. TRINGALI: Undaunted, defendants continue to

 19    act as if they are above the law. They wage a war of

 20    endurance against people who have never been charged with

 21    any crime. In response to your order last spring,
```

Notice how Tringali focuses on the facts that he contends will be established at trial and arranges these facts to tell a compelling story about the Haitians' continued detention.

Tringali/opening

22 defendants have simply refused to process the Haitians on

23 Guantanamo, rather than provide them access to counsel or

24 other procedural protections.

25   What will the evidence show:

1   Fact: Interdicted Haitians were brought directly

2   to the United States for medical screening until late

3   February 1992 when the Bush Administration decided for the

4   first time to process them in a separate, inferior and

5   discriminatory manner.

6   Fact: Only weeks earlier, the Bush Administration

7   had told both Congress and the Supreme Court that HIV

8   positive Haitians who had been screened-in would be brought

9   directly to the United States.

10   Fact: Even today interdicted Cubans—even those

11 who swim onto Guantanamo—are not medically screened

12 before coming to the United States.

13   Fact: All of the Haitians held on Guantanamo have

14 been screened-in, having been found to have a credible fear

15 of persecution if returned to Haiti.

16   Indeed, 115 of the 119 screened-in Haitians who

17 were subjected to a second interview without access to

18 counsel before such interviews were enjoined by the Second

19 Circuit were found by INS Asylum Officers to have a

20 well-founded fear of persecution if repatriated to Haiti.

Tringali/opening

21   Fact: The Haitians languish on Guantanamo where

22   many have been held captive for over a year.

23   Fact: They are confined to a prison camp,

24   surrounded by razor barbed wire, guarded by the military,

25   made to sleep on military cots for over a year, forced to

1   hang sheets from the ceiling to gain a semblance of

2   privacy, made to tie plastic garbage bags around the sides

3   of the huts where they live so that they do not get wet

4   when it rains.

5   Both the Centers for Disease Control and

6   Department of Health and Human Services have warned that

7   the operation of an HIV positive detention camp on

8   Guantanamo presents a "potential public health disaster"

9   and "is likely to result in significantly increased public

10   health risks" to the HIV positive Haitians.

11   Fact: The military doctors on Guantanamo

12   themselves admit that Guantanamo is ill-equipped to treat

13   individuals with serious illness and lacks specialists and

14   equipment necessary in treating AIDS patients.

15   Fact: The military has not objected to the

16   presence of lawyers or Haitian doctors on Guantanamo,

17   despite the statements of the Department of Justice in this

18   courtroom and elsewhere to the contrary, and, in fact the

19   military believes that both lawyers and Haitian doctors

It is important not to exaggerate facts, which can harm your credibility with the fact-finder. But it is good lawyering to choose vivid words that present the facts in the light most favorable to your client. Here, for example, Tringali uses "languish" and "held captive" to convey the Haitians' powerlessness.

Why does Tringali focus so much on the military's position on these issues?

Tringali/opening

20 could have served a useful role.

21   Fact: The military has urged that Camp Bulkeley

22 be closed.

23   Fact: The military has also urged that certain

24 individuals be medically evacuated because they could not

25 be adequately treated on Guantanamo, but the Department of

1 Justice has denied many of those requests. A denial

2 justified by the INS press spokesman in December [who]

3 remarked: "They're going to die anyway, aren't they?"

4   Your Honor will hear the testimony of Fritznell

5 Camy and Yanick [Mondesir]—two Haitians who have been held at

6 Camp Bulkeley, but who were finally allowed to enter the

7 United States for medical reasons. You will also hear the

8 deposition testimony of Johnny—Lambert Alexandre

9 [and Yvonne Pascal, who] remain confined to Camp Bulkeley.
    They

10 will tell you what it is like to serve an indefinite

11 sentence in the first U.S. government HIV prison camp.

12   You will hear from former government employees who

13 were assigned to Guantanamo, Ellen Powers and Sam Reep.

14 They will tell you what the Camp was like and how the

15 Haitians were processed and treated.

16   You will hear from Professor Deborah Anker of

17 Harvard Law School and Esther Cruz, who represent refugees

18 in political asylum cases in the United States. Both will

19 explain the role of lawyers in that process, particularly

20 for Haitians who are fleeing persecution in their

Tringali/opening

21 homeland.

22   Next, you will hear from Dr. Robert Cohen, an

23 Attending Physician at the AIDS Center at St. Vincent's

24 Hospital, Dr. Douglas Shenson, an Assistant Professor at

25 Albert Einstein College of Medicine who visited Guantanamo,

1 and Dr. Jonathan Mann, formerly Director of the World

2 Health Organization's Global Programme on AIDS and

3 currently a Professor at the Harvard School of Public

4 Health. These doctors will testify as to the medical needs

5 of AIDS patients, the inappropriateness of holding them in

6 a detention camp on Guantanamo, and that the admission of

7 the Haitians held there would not pose a public health

8 threat.

9   Finally, your Honor, we'll hear the deposition

10 testimony of Colonel Stephen Kinder—the one military

11 commander at Camp Bulkeley that defendants do not want to

12 call, and the one military commander they don't want you to

13 hear from. Colonel Kinder will testify as to the

14 frustration of the Haitians and his own without knowing

15 when or if they would be released and his unsuccessful

16 efforts to medically evacuate some of the more seriously

17 ill Haitians.

18   One year later, your Honor, the Haitians continue

19 to languish and grow increasingly sick, desperate and

20 suicidal on Guantanamo. There's much shame here. And it

21 is for that reason—and that reason alone—that

```
                           Tringali/opening

22    defendants will urge you again, as they have done before,

23    not to see the sadness in the eyes of the imprisoned

24    Haitians, not to hear the desperation in their voices, and

25    not to be moved by the human suffering they must endure.

 1    You refused to ignore it a year ago and you should refuse

 2    to ignore it again today. Thank you.

 3        THE COURT: Would you like to make an opening

 4    statement, Mr. Filppu?

 5        MR. FILPPU: Your Honor, I think the Court's well

 6    aware of the factual disputes between the parties and the

 7    implications of the facts, as we argue them, but I would

 8    prefer to reserve my opening statement until we start.

 9        THE COURT: Okay.
```

As mentioned in *Storming the Court,* Tringali normally took a straightforward approach in his opening statements. In this instance, however, and particularly in the final paragraph of his opening statement, he chose a more florid style because his audience included the media and thus the public. Imagine that you had to deliver the opening statement in *McNary.*[14] How might you have done things differently than Tringali? What would you have said in the opening minute of your statement? Do you see that to decide what you're going to say, you need a theory of the case? At the end of Tringali's opening, there is a brief exchange between Judge Johnson and Lauri Filppu. Why do you think Filppu decided not to deliver an opening statement? Was that the right decision? Why or why not?

13. Introducing Evidence at Trial. In the federal courts, the introduction of evidence, including witness testimony, is governed by the Federal Rules of Evidence. An understanding of these rules is critical for litigators; we'll provide a short introduction here to give you a feel for the basic application of the rules at trial.

You should understand four basic principles about the admissibility of evidence. First, to be admissible, evidence must be *relevant.* Evidence is relevant if it makes some fact in dispute more or less likely to be true. *See* Fed. R. Evid. 401. For example, in a tort

---

14. If you want to be a trial attorney, it should be evident that you're going to do a great deal of public speaking. If you're not the type to talk in class, you might want to start forcing yourself to participate more often. The only way to get comfortable with speaking in public is to do it!

action arising from a traffic accident, it is more likely that the defendant entered the intersection when the light was red if a credible eyewitness for the plaintiff testifies that he personally saw that the light was red for the defendant at the time of the accident. Second, evidence must be *material*—that is, it must bear on an element of a claim or defense in the case. Consider again the traffic accident suit. Would evidence that there had been a thunderstorm two weeks before the accident be material to the case? What if it was thundering and raining *during* the accident?

Third, evidence must be *reliable* (or, as it is sometimes called, "competent"). This means different things for different kinds of evidence. A document is competent, or reliable, if it can be shown that it actually is what it purports to be—and not, for example, a forgery or fake (see Note 17, later in this chapter). A witness is competent to provide particular testimony if it can be shown that his testimony is based on his personal knowledge. In the traffic accident case, for instance, if the witness is testifying that the light was red for the plaintiff, he must himself have been at the intersection and seen that the light was red, as opposed to having heard from someone else that it was red.

Fourth, evidence that meets all of the previous three criteria can nonetheless be excluded if its *prejudicial effect substantially outweighs its probative value*—that is, if the prejudice the evidence would cause substantially outweighs the value that it would have in helping the fact-finder decide the case. *See* Fed. R. Evid. 403. By contrast, if the probative value of the evidence is found to outweigh its prejudicial effect, the evidence will be deemed *admissible*. The fact-finder will then have the task of weighing its value in conjunction with the other admissible evidence when deciding the case. As an example, consider a tort action in which the plaintiffs, husband and wife, assert several claims, including loss of consortium as a result of injuries to one spouse from a car accident they allege was caused by the defendant. If there is evidence of extra-marital affairs by both plaintiffs, should that be admissible?

14. *Witness Testimony.*   Testimonial evidence at trial, as you no doubt know, is provided by witnesses testifying under oath on the stand. Direct examination is the questioning of a witness by the attorney who wishes to offer the witness's testimony in support of a particular claim or defense. Cross-examination is the process by which the opposing attorney challenges the accuracy and credibility of that witness's testimony. We consider each in turn.

a. *Direct examination.*   Examination of a witness is a critical skill that trial lawyers hone over many years. A lawyer's questions need to be short, clear, and direct and asked in a logical progression so as to arrange the pieces of the witness's testimony into a coherent, persuasive story for the fact-finder. Ideally, the attorney is able to develop a rhythm with her witness so that the questions and answers follow one another smoothly and naturally. At its best, the result is a seamless, compelling flow of testimony, and though it may all seem spontaneous to a layperson watching from the gallery, that is far from the case. It is, rather, the product of an experienced attorney who has done an expert job of preparing the witness before trial.

Such preparation is essential because potential problems abound when a witness takes the stand. Witnesses become nervous, testimony sometimes ends up being unclear, or the fact-finder (particularly in the case of a jury) may lose track of what the witness is saying. All of this is exacerbated by objections from opposing counsel, who may argue that the form or subject of the question posed to the witness violates the rules of evidence. For instance, attorneys conducting direct examinations must use nonleading questions—that is, questions that do not suggest the answer to the question within them ("How was the food at Camp Bulkeley?" rather than "Wasn't the food at Camp

Bulkeley awful?"). A leading question on direct almost always draws an objection from the other side; if the judge sustains it, the questioning attorney must rephrase the question on the spot or move on to another question.

Whatever the particular ground, an objection may not only eliminate certain testimony from the fact-finder's consideration, but can trip up the witness or the lawyer who is conducting the questioning—especially an inexperienced lawyer. In fact, some attorneys use objections purely to interrupt the flow of the opposing party's examination, although this isn't considered good practice. (Recall, for instance, how Adam Gutride struggled to examine Ellen Powers in the face of the numerous objections by government lawyer Ellen Sue Shapiro.[15] *See STC*, p. 252.) If the attorney feels an objection is legitimately warranted, however, the attorney must make it at that moment—or it is waived. If the trial court judge overrules the objection, it is at least on the record for appeal.

To give you a taste of a direct examination, we have reproduced below several portions of Mike Wishnie's questioning of plaintiffs' witness Samuel Reep on the first day of trial—March 8, 1993. Reep began by testifying that he was a Peace Corps volunteer in Haiti until the September 1991 coup, and that after the coup he left Haiti and went to work for the Justice Department on Guantánamo. Reep next testified that as a Justice Department employee, he served as a Creole translator during INS screening interviews. Then came the following testimony:

```
                    Reep-direct/Wishnie

                         * * * *

12    Q  Did you ever observe INS conduct first interviews of

13    refuguees?

14    A  Yes, I did.

15    Q  In what sort of places did they conduct these

16    interviews?

17    A  They conducted them in tents, in the hangar, sometimes

18    in stairwells of the hangar.

19    Q  Did the government or military personnel use these

20    stairwells during these interviews?
```

---

15. Objecting primarily for the purpose of throwing the opposing lawyer off balance can backfire even when the effort succeeds. Years after the *McNary* trial, Judge Johnson told Brandt Goldstein in an interview that he found Shapiro's conduct during Gutride's examination grating and counterproductive—not the sort of reaction counsel wants to elicit in the judge deciding the case.

Reep-direct/Wishnie

21   A Yes, they were public stairwells that went to the

22   civilian offices and some military offices on the floor

23   above. There was traffic just about all times going back

24   and forth.

Do you notice how clear and concise Wishnie's questions generally are? Crafting good questions is not as easy as it might initially seem. What was the purpose of Wishnie's question regarding the use of stairwells?

Reep's initial testimony went smoothly, but then Wishnie tried to elicit testimony from him about the workings of the credible fear screening interviews. The result was a series of objections from government lawyer David Kline . . . .

Reep-direct/Wishnie

* * * *

25   Q Mr. Reep, did some refugees have multiple first

1   interviews with INS?

2   A Yes.

3   Q How do you know?

4   A Being one of those that was interviewing, we saw

5   familiar faces and recognized names, and we would check our

6   records and see that in fact they had come through before.

7   In fact, it got to the point where we saw so many that when

8   a group would be gathered before we would bring them in to

9   interview, we would ask, have you been seen before.

10   MR. KLINE: I object and move to strike that

11   portion of the testimony. [This is] obvious hearsay when he

12   says "we did", "we knew", "we saw".

* * * *

```
                      Reep-direct/Wishnie

 9  Q  Mr. Reep, after someone said to you, I had a first

10  interview already, you just stated you checked the records.

11     What records did you check?

12  A  We would check—

13     THE COURT: When you say "we", who are you talking

14  about?

15     THE WITNESS: CRS, interview team.

16     THE COURT: You being one of them?

17     THE WITNESS: Yes.

18  BY MR. WISHNIE:

19  Q  Did you personally check records in these situations?

20  A  Yes, many times.

21  Q  What did you discover when you checked the CRS records?

22  A  I would see that this person had indeed passed through

23  on such and such a date that we had interviewed [him].
```

David Kline's first objection is that the testimony provided by Samuel Reep is "hearsay." In the most general of terms, that means the testimony is not based on Reep's personal knowledge—and, with some exceptions, is not admissible.[16] Given the rule that hearsay is not admissible, what word in Reep's testimony keeps getting him into trouble? The word "we." Why? Because Reep can only testify based on personal knowledge as to the names he recognized, the faces he'd seen before, and the records he checked; he cannot speak for the other translators and therefore cannot say "we." It's an easy mistake for a witness to make, because it's a common locution when relating a story about a group. In preparing Reep for his direct examination, you could simply tell him not to use "we," though he might well forget this instruction under the pressure of being on the stand. What additional advice might you give to help him avoid this problem?

Now consider the following testimony by Reep on direct examination and Kline's objection to this testimony.

---

16. The basic hearsay rule is that an out-of-court statement cannot be offered into evidence for the truth of the matter asserted in the statement. For instance, the plaintiff in an auto accident tort case could not offer a witness statement saying the light was green for the plaintiff—and then refuse to produce the witness in court. Nor could the plaintiff say, "I heard the witness say the light was green." The witness must come into court and testify as to the color of the light—and face cross-examination to test the accuracy and credibility of the testimony.

```
                    Reep-direct/Wishnie

                          * * * *

24  Q  Mr. Reep, did you personally meet or see other Haitians

25  who had been screened-in and then had another first

1   interview?

2   A  Yes, I did, many times.

3   Q  And in what circumstances?

4   A  Like I said, in the interview tent area I saw them many

5   times. There were times also that Haitians that were from

6   a screened-out camp would flag down a CRS member and say, I

7   was interviewed by CRS and now I hear I'm in a screened-out

8   camp, what is going on.

9       MR. KLINE: I object, your Honor. He's not

10  testifying about what he knows. He's testifying to persons

11  in the camp flagging down other CRS members and saying

12  things to them.
```

Do you understand the government lawyer's argument, in lines 9 through 12, as to why this is hearsay?

Wishnie also had some trouble with a question he asked about screened-in refugees who were found in the screened-out camp:

```
                    Reep-direct/Wishnie

1   Q  Did you ever have the experience of finding in the

2   records that someone was screened-in, but you had seen them

3   in a screened-out camp?

4   A  Yes.

5       MR. KLINE: Objection, your Honor, leading.
```

How might you revise the question to make it easier for the fact-finder to follow the testimony—and to get around the objection from Kline? (Hint: Split it up into several questions.) If you wish to read more of this trial testimony, you can find the full transcript on the book's website.

b. *Cross-examination.* Cross-examination gives opposing counsel the chance to probe the accuracy and credibility of a witness's testimony. This might be done by questioning the witness's perceptions about the events in question—for example, by asking an eyewitness about his poor eyesight—or by showing that the witness is biased in favor of one of the parties. Cross-examinations tend to be most effective when they are brief and focused on a few critical failings about the witness or his testimony. By careful, methodical questioning, the attorney aims to force the witness into a series of concessions that undermine—and ideally destroy—the testimony provided on direct. Done well, a cross-examination can be a thing of beauty . . . unless you're the witness or the opposing lawyer.

Recall that government lawyer Bob Begleiter conducted a very effective cross-examination of Bulkeley refugee Yannick Mondesir. *See STC*, pp. 249-51. With just a few questions, Begleiter was able to cast doubt on the veracity of Mondesir's testimony. For example, Begleiter asked Mondesir about Evans Paul, the former mayor of Port-au-Prince and the leader of the KID opposition party. What was her response? What kind of impact do you think this had on her claim of political persecution? On her overall credibility as a witness?

Preparation for a "cross" starts with diligent review of the witness's deposition testimony and the development of a basic outline of questioning. (A party must make available for deposition any witness that she intends to call at trial.) Opposing counsel will then listen with great care during direct examination of the witness to sharpen the focus of the cross, zeroing in on any newly revealed weakness or perhaps dispensing with a line of inquiry that seems unlikely to achieve much. When it comes time to conduct the cross, an attorney has more latitude than on direct—at least in some ways. For instance, leading questions are permitted on cross, while they are not allowed on direct. What do you think the reasoning is for that rule?

Still, there are limits to what the cross-examining lawyer can do. Most important, cross-examination is *limited to the subjects covered on direct*. If the attorney moves beyond those subjects, opposing counsel may object that the question is "beyond the scope of direct." As noted in *Storming the Court*, that is why Joe Tringali confined his direct examination of Fritznel Camy at the start of trial to so few topics. *See id.*, p. 249. Tringali wanted to give Judge Johnson a vivid impression of Guantánamo at the outset of the proceedings, but by asking Camy so little of real substance, he left Lauri Filppu with almost no latitude to conduct a meaningful cross.

The attorney who calls the witness usually defends her on cross-examination, objecting to questions that either seek to elicit evidence not permitted by the rules or are otherwise inappropriate. Lodging appropriate objections was the concern Tringali had in mind when he urged Adam Gutride to protect his witness during Ellen Sue Shapiro's cross-examination of Ellen Powers—but that is easier said than done. It takes plenty of practice to learn how to object to questions in a timely manner and to quickly and accurately explain the basis of one's objections if challenged to do so by the judge. Adam found this out the hard way, trying to voice objections as Shapiro pummeled his witness on cross. He finally managed to object to questions that exceeded the scope of the direct examination; he also could have objected to certain questions as argumentative. The judge recognized the potential objections anyway, however, barking out "sustained" even when Gutride was silent. Why do you think the judge did this? (See Judge Johnson's interview earlier in this chapter.)

Joe Tringali conducted several cross-examinations during the *McNary* case, including that of Lieutenant Jason Dillman. *See id.*, pp. 272-275. Refer back to the cited pages of the book and you will notice Tringali following one of the basic rules of cross-examination: If possible, never ask a question to which you don't know the answer. Tringali knows exactly where he is going with Dillman. With the use of highly circumscribed questions, Tringali forces him to recount what happened during the "predawn raid" that ended with Yvonne Pascal in the brig. Notice, too, the series of questions Tringali asks at the bottom of page 272 and the top of page 273 regarding fires, rock throwing, and other violence. Obviously, none of this was happening when the Haitians were asleep. What does Tringali accomplish by posing these questions?

INTERVIEW
JOE TRINGALI ON CROSS-EXAMINATION

What are your views on how to conduct a good cross-examination?

You should have two goals in mind when conducting a cross-examination. First, how do I neutralize or (even better) rebut any testimony of the witness on direct examination that may hurt my case? Second, can I use this witness to give helpful testimony for my case even if the witness was called to testify for the opposing side? With those two goals in mind, the cross-examination should be as concise and efficient as possible. Direct examinations often go on longer than the jury would like, so if you can come back on cross-examination with a short, focused, and effective cross-examination, you are likely to score points with the jurors (or the judge, if it's a bench trial).

As an illustration of some of the above principles, consider how I questioned Lt. Jason Dillman in the *McNary* trial [*See STC*, pp. 273-75]. Dillman testified about an early morning military operation (which plaintiffs dubbed a "pre-dawn raid") that led to a number of Haitians being confined in the military brig. Though we actually called Dillman to the stand, he was a hostile witness, and therefore my examination of him was done much as I would conduct a cross. And I got him to provide a lot of helpful testimony for our case. I had enough basic information about the pre-dawn raid before conducting the cross that I could ask him a series of brief questions about the events that painted things in a very bad light for the military. In addition, I kept the cross-examination brief and moved along at a rapid clip. We covered a lot of damning information in a short period of time.

How do you prepare for cross-examination?

If the witness has been deposed in the case or given any prior testimony, I read that testimony. Together with any helpful documents the witness authored or received, this testimony is the foundation of my cross-examination.

The main rule of cross-examination is not to ask a question to which you do not know the witness's answer. If you ask questions taken from the witness's prior testimony or documents, you will not violate that basic rule. I normally prepare a cross-examination binder for each witness that includes the prior testimony and key documents authored or received by the witness, as well as a cross-examination script that has specific references from the witness's prior testimony or documents for each answer I wish to elicit.

As an example, consider again the cross-examination of Lt. Dillman. I walked him through some details about the situation before the pre-dawn raid occurred, forcing him to answer a series of questions to which I knew the answer, such as the fact that there were no fires, rock throwing, or violence before the military entered Camp Bulkeley. By asking these questions, I forced him to set the stage for the conclusion that Bulkeley was peaceful before the soldiers came in and in chaos after they arrived.

How do you prepare your script? And do you ever improvise? If so, when?

Generally, I draft my questions with the aim of obtaining as much helpful testimony to my case as possible even though I am examining a hostile witness. To be effective, the question should give the witness little choice but to answer as I want based on prior testimony or documents. Usually, that means leaving the witness with no option but to respond with a simple "Yes" or "No" to a leading question that includes everything I would want the witness to say if I were calling the witness as my own witness on direct. Nothing goes perfectly, though, and you need to be ready to improvise when the witness gives an unexpected response. If you know the case as well as you should at the time of trial, you should be able to respond to any unexpected answers with questions that get your cross back on track.

In the case of the Dillman cross, you'll notice that I used a lot of yes/no questions. Things generally went smoothly, but there were a couple of times I had to improvise. A small example: At one point early on, I asked Dillman if the military made a "pre-dawn raid on Camp Bulkeley" [*STC*, p. 272]. Dillman was smart, and instead of answering yes, he challenged my characterization: "No. It wasn't a pre-dawn raid." [*Id.*]. I wanted to keep the rhythm of the cross-examination going, so I changed my question on the fly, using a more neutral formulation: "Did the military show up at Camp Bulkeley" early on Saturday morning? At this point, Dillman gave me the answer I wanted, and I was again headed in the direction I wanted to go.

What, in your view, is the biggest mistake a lawyer can make when conducting a cross-examination?

I think many lawyers would agree that the biggest mistake is asking one question too many. Often, when you are getting good admissions from a witness on cross-examination, you are tempted to press your luck and ask an additional question that was not asked previously of the witness (in prior testimony or documents). You should resist that temptation because you no longer control the cross if you are asking questions where the witness has not previously responded to that question. And, key to an effective cross-examination is that you, not the witness, are in control of the cross and the testimony elicited from the witness.

What are your aims when defending a witness who is facing cross-examination?

There are several aims. First, you want the witness to remain credible before the jury. If the witness suddenly changes her demeanor and is evasive or hostile, when on direct she was responsive and cordial, the jury will notice and it will detract from the witness's credibility and the points made by the witness on direct examination. Second, you want to have prepared your witness so he is not surprised by any questions he is asked or documents he is shown on cross. This requires careful preparation of the witness and conducting a mock cross of the witness. Third, you want to anticipate the more difficult questions the witness will be asked and be ready with a re-direct examination to neutralize any harmful testimony that is elicited on cross.

Unfortunately, there are times when things don't go your way. That was the case with our witness Yannick Mondesir [See STC, pp. 249-51]. We did the best we could to get her ready for the experience of a cross-examination—no easy task, given that she had only been in the United States a short while—but government lawyer Bob Begleiter managed to get her to act very defensively on the stand. Some people on our team feared that she did not come across as credible on some points of testimony. In the end, though, I don't think Begleiter did any real damage to our case, because his cross in no way rebutted our fundamental argument: The Haitians were being detained indefinitely in miserable conditions and without proper medical care in violation of the Constitution.

15. Expert Witnesses. One type of witness is subject to special evidentiary rules—the expert witness. An expert witness has specialized knowledge based on her education, training, or experience and thus may provide an expert opinion to assist the fact-finder in deciding a case. The rules on expert witnesses generally govern four issues: (1) the scope of what experts can testify about, (2) whether they are qualified to testify about that subject, (3) whether their testimony is relevant and reliable, and (4) the admissibility of the materials on which they rely to form their expert opinions. *See Daubert v. Merrell Dow Pharmaceuticals*, 509 U.S. 579 (1993).

To provide expert testimony, the witness must qualify as an expert under Rule 702 of the Federal Rules of Evidence. In the *McNary* trial, both sides relied on medical experts as expert witnesses. To establish their qualifications, the witnesses testified about their background, including education, board certifications, work experience, research, publications, awards, and committee work. The party offering the expert's testimony then asked the judge to designate the witness as an expert within his or her particular field. Such a designation enables the witness to render opinions in his or her area of expertise, including on hypothetical matters. (By contrast, witnesses offering nonexpert, or "lay," testimony are limited in the extent to which they may offer opinions.)

As an example of expert testimony, review the account in *Storming the Court* of the testimony of Dr. Jonathan Mann, a Harvard professor who specialized in epidemiology (the study of the spread of contagious diseases), with a subspecialty in AIDS.

See STC, pp. 256-57. You will see that Michael Ratner, who examined Dr. Mann, began by establishing his qualifications. Once Judge Johnson designated Mann as an expert, Ratner then asked for Mann's expert opinion about the epidemiological risk of allowing the Guantánamo Haitians into the United States. The essence of Mann's testimony was that admitting them to the United States would not pose a significant risk to the country's public health.

The government lawyers conducted almost no cross-examination of Mann. Rather, they introduced their own expert to testify about the risk of allowing the Haitians into the United States, leaving it for the judge to decide whom to believe in what is widely (and a bit cynically) called a "battle of the experts." The government lawyers did not use an epidemiologist, however—perhaps because, as Tringali and Koh conjectured, they couldn't find one willing to say what they wanted. Instead, they relied on Dr. Barbara Wolf, a physician with a specialization in pathology—the study of the causes, development, and consequences of disease—who made diagnoses of secondary infections in AIDS patients and performed autopsies of patients who had died of AIDS. Dr. Wolf testified that even among people who are aware that they are HIV positive, there are individuals who nevertheless have unsafe sex with uninfected (and unsuspecting) people. She also testified that some of the Haitians could be expected to engage in such behavior if they were admitted to the United States. Finally, Dr. Wolf testified about the high cost of treating AIDS patients and disagreed with Dr. Mann's statement that allowing the Haitians into the United States would not impose a significant burden.

Joe Tringali had the responsibility of cross-examining Dr. Wolf. Cross-examination of an expert witness, like that of any other witness, is generally intended to undermine the testimony provided on direct; however, there are differences in how to approach that task. In that regard, review the following excerpt of Tringali's cross of Wolf.

```
                    Wolf/cross/Tringali                    1640

                           * * * *

12  CROSS-EXAMINATION

13  BY MR. TRINGALI:

14  Q.  Dr. Wolf, are there any other diseases that cost as much

15  as AIDS over a lifetime?

16  A.  There are diseases that, in a given individual, can

17  result in equivalent costs, yes.

18  Q.  Dr. Wolf, you have no background in public health, is

19  that correct?

20  A.  That's correct.
```

21 Q.   And you have no background in epidemiology?

22 A.   That's correct.

23 Q.   And you have not provided HIV counseling to any
         patients?

24 A.   I have not counseled patients directly, that's
         correct.

25 Q.   And you know of Dr. Mann, is that correct?

                    Wolf/cross/Tringali   1641

 1 A.   Yes, I do.

 2 Q.   And you know that he is well-known and well-respected in

 3 the field of public health and AIDS?

 4 A.   Yes, he is.

 5 Q.   And that is a field in which you have no expertise?

 6 A.   That's true.

 7   MR. PAZAR: Your Honor—all right.

 8   THE COURT: You just wanted to stand up?

 9   MR. PAZAR: The witness was a little bit faster than

10 I was, your Honor.

11 Q.   Doctor, there are approximately 1.5 million Americans in

12 the United States who are HIV positive?

13 A.   That is approximately the current estimate, yes.

14 Q.   And the risk posed by the entry of each of the 215

15 Haitians on Guantanamo into this country is the exact same

16 risk already posed by each of the approximately 1.5 million

17 Americans already here?

18 A.   I'm sorry. Could you repeat that?

19 Q.   Sure. The risk posed by the entry of 215 Haitians from

20 Guantanamo who are HIV positive is the same risk already posed

Attorneys must stand up when they address the court. Here, Pazar stands to make his objection but isn't quite fast enough, and the witness answers before he can object to the question. We discuss this in more detail after this excerpt of trial testimony.

21 in this country by the 1.5 million Americans who are HIV

22 positive?

23 A.   In my opinion, that's an accurate assumption.

24 Q.   And it's also the same risk that's posed by those among

25 the 20 million tourists who enter our country each year who

                          Wolf/cross/Tringali   1642

1 are HIV positive, is that correct?

With this objection, Pazar is contending that Tringali has not established that the witness has a foundation of knowledge to answer the question. Note how Tringali responds by revising his line of questioning.

2   MR. PAZAR: Your Honor, there's no foundation. I

3 object.

4   THE COURT: I'll sustain [as to] the form of the
   question.

5 Q.   Do you know that tourists come into this country each

6 year without being HIV tested?

7 A.   Yes, I do know that.

8 Q.   Do you know that there are approximately 20 million

9 tourists who come into this country each year? That's the

10 estimate.

11 A.   I was not aware of that figure.

12 Q.   Whatever the number is, am I correct that the risk posed

13 by those individuals who are HIV positive, tourists who come

14 into this country, is also the same risk that is posed by

15 these 215 Haitians on Guantanamo?

16 A.   I think that's a reasonable assumption.

17 Q.   Now, HIV can be spread today in the United States by any

18 of 1.5 million people who are here and already infected?

19 A. Yes, although I would say with the exception of those who

20 are in terminally ill stages of disease, yes.

21 Q.   Many of those 1.5 million people have never been tested

22 and don't know they are HIV positive?

23 A.   That's correct.

24 Q.   And the only way to eliminate the risk in the United

25 States of an additional HIV infection, doctor, would be to

Wolf/cross/Tringali

1643

1 require mandatory testing and quarantine of all those who test

2 HIV positive, is that correct?

3   MR. PAZAR: Your Honor, again, I object. First,

4 there's no foundation laid; second, it's beyond the scope.

5   THE COURT: I'm going to allow it.

6 A.   I'm sorry. I don't think I understand it. Can you

7 repeat it.

8 Q.   To eliminate the risk through sexual transmission, the

9 only way you could do that is to test every person living in

10 the United States and then as to those who are HIV positive to

11 quarantine them so that you can be certain that they will not

12 pass the virus on to anyone else, if you want to eliminate the

13 risk?

14   THE COURT: Risk through sexual intercourse?

15   MR. TRINGALI: That's correct.

16 A.   To completely eliminate the risk, I guess in absolute

17 terms that could be considered correct. What we are trying to

18 do is to minimize the risk through education and behavioral

19 modification.

20 Q.   And as a doctor you are opposed to both mandatory testing

21 and quarantine, is that correct?

22 A.   Mandatory testing of the general population?

23 Q.   Correct.

24 A.   Yes, I am opposed to that.

25 Q.   And quarantine?

                    Wolf/cross/Tringali

                                                    1644

1 A.   Yes.

2 Q.   And you are also opposed to holding someone in prison for

3 no reason other than that they are HIV positive, is that

4 correct?

5   MR. PAZAR: Your Honor, again—

6   THE COURT: I'm going to allow it.

7 A.   Am I opposed to imprisoning someone on the basis solely

8 of HIV status?

9 Q.   Yes.

10 A.   Yes. I would be opposed to that.

11 Q. Doctor, if you increase the number of HIV positive people

12 in the United States from 1.5 million to 1,500,215, isn't it

13 correct that the increase in the U.S. HIV population [is]
        I guess

14 approximately 1/100 of one percent?

15 A.   I will have to accept your calculations.

16 Q.   I have a calculator for you, if you would like.

17   THE COURT: She's a doctor, not a mathematician.

18 She accepts it.

19   MR. TRINGALI: Okay. I have nothing further. Thank

20 you, doctor.

In what ways did Tringali's cross-examination differ from a cross-examination of a witness offering lay testimony? How did Tringali blunt Wolf's testimony about the burden that would supposedly be caused by the Haitians if they were to come to the United States? Do you think Tringali's strategy was effective? Why or why not?

Now consider government lawyer Charles Pazar's objection near the top of page 1643 of the trial transcript (lines 3-4). The question Tringali asked was, in fact, beyond the scope of the direct examination. Why would Judge Johnson allow it? In a bench trial, there isn't much risk of prejudice because the judge must often hear testimony to rule on its admissibility anyway. Thus, there is not much to be gained by having the testimony excluded after the judge has heard it and the presumption is that the judge will be able to give all the evidence its appropriate weight. Note that Pazar probably could have objected hear Tringali's question on page 1643, lines 20-21, and he finally did object again near the top of page 1644—but Judge Johnson allowed Tringali's question. If Pazar was not happy with the judge's rulings, what could he have done?

Consider also Pazar's attempt to interrupt Dr. Wolf on page 1641, line 7. What happened here? Pazar was intending to object before Dr. Wolf testified that she had no expertise in the field of public health and AIDS (perhaps entirely disqualifying her testimony), but Pazar wasn't fast enough with his objection. What could he have done at this point? He could have moved to strike the testimony—that is, remove it from the record—because it followed an objectionable question. The fact that there was no jury probably explains why Pazar didn't move to strike; as noted previously, the judge is presumably able to give all the evidence its appropriate weight—in this case, disregarding it. (Judge Johnson's comment to Pazar about standing up was meant to be humorous, and drew some laughter in the courtroom. Had a jury been present, it is unlikely that Judge Johnson would have made the joke.)

16. Testimony When the Witness Is Not Present.   A witness generally must deliver his testimony live in court so that the other side may test the credibility and accuracy of that testimony on cross-examination. Further, recall from Note 14 earlier in the chapter that a statement made outside of court is hearsay and usually inadmissible. In some circumstances, however, witness testimony can be offered at trial without the witness being present. In *McNary*, for example, the court allowed the students to read deposition testimony into the trial record. Why? Because the government refused to allow Yvonne Pascal and others designated as witnesses to leave Guantánamo to testify at trial. Rule 32 allows the use of deposition testimony at trial when a witness is unavailable, as long as the other party (here, the government) was represented at the deposition and the testimony is used only to the extent that it would be admissible had the witness testified in court. *See* Fed. R. Civ. P. 32. This rule was of obvious importance in *McNary*, since the plaintiffs would otherwise have had to rely only on the testimony of the Haitians paroled into the United States.

Class Exercise No. 2—Examination of a Witness

Your professor will divide you into teams of four so that you can prepare this exercise before class. One of you will play the part of Yvonne Pascal, another will play the part of Adam Gutride, a third will play the part of Lauri Filppu, and the fourth will be Judge Johnson. Imagine that Yvonne had been allowed to enter the United States to testify at trial. Gutride should conduct a direct examination of Yvonne regarding the conditions of the camp, and Filppu should conduct a cross-examination. If possible, the students playing Gutride and Filppu should

> try to make relevant objections during the other party's examination based on what they have learned about objections in this chapter, and Judge Johnson should rule on those objections. You may wish to review Yvonne Pascal's deposition testimony in Chapter Seven in connection with this exercise. You may also read the full transcript of Pascal's testimony on the book's website.

17. Other Evidentiary Matters. As explained in Note 13, documentary evidence must be "competent." To meet this requirement, the party introducing the document must show that the document, such as a personal datebook, a passport, or a bank check, is indeed what it purports to be. This process of providing a factual basis for the jury to infer that the document is what it purports to be is called laying a foundation for the document. A lawyer can lay the foundation for a document through witness testimony or by stipulation of the parties. Laying a foundation through witness testimony is often accomplished by asking the witness if he or she recognizes the document and, if so, to identify the document.

Laying the foundation is part of a more elaborate, quite ritualized procedure for offering documents into evidence through witness testimony. In general terms, this process involves marking the document as an exhibit, showing it to the other side, laying a foundation as described previously, and then asking that the document be admitted into evidence. The judge will then decide whether the document is admitted. The process of offering documents into evidence can be time-consuming, so parties often stipulate to the admission of each other's documents before trial. This is what happens in *McNary*, since there was generally little question about the authenticity and accuracy of the documents.

In addition to documentary evidence, the parties may rely on real evidence and demonstrative evidence. Although neither of these terms is defined in the Federal Rules of Evidence, you can think of real evidence as physical evidence, such as the allegedly defective product in a products liability suit, and demonstrative evidence as evidence that offers a "firsthand sense impression" about something in the case.[17] *See* Christopher B. Mueller & Laird C. Kirkpatrick, *5 Federal Evidence* § 9.22 (3d ed. 2007). In the *McNary* case, the most important piece of demonstrative evidence the plaintiffs introduced was the video of the military's pre-dawn sweep of Camp Bulkeley. Can you think of other kinds of demonstrative evidence that the plaintiffs might have presented at trial?

18. Closing Argument. Closing argument is the last impression that the attorney will leave with the jury or judge. It provides the attorney an opportunity to explain why the evidence compels a conclusion in her client's favor. Typically, a closing argument will go beyond a review of the evidence and include arguments both as to how the facts support the party's position and how the law applies to those facts. An attorney will generally return to her theory of the case, focusing on the broader story that the evidence tells, emphasizing the credibility of witnesses with favorable testimony, and seeking to undercut the opposition's evidence and arguments.

---

17. Demonstrative evidence encompasses real evidence because physical objects that play a role in the events leading to the suit also convey a firsthand sense impression about something at issue in the case. *See* MUELLER & KIRKPATRICK, 5 FEDERAL EVIDENCE § 9.22 (3d ed. 2007).

The closing arguments in *McNary* immediately followed the cross-examination of Jason Dillman. Brief portions of those arguments from Lauri Filppu and Joe Tringali appear on pages 275-76 of *Storming the Court*. Can you point to a moment when Filppu draws inferences from the evidence—specifically, the testimony of Dr. Barbara Wolf (which was not included in the book)? Can you identify a point at which Tringali argues that the government's evidence supports the plaintiffs' due process claim? As with much of the rest of the trial, the fact that this was a bench trial allowed more exchange between the judge and the attorneys than there might otherwise have been because there was no risk of prejudicing the jury. For example, you'll notice that Judge Johnson actually challenges Filppu in the middle of his argument. *See STC*, p. 276. That would almost certainly not have occurred if *McNary* had been a jury trial.

19. Reaching a Verdict.   After closing arguments in a jury trial, the judge will charge the jury by reading a statement about the law that the jurors should apply in reaching their decision. These jury instructions will have been agreed to by the parties in advance during a charging conference with the judge. *See* Fed. R. Civ. P. 51. Remember that the judge and jury have two different roles in a jury trial: The judge determines the law and the jury finds the facts. The jury instructions are the judge's opportunity to explain the law that the jurors must apply once they have made their factual findings.

In a bench trial, such as the *McNary* case, the judge determines both the law and the facts. Rule 52(a) requires the court to separately state its findings of fact and its conclusions of law. In advance of issuing its decision, the court will generally ask the parties to submit proposed findings of fact and conclusions of law. These submissions resemble judicial opinions written in favor of the side who prepared it. In many instances, judges (and their law clerks) will rely on the prevailing party's filing when drafting the real opinion. Consistent with this widespread practice, Judge Johnson seems to have relied on the plaintiffs' proposed findings and conclusions in *McNary*, for his decision in plaintiffs' favor shares a number of similarities with their filing. Does this practice seem problematic to you? Why or why not? If you are troubled by it, why? Does it affect your response to recall that federal judges are each responsible for many hundreds of cases at a time?

20. Motions After Judgment.   After judgment has been entered (but no more than ten days afterward), a party can move for a new trial under Federal Rule 59. In a jury trial, granting such a motion means that a new jury must be selected and the entire trial then begins anew. In a bench trial, however, the judge can simply re-open the judgment and take additional testimony, either amending the findings of fact and conclusions of law or making new ones. *See* Fed. R. Civ. P. 59(a)(2). There are many grounds on which a motion for a new trial or other relief from judgment might be based, including manifest errors of law, a verdict against the weight of the evidence, unfair surprise, newly discovered evidence, or evidentiary errors that are not "harmless." *See* Fed. R. Civ. P. 59, 60. If an error is harmless, it means that it did not affect the parties' rights and therefore will be disregarded. *See* Fed. R. Civ. P. 61. No motion for a new trial was made in *McNary*. Beyond a motion for a new trial, a losing party has other options following the entry of judgment against it. Chapter Nine, which discusses appeals, will explore those options and how the government's strategic use of the right to appeal led to the surprising endgame in *McNary*.

INTERVIEW
MICHAEL RATNER ON LITIGATION VERSUS LOBBYING AS A STRATEGY TO ACHIEVE CHANGE*

In the *McNary* case, you relied on both litigation and on lobbying to try to win the freedom of the Haitians on Guantánamo (and to reverse the direct return policy). As a public interest litigator who has devoted most of his career to suing governments and governmental actors, when do you think litigation is most likely to succeed?

If an issue is particularly controversial, litigation—while still an uphill climb—may be the best way to achieve change. It's not that litigation is likely to succeed in all such cases. The road is long and difficult, and in some instances, it simply will not work. For example, we never have, and never will, stop a president from going to war through litigation. But when individual rights are at stake, rights that can be grounded in the Constitution, and there are politically charged and contentious disputes surrounding those rights, litigation can be the most effective way to lead the fight.

Take the *McNary* case. Lobbying the INS to repeal its rule excluding all HIV-positive aliens (which would have allowed the HIV-positive refugees on Guantánamo to come to the United States) was a non-starter with the George H.W. Bush administration. So was trying to persuade the president to reverse his direct return policy. The lesson is that controversial issues, from certain social issues to debates that play out as national security issues, are difficult to win by lobbying, whether you're dealing with an administrative agency, the White House, or Congress.

If you want to change a policy in such instances, it's necessary to give an administration, even a favorable one, some cover—and an effective way to do that is to prevail in court (if you can manage it). For example, we finally shut down the HIV camp at Guantánamo by winning our case in federal district court in Brooklyn. Judge Johnson's ruling gave the Clinton administration the chance to say it was simply obeying a court order. In contrast, the Supreme Court ruled against us in the direct return policy case—and it took over a year before the Clinton administration altered that policy.**

This does not mean that lobbying is hopeless, even on major social issues. If we're in litigation and a member of Congress gives a speech in favor of our position or if a committee holds hearings on a relevant issue, it helps create an atmosphere of making acceptable what many think is impossible as a policy matter—and it may even influence the courts. My colleagues at the Center for Constitutional Rights

---

* Mr. Ratner was interviewed before Barack Obama was elected President of the United States.

** Of course, there were some key differences in the two cases that made winning the Guantánamo litigation easier. In closing Guantánamo, the administration was simply allowing a few hundred refugees into the United States. It was changing no major policy. In contrast, reversing the forcible return program implicated larger domestic and foreign policy considerations, as well as future electoral politics in states like Florida. Given all that, I believe there's almost no way we could have won that case for a group with as little political support as Haitian refugees.

(CCR) and I use every tool at our disposal. We couple litigation with lobbying and protest and media outreach. Even when we think litigation is the best approach, we don't think lobbying—or any other form of advocacy—should be ignored. Lobbying just shouldn't lead the struggle, particularly on really controversial issues.

You often face difficult odds in the cases that you file. Given how hard it can be to win in court, how do you define success in litigation?

I would define success as standing up in court for what is right and for trying to maximize those rights guaranteed by the Constitution and the various human rights declarations and treaties binding on the United States. Our goal at CCR is to create a country and a world where rights that are *said* to be fundamental are *treated* as fundamental.

The key point is that we do not always need to win a case to move our society in the direction of justice and right. CCR and I will sometimes litigate even if we believe we may lose the case either because the case law is more or less against us or the immediate social and political environment makes a victory unlikely at that moment in time. I believe it is necessary to stand up against the denial of rights even when the odds are stacked against us—as they were in *McNary* and when we filed our post-9/11 Guantánamo cases.*** Going to court to challenge a denial of rights not only provides a legal basis for addressing the issues, it sends an important message to politicians, the legal community, the media, and the general public. In other words, litigation can shine a spotlight on the issues, bringing them into public consciousness—especially in the litigious United States.

When do you think the "inside" strategy of lobbying—in contrast to the "outside" strategy of litigation—is most likely to succeed? Given your experience in *McNary*, do you believe lobbying can *ever* succeed when you are pressing a controversial position? Why or why not?

I am not sure with the current politics in Congress and the country as a whole that lobbying on controversial issues from the progressive side can win. Even with a Democratic Congress we failed to stop the expansion of the Foreign Intelligence Surveillance Act (FISA). Liberal senators, including [then-Senator] Barack Obama, caved on the FISA amendments for fear of being perceived as weak on national security. In such highly charged political circumstances, a court is better suited than Congress to focus on the limitations our Constitution places on government power. A court's job is to interpret and enforce the Fourth Amendment, and it can do so free from the pressure of election results.

Nevertheless, as I've stressed above, courts alone are not enough. Public protest, articles, media, and lobbying are all necessary to win many of these battles. But my experiences with *McNary* reinforced my skepticism about lobbying as a winning strategy. When we began the case, we were told by AIDS lobbyists not to litigate the HIV ban on aliens; they thought there was a good chance of lifting the exclusion in Congress. I thought they were crazy. I never believed Congress would

---

*** CCR has represented a number of Guantánamo detainees since 2002.—Eds.

agree to lift the ban, mainly because of prejudice toward gays and fears about people who are HIV positive.

Has your approach to either litigation against the government or lobbying within government changed in light of your experiences in *McNary*?

My approach to litigation remains the same: Litigate and fight on principle. Even in litigation, there can be positions taken that compromise principle. I will not do it. For instance, we did not argue the post-9/11 Guantánamo cases in a way that was expedient. We could have argued that habeas corpus rights applied only to those people held at Guantánamo, which is under the exclusive jurisdiction and control of the United States. But we did not limit our argument that way. Instead, we insisted that everyone in the custody of the United States, no matter where in the world they were held, had that right. This position did not, I must admit, come easily. There was a fight within our litigation team about whether to limit our argument to Guantánamo, but in the end, we stood firm on the broader view of habeas corpus rights.

When it comes to lobbying, *McNary* reinforced my general view of never trusting a politician. In late 1992 and early 1993, we could not have been closer to the Clintons and the transition team. We knew so many people and had such good relationships with them. But in the end, none of that helped us, because freeing the Haitians at Guantánamo was too controversial. So despite all our contacts within the incoming administration, we had to go back to court and litigate. Whether in court or by protest, it's our job to make politicians do the right thing.

What advice do you have for a young public interest attorney launching her first lobbying effort on a controversial issue?

Be careful. Chatting with members of Congress and their aides can be intoxicating. It gives you a sense of power, and you can get caught up in striking political deals that are unacceptable if evaluated according to your core principles. Stay in touch with your clients to keep you focused on what they want and need. One problem with some public interest lobbyists in D.C. is they have no real human clients, in the sense of individual people who are suffering and need their help. As a result, I think some of those lobbyists don't fully understand what's at stake when they're "compromising away" someone's rights. My view is that you should get out of Washington as much as possible and see what's happening on the ground. It often appears that change happens in Washington, but I think most real change does not.

CHAPTER NINE

Appeal and Settlement

INTRODUCTION

The final judgment of a U.S. district court does not necessarily mark the end of a lawsuit. If a party believes that the court's judgment is in error, she has the right to appeal the case to the federal court of appeals. As you'll recall from Chapter One, there are 13 federal appellate, or "circuit," courts. The Second Circuit, for instance, hears appeals from the federal courts in Connecticut, Vermont, and New York—and thus was responsible for hearing any appeal in the *McNary* case. The federal courts of appeals have the power to review federal district court rulings and to affirm, reverse, or modify them. The federal appellate courts played a crucial role in *McNary*, shaping the litigation throughout the case, and, as we will see, dramatically affecting the final outcome and legacy of the litigation.

Disputes at the appellate level tend to focus on the law rather than the facts, often zeroing in on a few discrete legal principles that the losing party believes the trial court misconstrued or misapplied. Because there is no new fact-finding done at the appellate level, there are no juries. Appeals are traditionally heard by panels of three judges, who read the written briefs submitted by each side and then hear oral arguments from the attorneys, who usually have 10 to 20 minutes each to make their case. Private lawyers who argue appeals often specialize in appellate practice, and the Department of Justice has special divisions for arguing civil and criminal appeals. Cases are decided by a majority vote and may be accompanied by one or more concurring or dissenting opinions.[1] Given the focus on legal issues and the often scholarly tone of oral arguments, the appellate process rarely has the dramatic flair of a trial—but it is every bit as critical. An appellate ruling on a single issue of law can destroy the winner's

---

1. A concurring opinion is a separate opinion written by a judge who agrees with the judgment but often on grounds different from those expressed in the majority opinion. The concurring judge might agree with the majority opinion but want to write separately to elaborate on or emphasize something not contained in that opinion, or she may agree only with the outcome and write separately to explain the different rationale on which she relied. This latter form of concurrence is called "concurring in the judgment."

hard-fought trial victory, giving the losing party a new trial on some or all of the issues—or perhaps even an outright victory in the case.

Keep in mind, however, that a decision by the court of appeals is not necessarily the end of the case. The losing party at the appellate level can request a rehearing of the case by the original panel of judges that heard the case or can seek a rehearing *en banc*, which calls for all of the judges in a circuit to decide the case.[2] Rehearings of either sort are relatively rare occurrences. The losing party also has another option: filing a petition for a *writ of certiorari* (also called filing a "cert petition"), with the Supreme Court. The Supreme Court's review of almost all cases is discretionary—that is, there is no right to review by the Supreme Court. Such review is rarely granted. As discussed in Chapter One, approximately 80 cert petitions are granted each year.[3]

This chapter will discuss the appeals process following final judgment as well as the separate but related topic of interlocutory appeals, which take place before the district court has entered a final judgment. The early months of the litigation gave rise to several interlocutory appeals and produced some of the most intriguing moments in the litigation.

We begin with an example of a notice of appeal—in this instance, the notice filed by the government on August 9, 1993, after conclusion of the trial before Judge Johnson.

NOTICE OF APPEAL IN *McNARY*

```
RLB:cs                                          RB 7052
RB3_138.NOA


UNITED STATES DISTRICT COURT
EASTERN DISTRICT OF NEW YORK

----------------------------------------X

HAITIAN CENTERS COUNCIL, INC., NATIONAL      NOTICE OF APPEAL
COALITION FOR HAITIAN REFUGEES, INC.,
IMMIGRATION LAW CLINIC OF THE JEROME N.      Civil Action
FRANK LEGAL SERVICES ORGANIZATION, OF        No. CV-92-1258
NEW HAVEN CONNECTICUT; DR. FRANTZ
GUERRIER, MILOT BAPTISTE, KENNEDY            (Johnson, J.)
AUSTIN and YVONNE PASCAL ON BEHALF
OF THEMSELVES AND ALL OTHER SIMILARLY
```

2. If a court of appeals has more than 15 judges, the judges traditionally do not all sit for an *en banc* hearing. For instance, the Ninth Circuit has 28 active judges (the number will increase to 29 by the end of 2009); *en banc* hearings in that circuit are composed of a random selection of 15 judges.

3. The Supreme Court may decide to grant cert in a case because, among other things, there is a conflict between the decisions of two or more federal courts of appeals on an important matter or because there is a conflict between a state court of last resort (usually known as the state's supreme court) and another such court (or a federal court of appeals) on an important federal question. *See* Sup. Ct. R. 10. If you are interested in learning more about Supreme Court practice, the definitive guide is EUGENE GRESSMAN ET AL., SUPREME COURT PRACTICE (9th ed. 2007). Many lawyers still refer to this widely admired work as "Stern and Gressman," though Robert L. Stern, a co-author of the first eight editions, died in 2000.

SITUATED; LENER MICLIS and CLAUD
KENOL ON BEHALF OF THEMSELVES AND
ALL OTHERS SIMILARLY SITUATED,

        Plaintiffs,

    - against -

CHRIS SALE, ACTING COMMISSIONER,
IMMIGRATION AND NATURALIZATION
SERVICE; JANET RENO, ATTORNEY
GENERAL; IMMIGRATION AND NATURALIZATION
SERVICE; WARREN CHRISTOPHER, SECRETARY
OF STATE; REAR ADMIRAL ROBERT KRAMEK
AND ADMIRAL KIME, COMMANDANTS, UNITED
STATES COAST GUARD; AND COMMANDER, U.S.
NAVAL BASE, GUANTANAMO BAY,

        Defendants.

--X

Notice is hereby given that CHRIS SALE, ACTING

COMMISSIONER, IMMIGRATION AND NATURALIZATION SERVICE, JANET

RENO, ATTORNEY GENERAL; IMMIGRATION AND NATURALIZATION SERVICE;

WARREN CHRISTOPHER, SECRETARY OF STATE; REAR ADMIRAL ROBERT

KRAMEK AND ADMIRAL KIME, COMMANDANTS, UNITED STATES COAST GUARD;

AND COMMANDER, U.S. NAVAL BASE, GUANTANAMO BAY, defendants above

named, hereby appeal to the United States Court of Appeals for the

Second Circuit from the Memorandum and Order granting permanent

injunctive relief issued in this action on June 8, 1993.

Dated: Brooklyn, New York
       August 9 , 1993

                ZACHARY W. CARTER
                United States Attorney
                Eastern District of New York
                One Pierrepont Plaza
                Brooklyn, New York 11201

    By: _____
                ROBERT L. BEGLEITER
                Assistant U.S. Attorney

                _____
                SCOTT DUNN
                Special Assistant U.S. Attorneys

```
JANET RENO
Attorney General

LAURI STEVEN FILPPU
Deputy Director
P.O. Box 878
Ben Franklin Station
Washington, D.C. 20044
    (Of Counsel)
```

NOTES AND COMMENTS

1. The Mechanics of Appeal.   In civil cases between private parties, a notice of appeal must be filed within 30 days after the entry of the judgment or the order that is the subject of the appeal. Fed. R. App. P. 4(a)(1)(A). However, when the United States or its officers or agencies are parties to an action—as was the case in *McNary*—any party may file an appeal within 60 days after the entry of judgment. Fed. R. App. P. 4(a)(1)(B). The government's notice, as you see, is dated August 9, 1993—exactly 60 days after Judge Johnson issued his decision. Why do you think extra time is granted when the government is a party?

Under Federal Rule of Appellate Procedure 4(a)(1)(A), the party pursuing the appeal, referred to as the appellant, must first file a notice of appeal (and a certain number of copies) with the clerk of the district court from which the order or judgment is being appealed. (The party defending the ruling is the appellee.) The required contents of the notice of appeal are specified in Appellate Rule 3(c); the appellant must identify the party taking the appeal, the judgment or order being appealed, and the court to which the appeal is being taken. If you refer to the government's notice of appeal reproduced on the previous page, you will see that all of the required elements are included—but not much else. The notice of appeal is little more than a piece of paper indicating a party's intention to appeal. The substantive arguments in the case are reserved for the briefs and oral argument.

Once the notice of appeal is filed, the district court clerk sends the notice to the appeals court clerk, who is responsible for docketing the appeal in the court of appeals. The appeals court clerk then sets a briefing schedule and, where appropriate, a date for oral argument (some appeals are decided solely on the briefs). The briefing and argument process at the court of appeals level moves at a relatively slow pace. The parties are generally given several months to finish their briefs, with oral argument scheduled many weeks or even a few months after the briefs are due.[4] This gives the judges assigned to the case (and their law clerks) time to review the issues involved. Once the court has heard oral argument, it may take several months, or even longer in some instances, for the court to issue a decision.

2. Interlocutory Appeal. The government's appeal of Judge Johnson's preliminary injunction ruling in April 1992, just three weeks after *McNary* was filed, is

---

4. The appellant is also responsible for filing an appendix to the brief, containing relevant docket entries and portions of the pleadings, the judgment or order, and other parts of the record below. Fed. R. App. P. 30. Both the appellant and the appellee designate materials to include in the appendix.

an example of an interlocutory appeal. An interlocutory appeal is an appeal taken before the district court has finally disposed of the case. Normally, district court orders can be appealed only after the court has reached a final decision. This is what is known as the *final judgment rule*. *See* 28 U.S.C. § 1291. A final decision is a district court decision that "'ends the litigation on the merits and leaves nothing for the court to do but execute the judgment.'" *Coopers & Lybrand v. Livesay*, 437 U.S. 463, 467 (1978) (quoting *Catlin v. United States*, 324 U.S. 229, 233 (1945)). Some examples of final decisions include a dismissal for failure to state a claim upon which relief may be granted under Rule 12(b)(6), an entry of summary judgment under Rule 56, and a final judgment following trial, as in *McNary*.

The rationale for the final judgment rule, as one commentator explains,

> is based upon the policy of avoiding piecemeal review of issues as they arise in the trial court. If the system permitted a disgruntled party to appeal each issue as it came up, the trial court proceedings could be delayed markedly. . . . In addition, the final judgment rule ultimately avoids appellate review of many issues altogether. That is, a litigant who feels that the trial judge made various errors, but who ultimately wins the case, will not appeal.

Richard D. Freer, *Introduction to Civil Procedure* 758 (2006).

A district court ruling on a preliminary injunction occurs *before* a final decision on the merits. Can such a ruling be appealed under the final judgment rule set out in 28 U.S.C. § 1291? No, because it is not a final judgment. There are, however, exceptions to the final judgment rule. Section 1292 of Title 28 of the U.S. Code provides appellate courts with statutory authority to hear appeals of certain kinds of interlocutory orders—orders issued prior to final judgment.[5] Section 1292(a)(1) permits appeals of interlocutory orders "granting, continuing, modifying, refusing or dissolving injunctions." By its terms, then, section 1292 authorizes a party to seek appellate review of a preliminary injunction order. Why might Congress have created this exception to the final judgment rule? Can you explain how your suggested rationale for the rule applies to the *McNary* case?

Recall that, before the preliminary injunction order, Judge Johnson issued a temporary restraining order (TRO) against the government. *See STC*, pp. 88-89. The Justice Department, however, did not appeal that order. Why? Review the language of Section 1292(a)(1) carefully: It contains no reference to a TRO. Generally, a TRO cannot be appealed. *See, e.g., Clarkson Co., Ltd. v. Shaheen*, 544 F.2d 624, 627 n.4 (2d Cir. 1976). Why might that be the case?

3. Stay Orders.   In addition to the final judgment rule and the statutory exceptions to that rule, there is one other procedural device that figured prominently in

---

5. There are also judicially-created exceptions to the final judgment rule, including what is known as the collateral-order exception. *See Cohen v. Beneficial Industrial Loan Corp.*, 337 U.S. 541 (1949). Under the collateral-order exception, orders other than a final judgment can also be appealed if they "conclusively determine the disputed question, resolve an important issue completely separate from the merits of the action, and [are] effectively unreviewable on appeal from a final judgment." *Coopers & Lybrand v. Livesey*, 437 U.S. 463, 468 (1978). For example, the Supreme Court has held that an order requiring a defendant to bear 90 percent of the costs of providing notice to a class in a class action lawsuit (*see* Chapter Ten, Note 7) could be appealed under the collateral-order exception. *Eisen v. Carlisle & Jacquelin*, 417 U.S. 156, 172 (1974). The order conclusively determined the issue of cost and was separate from the merits of the case. In addition, the issue was too important to postpone because the defendant, if it prevailed on the merits, would have been unable to recover the costs of the notice. JACK H. FRIEDENTHAL ET AL., CIVIL PROCEDURE 626-27 (4th ed. 2005).

the appellate journey of *McNary*: the stay. *See* Fed. R. Civ. P. 62(c); Fed. R. App. P. 8. A stay puts a temporary hold on some or all of the litigation, including the enforcement of court orders. A party may seek a stay in a variety of circumstances. In *McNary*, the government sought stays to prevent various orders by Judge Johnson, including his first preliminary injunction order, from taking effect. Stay practice generally operates much more quickly than the appeals process, which, at a bare minimum, usually takes weeks, even if the proceedings are expedited. A stay of a district court's preliminary injunction order can be entered by the district court itself, but if the motion for a stay is denied, the moving party can seek appeal of that ruling, going first to the court of appeals and ultimately to the Supreme Court.

After Judge Johnson issued the preliminary injunction in *McNary* on April 6, 1992, temporarily barring the return of Haitians from Guantánamo to Haiti, the Justice Department immediately filed a motion with Judge Johnson seeking a stay of his order. In deciding whether to grant the stay, a district court must conduct an analysis similar to the analysis used to decide whether to grant a plaintiff's request for injunctive relief. *See* Chapter 5, Footnotes 3 & 9. In the Second Circuit, for instance, the district court is required to consider: "(1) whether the stay applicant has made a strong showing that he is likely to succeed on the merits; (2) whether the applicant will be irreparably injured absent a stay; (3) whether issuance of the stay will substantially injure the other parties interested in the proceeding; and (4) where the public interest lies." *United States v. Eastern Airlines, Inc.*, 923 F.2d 241, 244 (2d Cir. 1991). Because Judge Johnson essentially had balanced those factors in the plaintiffs' favor when granting their request for injunctive relief, he denied the government's motion for a stay the next day.

Justice Department lawyer Paul Cappuccio then sought a stay from the Second Circuit. *See STC*, p. 111. (Stay applications in such a situation are often filed within hours of an adverse decision from the court below. Indeed, lawyers may already have the papers drafted and ready for filing before the lower court has made its decision.) After a hasty oral argument, however, the Second Circuit denied the stay application as well. *See id.*, pp. 114-15. When that failed, Cappuccio went to the Supreme Court to seek the stay. *See id.*, pp. 115-16. Conventional wisdom suggests the Supreme Court would defer to the lower courts, which were more familiar with the developing facts of the case. Nevertheless, Cappuccio had a gut instinct that the Supreme Court would issue the stay, and he proved right.[6] In a 5-4 ruling, the Justices decided in favor of the government. What does the Supreme Court's decision suggest about how the Justices viewed the merits of the case? In that connection, consider a memorandum that Justice Clarence Thomas circulated to the rest of the Supreme Court explaining his vote on the issue.[7]

---

6. In an interview with Brandt Goldstein, Cappuccio recalled telling his colleagues that in his view, the Supreme Court "knew this case was out there," and that the Justices were not comfortable with Judge Johnson's preliminary injunction. Cappuccio had clerked for two years at the Supreme Court and was knowledgeable about its inner workings and the personalities of the various Justices. For a controversial account of Cappuccio's role as a law clerk—and one that Cappuccio himself disputes—see EDWARD LAZARUS, CLOSED CHAMBERS: THE RISE, FALL, AND FUTURE OF THE MODERN SUPREME COURT 315, 321-22 (1998).

7. A copy of Justice Thomas's memorandum can be found in the Harry A. Blackmun Papers at the Library of Congress. Justice Blackmun's papers became public in 2004, five years after his death. The papers include a remarkable collection of memoranda, letters, and other documents that shed light on the Supreme Court's procedures and decisions during the period when Blackmun was a Justice. For more information about the Blackmun Papers, see http://www.loc.gov/rr/mss/blackmun/.

Supreme Court of the United States
Washington, D. C. 20543

CHAMBERS OF
JUSTICE CLARENCE THOMAS

April 22, 1992

Re: No. A-775, *McNary* v. *Haitian Centers Council, Inc.*

Memorandum to the Conference

I have received an application for a stay pending an appeal to the Second Circuit of an order issued by the Eastern District of New York (Johnson, J.) in *Haitian Centers Council, Inc.* v. *McNary*. I hereby refer the matter to the Conference.

* * * *

In deciding whether to grant a stay pending appeal, we must consider "(a) whether irreparable injury may occur absent a stay; (b) the probability that the District Court was in error . . . ; and (c) the public interests that may be affected by the operation of the [injunction]." *Republican State Central Comm.* v. *Ripon Soc'y*, 409 U. S. 1222, 1224 (1972) (Rehnquist, Circuit Justice). With respect to irreparable injury, the government argues first, that the district court's order has directly inspired more Haitians to flee the country and has interfered with the sensitive political and military aspects of the continuing interdiction program; and second, that Judge Johnson, rather than maintaining the status quo, has in effect decided the merits by ordering immediate access to the interdictees. The government for the most part reiterates these concerns in arguing that the public interest favors its position. Respondents maintain that the denial of a stay will not cause irreparable injury, arguing that Judge Johnson's order has had no appreciable effect on flight from Haiti. Respondents also maintain that the public interests favor their position, for any rescreened interdictees would be returned to Haiti. With respect to the merits, the government argues that it is overwhelmingly probable that it will prevail in the Second Circuit. The government first contends that *HRC* should have been accorded res judicata effect here. Even so, the government argues, aliens interdicted outside the United States enjoy no Fifth Amendment due process rights, and the organizations enjoy no First Amendment speech rights to communicate with extraterritorial aliens, especially, the government stresses, on a military base. Respondents challenge the assertion that *HRC* bars their claims here and argue, moreover, that the claims that they have raised do not present a political question unsuitable for judicial resolution. Respondents then argue that the interdictees do enjoy the protection of the Fifth Amendment, given that Guantanamo Bay is under the jurisdiction of the United States, and that the organizations do have First Amendment rights to communicate with the interdictees.

Even if *HRC* does not have res judicata (or collateral estoppel) effect, it seems to me, respondents would probably lose on the merits. (The government does not pursue the argument that respondents' claims are political questions, and thus I don't discuss it.) In his *HRC* memorandum of January 30, Justice Kennedy doubted whether a right of access, assuming one existed on a military base, would support an injunction preventing repatriation. I agree with Justice Kennedy's analysis and in addition find persuasive the Eleventh Circuit's thorough reasoning, on precisely the same point, in *HRC*. See 953 F.2d 1498, 1511–1515 (1992); see also *Ukrainian-American Bar Ass'n* v. *Baker*, 893 F.2d 1374 (CADC 1990). Respondent's Fifth Amendment claim is, in my view, equally unlikely to find favor on appeal. We have consistently rejected the argument that the Fifth Amendment applies to aliens outside American territory, *e.g.*, *United States* v. *Verdugo-Urquidez*, 494 U.S. 259, 269 (1990), even if under American military control, see *Johnson* v. *Eisentrager*, 339 U.S. 763 (1950), and neither Judge Johnson's opinion nor respondents' brief have made out for me a persuasive case to the contrary.

The considerations going to both irreparable injury and to the public interest seem to me similar to those that we weighed during the pendency of *HRC*. Now, as then, I find the balance of the equities close, and I remain deeply concerned about the allegations of mistreatment of those repatriated, but I conclude that the balance favors the granting of a stay pending appeal. In place, the injunction will disrupt the government's repatriation plan. Finally, I share the concerns that the Chief Justice expressed in his own *HRC* memorandum, that the courts not interfere with the Executive's exercise of its power over foreign affairs and the military.

For these reasons, I vote to grant the application for a stay of all of the district court's order pending a decision by the

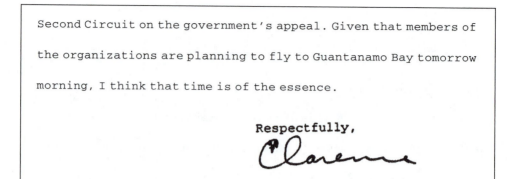

How did Justice Thomas analyze the factors the Supreme Court must consider when deciding whether to grant a stay?[8] Do you agree with Justice Thomas's assessment of the irreparable injury and public interest factors? Why or why not? Are you surprised by the brevity of the analysis? Keep in mind that the Justices work to make these decisions very quickly and are already overloaded with work on other cases.

Recall that after the first round of litigation, which culminated in the Supreme Court's decision to grant the government's request for a stay, the Bush administration changed its policy with respect to Haitian refugees. Under what became known as the direct return policy, the Coast Guard intercepted boats leaving Haiti, collected the passengers aboard, and returned them to Port-au-Prince instead of taking them to Guantánamo for screening interviews. *See STC*, p. 129. This led to another flurry of litigation in the summer of 1992 before Judge Johnson, the Second Circuit, and the Supreme Court. *See id.*, pp. 136-43. Judge Johnson ruled in favor of the government (though he was critical of the direct return policy), but the Second Circuit reversed, holding that the policy violated the "no return" command of Section 243(h)(1) of the Immigration and Nationality Act.[9] *Haitian Centers Council, Inc. v. McNary*, 969 F.2d 1350 (2d Cir. 1992). The Second Circuit ordered the district court to prevent the government from returning intercepted Haitians to Haiti.

The Supreme Court then issued a stay of the Second Circuit's judgment. *McNary v. Haitian Centers Council, Inc.*, 505 U.S. 1234 (1992). The ruling was 7-2, with Justices Blackmun and Stevens dissenting. Justice Blackmun wrote that the government's likelihood of success on the merits was no better than even, given that the judges in the courts below in both *McNary* and *Baker* had split equally on whether Section 243(h)(1) applied in international waters. *Id.* (Blackmun, J., dissenting). Blackmun went on to stress that "the Government has offered a vague invocation of harm to foreign policy, immigration policy, and the federal treasury, [but] the plaintiffs in this case face the real and immediate prospect of persecution, terror, and possibly even death [if returned to Haiti]." *Id.* Do you agree? Think about this from the government's perspective. How might you make more specific the harm to the government? What counter-argument can you offer against Justice Blackmun's view of the harm that the plaintiffs faced?

---

8. Notice that Justice Thomas sets out a different formulation than the Second Circuit of the test for deciding whether to grant a stay, but his analysis of element (b) amounts to the Second Circuit criterion of whether the stay applicant has made a strong showing that he is likely to succeed on the merits.

9. 8 U.S.C. § 1253(h)(1).

Jean-Bertrand Aristide, the then-exiled president of Haiti, with Dr. Hesung C. Koh (Harold Koh's mother), Harold Koh, and Mary-Christy Fisher (Koh's wife), April 24, 1994. Aristide spoke at Yale Law School several months before he was restored to power in Haiti by the United States military. Photographer unknown.

    4. Standards of Review on Appeal.   After the August 1992 stay order issued by the Supreme Court in the direct return case, there were no more interlocutory appeals or stay applications, so we turn now to the end of the trial in the Guantánamo case. As noted previously, the government appealed the final judgment entered by Judge Johnson in June 1993. Ultimately, the plaintiffs and the government settled the case before the Second Circuit could hear the appeal. *See* Note 7. Had the appeal gone forward, however, the Second Circuit would have reviewed the district court's decision according to well-settled appellate standards of review. As the Supreme Court has explained, for "purposes of standard of review, decisions by judges are traditionally divided into three categories, denominated questions of law (reviewable 'de novo'), questions of fact (reviewable for clear error), and matters of discretion (reviewable for 'abuse of discretion')." *Pierce v. Underwood*, 487 U.S. 552, 558 (1988).

    Black's Law Dictionary defines de novo as "[a]new" or "afresh." *Black's Law Dictionary* 467 (8th ed. 2004). In the context of appellate litigation, that means that the court of appeals need not defer to the conclusions of law reached by the district court—hence the court of appeals reviews legal questions "as if [they] had come to the courts for the first time." *Zervos v. Verizon New York, Inc.*, 252 F.3d 163, 168 (2d Cir. 2001). Can you think of a question of law from the district court's final decision after trial in *McNary* that would be reviewed de novo by the Second Circuit?

    The district court's factual findings are subject to a different, less exacting standard of review. With respect to questions of fact—for example, whether the light was red for the plaintiff or the defendant in a traffic accident, or whether a particular witness's testimony is credible—the district court's findings are accorded deference by the court of appeals. As you know from Chapter Eight, either the jury or judge may serve as the finder of facts in the district court; in *McNary*, Judge Johnson was the fact-finder. Under Federal Rule of Civil Procedure 52(a), he was required to state his factual findings, which could not be set aside unless the Second Circuit determined they were "clearly erroneous." Fed. R. Civ. P. 52(a)(1), (6). The Supreme Court has stated that a "finding is 'clearly erroneous' when although there is evidence to support it, the reviewing court on the entire evidence is left with the definite and firm conviction that a mistake has been committed." *United States v. United States Gypsum Co.*, 333 U.S. 364, 395 (1945). Why do you think the standard of review for findings of fact involves less scrutiny than the standard of review for conclusions of law?

Just as the district court's factual findings enjoy deference, so, too, do the discretionary decisions made by the district court in the course of managing the case. The district court judge enjoys discretion on a host of issues. At the pretrial phase, this discretion extends to, among other matters, determining the discovery schedule, ruling on discovery motions and requests to amend pleadings, and managing the pretrial conference. During trial, some of the decisions within the court's discretion include deciding whether to grant a continuance, ruling on evidentiary motions, and reviewing post-trial motions for relief such as the grant of a new trial. Only if the district court judge "abuses" her discretion—that is, makes a decision so arbitrary or unreasonable as to be clearly mistaken—will a court of appeals set aside the district court's decision on such an issue.

5. New Evidence on Appeal.   As noted at the beginning of this chapter, the focus on appeal is on the law, not the facts. Indeed, as a general matter, the introduction of new facts is prohibited on appeal. It is the responsibility of the fact-finder in the lower court to make factual determinations—to weigh the evidence and to assess the credibility and perceptive accuracy of witnesses, among many other things. In that regard, the most controversial aspect of the government's initial stay request (from the perspective of the plaintiffs) was its introduction of new factual information in its stay application to the Supreme Court. This new information was presented in the form of a declaration by Donna Hrinak, a State Department official. Hrinak asserted that the plaintiffs' lawsuit—specifically "the injunctive relief ordered by the District Court"—increased the "outflow of Haitians from Haiti." Declaration of Donna Hrinak, April 20, 1992, paragraph 3. Hrinak's declaration was offered in support of the government's argument that the litigation produced a "magnet effect" and encouraged Haitians to flee their country. *See STC*, pp. 114-15. The declaration is reproduced here, along with statistical information that Hrinak offered in support of her contentions.

DECLARATION OF DONNA HRINAK

1. I am the Deputy Assistant Secretary for Mexico and Caribbean Affairs, Bureau of Inter-American Affairs, U.S. Department of State. In this position, my responsibilities include oversight of U.S. relations with Haiti.

2. As is more fully detailed in the attached certified copy of the Coast Guard's daily report of Haitian boat migrant interdiction, almost 4,000 Haitian boat migrants have been interdicted by Coast Guard cutters since April 1. Of this number, 1,377 have been interdicted in the past four days alone, e.g. April 16-19. This represents a dramatic increase over the number of Haitians who took to the open sea before this lawsuit was filed and before the District court first issued injunctive relief in this case on March 27, 1992.

3. It is my considered judgment, as a representative of the State Department, that the injunctive relief ordered by the District Court in this case has contributed in significant part to the increased outflow of Haitians from Haiti.

4. Since the September 1991 coup d'etat in Haiti, the State Department through its Embassy in Port-au-Prince has monitored the economic and political conditions in that country—including the level of violence and persecution. Based on our information, we have no reason to believe that the level of political violence in Haiti has significantly increased nor that economic conditions have markedly deteriorated since this lawsuit was filed in late March 1992.

5. Nonetheless, as indicated above, the number of interdictions of Haitian boat migrants has increased dramatically since this lawsuit was filed. Indeed, there is a general correlation between the number of interdictions made by the Coast Guard and the pendency of litigation in United States courts and the issuance of injunctive relief in this action and in Haitian Refugee Center v. Baker.

6. This correlation is startling. As is demonstrated by the attached certified copy of the Coast Guard's interdiction report, in the two weeks prior to this Court's January 31, 1992 stay of the District Court's order in the Haitian Refugee Center v. Baker litigation, over 6,000 Haitians were interdicted by the Coast Guard. By contrast, in the two weeks immediately following this court's January 31 stay, only 560 Hiatians were interdicted.

7. The same correlation exists in this litigation. In the first three weeks of March, there were only 211 Haitians interdicted. On March 24, the present action was filed, and on March 27, the District Court entered injunctive relief against the United States. During the last week of March, there were 947 Haitians interdicted.

8. The situation in April has grown even worse. In the first 15 days of April, there were 2,551 Haitians interdicted. In the last four days alone, there have been an additional 1,377 Haitians interdicted.

9. In my view, the mere existence of pending litigation, and particularly the existence of any kind of injunctive relief against

the United States Government, acts as a magnet for Haitians to leave Haiti.

I declare under penalty of perjury that the foregoing is true and correct.

Washington, D.C.   April 20, 1992

INTERVAL	#INTERVIEWED	#SCREENED-IN	SCREEN-IN PERCENTAGE
STATISTICS PROVIDED BY INS TO BERMAN			
APRIL			
6-8	231	11	4.8
8-9	109	13	11.9
9-11	248	24	9.7
11-12	115	9	7.8
12-13	133	5	3.8
13-14	37	8	21.6
14-15	159	24	15.1
6-15	1132	96	8.5
STATISTICS PROVIDED BY STATE DEPT. TO BERMAN			
APRIL			
1-8	466	45	9.7
8-12	1921	48	2.5
1-12	2387	93	3.9

NOTE: Figures from both the INS and the State Department indicate that the overall screen-in rate from the coup (9/91) until April 1, 1992 was 39%.

DATE	NO. INTERDICTED	NO. REPATRIATED	COURT ACTION
MARCH			
9	55	512	
10	134	0	
11	0	525	
12	22	0	
13	0	299	

DATE	NO. INTERDICTED	NO. REPATRIATED	COURT ACTION
14	0	0	
15	0	0	
16	0	0	
17	0	97	
18	0	0	
19	0	0	
20	0	0	
21	0	0	
22	0	0	
23	0	0	
24	0	0	
25	141	0	
26	61	0	
27	0	0	TRO entered
28	28	126	
29	231	0	
30	99	80	
31	387	0	
APRIL			
1	135	0	
2	242	0	
3	84	0	
4	28	197	
5	18	0	
6	177	224	PI entered
7	350	0	
8	62	245	PI stay denied(DCt)
9	206	0	
10	273	206	
11	134	0	
12	34	0	
13	568	0	
14	142	260	PI stay denied (2d Cir)
15	98	0	
16	461	251	
17	297	0	
18	435	0	
19	184	0	
20	248	0	
21	510	0	
22	561	0	PI stayed (S. Ct.)
23	71	128	
24	313 (I)	153(I)	
25	313 (II)	153 (II)	
26	313 (III)	153(III)	
27	155	0	

DATE	NO. INTERDICTED	NO. REPATRIATED	COURT ACTION
28		58	
29			
30			
MAY			
1			
2			
3			
4			
5			
6			
7			
8			
9			

    * Roman Numeral (I, II, Etc.) mean that we have one number for those days combined, usually a weekend.

What makes the introduction of Hrinak's new declaration about the magnet effect problematic on appeal? The plaintiffs never had an opportunity to cross-examine Hrinak and Judge Johnson never had a chance to evaluate the credibility of her testimony. Harold Koh made these points in a letter faxed to the Supreme Court two days after Hrinak made her declaration. (Koh sent the letter to the Chief Deputy Clerk of the Supreme Court, with the hope that the clerk would circulate the letter to the Justices. Koh was operating in an uncertain procedural world. There was no obvious motion, application, or other means under the Supreme Court's rules that he could have used to challenge the government's use of the declaration.) Koh's letter is reproduced here.

YALE LAW SCHOOL
BOX 401A YALE STATION
NEW HAVEN, CONNECTICUT 06520-7375

HAROLD HONGJU KOH
Professor of Law
(203) 432-4932
Telefax: (203) 432-8260

<u>BY FAX</u>
April 22, 1992

Mr. Francis J. Lorson, Esq.
Chief Deputy Clerk
United States Supreme Court
One First St., N.E.
Washington, D.C. 20543

RE: Gene McNary, et al. v. Haitian Centers Council, Inc., et al.
       (Civ. No. 92-1258 E.D.N.Y 1992), <u>appeal pending</u>, No. 92-6090
       (2d Cir. 1992) (Second Circuit argument scheduled May 7 or 8, 1992)

Dear Mr. Lorson:

We understand that the Solicitor General's application to Justice Thomas, as Second Circuit Justice, for a stay pending appeal to the Second Circuit of Judge Sterling Johnson's preliminary injunction order in this case has been referred to the Conference. We respectfully request that you transmit this letter to the full Court for its consideration.

Attached to the Government's application at page 190 is the uncross-examined Declaration of Donna Hrinak, Deputy Assistant Secretary of State for Mexico and Caribbean Affairs, Bureau of Inter-American Affairs, dated April 20, 1992, which was not part of the record before the District Court in this case. Ms. Hrinak's declaration cites recent Coast Guard figures regarding the interdiction of fleeing Haitians, claims "that the injunctive relief ordered by the District Court in this case has contributed in significant part to the increased outflow of Haitians from Haiti," <u>id</u>. at 190, and concludes that "the mere existence of pending litigation, and particularly the existence of any kind of injunctive relief against the United States Government, acts as a magnet for Haitians to leave Haiti." <u>Id</u>. at 193.

As we noted on page 12 of our Memorandum requesting Summary Denial of the Government's Extraordinary Application for a Stay Pending Appeal, after a five and one-half hour hearing that included live testimony, Judge Johnson's preliminary injunction opinion found the Government's evidence regarding such a "magnet effect" to be "inconclusive." PI Op. at 12. At the preliminary injunction hearing, the Government presented absolutely no evidence to link the increased number of Haitian interdictees with the District Court's order. On the other hand, respondents presented numerous reasons why Haitians have been inter-dicted in larger numbers in the last few weeks, including evidence that substantial numbers of Haitians who had landed in Cuba had recently been expelled onto the high seas by Castro. <u>See</u> Pl. Exh. # 69 at 62; PI Transcript at 108–11.

Given this background, the Hrinak Declaration filed yesterday appears to be yet another Government attempt to use uncross-examined, extra-record affidavits manufactured for the purpose of appellate litigation to mislead the Supreme Court to stay the District Court's lawful order. The Government has now failed to stay that order on four successive occasions, twice before Judge Johnson and twice before the Second Circuit (Pratt, Timbers & Mukasey, JJ.). In <u>Haitian Refugee Center v. Baker</u>, 112 S.Ct. 1245 (1992), an earlier case before this Court, the Solicitor General's successful January 31, 1992 application to this Court for a stay of the District Court's injunctive relief similarly relied upon untested allegations in extra-record affidavits that did not survive subsequent cross-examination.*

---

*For example, the Solicitor General filed the affidavit of Admiral William P. Leahy, Jr. before the Supreme Court, affirming that having counsel from the Haitian Refugee Center present on Coast Guard cutters would interfere drastically with operations. Upon later deposition, Admiral Leahy testified that his own 14 year-old son had spent two weeks on a Coast Guard cutter during an operational law enforcement mission. Similarly, Assistant Secretary of State Bernard Aronson declared that he had

To forestall another round of such Government misconduct, following the filing of the stay application yesterday, respondents sought a status conference with Judge Johnson, on the record, and requested that he permit us to take the deposition of Ms. Hrinak immediately, so as [to] cross-examine her with regard to the "magnet effect" allegations made in her declaration. Judge Johnson expressed concern on the record that the Government appeared to be "stacking the deck," by including for the first time in a stay application before this Court a declaration that had not been subject to cross-examination. Accordingly, Judge Johnson directed the Government to inform this Court that the Hrinak Declaration had been generated for the first time on appeal and had not been part of the record before the District Court. Judge Johnson further advised repondents to move before this Court either to strike the Hrinak Declaration from the record or, in the alternative, to supplement the record before this Court with a deposition of Ms. Hrinak or counter-declarations regarding the so-called "magnet effect."

Accordingly, respondents hereby request that this Court take judicial notice of the attached "Chronology of Events in Haiti Since March 18, 1992," drawn from the wire services and newspaper accounts. See Appendix A. These events, which include the collapse of an international plan for returning President Aristide to Haiti and a new wave of violence and beatings by the Haitian military, are also recounted in the attached Declaration of Jocelyn McCalla of the National [Coalition] for Haitian Refugees, who has just returned from seven days in Haiti. See Appendix B. The events recounted in these appendices wholly rebut the Government's unfounded claim of irreparable injury from the District Court's order by providing ample reason, wholly unrelated to that order, why Haitians might have begun to flee Haiti in enlarged numbers in late March.

Now that the Court as a whole is considering the Government's stay application, respondents reiterate their request that that application be summarily denied, or that respondents be given an opportunity to file a responsive memorandum of law within twenty-four hours of the Court's call for a response. Respondents reiterate that the only issue raised by this stay is whether our clients—three legal service organizations and their Haitian clients, who are being held in custody, incommunicado, and against their will on territory subject to complete U.S. jurisdiction and control—will have an opportunity to talk to one another before the Second Circuit resolves the appeal.

Given that thirty-four credible asylum applicants will be sent back just as soon Judge Johnson's order is stayed; that conditions in Haiti appear to be rapidly deteriorating; that respondent Haitian Service Organizations are suffering daily and irreparable injury to their First Amendment rights because the Government denies them access to their clients; that no probative evidence has been offered regarding any magnet effect caused by Judge Johnson's order; that that order does not affect the Government's power to repatriate Haitians who have been "screened-out," i.e., found not to have a credible fear of political persecution, or even "screened-in" (so long as they have been adequately counseled); that no certiorari petition is or will soon be pending before this Court; that the Second Circuit is already scheduled to hear an expedited appeal in this case in about two weeks; and that the Government's arguments against the order have already been rejected six successive times, without dissent, by two federal courts, respondents again respectfully urge this Court to deny the stay requested in this case.

"credible reports" that as many as 20,000 Haitians were "massing on one of Haiti's coasts preparing to depart by sea for the United States." In subsequent deposition, however, Aronson conceded that "massing" was "an ambiguous term," that they were not "gathered in some huge group," and that he could not be sure of how many there actually were. See generally HRC v. Baker, Plaintiffs' Application to Stay the Mandates of the United States Court of Appeals for the Eleventh Circuit Pending Certiorari at 31–41.

Very truly yours,

Harold Hongju Koh (signature)

Harold Hongju Koh
Counsel for Plaintiffs
Haitian Centers Council,
Inc., et al.

Appendix A: Chronology of Recent Events in Haiti Since March 18, 1992
Appendix B: Declaration of Jocelyn McCalla

cc: The Honorable Sterling Johnson, Jr., EDNY
       Scott Dunn, Esq., AUSA-EDNY
       Ronald Mann, Esq., Solicitor General's Office, DOJ
       John F. Daly, Esq., Civil Appellate, DOJ
       Robert Bombaugh, Esq., OIL-DOJ

Notice that Koh has responded by introducing new factual information of his own, forcing the Supreme Court to start acting like a trial court by weighing the evidence and making a factual determination—precisely what the rule against introducing new evidence on appeal is meant to prevent. Now that you have read the Hrinak declaration and Koh's response, put yourself in the role of the fact-finder: Do you find the government's magnet effect claims persuasive? If, as plaintiffs' counsel, you could depose Hrinak, what questions would you ask her to undermine her contentions? What other documents might you request from the government? If you were serving as a lawyer for the government, how might you have responded to Koh's letter? As a government lawyer, who might you have deposed to challenge the evidence that Koh provides in his letter?

6. *Appealing the Judgment in* McNary.   The appeal filed by the government in the *McNary* case presented some interesting questions about litigation strategy. By the time the government appealed in August 1993, all of the Haitians had been flown to the United States and Camp Bulkeley had been shut down. *See STC*, p. 298. The Clinton administration nevertheless appealed because it did not want Judge Johnson's decision to remain on the books as a legal precedent that might constrain the executive branch's ability to act in the future.[10]

Consider how each side saw the case at that time, starting with the perspective of the Yale team. Judge Johnson has ruled convincingly in your favor, and this victory in the trial court entitles plaintiffs' counsel to an award of attorneys' fees under the Equal

---

10. If Camp Bulkeley had been shut down and the Haitians had been released, hadn't the government already conceded the case? To put it another way, why could the government appeal when the case appeared to be over? The government's decision to release the Haitians but then appeal meant that it was, in effect, voluntarily ceasing unlawful behavior that it might later resume. Such circumstances constitute an exception to the mootness doctrine, thus ensuring that the Second Circuit could have heard the case. *See United States v. W.T. Grant*, 345 U.S. 629, 632 (1953).

Access to Justice Act, 28 U.S.C. § 2412—as long as the trial court decision is upheld on appeal. In addition, your clients have obtained the relief they sought: release from government detention on Guantánamo and entry into the United States. What remains of the case—the award of fees and the precedent—will now be at stake at the Second Circuit, which has proven quite sympathetic to the Haitians, and could potentially end up before the Supreme Court, which has not seemed sympathetic at all. Would you want to continue litigating or would you attempt to settle what is left of the case?

Now put yourself in the position of the government. The pending notice of appeal provides an opportunity to get the district court's judgment in favor of the plaintiffs reversed. What are your prospects on appeal? On the one hand, there is little chance that the Second Circuit will set aside any of the *factual* findings made by the district court. (Can you explain why that might be the case? *See* Note 4.) Moreover, the Second Circuit consistently has sided with the plaintiffs on legal questions during interlocutory appeals and stay applications. On the other hand, the Supreme Court has just as consistently sided with the government. But will the Court exercise its discretion and grant certiorari to review a Second Circuit decision in favor of the plaintiffs?

The uncertainty about the outcome of an appeal led the government to propose a settlement offer to the plaintiffs' counsel—and that same uncertainty led plaintiffs' counsel to accept the offer. Review pages 298-300 of *Storming the Court* as background and then read the settlement agreement signed by the parties and submitted to Judge Johnson in early 1994, reproduced here along with the judge's order approving the settlement.

```
UNITED STATES DISTRICT COURT
EASTERN DISTRICT OF NEW YORK
- - - - - - - - - - - - - - - - - - - - - - - - - - - - - - - - - - - - - X
HAITIAN CENTERS COUNCIL, INC.,            :
NATIONAL COALITION FOR HAITIAN
REFUGEES, INC., IMMIGRATION LAW           :
CLINIC OF THE JEROME N. FRANK
LEGAL SERVICES ORGANIZATION, OF NEW       :
HAVEN, CONNECTICUT; DR. FRANTZ
GUERRIER, MILOT BAPTISTE, KENNEDY         :
AUGUSTIN and YVONNE PASCAL
on behalf of themselves and all           :
other similarly situated;
LENER MICLIS and CLAUD KENOL              :
on behalf of themselves and all
others similarly situatued,               :
                                                   STIPULATED ORDER
                              Plaintiffs, :        APPROVING CLASS
            - against -                   :        ACTION SETTLEMENT AGREEMENT

                                                   92 Civ. 1258 (SJ)
```

```
DORIS MEISSNER, COMMISSIONER,              :
IMMIGRATION AND NATURALIZATION
SERVICE; JANET RENO, ATTORNEY              :
GENERAL; IMMIGRATION AND
NATURALIZATION SERVICE; WARREN             :
CHRISTOPHER, SECRETARY OF STATE;
REAR ADMIRAL ROBERT KRAMEK and            :
ADMIRAL KIME, COMMANDANTS,
UNITED STATES COAST GUARD; and            :
COMMANDER, U.S. NAVAL BASE,
GUANTANAMO BAY,                            :

                          Defendants.     :
- - - - - - - - - - - - - - - - - - - - - - - - - - - - - - - - -x
```

On January 18, 1994, this Court provisionally approved the
Stipulated Settlement Agreement (annexed as Exhibit A) submitted by
the parties. Published notice of the pendency of the Settlement
Agreement and of the fairness hearing was given to class members as
provided in the Court's January 18, 1994 Order Preliminarily
Approving Stipulated Settlement Agreement and Directing Notice to
Class by counsel for the plaintiffs in the manner set forth in the
Affidavit of Joseph F. Tringali, filed on February 8, 1994. On
February 22, 1994, the Court held a fairness hearing to consider any
objections to the proposed Settlement Agreement.

The Court having found that, as the parties have stipulated,
the defendants have fully complied with all orders entered in this
case and that plaintiffs are entitled to no further relief of any kind
in this action, and having made an independent determination under
Fed. R. Civ. P. 23(e) that the Settlement Agreement is a fair, adequate and reasonable settlement of this action, it is hereby

ORDERED that the Settlement Agreement annexed hereto is
approved; and it is further

ORDERED that the Court's Interim Order of March 26, 1993, and the Order of June 8, 1993 (as clarified on July 9, 1993), including all of the declaratory and injunctive relief ordered by the district court, are vacated, and it is further

ORDERED that, pursuant to paragraph 3 of the Settlement Agreement, the instant action is dismissed in its entirety with prejudice, except that (i) the dismissal shall be without prejudice to potential future members of the certified class, i.e., "all Haitian citizens who . . . will be 'screened-in' " and who "will be detained", and (ii) the Court retains continuing jurisdiction as provided for in paragraph 3 of the Settlement Agreement which jurisdiction over this action shall be terminated upon full satisfaction of the terms set forth in paragraph 5 of the Settlement Agreement; and it is further

ORDERED that the payment of attorneys' fees, expenses and the taxation of costs shall be made as provided in paragraph 5 of the Settlement Agreement and the equal sharing of costs incurred in providing class notice shall be made as provided in Paragraph 3 of the Settlement Agreement. Upon entry of this Order, defendants shall pay to Simpson Thacher & Bartlett, in full satisfaction of all past, pending and potential future claims for attorneys' fees, expenses and costs arising out of this action, the sum of $595,553.25 for fees and expenses under the Equal Access to Justice Act, 28 U.S.C. § 2412(d), and the sum of $38,546.75 for costs under 28 U.S.C. § 2412(a). (These costs are for the kinds of expenditures set forth in 28 U.S.C. § 1920, which is made applicable to the United States by 28 U.S.C. § 2412(a).)

Dated: February 22, 1994

                                    Sterling Johnson, Jr.
                                    United States District Judge

SETTLEMENT AGREEMENT

Re: Haitian Centers Council, Inc., et al. v. Chris Sale,

      Acting Commissioner, INS, et al., No. CV-92-1258,

      (E.D.N.Y.), appeal pending, No. 93-6216 (2d Cir.)

All of the parties to the above-referenced case, through

their undersigned counsel, hereby agree to the following terms for

resolving any and all claims and issues pending in this action:

1. The parties stipulate that the defendants-appellants

(hereinafter "the Government") have fully complied with all orders

entered in this case and that plaintiffs are entitled to no further

relief of any kind in this action.

2. The parties will stipulate to the withdrawal of the Gov-

ernment's appeal in No. 93-6216, without prejudice, subject to

reinstatement by written notice to the Clerk of the Court, so that

this settlement can be fully executed. This stipulated withdrawal

shall be without costs and without attorneys' fees to any party.

Costs and attorneys' fees will be paid under this agreement only as

provided under Paragraph 5, infra.

3. If the court of appeals approves the stipulated with-

drawal, the parties will jointly move that the district court vacate

the Interim Order of March 26, 1993, and the Order of June 8, 1993 (as

clarified on July 9, 1993), including all of the declaratory and injunctive relief ordered by the district court, and dismiss this action in its entirety with prejudice—except that the dismissal shall be without prejudice to potential future members of the certified class, _i.e._, "all Haitian citizens who * * * will be 'screened in'" and who "will be detained." In the event that further proceedings are conducted in the district court under Federal Rule of Civil Procedure 23(e), plaintiffs will take full responsibility for providing whatever notice may be required to the class members, except that one-half of any costs incurred in providing such notice shall be paid by the Government. The district court shall retain jurisdiction solely to the extent necessary, if any, to enforce the terms of this agreement. Upon full satisfaction of the terms set forth in Paragraph 5, _infra_, all district court jurisdiction over this action shall be terminated.

4. If the district court grants in full the joint motion described in Paragraph 3, _supra_, the Government shall not reinstate its appeal in No. 93-6216, and the appeal shall thereafter be deemed withdrawn with prejudice. If the district court does not enter the order jointly requested by the parties, the Government shall reinstate its appeal.

5. Upon entry of the order jointly requested by the parties, as described in Paragraph 3, _supra_, the Government shall pay to plaintiffs the sum of $634,100.00 in full satisfaction of all past, pending and potential future claims for attorneys' fees, expenses and costs arising out of this action. Payment of these fees, expenses and costs shall be contingent upon the district court's entry of such order.

HAROLD HONGJU KOH, ESQ.
Lowenstein International Human
  Rights Clinic
127 Wall Street
New Haven, Connecticut 06520

MICHAEL RATNER, ESQ.
Center for Constitutional Rights
666 Broadway
New York, New York 10012

LUCAS GUTTENTAG, ESQ.
Immigrants' Rights Project
American Civil Liberties Union
132 West 43rd Street
New York, New York 10035

JOSEPH TRINGALI, ESQ.
Simpson, Thacher & Bartlett
425 Lexington Avenue
New York, New York 10017

ROBERT RUBIN, ESQ.
Lawyers' Committee for Civil
  Rights of the San Francisco
  Bay Area
301 Mission Street, Suite 400
San Francisco, California 94105

Attorneys for the
  Plaintiffs-Appellees

FRANK W. HUNGER
Assistant Attorney
  General
ZACHARY W. CARTER
United States Attorney

MICHAEL JAY SINGER
Assistant Director
  Appellate Staff

ROBERT M. LOEB
Attorney, Appellate
  Staff
Civil Division, Room
  3343
Department of Justice
Washington, D.C. 20530

Attorneys for the
  Defendants-Appellants

By: _Harold Hongju Koh_
     HAROLD HONGJU KOH

DATE: _October 21, 1993_

By: _Michael Jay Singer_
     MICHAEL JAY SINGER

DATE: _October 20, 1993_

What did each party obtain through the settlement? What did each party give up? Do you believe the plaintiffs' counsel made the right decision in agreeing to the settlement? Why or why not? What about the government? Why or why not?

INTERVIEW
LISA DAUGAARD ON CLIENT-CENTERED LAWYERING

One hears the term "client-centered lawyering" a great deal in the public interest law world. What does client-centered lawyering mean to you?

It means learning enough about the client to have a real dialogue with her about her objectives for the representation; providing the best advice you can about the client's options and the likely outcome of each possible approach; and then truly being guided by the client's priorities for the representation. Sometimes, that is not the same as following the strategy you (as the lawyer) believe is most likely to prevail in court.

For example, in my current work as a public defender, I might have a client charged with domestic violence who is factually innocent, but does not want me to cross-examine his partner about her recent drug and prostitution activity, even though I believe doing so would likely lead to an acquittal. It may be that for the client, preserving his relationship with his partner or honoring her struggle to move beyond past problems is an even more important goal than winning his case. In such a case, client-centered lawyering means foregoing a blistering cross-examination, and maybe an acquittal, to advance his most important objective.

To what extent did the Yale team's representation of the Haitians reflect client-centered approach to lawyering?

Initially, it was impossible to be client-centered, because—through no fault of ours—we had no access to our clients, and vice versa. We had to discern our clients' objectives third-hand, through very general assertions by intermediaries that they wanted help with their situation. [For example, the fax from Father Jacques Fabré on Guantánamo, alerting the National Coalition for Haitian Refugees that several Haitian detainees sought "help"—which Yale interpreted to mean legal assistance.—Eds.] Later, when we had more regular contact with the refugees, it was possible to debate what course we should pursue based on the stated objectives of the clients. Ultimately, after much debate, we did adopt the clients' position that the remedy we were seeking was their release, rather than, for example, ensuring that lawyers could represent them on Guantánamo for futile pseudo-asylum hearings. Consistent with our clients' desires, our final position at trial was that release was the remedy for all of the asserted violations of law. We were no longer seeking intermediate remedies, such as improving access to the camp or camp conditions.

How (if at all) did Yale's representation of the Haitians fail to reflect a client-centered approach?

In several ways. To start with perhaps the most wrenching example, when the Supreme Court lifted the stay on uncounseled asylum processing and repatriation [described in Chapter 4 of *STC*], many refugees, including our named plaintiffs, refused to participate in the hearings without lawyers. We did not seek emergency court intervention to protect them, out of concern that doing so would have jeopardized the rest of our case. We might have been able to do so, by filing a habeas corpus petition [the right to test the legality of one's detention, *see STC*, pp. 116-18], though it was far from clear that we would succeed. But some people on the team felt that doing so might have alienated Judge Johnson, thus hurting the prospects of the rest of our clients who were still detained on Guantánamo, with no guarantee of helping those who were being repatriated. And so we did nothing.

Yet those clients we failed to protect were holding fast to the position *we* had taken in the litigation—that there was something important about having a lawyer for an asylum interview. And as a direct consequence, they were repatriated to Haiti. Had our approach been more client-centered, we either would have found a way to harmonize the interests of all the clients or taken seriously that we had a real conflict of interest—even though it was highly unlikely that we could have found counsel for the returnees on such short notice.

A second instance involves our initial meeting with all our clients at Guantánamo in fall 2002. Camp President Michel Vilsaint wanted to know whether our litigation plan involved seeking their release from the camp, or whether we were just seeking lawyers and improved screening processes. Though there was internal dissension about how to respond, our official answer ended up being that there was no reason to believe we could secure their release through litigation. This answer damaged the embryonic relationship between the legal team and the clients. It also failed to grasp that the Haitians did not have incremental objectives; their only goal was release from the camp, ideally to the U.S. but if not, to anywhere other than Guantánamo. In my view, our response did not take seriously at the time that we needed to find a way to pursue the actual objective of our clients.

A third example: In late January 1993, our clients decided not to wait any longer for us to free them in court or for President Clinton to free them through an executive order. Instead, they used what little power they had to try to help themselves. So they launched a hunger strike. The initial response of many on the team was to try to talk the clients out of this approach. A client-centered view would, I think, have suggested that the clients had soberly and correctly assessed the situation and concluded that the strategies we were employing at the time were unlikely to achieve their release. Though the hunger strike made us uncomfortable, a client-centered response would have been to change our litigation strategy to focus on release and to publicize the hunger strike. Eventually, the team did publicize the strike and organized rolling solidarity hunger strikes on campuses and elsewhere across the country.

The Haitians did not always agree among themselves about what they wanted from the lawyers. Can you describe one of these conflicts?

In addition to the discussions above, when we finally prevailed at trial and Judge Johnson ordered the refugees released, the "guerrilla" social workers who were helping us resettle the Haitians returned to Guantánamo and began to assess our clients for placement in U.S. cities. (I refer to them as "guerillas" because they made things work out for our clients even when normal policies and protocols would have made it impossible.) They discussed where clients might already have family members in the United States, and other needs, to determine the best placement—Miami, New York, Boston, or elsewhere.

In at least one case, they determined that abuse within the family made it inappropriate to place both parents together with their child—the mother did not want to continue to live with her child's father, but he insisted they stay together. The social work team made the decision that the mother would be placed separately from the father. The emergency nature of the situation made it impossible to handle this in the way a possible conflict might normally be handled—getting a different team involved on the part of the father to best represent his interests. It was imperative to get him out of Guantánamo before the government decided to appeal Judge Johnson's order.

What can new lawyers learn from the *McNary* case about working on a large public-interest litigation team?

One of the strengths of our team was that, even when there were vehement differences of opinion among us, once a decision had been made, we were all wholeheartedly committed to trying to make that approach work. Thus, there was not much room for individual students or lawyers to adopt a separate approach to managing our relationship with the clients. My view of what that relationship should be did not always prevail. But even though I still think my view was right, I accept (and accepted at the time) that all of my colleagues on the legal team were deeply sincere about their views of how we should proceed and were operating with the purest of intentions in a desperate effort to rescue people who had everything stacked against them. I think we did a good job collectively of listening to each other and learning from our mistakes, which included developing, over time, a more client-centered orientation.

What advice do you have for new lawyers about managing client relationships?

Avoid paternalism. If you are in any sort of legal services, public defense, or civil rights practice, representing people who are unable to pay your fee, treat the client's view of the goal of representation with as much deference and respect as you would if it were someone who was writing a check for your fee and could easily walk down the street and retain someone else who would pay more attention to her objectives.

7. *Settlement Offers.*   In addition to the settlement offer at the end of the case, which the plaintiffs accepted, you will recall that Paul Cappuccio made a settlement offer in September 1992 that would have allowed the Haitians access to counsel to represent them in their asylum hearings at Guantánamo. *See STC*, pp. 157-58. If a settlement offer is made in the course of a civil suit, a lawyer is generally obliged to communicate that offer to her client. This obligation is governed by the ethics rules of the state in which the lawyer is practicing. *See, e.g.*, Lisa G. Lerman & Philip G. Schrag, *Ethical Problems in the Practice of Law* 278 (2d ed. 2008). In most jurisdictions, once a settlement offer is made, the lawyer typically communicates the offer to the client and counsels the client as to the relative merits of accepting or rejecting the settlement offer.

The final decision of whether to accept or reject the offer, or to make a counter-offer, rests entirely with the client. A few jurisdictions take an alternative position, treating the client's act of hiring a lawyer as an implicit grant of settlement authority to the lawyer. *See id.* In jurisdictions following this minority rule, a lawyer has no obligation to communicate a settlement offer to the client.

The *McNary* case was filed in the Eastern District of New York, which subjects lawyers under its jurisdiction to the New York State Rules of Professional Conduct ("NYRPC").[11] *See* E.D.N.Y. Local R. 1.5(b)(5). Attorneys licensed to practice in New York would also be subject to these rules by virtue of their bar admission. NYRPC takes the majority position that lawyers must communicate settlement offers to their clients. Accordingly, the Yale team was obligated to communicate both the September 1992 and the post-trial settlement offers to their clients, and Koh and the other plaintiffs' attorneys could have been subject to disciplinary sanctions had they failed to do so.

To understand how the September 1992 settlement offer was communicated to the Haitians, a bit of background is necessary. In most suits, settlement can be quite simple. If an offer of settlement is accepted, the parties file a stipulation of dismissal, and that is the end of the matter. *See* Fed. R. Civ. P. 41(a)(1)(A)(ii). In the case of a class action suit like *McNary*, however, the settlement process is much more complicated. Any settlement in a federal class action must comply with Rule 23(e) of the Federal Rules of Civil Procedure, which imposes several requirements that do not apply to non-class actions. For example, the settlement of a class action suit must be approved by the court. Fed. R. Civ. P. 23(e). Before approving a settlement, the court must conduct a hearing to determine whether the proposed settlement would be "fair, reasonable, and adequate." Fed. R. Civ. P. 23(e)(2).

The court's primary concerns in this hearing are ensuring that passive or absent class members are protected and adequately represented and avoiding collusion between the parties who are actively taking part in the action. 7B *Federal Practice and Procedure* § 1797.1 (3d ed. 2005 & Supp. 2008). Courts can take a variety of factors into consideration in evaluating fairness, including the suit's likelihood of success and the amount proposed in the settlement. *Id.* As you can see from Judge Johnson's order, reproduced above, he held a fairness hearing on the final settlement proposed in *McNary* and concluded that the agreement was "a fair, adequate and reasonable settlement of this action."

The court must also direct that notice be provided "in a reasonable manner" to all class members who would be bound by the proposed settlement, and any class member may object to the proposed settlement.[12] Fed. R. Civ. P. 23(e)(1), 23(e)(5). Judge Johnson's order indicates that published notice was provided to the members of the

---

11. In 2009, New York adopted the New York Rules of Professional Conduct, which replaced the New York Code of Professional Responsibility. The Code was in effect during the *McNary* lawsuit.

12. In addition, the parties seeking the court's approval of a settlement must file a statement identifying any agreement they have made in connection with the proposed settlement. Fed. R. Civ. P. 23(e)(3). This requirement does not change the basic obligation to disclose the terms and conditions of the settlement; it "aims instead at related undertakings that, although seemingly separate, may have influenced the terms of the settlement by trading away possible advantages for the class in return for advantages for others." Rule 23 Advisory Committee Notes, 2003 Amendments.

McNary class who would have been bound by the judgment.[13] How would you evaluate the reasonableness of notice provided in this manner?

With respect to the settlement, consider the distinctive situation of the plaintiffs in *McNary*. The class members who had already been admitted to the United States now had all the relief they sought. They had been released from Guantánamo (and from United States custody generally), were physically present in the United States and enjoying freedom of movement, and were receiving adequate medical care, and those not already granted asylum after a hearing on Guantánamo had the assistance of counsel in preparing for their asylum hearing. Accordingly, it seems unlikely that any of this group of plaintiffs would have objected to the settlement. As it turned out, none did.

A trickier situation was presented with respect to a different subset of the class: those Haitian citizens who *in the future* would "be 'screened in' " and "detained" under any United States-Haitian interdiction policy in place after the case settled. Settlement Agreement, *Haitian Centers Council, Inc. v. Sale*, October 21, 1993, ¶ 3. Who were these class members? No one could possibly know, since at the time, the Clinton administration was still interdicting Haitians and returning them directly to Haiti. Assuming, however, the administration were later to change its policy, reopen Guantánamo, and again begin screening in and detaining Haitians, plaintiffs' counsel wanted to ensure that those Haitians' claims would not be barred by the settlement. As a result, the settlement agreement stipulated that the *McNary* case would be dismissed *without prejudice* as to those potential future class members—meaning that the case could be refiled on behalf of those individuals if the administration did, in fact, adopt such a policy.[14]

> **Class Exercise No. 3—Oral Argument Exercise**
> Consider the previous points as you work through the following class exercise. Your professor will divide you into teams so that you can prepare in advance of class.
>
> Imagine you are a student in the Lowenstein Clinic. The *McNary* trial is over and Judge Johnson has issued his final decision in favor of the plaintiffs. The government has appealed the final judgment to the Second Circuit. Assume that the case did not settle and Judge Johnson did not vacate the final opinion. Half of the teams should prepare to represent the plaintiffs in an appellate argument before the Second Circuit, and the other half should prepare to represent the government.
>
> Your argument will focus on a due process claim with respect to conditions of confinement—apart from the issue of adequate medical care. The plaintiffs' amended complaint did not clearly set forth a separate due process

13. The authors have not been able to locate a copy of Joe Tringali's affidavit describing the notice provided with respect to the settlement agreement. Nevertheless, Tringali, Harold Koh, and Mike Wishnie all recall that the settlement agreement was published in one or more New York-based Haitian newspapers.

14. As it turned out, the Clinton administration reversed the direct return policy in June 1994, and, after a brief period of time during which the INS processed some asylum claims of interdictees, the administration reopened Guantánamo as a safe haven for Haitian refugees—allowing them to stay there, but *not* permitting them to seek asylum in the United States. Koh and some Yale students were part of a large contingent that challenged the policy but lost on appeal at the Eleventh Circuit. *See Cuban American Bar Ass'n, Inc. v. Christopher*, 43 F.3d 1412 (11th Cir. 1995).

claim based on conditions of confinement. Nevertheless, assume that such a claim was part of the amended complaint, and recall that at trial, the plaintiffs presented evidence on the conditions of their confinement, including the testimony of Fritznel Camy (*STC*, pp. 248-49), Yanick Mondesir (*id.*, pp. 249-51), and Ellen Powers (*id.*, pp. 252-54). The government presented evidence to rebut these claims, including the testimony of Colonel Joe Trimble (*id.*, pp. 268-70) and Lieutenant Jason Dillman (*id.*, pp. 272-75). The plaintiffs also submitted documentary and demonstrative evidence on conditions of confinement during their cross-examinations of Trimble and Dillman, as described in *Storming the Court.*

Assume that Koh and Tringali have divided the issues that are on appeal among a number of different students in the Lowenstein Clinic. You are responsible for arguing only one issue to the Second Circuit—conditions of confinement. That is, assume that the rest of the Yale team is preparing arguments on the remaining issues in the case, including the issue of medical care and the legal question of whether the due process clause applies to the detainees on Guantánamo. For purposes of this exercise, do not address the issues of medical care or the application of the due process clause to the detainees on Guantánamo.

To prepare your argument, you should begin by reviewing the factual findings Judge Johnson made with respect to the conditions of confinement on Guantánamo. *See Haitian Centers Council, Inc. v. Sale*, 823 F. Supp. 1028 (E.D.N.Y. 1993). Judge Johnson's decision did not discuss the legal standard for evaluating whether the conditions of confinement on Guantánamo satisfy the requirements of the due process clause or the application of that standard to the case at hand. Therefore, please assume that his decision also includes the following paragraphs:

> The standard for evaluating a challenge by an unadmitted alien to the conditions of the alien's non-punitive confinement has not been established in the Second Circuit. *Arar v. Ashcroft*, 532 F.3d 157, 189 (2d Cir. 2008). In *Arar*, the Second Circuit identified two possible frameworks that courts in this circuit might use to evaluate such challenges. The first is the standard that is currently used by the Fifth and the Eleventh Circuits. Under this standard, conditions of confinement violate the due process clause only if they constitute "gross physical abuse." *Id.* Arar's claim failed under this standard. The Second Circuit observed that Arar's claim would also fail under the more lenient standard that the Second Circuit has "traditionally taken when evaluating substantive due process challenges to conditions of pre-trial confinement. This approach looks to whether the challenged conditions amount to 'punishment that may not constitutionally be inflicted upon [pre-trial] detainees *qua* detainees.'" *Id.* (quoting *Bell v. Wolfish*, 441 U.S. 520, 539 (1979)) (alterations in original).
>
> The Second Circuit explicitly reserved the question of "whether an unadmitted alien challenging the conditions of confinement has rights beyond the right to be free of 'gross physical abuse at the hands of state [and] federal officials.'" *Id.* at 190 (quoting *Lynch v. Cannatella*, 810 F.2d 1363, 1374 (5th Cir. 1987)) (alteration in original).
>
> I conclude that unadmitted aliens challenging the conditions of their confinement are entitled to more than just the right to be free of gross

physical abuse. In reaching this conclusion, I am adopting the second of the two tests identified by the Second Circuit in *Arar*. The plaintiffs are not like the stowaways in *Lynch v. Cannatella*, who affirmatively hid themselves on a barge with the aim of entering the United States illegally and who alleged they were abused when they were then transported back to Jamaica by the barge owner. *Lynch*, 810 F.2d at 1367-68. Rather, the unadmitted aliens here are individuals who fled Haiti and were interdicted by the U.S. Coast Guard in international waters, transported to a U.S. military base on territory under the exclusive jurisdiction and control of the United States, and imprisoned in camps there for well over a year. The plaintiffs have a legitimate connection to the United States that was created by the actions of the U.S. government and which has only increased during the time of their confinement. They are clearly entitled to greater due process rights than the stowaways described in *Lynch*. Rather, the plaintiffs are much more like the pretrial detainees in *Bell*; even though the government may assert an interest in detaining them, it may not inflict punishment on them without due process of law. *Bell*, 441 U.S. at 535-37.

Thus, the proper standard for evaluating the plaintiffs' claims is whether the conditions "amount to punishment of the detainee," which may not be imposed without due process of law. *Id.* at 535. In making this determination, the court must evaluate "whether the disability is imposed for the purpose of punishment or whether it is but an incident of some other legitimate governmental purpose." *Id.* at 538. A plaintiff can demonstrate that conditions of confinement amount to punishment if, for example, the detention facility has "expressed an intent to punish" or "a restriction or condition is not reasonably related to a legitimate goal." *Id.* at 538, 539; *see also Arar*, 532 F.3d at 190.

I find that the conditions of confinement experienced by the refugees on Guantánamo, as described in my findings of fact, are not reasonably related to a legitimate governmental purpose. Accordingly, I find that they constitute punishment and therefore violate the due process rights of the plaintiffs.

You will want to review the cases cited by Judge Johnson: *Arar, Bell,* and *Lynch*. You will also need to review the evidence, described in *Storming the Court*, that was presented to the judge during the trial regarding the conditions of confinement on Guantánamo, as well as the judge's factual findings with respect to these conditions. Unless your professor instructs you otherwise, do not do any other research for this assignment.

There are three questions that you will need to address in making your argument to the Second Circuit.

- The first question you must address is whether Judge Johnson identified the correct legal standard for evaluating a challenge by an unadmitted alien to the conditions of the alien's non-punitive confinement. Review Note 4, above, to remind yourself what standard of review the Second Circuit will use to evaluate questions of law.
- The second question you must address is whether Judge Johnson's factual findings with respect to the conditions of confinement on

Guantánamo were correct. Here, too, you must make your argument with the relevant appellate standard of review in mind. *See* Note 4.

- The third question you will need to address is whether Judge Johnson properly applied the appropriate legal standard to his factual findings in deciding that the conditions of confinement on Guantánamo violated the due process clause. The Second Circuit will review the question of whether a district court erred in its application of law to facts under the "de novo" standard. *See United States Fidelity & Guaranty Co.*, 545 F.2d 1330, 1333 (2d Cir. 1976).

Because there are other issues for the team to argue, you will have only 15 minutes to argue the conditions of confinement issue to the Second Circuit.

CHAPTER TEN

Preclusion

INTRODUCTION

To paraphrase the saying, all things, both good and bad, must come to an end—including litigation. We expect litigants in our adversarial system to fight zealously, but at some point, the case is decided and judgment is entered. Regardless of the outcome, the parties' dispute—at least in court—is forever put to rest. There's no going back to the judge with additional arguments or claims. This idea of finality is what Harold Koh was trying to communicate to his students when he told them that litigants in American courts have "one bite at the apple." *STC*, p. 37.

The legal doctrines based on the concept of finality are traditionally known as *res judicata* ("a thing decided") and *collateral estoppel*—or, in the modern phraseology, *claim preclusion* and *issue preclusion*. Together, they are often referred to as the doctrines of *preclusion* or *former adjudication*. All of this terminology will be discussed later in the chapter. At the outset, what you should understand is the basic "one bite" idea of former adjudication—and the fact that it played a major role in *McNary*. Indeed, before the Yale team even filed its complaint, Harold Koh and some of the students feared that it might be too late to bring suit on behalf of the Haitian refugees because of the principles of preclusion—claim preclusion, in particular. *See id.*

Why? As you'll recall from *Storming the Court*, the government already had prevailed in an earlier action brought on behalf of Haitian refugees—*Haitian Refugee Center v. Baker*, which had been filed in federal district court in Miami by immigration expert Ira Kurzban and his colleagues. That case ultimately was decided by the Eleventh Circuit in February 1992, before the Yale team went to court in Brooklyn. Because *Baker* had already been filed, litigated, and disposed of when Lisa Daugaard and Michael Barr approached Harold Koh about helping the Haitians, one of Koh's primary concerns about bringing a new case was that *Baker* might preclude it. Accordingly, much of the Yale team's initial efforts went to convincing Judge Johnson and then the Second Circuit that the doctrine of claim preclusion did not, in fact, bar the plaintiffs' claims.

In this chapter, we will explore the principles of preclusion and their impact on the *McNary* litigation, focusing on the concept of claim preclusion, which played a central part in the case. We also will examine issue preclusion, which had a relatively minor role. Before we begin, however, it is important to point out a fundamental tension created by the role of former adjudication in our system. We have previously emphasized the equitable and flexible qualities of the Federal Rules—the liberal approach to pleading, the broad discovery rules, the emphasis on deciding cases on the merits. This orientation reflects the primary goal of the rules: to promote outcomes that are just because they are factually accurate and legally correct. As we have noted, however, a lawsuit must inevitably, if only eventually, end—and once the case is over, a party is entitled to peace (what the courts sometimes call "repose"). Preclusion establishes the limits on litigation and protects the value of finality.

This is where the tension arises, because finality and accuracy do not always go hand in hand. What if the court's decision is wrong? A losing party can appeal, of course; indeed, appeal is the losing party's principal recourse.[1] But what if the appellate court's decision is also wrong, and the U.S. Supreme Court refuses to hear the case? In such an instance, preclusion nevertheless bars the losing party from starting over and re-filing her complaint with the same claims against the same defendant. The prevailing party is entitled to repose, despite the unjust or incorrect result in court.

Does this seem fair to you? Shouldn't the losing party have another chance to rectify an incorrect judgment? If the only goal of our judicial system were to obtain a correct decision, there would *always* be another opportunity to challenge decisions or re-litigate claims. Accuracy, however, is not the only goal of our system. Ensuring finality can be nearly as important as arriving at a correct outcome. Finality grants parties the assurance that they will not be sued again, conserves judicial resources by requiring that claims be decided once and only once, and protects the integrity of final judgments by avoiding the possibility of inconsistent subsequent rulings.

NOTES AND COMMENTS

1. Procedural Considerations.   We turn first to claim preclusion, or res judicata.[2] Claim preclusion, the broader of the two former adjudication doctrines, bars the relitigation of a legal claim. To repeat Harold Koh's capsule summary: Litigants get only one bite at the apple.

The first procedural aspect of claim preclusion to understand is that it must be raised as an affirmative defense under Rule 8(c)—and this has important implications. Recall the discussion of affirmative defenses from Chapter Three: They generally must be raised in the answer (or another responsive filing) or *they are waived*. The defendant has the burden of pleading and proving the affirmative defense of claim preclusion. What did this mean in *McNary*? As the party asserting the defense, the government was responsible for persuading Judge Johnson that the plaintiffs' suit was precluded.

---

1. Appeals are discussed in Chapter Nine. A party can also move for a new trial under Rule 59 or relief from a judgment or order under Rule 60, as discussed in Chapter 8, Note 20.

2. Some courts, particularly in older decisions, use the term res judicata to refer to both doctrines of former adjudication—claim preclusion and issue preclusion. In this book, however, we will use res judicata to refer only to claim preclusion.

A second procedural consideration: Claim preclusion is not limited to instances in which a party tries to relitigate a claim in the same court in which the claim was initially litigated. The doctrine also applies if the party asserts the same claim in a different court the second time around. If the first case is filed in a state court and a final judgment is entered, a second court in another state must respect that judgment under the Constitution's full faith and credit clause. *See* U.S. Const. art. IV, § 1.

A similar practice is followed in the federal courts, although under different legal authority: Federal common law requires federal courts to respect the judgments of other federal courts. Recall that the *Baker* case was litigated in the United States District Court for the Southern District of Florida. As a result, the final judgment in the federal court in Florida would prevent relitigation of the same claims in any other federal court, including the United States District Court for the Eastern District of New York.

2. Elements of Claim Preclusion.   We now turn to the basic operation of the claim preclusion doctrine. For the judgment in a first lawsuit to bar the filing of a second lawsuit, three criteria must be met: (1) the claim in the second matter must be the same claim raised in the first lawsuit, (2) the parties in the second action must be either the same parties as those in the first action or "in privity" with the parties in the first action, and (3) the prior judgment must be valid, final, and on the merits. The following notes will examine each of these requirements in turn.

3. Same Claim Requirement.   For claim preclusion to apply, the claim in the second action must be the same claim litigated in the first action. Consider *Baker*, for example. In that case, Haitian refugees interdicted on the high seas by the United States and detained on Guantánamo sued for violations of their constitutional and statutory rights and to prevent repatriation to Haiti. Under the most straightforward application of claim preclusion, Haitian refugees who were plaintiffs in the *Baker* case would be prevented from making those same arguments in a second case against the United States.

But that is not the end of the inquiry as to what arguments the *Baker* plaintiffs would be barred from making. The concept of a "claim" is actually broader than you might imagine. Under preclusion doctrine, a "claim" refers not only to any rights to relief the plaintiff actually raised in the first suit but also *to all related rights that the plaintiff could have raised*—even if the plaintiff never mentioned them. This point naturally leads us to another question: How do we decide what could (and therefore should) have been raised by the plaintiff in the first suit?

To answer this question—and thus define the scope of the "claim" barred by claim preclusion—most courts today follow the "transactional test" set out in the *Restatement (Second) of Judgments.*[3] The transactional test defines the "claim" in terms of the event or occurrence that caused the harm giving rise to the lawsuit. Generally, all of the plaintiff's rights arising out of that event or occurrence constitute

---

3. *See* RESTATEMENT (SECOND) OF JUDGMENTS § 24(1) (1982) (explaining that a valid, final judgment in the first lawsuit extinguishes "all rights of the plaintiff to remedies against the defendant with respect to all or any part of the transaction, or series of connected transactions, out of which the action arose"). The transactional test is followed by so many federal courts today that it can be viewed as the "predominant federal rule," although different courts articulate the test in different ways. 18 FEDERAL PRACTICE AND PROCEDURE § 4407 (2d ed. 2002). However, there are a few courts that use other criteria in determining whether the second suit involves the same claim for purposes of claim preclusion, such as whether the second suit involves different legal rights and duties. *See id.*

one claim and must be raised in a single lawsuit.[4] To bring two separate suits on different aspects of the same claim is called "splitting a claim" and is not permitted under the doctrine of claim preclusion.

In applying the transactional test, courts take into account a number of pragmatic considerations, including (1) whether the facts giving rise to each claim are closely connected in time, space, origin, or motivation, (2) whether the facts form a convenient trial unit, and (3) whether treating the facts as a single claim would conform to the parties' expectations and business practices. *Restatement (Second) of Judgments*, § 24(2); *see also* Jack H. Friedenthal et al., *Civil Procedure* 666 (4th ed. 2005).

What does it mean for facts to be closely connected in time, space, origin, or motivation? If, for example, officials violently throw a man out of a baseball stadium because they say he is drunk, then the facts giving rise to his claims for assault and slander would be closely connected along these four dimensions. As to the second factor, two issues may form a convenient trial unit if there is an overlap in evidence—that is, if proving the facts relevant to both issues would require many of the same witnesses and documentary evidence, for example. The third factor (conforming to the parties' expectations and business practices) generally is relevant only in claims arising out of a contractual relationship. For instance, if the parties to a business deal would have expected two separate agreements to be treated as one business transaction—such that the plaintiff would have asserted rights based on these obligations either together or not at all—the court will be more likely to treat them as part of the same transaction or occurrence for purposes of claim preclusion.[5]

The transactional test is highly fact-specific and it is often difficult to predict how a court might rule in any particular set of circumstances. There are, however, a number of commonly occurring situations in which courts generally agree on the application of the transactional test. Let's look at one of those situations: an individual who was in a car accident suing once for damages to his car and a second time for personal injuries. Under the transactional test, would this be permitted? Think back to the test. Are the facts at issue in these two suits closely related in time, space, origin, or motivation? And what evidence would the two suits share? (Remember to be specific about what particular evidence the two suits would share and why.)

4. Same Claim: Subsequent Developments.   What if the plaintiff in the previous example does not know the extent of her injuries when she brings suit for damage to her car? For example, she may have sustained a head injury, but the full consequences of that head injury do not become apparent until later. The law of preclusion requires the plaintiff to bring suit for all then-existing injuries, even if the magnitude of the injury is not yet known. What do you think the purpose of this rule is? In addition, the law of preclusion prevents newly discovered facts or subsequent changes in the law from serving as the basis for a second suit by the plaintiff once the first suit is over. Does this rule seem fair to you? What do you think the rationale for the rule is?

Despite these limitations, it *is* possible for the plaintiff to bring a second suit—even one closely related to the first—to seek recovery for injuries arising out of events

---

4. For exceptions to the general rules of claim preclusion, see RESTATEMENT (SECOND) OF JUDGMENTS § 26.

5. There is some circularity in the parties' expectations element of the test; party expectations are in part a function of prior court rulings.

that occurred *after the first lawsuit*. In the words of a Second Circuit case cited by Judge Johnson in *McNary*,[6] a previous judgment "cannot be given the effect of extinguishing claims which did not even then exist and which could not possibly have been sued upon in the previous case." *Prime Mgt. Co. v. Steinegger*, 804 F.2d 811, 816 (2d Cir. 1990) (citation omitted). For instance, following a tort action arising from an auto accident, if the defendant negligently drove into the plaintiff's car the day after the jury verdict regarding the first accident, the plaintiff would be free to bring a second suit for injuries resulting from that collision. Casting this point in the terms of our transactional test, even though the second accident involves the same parties, it nevertheless constitutes a separate transaction and therefore gives rise to a separate claim.

Sometimes referred to as "changed circumstances," the occurrence of new events after the first lawsuit is over played a critical role in *McNary*. Start by considering the distinction between plaintiffs who had been "screened in" and those who had been "screened out." At the time of *Baker*, a number of individuals had been "screened in" as potential refugees who might face political persecution were they returned to Haiti. These screened-in Haitians were not the focus of *Baker*. Plaintiffs' counsel did not challenge the treatment of the screened-in Haitians at the time because they were being flown to the United States to undergo a full asylum hearing with the assistance of counsel. Rather, plaintiffs' counsel in *Baker* brought suit to ensure that Haitians who had been screened *out* obtained access to counsel and appropriate review of their asylum claims—and to enjoin their return to Haiti until their cases had been reviewed. After three frantic months of litigation, the Eleventh Circuit ordered the district court to dismiss the suit for failure to state a claim upon which relief could be granted. *Haitian Refugee Center, Inc. v. Baker*, 953 F.2d 1498 (11th Cir. 1992). Plaintiffs' petition for a writ of certiorari from the Supreme Court was denied on February 24, 1992. *Haitian Refugee Center, Inc. v. Baker*, 502 U.S. 1122 (1992).

Then a new development occurred. Five days after the Supreme Court's denial of certiorari, the government instituted new interview procedures on Guantánamo, as set forth in a memorandum, reproduced here, by the general counsel of the INS, Grover Joseph Rees. A few days later, a sympathetic INS official leaked the memorandum to a human rights lawyer in New York named Arthur Helton. Helton then passed it on to an attorney familiar with the Yale team. Review the Rees memorandum carefully.

Subject	Date
Interviews of "Screened In" Persons Subject to Medical Exclusion	February 29, 1992

To	From
John Cummings INS/GTMO	Grover Joseph Rees General Counsel

---

6. *Haitian Centers Council, Inc. v. McNary*, 1992 WL 155853, at *5 (E.D.N.Y. Apr. 6, 1992).

As you know, there are a number of persons at the naval base in Guantanamo who have been "screened in" as possible refugees but who have been determined to have a communicable disease of public health significance.

The Immigration and Nationality Act (INA) requires that persons with communicable diseases of public health significance "shall be excluded from admission into the United States." INA § 212(a)(1). With respect to persons who are determined to be refugees, however, the Act provides that the Attorney General may waive the medical exclusion "for humanitarian purposes, to assure family unity, or when it is otherwise in the public interest." Id. § 207(c)(3). Such a waiver must be in writing and shall be granted only on an individual basis following an investigation. Id.

The Act further provides that the Attorney General may temporarily parole aliens into the United States "for emergent reasons or for reasons deemed strictly in the public interest." Id. § 212(d)(5)(A). Such parole does not constitute an admission into the United States and confers no immigration or refugee status. Id. Moreover, a person who is a refugee may be paroled into the United States (rather than admitted as a refugee under the formal refugee admission process) only when the

Attorney General finds parole to be

"require[d]" by "compelling reasons in the

public interest." Id. § 212(d)(5)(B).

With respect to a person whose application for

parole is premised on the possibility that he or

she may be a refugee, but who has been determined

to have a communicable disease of public health

significance, the judgment with respect to

whether parole is required by "compelling rea-

sons in the public interest" should be informed

by the same factors that would justify a waiver of

the medical exclusion if the person were to seek

admission as a refugee. That is, the waiver must

be justified "for humanitarian purposes, to

assure family unity, or when it is otherwise in

the public interest." Id. § 207(c)(3).

At a minimum, this requires a determination that

the person is in fact a refugee.

Accordingly, any person "screened in" as a

possible refugee who has been determined to have

a communicable disease that is not curable should

be given an interview to determine whether he or

she is a refugee within the definition of

INA § 101(a)(42). In the case of a Haitian national

in Guantanamo, this definition requires a

finding that the person is unable or unwilling to return to Haiti, because of a well-founded fear of persecution on account of race, religion, nationality, membership in a particular social group, or political opinion. This finding is identical to that required to grant asylum or refugee status. The interview should therefore be identical in form and substance, or as nearly so as possible, to those conducted by asylum officers to determine whether asylum should be granted to an applicant already in the United States.

How might these interviews, which were conducted on Guantánamo, be different from the interviews conducted in the United States?

Interviews should be conducted according to the usual standards and techniques for asylum interviews. See Interview Checklist, INS Asylum Branch Procedures Manual and Operations Instructions, p. 121 (March 1992). An Asylum Assessment should be prepared for each applicant, in accordance with the assessment format set forth in the Procedures Manual and Operations Instructions. See id. at 124-25. All assessments should be forwarded to the Director of the Asylum Branch. When the interviewing asylum officer determines that an applicant is not credible, or that the facts adduced in the interview are insufficient, even if true, to establish a well-founded fear of persecution within the definition of the Act, this determination should be noted in the assessment along with the reasons therefor. When the interviewing officer determines that an applicant appears credible and that the facts adduced would, if true, establish a well-founded fear of persecution, the assessment will be forwarded to the State Department for information concerning the accuracy of the applicant's assertions about his or her experiences and about country conditions. See 8 C.F.R. § 208.11.

These procedures should be followed only with respect to persons whose communicable diseases of public health significance are not curable. Persons whose diseases are susceptible of prompt treatment and cure, and who would not thereafter be medically excludable, should be handled in accordance with established procedures pending further guidance.

What changes does the Rees memorandum institute? Which plaintiffs in *McNary* were subject to these new procedures? Do you recall the meaning of a "communicable disease of public health significance?" *See STC*, p. 56. The critical question for the *McNary* case is: Did the procedures instituted by the Rees memorandum constitute "changed circumstances" such that claim preclusion should not bar a new lawsuit after *Baker*? Why or why not?

Consider how the level of generality at which you analyze the question may affect your answer. If the question is whether the plaintiffs in *Baker* and *McNary* both challenged INS interviewing procedures under the Immigration and Nationality Act, the answer seems to suggest the application of claim preclusion. If the question is instead *what* interviewing procedures the plaintiffs in *Baker* and *McNary* were challenging, however, the answer seems to point in the other direction. How do you justify the level of generality at which you analyze the question?

5. Same Party Requirement.   Claim preclusion can operate only between the same parties. A claim brought by one party may not be barred because of an earlier lawsuit brought by another party. Consider, for example, the case of two passengers on a bus who are injured when their vehicle is hit by a truck. If the first passenger sues the truck driver, that suit will not bar the second passenger from filing her own suit against the truck driver. What is the rationale for this rule? In fact, the rationale has a constitutional basis in the due process clause.

The identity of the parties was a significant issue in determining the application of claim preclusion in *McNary*. In addition, *McNary* involves a twist on this issue because both *Baker* and *McNary* were class actions. We will discuss in Note 7 in this chapter the identity of the Haitian plaintiffs in the two cases and how that bears on the application of claim preclusion. For the moment, however, consider some of the other plaintiffs in the *McNary* case—in particular, the lawyers themselves. Remember that in *McNary*, one of the ways in which Koh sought to avoid claim preclusion was to include as plaintiffs new lawyers asserting their own First Amendment right to meet with their clients. *See STC*, pp. 37-38. Why would these plaintiffs avoid claim preclusion?

The requirement of identity of parties sometimes implicates the concept of "privity." Privity refers to a close relationship between two or more parties that share an interest in a legal claim brought by only one of the parties. Claim preclusion bars a second suit on the same claim by someone who is in privity with the original party who asserted the claim. For example, one who inherits land from another person is in privity with the prior owner and cannot relitigate previously decided claims relating to the property. An individual may also be in privity with a party to a previous lawsuit if the second party substantially controlled the first litigation or was a representative of the first party. In the *McNary* case, for example, the government initially contended that Haitian Centers Council in Brooklyn (the lead plaintiff in *McNary*) was in privity with the Haitian Refugee Center in Miami (the lead plaintiff in *Baker*), although after initial discovery it conceded that this was not the case. *Haitian Centers Council, Inc. v. McNary*, No. 92 Civ. 1258, 1992 WL 155853, at *4 (E.D.N.Y. Apr. 6, 1992). The organizations are, in fact, entirely separate and neither controls the other. But if it had turned out, say, that Haitian Centers Council had dictated the *Baker* litigation strategy, it is possible that Haitian Centers Council would have been bound by the *Baker* judgment—and thus barred by claim preclusion from bringing the *McNary* case.

6. Requirement of a Valid and Final Decision on the Merits.   The third and final element of claim preclusion is that the judgment must be valid, final, and on the merits. Valid means that it was entered by a competent court. For example, generally speaking, a judgment entered by a court that does not have subject matter jurisdiction or personal jurisdiction over the defendant would not be valid and therefore would not be entitled to preclusive effect.[7] The judgment must also be final. Finality requires

---

7. If, however, the issue of jurisdiction was (or could have been) raised and decided in the first suit, other courts generally will respect this decision—even if it is not correct—in accordance with the principles of full faith and credit. An exception applies when a default judgment is entered against a defendant who

only that there be nothing left to do in the case except enter judgment. *See* Jack H. Friedenthal et al., *Civil Procedure* 684. Interlocutory orders, preliminary injunctions, temporary restraining orders, and pretrial rulings are generally not final for purposes of claim preclusion.[8]

Finally, the judgment must be "on the merits." This requirement can be deceiving because it does *not* mean that there has to have been a full trial for claim preclusion to apply. Instead, what is important is that there was an *opportunity* to litigate the merits. For example, while a judgment after a full jury trial is clearly "on the merits," so is a ruling granting a summary judgment motion under Rule 56. In the federal courts and the courts of many states, dismissal for failure to state a claim upon which relief can be granted is generally on the merits, unless the court specifies that the dismissal is without prejudice. *See* Fed. R. Civ. P. 41(b). The *Baker* case was dismissed for failure to state a claim under Rule 12(b)(6) and was therefore a dismissal on the merits. Dismissals for lack of jurisdiction, improper venue, or nonjoinder or misjoinder of parties are not on the merits. *See id.*

7. Claim Preclusion in Class Actions.   Now that you have a basic understanding of claim preclusion, we can begin to think about its application to the *McNary* case in more detail. Remember the initial strategy session about filing a new suit that Koh had with the law students? *See STC*, pp. 36-41. In that session, student Paul Sonn presented his research on whether the *Baker* decision would preclude a second lawsuit on behalf of the Haitian refugees. Part of the challenge of getting around *Baker* was the fact that, as Sonn noted, *Baker* was a class action lawsuit—a case in which many plaintiffs sought to join together and sue a common defendant. *McNary*, too, was a class action suit. To understand the operation of claim preclusion in *McNary*, therefore, a brief discussion of class actions is necessary. As you review this note, consider the possible advantages of the class action form. What purposes do you think it served in *Baker* and *McNary*?

As just noted, a class action lawsuit is one in which a large number of individuals who generally have the same claims against a defendant sue together as a group (which may include dozens, thousands, hundreds of thousands, or even more). The primary rationale for class action litigation is efficiency—both litigants and the judicial system are spared repeated litigation of the same claims and issues. The group of plaintiffs is called a class, and the composition of the group is determined by the "class definition." Anyone who falls within the definition of the class is a plaintiff in the lawsuit, although not all of the plaintiffs participate directly in the lawsuit. Rather, a few members of the class are chosen as "named plaintiffs" and they represent all of the people within the class.

For example, imagine a consumer protection law action against Ace Cell Phone Company for overcharging customers during the first half of 2008. The class of plaintiffs could be defined to include "any individual who had a contract for cell phone service with Ace Cell Phone Company at any point between January 1, 2008, and

---

contends that there was no personal jurisdiction over her in the forum state and who never appeared to contest the lawsuit. In this situation, a defendant may "collaterally attack"—that is, challenge in a separate suit—a default judgment for lack of personal jurisdiction. *See Pennoyer v. Neff*, 95 U.S. 714 (1878).

8. However, if a case is on appeal, or if the time for filing an appeal has not yet expired, most jurisdictions will treat the lower court judgment as final for claim preclusion purposes. Jack H. Friedenthal et al., Civil Procedure 685.

Bible signed and presented to Harold Koh and the plaintiffs' litigation team by the Haitians held at Camp Bulkeley. Photographer unknown.

June 30, 2008, inclusive." All of the people who had cell phone contracts with Ace Cell during this time period will be plaintiffs, but not all will actively participate in the lawsuit. Instead, a few cell phone users who had Ace Cell contracts during the relevant time period will become named plaintiffs and they will represent the interests of the entire group of plaintiffs.

Class action lawsuits are governed by Rule 23. That rule specifies the conditions under which a class may be certified—that is, recognized and permitted to proceed as a class—and when individual class members are entitled to notice and, in some types of class actions, an opportunity to say that they do not want to be part of the class (a process known as opting out, after which a litigant can instead sue individually). Rule 23 sets out four requirements for a lawsuit to be certified by the court as a class action: numerosity, commonality, typicality, and adequacy of representation. Fed. R. Civ. P. 23(a). Briefly, numerosity requires that there be so many plaintiffs that joinder is "impracticable"; commonality requires that there be questions of law or fact common to the class; typicality requires that claims or defenses of the representative parties be typical of those of the class; and adequacy of representation requires that the representative parties (the named plaintiffs) fairly and adequately protect the class interests. Fed. R. Civ. P. 23(a)(1)-(4). In addition to meeting all four requirements set forth of Rule 23(a), a class must meet *one* of several alternative requirements set forth in Rule 23(b) in order to be certified. The class in *McNary* was certified under Rule 23(b)(2), which is appropriate when plaintiffs are seeking equitable relief and the defendant "has acted or refused to act on grounds that apply generally to the class." Fed. R. Civ. P. 23(b)(2). In *McNary*, the equitable relief requested initially was access to attorneys during asylum hearings and later, of course, evolved into demands for proper medical care and release from Guantánamo.

If the court certifies a class, then the litigation will proceed as a class action, with the named plaintiffs representing the interests of the class. If the plaintiffs prevail, then every member of the class is entitled to the injunctive relief sought and a proportionate share of the damages awarded. What matters for the purposes of claim preclusion in *McNary* is that regardless of the outcome, the judgment in the first lawsuit bars *the entire class from suing again on the claims that were or could have been litigated in the action*. That is because all of the class members are considered to be plaintiffs for purposes of claim preclusion. As a result, as long as the criteria of Rule 23 are met, a judgment in a class action will bind all class members—even if they did not actively participate in the litigation of the lawsuit. Can you see why this might make it difficult for the plaintiffs in *McNary* to avoid the preclusive effect of *Baker*?

There are, however, limits on the binding effects of a class action. For example, if an individual who seeks to file suit was *not* a member of the class in the first case, she has not had her day in court. To prevent her from litigating her own claim would violate her due process rights. *See Hansberry v. Lee*, 311 U.S. 32 (1940).[9] That is the question at the heart of whether claim preclusion should apply in *McNary*.

8. Claim Preclusion and McNary. Armed with a basic outline of how a class action works and its interaction with claim preclusion, you should recognize that to determine the preclusive effect of *Baker* on *McNary*, it is necessary to ascertain the scope of the *Baker* class. If the classes are different, then there can be no claim preclusion because the parties in the first and second case are not the same. On December 3, 1991, the district court in *Baker* certified the plaintiff class as "all Haitian aliens who are currently detained or who in the future will be detained on U.S. Coast Guard Cutters or at Guantánamo Naval base who were interdicted on the high seas pursuant to the United States Interdiction Program and who are being denied First Amendment and procedural rights." *Haitian Centers Council, Inc. v. McNary*, 969 F.2d 1350, 1354 (2d Cir. 1992). Review this language very carefully.

Now, compare this definition with the definition of the plaintiffs' class in *McNary*. On April 6, 1992, Judge Johnson conditionally[10] certified the class in *McNary* as consisting of "[a]ll Haitians who have been or will be 'screened in'." *Id.* (quoting *Haitian Centers Council, Inc. v. McNary*, 969 F.2d 1326, 1336 (2d Cir. 1992)); *see also Haitian Centers Council, Inc. v. McNary*, No. 92 Civ. 1258, 1992 WL 155853, at *10 (E.D.N.Y. Apr. 6, 1992). In his final opinion in the case after the trial, Judge Johnson officially certified the class as " '[a]ll Haitian citizens who have been or will be 'screened-in'—including those who have been or may be subject to or who have resisted additional screening procedures—who are now, will be or have been detained on Guantánamo Naval Base, or any other territory subject to United States jurisdiction

---

9. There is also the possibility of a class definition being "overly broad" if the interests of certain plaintiffs were not adequately represented by the named plaintiffs in the first suit (say, because the claims of the named plaintiffs were not typical of those other plaintiffs). The kind of representation at issue here is not legal representation; rather, the claims of the parties who serve as lead plaintiffs in the suit must be *representative of the claims* of the other plaintiffs in the class. Here, too, it would violate due process to hold that those inadequately represented plaintiffs are precluded from bringing their own claims.

10. The court's certification was conditional because at the time, the government challenged certain of the plaintiffs' factual allegations relating to the class. The court authorized the government to take discovery on those issues and stated an intention to hold a hearing as to whether the class certification should be modified. *Haitian Centers Council, Inc. v. McNary*, No. 92 Civ. 1258, 1992 WL 155853, at *10 (E.D.N.Y. Apr. 6, 1992). However, no subsequent hearing on the issue was held.

or Coast Guard cutters'" pursuant to Rules 23(a) and 23(b)(2). *Haitian Centers Council, Inc. v. Sale*, 823 F. Supp. 1028, 1039 (E.D.N.Y. 1993) (citation omitted) (alteration in the original). Again, review the language very carefully. What are the characteristics of the class that the named plaintiffs in *McNary* represented? Are members of the class of plaintiffs identified in *McNary* also individuals who would have fallen within the definition of the plaintiff class in *Baker*? Why or why not? What language in the two class definitions supports your argument?

> **Class Exercise No. 4**
> Consider the previous points about claim preclusion in connection with the following class exercise. Your professor will divide you into teams so that you can prepare the exercise before class. Half of the teams should prepare to play the role of plaintiffs' counsel in *McNary* and the other half should prepare to play the role of attorneys for the government. Be ready to argue whether the *McNary* lawsuit is barred, in whole or in part, under the doctrine of claim preclusion as a result of the final judgment in *Baker*. Based on the principles we have examined in this chapter, develop the best arguments you can on behalf of your clients and prepare rebuttals for the counter-arguments that you anticipate the other side will make.

9. Stare Decisis.   A final point about claim preclusion: It must be distinguished from the principle of stare decisis. Stare decisis refers to the effect of prior decisions on later litigation involving completely different parties. The principle of stare decisis, also referred to as precedent, essentially means that "like cases should be decided alike within a single jurisdiction." Jack H. Friedenthal et al., *Civil Procedure* 648. Claim preclusion bars relitigation between parties to promote judicial efficiency and provide repose for individual litigants, while stare decisis fosters consistent application of the law, thus helping to ensure stability and predictability in our legal system.

Stare decisis is therefore both broader and narrower than preclusion doctrine. How is stare decisis broader? As just noted, while preclusion requires some identity of parties, stare decisis applies in cases involving different parties. For example, *Brown v. Board of Education*[11] is binding as a matter of stare decisis in cases involving school districts and students other than those in *Brown*. How is stare decisis narrower than claim preclusion? Stare decisis only applies to issues of *law*. Issues of fact are relevant to stare decisis only to the extent that they make a later case similar to an earlier one and therefore subject to the decision of the earlier court. In addition, stare decisis is more flexible because on occasion, a court may overrule earlier precedent.

10. Issue Preclusion—Introduction.   We now turn from claim preclusion to issue preclusion, which is also known as collateral estoppel. Although it figured less prominently in *McNary* than claim preclusion, issue preclusion did play a role in the government's defense. To analyze that role, we must first explain the basic contours of the doctrine. Issue preclusion and claim preclusion are related, but quite different, concepts. Once a claim has been litigated, claim preclusion prevents successive or repetitive lawsuits with respect to the same *claim*. If the plaintiff forgot to raise a

---

11. 347 U.S. 483 (1954).

part of that claim in the first suit, the law does not allow him to bring a second suit on that overlooked aspect. In contrast, issue preclusion prevents the parties from rehashing particular issues: It bars the relitigation of a specific question of law or fact that was actually litigated and decided in a prior proceeding.

For example, consider the case of two children on a school bus who are injured when the bus runs a red light and hits a car traveling through the intersection. The parents of one of the injured children sue the school bus driver. The court, finding the driver negligent because he ran the red light, awards damages to the plaintiffs. Under issue preclusion, the parents of the second child can sue the bus driver in a second action—and rely on issue preclusion to establish that the bus driver was negligent rather than having to litigate the issue of the driver's negligence anew. Similarly, the driver of the car who was hit by the school bus could bring his own tort action against the bus driver and attempt to rely on issue preclusion to establish the driver's negligence.

The school bus accident case highlights two important contrasts between issue preclusion and claim preclusion. First, all that is in question regarding issue preclusion is the *issue* of negligence, not the entire tort claim. Thus, even where issue preclusion applies, it will not completely resolve or bar the second case. There may still be a number of other disputed issues between the parties that must be litigated. For instance, the plaintiff in the second lawsuit must still prove causation and damages; he or she will simply have the benefit of a factual finding that the bus driver's conduct was negligent. A second key contrast between claim preclusion and issue preclusion is that issue preclusion, at least in the modern era, does *not* require that the parties in the first and second cases be identical. The second suit in the school bus accident example involved a second child who was not a party in the first case. In such an instance, as you know from the previous discussion, *claim* preclusion could not have applied. The use of issue preclusion by a new party (as in the school bus accident case) is called non-mutual issue preclusion.[12]

11. The Elements of Issue Preclusion. The application of issue preclusion requires four elements. The issue in question must be: (1) identical in the first and second cases, (2) the subject of a valid and final judgment, (3) actually litigated by the parties, and (4) necessary to the judgment.[13] *See* Jack H. Friedenthal et al., *Civil Procedure* 708.

---

12. Traditionally, issue preclusion, like claim preclusion, required that the parties be identical. Many jurisdictions have relaxed this "mutuality" rule and now allow issue preclusion to be asserted by someone who was not a party to the first suit, as long as it is asserted against someone who was a party to the first suit. *See Parklane Hosiery Company v. Shore*, 439 U.S. 322 (1979). Issue preclusion can either be used offensively by a new plaintiff seeking to use a prior judgment against a defendant who was a party to the prior lawsuit (as in the school bus accident above), or defensively by a new defendant seeking to prevent a plaintiff from relitigating issues resolved against her in a prior suit. The application of offensive non-mutual issue preclusion depends on several factors laid out in the *Parklane* case that will not be dealt with here. It is important to remember, however, that issue preclusion can only be asserted against a party who was a party to the first lawsuit and therefore has had his day in court.

13. Commentators and courts often include a fifth requirement, which is that the fact-finder (whether judge or jury) must have actually considered and decided the issue in question. (Note the overlap with the requirement that the issue was necessary to the judgment. If it was necessary to the judgment, it must have been decided.) This "actually decided" requirement is most often a problem when a jury issues a general verdict, meaning that it simply finds for the plaintiff or defendant with no further explanation—leaving it unclear whether, for example, a plaintiff in a negligence case lost because the jury concluded she had suffered no damages or because the jury concluded she was contributorily negligent. In this instance, the

The first requirement is that the issues litigated in the first and second cases must be *identical.* For instance, in the school bus example, the two lawsuits involving the children presented an identical issue: Was the school bus driver negligent in the way that he drove the bus? As we will see later, the question of whether the issues in *Baker* and *McNary* were identical played a role in the court's decision that issue preclusion did not apply in *McNary.* The second requirement—that the issue in the first case be the subject of a valid, final judgment—was discussed previously in Note 6 in connection with claim preclusion. The same requirements for a valid, final judgment set out in that note apply to issue preclusion as well.

The third requirement for issue preclusion is that the issue must have been *actually litigated.* This means that the issue must have been the subject of an adversarial presentation—the parties must actually have raised and disputed the issue.[14] "A judgment is not conclusive in a subsequent action as to issues which might have been but were not litigated and determined in the prior action." *Restatement (Second) of Judgments* § 27, Comment e. The purpose of the "actually litigated" requirement is to ensure that a party has had an opportunity to be heard fully on an issue.[15] For example, if the first action is decided through a default judgment, issue preclusion ordinarily will not apply because no issues were actually disputed. The *Restatement* elaborates that "[t]here are many reasons why a party may choose not to raise an issue." *Id.* Can you think of some?

The fourth requirement means that the issue must also have been a *necessary basis* for the judgment in the first action. This requirement is related to the incentives of the parties in the first action. For instance, in a commercial dispute between two parties, assume that the trial court finds that the defendant breached its contract with the plaintiff, but dismisses the claim because the plaintiff filed the case after the statute of limitations expired. In this instance, the ruling on the breach was *not necessary* to the court's decision. The problem here is that the defendant has no incentive—and indeed as the prevailing party may not be permitted—to appeal the finding that there was a breach of contract, and the plaintiff has no reason to challenge the finding that the defendant breached its contract because that finding was favorable to its position. Because the case will not be heard on appeal, the finding was "not subject to full judicial scrutiny," and as a policy matter, issue preclusion would not be appropriate. Richard D. Freer, *Introduction to Civil Procedure* 541 (2006). A second policy consideration supports this view: The fact-finder may not have devoted sufficient attention to an issue—such as the breach of contract in our example—that was unnecessary to the judgment. *Id.*

12. Issue Preclusion in McNary.   As you may recall, the government changed its Haitian refugee policy several times during the time period covered by *Storming the Court.* These changes led to three different legal challenges: first the *Baker* litigation

---

question of contributory negligence might not have been actually decided by the jury. In contrast, a jury issuing a special verdict must answer specific questions about the defendant's or plaintiff's case, clarifying the reasoning underlying the verdict.

14. Contrast this requirement with the rules of claim preclusion, according to which a claim can be precluded even if it was never raised in the first action.

15. Further, "if preclusive effect were given to issues not litigated, the result might serve to discourage compromise . . . and thus to intensify litigation." RESTATEMENT (SECOND) OF JUDGMENTS § 27, Comment (e).

and then two separate cases in *McNary*—the due process case before Judge Johnson about conditions and detention on Guantánamo and the case heard by the Supreme Court on the direct return policy established by President Bush's May 1992 executive order. Judge Johnson primarily analyzed the preclusion issues in *McNary* in terms of claim preclusion, much the way we analyzed it earlier in this chapter. But the Second Circuit also addressed issue preclusion in *McNary*, mostly in connection with the plaintiffs' challenge to the direct return policy. We will therefore consider issue preclusion specifically in the context of the direct return case.

After Judge Johnson denied the plaintiffs' request to enjoin the direct return policy in early June 1992, plaintiffs appealed to the Second Circuit. On appeal, the Second Circuit considered whether issue preclusion prevented plaintiffs from relitigating (among other issues) the extent to which the Immigration and Nationality Act (INA) applied beyond American territorial waters. *See Haitian Centers Council, Inc. v. McNary*, 969 F.2d at 1354-57. Tracking the elements of issue preclusion, the government argued that the issue of whether the INA had extraterritorial application was: (1) identical to the INA issue raised in *Baker*, (2) the subject of a valid and final judgment by the Eleventh Circuit (followed by a denial of certiorari by the Supreme Court), (3) actually litigated by the parties in *Baker*, and (4) necessary to the Eleventh Circuit's judgment, which had denied all relief sought by the *Baker* plaintiffs.

The Second Circuit, however, ruled that issue preclusion did not apply for two reasons. First, the court relied on the "changed circumstances" exception, which applies to issue preclusion as well as to claim preclusion. The court explained that the May 1992 direct return order constituted changed circumstances after *Baker*, thus warranting a new determination as to the INA's extraterritorial application. *Id.* at 1356. The court emphasized that the government had made certain representations to the Supreme Court during the *Baker* case about its policies on Haitian refugees, but had then changed those procedures after the litigation ended:

> [W]hen the United States (a) resists Supreme Court review [in *Baker*] on a dramatic issue of such public import . . . by representing that there will be screening of intercepted aliens followed by full consideration of asylum rights, (b) achieves the desired denial of *certiorari*, and then (c) embarks on a completely contrary policy, that is a change of the type that ought to permit an inferior court, unfettered by estoppel, to adjudicate the merits of a new case based on the new circumstances.

Id. at 1357.

Note that the court's analysis can also be construed as determining that the issue itself was actually not the same in both cases. In *Baker*, the issue was whether the INA applied extraterritorially to require more careful screening procedures than those actually afforded to Haitians who were screened out. *See Haitian Refugee Center v. Baker*, 953 F.2d 1498 (11th Cir. 1992). In the *McNary* direct return case, the issue was whether the INA applied extraterritorially to prohibit the president's direct return policy. Because these two issues were not identical, issue preclusion did not apply.

Second, the court found that the plaintiffs in *McNary* were not part of the class in *Baker* and therefore could not be bound by the *Baker* judgment. The Second Circuit explained that the *Baker* class was defined by interdiction procedures that were later changed by the president's May 1992 direct return order. According to the certification order in *Baker*, the class in that case was defined as "all Haitian aliens who are currently detained or who will in the future be detained on U.S. Coast Guard cutters or at Guantánamo Naval base who were interdicted on the high seas pursuant to the United States Interdiction Program and who are being denied First Amendment and procedural rights." *McNary*, 969 F.2d at 1354. The court reasoned that because of the procedural changes instituted by the direct return order, the *McNary* plaintiffs were not being interdicted pursuant to the same "United States Interdiction Program" identified in *Baker*. As a result, the court concluded that the *McNary* plaintiffs were not part of the *Baker* class and thus were new parties. *Id.* at 1355. Do you agree with this ruling? Why or why not?

Because the Second Circuit determined that the *McNary* plaintiffs were new parties, they were entitled to their day in court—even though the government had prevailed in *Baker* on the issue of the extraterritorial application of the INA. To understand why, recall from the discussion in Footnote 12 above that a defendant cannot assert issue preclusion against a plaintiff who was not a party to the prior action. That was the case in *McNary*, and the court therefore ruled that the plaintiffs could proceed. Reviewing the two grounds that the court relied on to deny application of issue preclusion, can you explain how they are related? In light of your answer, do you think it was necessary for the court to provide two different reasons for its ruling? Why?

INTERVIEW
MICHAEL WISHNIE ON HOW *McNARY* AFFECTED THE BIG PICTURE FOR HIM

How did working on *McNary* influence . . .

1. Your view of litigation focused on local problems versus litigation focused on problems of an international scope?

I remain committed to using litigation primarily to solve problems that arise locally. I'm not really a genuine *international* human rights lawyer—I'm not sure that I've ever represented someone who is truly overseas, for instance, in a matter before a foreign or international tribunal (I'm not counting my clients on Guantánamo, in the 1990s or now, as being truly "overseas").

But *McNary* did open my eyes to the strategies and tactics used by international human rights lawyers—and how I could use them while focusing on domestic issues. In a number of cases, for example, my students and I have included either international or foreign law claims, together with domestic causes of action. For instance, where our clients are the victims of trafficking or forced labor, we have at times included a claim under international law via the Alien Tort Claims Act [28 U.S.C. § 1350, which grants federal district courts jurisdiction over tort claims committed in violation of the "law of nations or a treaty of the United States," even if both plaintiff and defendant are foreign nationals].

Or, in another example, when I was at NYU my students and I represented clients seeking to reform the flawed New York State workers' compensation system. As part of a multipart strategy, we advised our clients that they might petition for relief under the North American Free Trade Agreement (NAFTA) labor rights side-agreement. Under this agreement, workers in one NAFTA nation (say, the U.S.) can bring a proceeding in another signatory nation (such as Mexico) to enforce their own nation's domestic labor laws. We prepared a petition challenging delays in the New York workers' compensation system, and immigrant workers from New York filed it in Mexico—which launched a wide-ranging investigation. New York State retained private counsel to defend the proceeding, which received significant media attention, boosting our campaign for legislative change at the state level. This is the sort of international law strategy, in the service of a domestic rights agenda, that would not have occurred to me before *McNary*. (In fact, it was another team member, Graham Boyd, who had first alerted me to the potential of the NAFTA side labor agreement.)

But I continue to believe that working locally is the best way to ensure accountability of lawyers to the clients and communities they serve, and genuinely to advance social and economic justice. So my cases focus on local problems.

2. Your view of what makes a good lawyer?

I think that *McNary* really expanded my understanding of what makes a good lawyer. I'd never worked with any of the lawyers on the case before—Harold Koh, Joe Tringali, Michael Ratner, Lucas Guttentag, Robert Rubin—and I benefited from seeing lawyers with different styles, strategic impulses, and core values each approach a particular problem. It opened my eyes to the different strategic choices that were available at any given juncture in a case. It wasn't a matter of right or wrong answers, but of the different ways that a problem could be handled. And I didn't come out wanting to be a lawyer who was just like Harold, Joe, Michael, Lucas, or Robert, but instead, as a combination of some of the best qualities I saw in each of them. To name just a few of the qualities I have in mind: an inexhaustible capacity to keep on working for the client no matter the circumstances; political creativity and a willingness to stand on principle, even if there isn't much supporting legal precedent; the value of excellent preparation and meticulous attention to detail; and the importance of seeing both individual issues and the big picture.

3. Your career plans and ambitions?

One thing *McNary* definitely did was make me want to learn how to litigate, and that was a change in short-term priorities for me. So right when I graduated, I decided to get a job that would put me in the courtroom all the time. I took a job with the Legal Aid Society of New York, in the Brooklyn neighborhood office, handling housing and welfare cases. I tell you, the Brooklyn Housing Court at 141 Livingston Street was a long way from the United States Supreme Court, but the position offered me an opportunity to work directly with clients (mostly tenants and tenant associations), and got me into court probably three or four days each week, arguing cases and negotiating deals. If I'd gone directly to, say, the ACLU instead, I would generally have been the third or fourth person assigned to a case, without the immediate responsibility to develop my own judgment and skills, and to exercise judgment personally on behalf of clients. I wanted to be up on my feet in the rough and tumble of daily litigation.

Second, the *McNary* case and my work in other legal clinics during law school got me thinking about combining legal work with an earlier interest of mine—teaching. I'd long been interested in teaching, having done it on a volunteer basis during college and law school. I'd also taught English for two years in China. Once I got to law school and spent time working in a clinic, I realized that being a clinical professor might be a great way to combine law practice and teaching. The *McNary* case, which came after I'd already done some work in other clinics— landlord-tenant cases, an asylum case, some union organizing work—really confirmed for me that I'd love an opportunity to try clinical teaching.

You initially expressed some skepticism about getting involved in *McNary*, but you became a committed member of the litigation team. What were the most important lessons you learned from working on the case?

I think that there were a few things I took away from *McNary* that most influenced my professional life.

One, I came to law school dubious about the effectiveness of litigation. I thought of litigation as slow, highly resource-intensive, and a very blunt instrument for attempting to solve complex social problems. And with a conservative judiciary after many years of appointments by Presidents Reagan and Bush, I thought litigation was even more unlikely to be successful in achieving social, economic, or racial justice. Instead, I believed change would more likely result from long-term strategies aimed at organizing, popular education, and eventually legislative change. I came to law school because I thought I would learn skills that could make me more effective at pursuing these other strategies.

McNary changed my view. I still believe litigation is resource-intensive and often too blunt an instrument to accomplish meaningful, lasting change. But *McNary* taught me that sometimes—*sometimes*—litigation can solve problems and advance social causes. So I decided that I wanted to develop litigation skills as one of the strategies I could deploy on behalf of clients and causes.

For me, the second lesson of *McNary* is that litigation alone is not enough. You can't focus only on the courtroom. Had we merely litigated the Guantánamo case, we would have lost. Because even if the Second Circuit had affirmed Judge Johnson's judgment ordering the release of the refugees, I think we all recognized the very real possibility that the government would have petitioned for certiorari. And if it had, that the Supreme Court would likely have granted cert and eventually reversed and ruled for the government. But we created political pressure on the Clinton administration to let the decision stand. We engaged with local and national politicians and officials, in legislatures and executive branch agencies, pressed the refugees' case in the media, collaborated with community-based and student organizations, and reached out to the general public. If we hadn't done those things, I think the government may well have decided to keep litigating rather than to seize the opportunity presented by Judge Johnson's decision after trial. Our clients might never have reached the United States.

Lesson three is broader—and that lesson is that social justice work is hard, but it's a lot easier and a lot more fun when you're doing it with friends and people you respect. I really loved working with Lisa and Graham and Ray and Paul and Michael and Sarah and all the other students and lawyers involved. I learned that I could do so much more working in collaboration with others than I ever could have hoped to accomplish alone. And it made me a better lawyer. Looking back, I'm really amazed by how hard we worked and how hard we pushed each other. So after law school, I set out to find other professional contexts where I could work with others whom I respected but also whom I simply enjoyed spending time with. If you're going to raise a little hell, why not do it with people you like?

Yale Law School Graduation, May 25, 1992. From left to right are Lisa Daugaard, Michael Barr, Harold Koh, Ray Brescia, Graham Boyd, and Sarah Cleveland. Photographer unknown.

Index